STRANGERS NO MORE

STRANGERS NO MORE

IMMIGRATION AND THE CHALLENGES
OF INTEGRATION IN NORTH AMERICA
AND WESTERN EUROPE

RICHARD ALBA AND NANCY FONER

PRINCETON UNIVERSITY PRESS
PRINCETON AND OXFORD

press.princeton.edu
Jacket photograph: Pedestrians on the Albert Cuyp Market, a popular street in
Amsterdam, August 8, 2011, © Herman Wouters/The New York Times/Redux

ISBN 978-0-691-16107-5
Library of Congress Control Number: 2015932635

British Library Cataloging-in-Publication Data is available

This book has been composed in Minion Pro

Printed on acid-free paper ∞

Printed in the United States of America

1 3 5 7 9 10 8 6 4 2

CONTENTS

PREFACE

Strangers No More is a book about immigration—the massive waves of post–World War II immigration that brought millions of newcomers to the two sides of the Atlantic and are remaking the societies of North America and Western Europe. By now, the children and, in some cases the grandchildren, of the immigrants are as numerous as the immigrants themselves. These individuals can no longer be described as strangers to these societies. Yet, as we have found in the process of writing this book, nowhere are they—or, more accurately, the majority of them—completely integrated in the sense that they are recognized as fully belonging to the countries they call home and share the same opportunities open to citizens from long-established families. This is especially so for the groups we describe as "low status," such as Mexicans in the United States or Turks in several European countries. The immigrants in these groups typically brought low levels of education from their home countries and took jobs on the bottom rungs in the advanced economies to which they moved, and they, and their children, are distinguished by ethnic, racial, or religious differences from members of the long-standing native majorities.

The book is also concerned with the societies where immigrants have come to live and their descendants are growing up, specifically, with Canada, France, Germany, Great Britain, the Netherlands, and the United States. While our focus is on these six countries, we believe that by studying them we can also shed light on changes in the other countries of the North Atlantic region that have taken in substantial numbers of immigrants during the past sixty years. The demographic destiny of all these countries during the next quarter of a century is unmistakable: their populations of adults in their prime—in the ages when they rear families, are at the peak of their earning power, and engage most fully in civic activity—will become much more diverse, as post–World War II baby boomers age and youthful cohorts, containing many members who grew up in immigrant homes, mature. In a very real sense, the future vitality of these societies—in cultural, economic, and social terms—will be bound up with the integration of their immigrant-origin groups, including those of low status.

We began working together on this book seven years ago, as soon as we became colleagues at the City University of New York. We did not then expect that it would take us so long to complete this project, but we underestimated the effort involved to clarify for ourselves the situations of multiple groups in six countries across a variety of institutional domains, from the labor market to the polity and school system, and on topics ranging from religion and race to identities and intermarriage. Such a lengthy effort has inevitably involved the help of many along the way. We are grateful to those who read the manuscript and provided us with feedback to improve it. They include Irene Bloemraad, Jan Willem Duyvendak, and one anonymous reader for Princeton University Press. Thomas Faist, Irena Kogan, Leo Lucassen, and Jeffrey Reitz also read portions of the manuscript. We owe thanks, as well, to Jørgen Carling, Ellen Kraly, and Jennifer Lee for welcoming an article derived from the book for the fiftieth anniversary issue of *International Migration Review*; their comments on the article helped us also in revising the book manuscript.

A great many friends and colleagues in the immigration field have been a source of ideas and insights. It is not possible to name them all here, for there are so many, and we would not want to leave anyone off the list. We do, however, want to acknowledge our debt to a number of institutions and people who have played a more direct role in the development and writing of the book.

This book depends on empirically informed comparisons, and obtaining the most relevant and up-to-date data was an enormous challenge, one that we could not have met with only our own resources. We had a lot of help. Some essential data tasks were carried out at our home base, the City University of New York, by David Monaghan, Joseph Pereira, and Guillermo Yrizar Barbosa, and in Albany, where Richard Alba was formerly a faculty member, by Jeffrey Napierala and Ruby Wang. Critical U.S. data were supplied by the Center for Urban Research and the Luxembourg Income Study at CUNY and by the Center for Social and Demographic Analysis in Albany. Yaël Brinbaum and Yaojun Li created special tabulations for us with French and British data, respectively.

Many colleagues elsewhere gave us critical assistance in identifying data. For data on Canada, we must thank Monica Boyd; for France, Yaël Brinbaum and Roxane Silberman; for Germany, Cornelia Kristen and Karen Schönwälder; for Great Britain, Neli Demireva, Anthony Heath, Ron Johnston, Raya Muttarak, Ceri Peach, and Maria Sobolewska; for the Netherlands, Laure Michon, Liza Mügge, Leen Sterckx, and Floris Vermeulen.

Each of us came to this project with a history of interest in immigration outside the United States and in comparative investigations of the immigrant and second-generation experience. For Alba, this history began with two long stays in Germany, thanks to the Fulbright program. His burgeoning interest in immigrant groups in Germany developed through conversations and collaborations with colleagues in Mannheim, especially Hartmut Esser, Johann Handl, and Walter Müller. Subsequently, he spent time in Paris and learned a great deal about the French situation from Roxane Silberman and from her colleagues at the Maurice Halbwachs Center. Also memorable is his visit to an immigrant *banlieue* in the company of Michèle Tribalat. A series of comparative analyses deepened his interest and knowledge. He is indebted to the financial support for them provided by a John Simon Guggenheim Memorial Foundation Fellowship, a German Marshall Fund Fellowship, and research grants from the U.S. National Science Foundation and Russell Sage Foundation.

The foundational project, which fed directly into a chapter in the current book, concerned the education of the second generation in the United States and five European countries. Co-directed with Jennifer Holdaway of the Social Science Research Council (SSRC), the project tutored Alba in the institutional intricacies that structure opportunities for and impediments to integration. The project was a massive group effort, involving twenty-five senior and junior scholars. All of them contributed to the knowledge gained through the comparisons, but Alba is most grateful to the international team of senior scholars: in addition to Holdaway, they include Mikael Alexandersson, Silvia Carrasco, Maurice Crul, Margaret Gibson, Anthony Heath, Roxane Silberman, Carola Suárez-Orozco, and Mary Waters. Frans Lelie, though not formally a collaborator, deserves special mention for her numerous efforts in support of this project and for her generous and informative reception of Alba in Amsterdam.

Nancy Foner's interest in comparative immigration—and the role of America's racial legacy in shaping the contemporary U.S. immigrant experience—goes back many years, initially to in-depth research on West Indian migrants in London and New York City and, later, to comparisons of different historical U.S. eras, in particular New York's two great waves of immigration.

In the past decade, Foner's understanding of immigrant integration in comparative perspective has been deepened by involvement in a number of projects and institutions on both sides of the Atlantic. In the United States, she owes a debt to the Russell Sage Foundation, and its then-president Eric Wanner, for providing an intellectual home during a year as an associate scholar—and a place where she could engage in conversations with a broad range of immigration scholars, including Maurice Crul, Kay Deaux, Douglas Massey, and Mary Waters. The foundation also funded a conference, organized with Patrick Simon, on immigration, national identity, and integration in North America and Europe. Thanks to Patrick for his role in initiating the conference, to senior program officer Aixa Cintron for helping to make it happen, and to the contributors, among them Irene Bloemraad, Thomas Faist, Gary Gerstle, Nasar Meer, Deborah Schildkraut, and Marieke Slootman, whose research on identity issues contributed to the development of one of this book's chapters. Foner is also grateful to the CUNY Graduate Center Advanced Research Collaborative and its director, Donald Robotham, for providing a year off from teaching as we were completing the book.

Foner has learned a great deal about immigration issues in Europe from colleagues at the Max Planck Institute for the Study of Religious and Ethnic Diversity in Göttingen, including its director, Steven Vertovec, as well as Matthias Koenig, Karen Schönwälder, Susanne Wessendorf, and fellow advisory group members Robin Cohen, Ralph Grillo, and Daniel Hiebert. Thanks, too, to

Christophe Bertossi, with whom Foner directed an SSRC dissertation proposal development workshop on transatlantic comparisons of multiculturalism, immigration, and identity; to Josh DeWind, the indefatigible SSRC program director, who raised probing questions at the meetings; and the doctoral students who were developing research projects on comparative U.S.-Europe immigration topics. Foner also owes a debt to many Dutch colleagues who have helped her better understand the Dutch context and who, over the years, have welcomed her at the University of Amsterdam's Institute for Migration and Ethnic Studies and as a visiting scholar in the urban studies program: Maurice Crul, Leo Lucassen, Rinus Penninx, and Floris Vermeulen. A special thanks to Jan Rath, Jan Willem Duyvendak, and Rogier van Reekum, with whom she also worked on a project comparing the consequences of immigration in New York and Amsterdam.

At our own institution, the City University of New York, our many colleagues have provided a stimulating intellectual environment in which to work on this book. A special word of appreciation to Philip Kasinitz for his astute insights as well as good cheer and humor, and to John Mollenkopf, with whom we share a commitment to transatlantic comparisons of immigration.

It has been a pleasure to work with the editorial staff at Princeton University Press. We would like to thank Eric Schwartz, senior editor at the press, for his enthusiasm for the project and helpful advice, as well as for guiding the manuscript through the acceptance process with great expertise. We were fortunate that senior editor Eric Crahan took over when the "first" Eric departed for a position at another press. We are also grateful to editorial assistant Ryan Mulligan, senior production editor Brigitte Pelner, and copyeditor Linda Truilo for their help along the way.

Last but certainly not least, we would like to thank members of our families. Richard Alba could not have sustained the lengthy and intensive effort required for this book without the loving support of Gwen Moore, and Michael and Sarah Alba. Nancy Foner is grateful to her husband, Peter Swerdloff, for his unfailing support, her mother, Anne Foner, who has always been there as a sounding board, and her daughter, Alexis, for, among other things, her writerly advice.

STRANGERS NO MORE

CHAPTER 1

STRANGERS NO MORE

The Challenges of Integration

Immigration is transforming Western Europe and North America. The origins of this massive inflow date back to the middle of the twentieth century, a period of recovery and expansion after the devastations of worldwide economic depression and war. The numbers are astounding. The United States has the largest foreign-born population of any country in the world, with around forty million immigrants (as of 2012), while the combined member states of the European Union are home to approximately 50 million people who have moved across borders and are living outside the country of their birth. In the United States, immigrants and their children account for nearly a quarter of the population, and the figure is even higher in Canada; in the largest Western European countries, it is generally about a fifth.

If the numbers are impressive, their implications are even more remarkable. Western Europe, on one side of the Atlantic, and the United States and Canada, on the other, all have to deal with incorporating millions of immigrants whose cultures, languages, religions, and racial backgrounds often differ starkly from those of most long-established residents. In Europe, societies that previously thought of themselves as homogeneous have seen the rise of ethnic, religious, and racial diversity. In Canada and the United States, immigration has long been part of the national story, but immigrants now hail from new places and are seen, in racial and ethnic terms, as more different than ever before.

How European and North American societies are to meet the challenges of this new diversity is one of the key issues of the twenty-first century. A central question is how to integrate immigrants and their children so that they become full members of the societies where they now live. Full membership means having the same educational and work opportunities as long-term native-born citizens, and the same chances to better their own and their children's lot. It also means having a sense of dignity and belonging that comes with acceptance and inclusion in a broad range of societal institutions. The struggle for inclusion is likely to become ever more intense in the coming decades in the context of shifting demographics in Europe and North America. There is every sign that there will be a continued demand for immigration, creating inflows of new arrivals in the years ahead, and, at the same time, young people of immigrant origin will constitute a larger and larger share of young adults.

The challenges of integration are complicated by the widespread resistance of natives to immigrants and their children. There are anxieties about whether the newcomers will fit in and fears that they will undermine the basic foundations of established ways of life. These concerns are prominent in popular writings and the media. They are evident in opinion polls. They feature in some academic writings. And they have been voiced and exploited by politicians.

A widely acclaimed 2009 book by journalist Christopher Caldwell, *Reflections on the Revolution in Europe*, argues that immigration there is exacting a "steep price in freedom" and bringing "disorder, penury, and crime." Princeton Islamic scholar Bernard Lewis has said that by the end of this century Europe will be "part of the Arab West, the Maghreb." On the other side of the Atlantic, massive waves of Hispanic immigration, according to the late Harvard political scientist Samuel Huntington, are eroding America's national identity, and, if continued, will turn the United States into a country of two languages, two cultures, and two peoples without a shared historic cultural core. In the American media, Mexican immigrants and their children are often portrayed as unwilling to integrate—"unassimilable separatists"—and as a threat to existing institutions.[1]

National opinion polls reveal a high level of concern. About half of Americans and Europeans polled in a 2011 survey said that immigration is more of a problem than an opportunity.[2] Anxieties about newcomers' ability to integrate have spilled over into the political sphere as well. In Europe, anti-immigrant rhetoric is a staple of right-wing politicians and political parties. In 2014, France's xenophobic National Front came in ahead of all the country's other parties in the European Parliament elections with a quarter of the vote. The Netherlands' Geert Wilders, who has called for an end to Muslim immigration and the banning of the Koran, was voted the second most popular politician in his country in two national polls in 2009; and his Party for Freedom topped the polls four years later. In the United States, nativistic fears have been pivotal in many state and local elections, especially in places like Arizona, at or near the border with Mexico.

This book gets behind the rhetoric, exaggerations, and fear-mongering to examine what is really happening and why. The core issue is the integration of immigrants and their children. We approach this issue through a comparative—transatlantic—perspective.

As one might expect, the comparison reveals parallels as well as differences in how immigrants and their children are faring in Europe and North America and in the opportunities provided within different institutional arenas. But it does more than this. The value of comparing societies is that it enables us to spot where integration seems to be proceeding successfully and where it is not. Systematic comparison is essential, we believe, if lessons are to be drawn from the experience with immigration in diverse societies. Indeed, comparison lends itself to exploring ideas about borrowings, or features of institutions in one or more societies that appear worthy of emulation in another.

Comparisons cast differences into sharper relief; in particular, they bring out the distinctive ways that societies meet similar challenges of integration and shed light on unexpected outcomes. As a consequence, they give us new perspectives on each country and can offer new insights into each country's own internal dynamics. To paraphrase sociologist Reinhard Bendix, a comparative lens increases the visibility of processes and structures in one society by highlighting similarities and differences with another. It can reveal features that, because they are more or less "constant" within a society, like its political system, might otherwise be ignored or taken for granted. A comparative approach, as historian George Fredrickson observes, thereby enlarges our understanding of the institutions and processes being compared.[3]

Comparing the European and North American immigrant experiences highlights an array of historically rooted and durable social, political, and economic structures and institutions—from educational and political systems to legal frameworks and religious arrangements—that create barriers, as well as possible bridges, to integration for immigrants and their descendants in different societies. It points, as well, to the impact of other factors, including characteristics of the immigrant flows to each country, the nature of specific government policies, and a range of current social and economic trends. While there are definite transatlantic contrasts, no simple and consistent North America-Europe divide emerges; national differences within Europe and within North America matter. At the same time, there are some remarkable similarities among countries with very different institutional structures and immigration histories. To put it another way, there are no clear-cut winners or losers: each society fails and succeeds in different ways. Our goal is to identify the factors that impede or facilitate integration and to understand how they operate—and why—in distinctive national contexts.

Our comparison encompasses six key countries. On the North American side, one is the United States. This is hardly surprising given its size and importance as an immigration society and that we are U.S.-based sociologists who have spent much of our careers exploring immigration's impact there. We also include Canada, which, like the United States, is a classic settler society, but with significant contrasts, including different integration and admissions policies. Canada is often touted as a model of successful integration so that adding it to the mix helps to better understand the dynamics of immigrant inclusion and evaluate claims about immigrant integration there.

In Western Europe, the countries in our study are Britain, France, Germany, and the Netherlands. All four have received huge numbers of immigrants since the end of World War II. Indeed, taken together, they are home to half of the European Union's foreign born. The four countries represent a range of institutional approaches to immigration, and a substantial literature is available about immigrants and their children in each of them. An added advantage is that one of us has done research on immigrants and their children in France and Germany, the other has written about immigration in Britain and the Netherlands.[4]

In each country, our focus is mainly on groups we describe as "low status," such as Mexicans in the United States, North Africans in France, and Turks in Germany. The immigration flows to most countries, of course, are diverse and include groups with considerable human capital, whose members often take well-paid and prestigious positions, for example, in medicine and engineering. (One of every three immigrants to the United States is university educated; and a number of professions, such as those in science and engineering, are disproportionately staffed by these immigrants, who come mostly from Asia.[5]) But many immigrant groups are dominated by individuals arriving with low levels of education, who typically end up in poorly paid, sometimes off-the-books jobs that are frequently dirty and sometimes dangerous and demeaning. These immigrants are also stigmatized because of their ethnicity or race; they stand out because they look different in the eyes of the native majority and because they have different cultural backgrounds and, in some cases, religions. Members of low-status groups face the greatest barriers to integration in both the immigrant and the second generations. Our focus on these groups takes in large portions of the immigrant-origin populations in all the countries we study except for Canada, whose entry policies have been unusually selective. In Canada, the best approximation we can find are the groups labeled "visible-minority" immigrants, a term used there to refer to nonwhites, mostly from Asia and many well educated.

We explore the dynamics of integration in multiple ways. Our analysis runs the gamut from understanding the progress of those with immigration backgrounds in terms of educational attainment and political office to the impact and extent of residential segregation and growing economic inequality. We investigate the role of national identities and intermarriage as well as the barriers based on race and religion. This examination to a large degree draws upon a synthesis of the existing research literature, but it also incorporates our own analyses of both quantitative and qualitative data.

WHAT IS INTEGRATION?

Integration lies at the heart of our analysis. It is therefore important to clarify what we mean by the concept as well as to spell out some of our basic assumptions about the dynamics of change among immigrants and their children. "Integration," as we understand it, refers to the processes that increase the opportunities of immigrants and their descendants to obtain the valued "stuff" of a society, as well as social acceptance, through participation in major institutions such as the educational and political system and the labor and housing markets. Full integration implies parity of life chances with members of the native majority group and being recognized as a legitimate part of the national community. (By "native majority" we mean, in North America, later-generation Americans or Canadians of European descent and, in European countries, those with long-established ancestry; unless otherwise indicated, we use the term "native" to refer to those born in a country to parents who were also born there, while the phrase "immigrant origin," includes both immigrants and their descendants.)

For members of low-status immigrant groups, integration processes over time—often, across generations—tend to improve their economic, social, and political situations. The integration concept also applies to groups in which many arrive with higher status than is average for the native majority; it has to do with their ability to gain positions in key institutional sectors commensurate with their qualifications and talents so that, for example, an immigrant surgeon is not relegated to a low-level healthcare position and her professional abilities are acknowledged by colleagues, staff, and patients.

Integration occurs in relation to a "mainstream" society. The mainstream can be thought of as encompassing those social and cultural spaces where the native majority feels "at home" or, in other words, where its presence is taken for granted and seen as unproblematic. The mainstream includes public institutions such as schools and government, more informal social settings such as neighborhoods inhabited in large numbers by the native majority, and accepted ways of behaving, which, needless to say, typically differ to some extent among different native subgroups (as defined, for example, by social class or region). While the native majority is found in mainstream settings as a matter of definition, these need not be exclusive in ethnic and racial terms; members of other groups, such as Muslim or Latin American immigrants and their children, may enter them and be accepted. The terms under which this can happen determine the ease or difficulty of integration.

Moving to and settling in Europe or North America inevitably involves change on the part of immigrants as they adjust to life there, and this is especially so when they come from societies with customs, values, and institutions that differ markedly from those in the new country. At the most basic, immigrants typically learn to eat different foods than they are used to and to speak new languages. The children who grow up in immigrant homes are affected more profoundly by the culture and institutions around them than the immigrants themselves, who arrived as adults and spent their formative years steeped in home-country ways. The children, learning from their peers in school or on the street and from the mass media, acquire tastes and knowledge that make them quite different from their immigrant parents. Usually, the children have at least as much in common with their native majority age-mates as they do with their own parents, as they listen to popular music, for example, and adopt the latest fashion styles. As they mature, they may begin to distance themselves in other ways from immigrants, taking jobs in the mainstream labor market that put them in a world beyond their parents' ken. They usually go much further in school than their parents, at least when the parents are low-wage immigrants from such regions of the world as Latin America or Africa.

The changes may not all be beneficial or benign; some can have negative repercussions for immigrants and their children. Low-status immigrants in Europe and North America are commonly confined to the bottom rungs of the job ladder. Too often, they confront racial or ethnic prejudice and discrimination from members of the native majority. So may their children who, owing to disparate treatment in schools and the labor market, sometimes drop out of school or occasionally turn to illicit activities; either may be an early step on a pathway to permanent disadvantage. When members of a particular group are stigmatized on the basis of race and ethnicity and disadvantaged in educational and employment opportunities—on a large scale—these are signs of its emergence as an ethnoracial minority or, as in the United States, of possible assimilation into an existing minority population.[6]

Changes do not take place in only one direction. The presence of immigrants and the second generation alters the communities in which they live and, in some ways, the larger society as well. An obvious form of impact is on food, as immigrant cuisines, often modified for European or North American tastes, enrich the offerings in the new society. The Turkish *döner kebab* has become the most popular fast food in Germany, and more salsa than ketchup is sold in the United States. But the impact can be much deeper as new attitudes and values seep into the mainstream culture.[7] If we look back in time in the United States, for example, the educational advance of Jews in the mid-twentieth century had a huge impact on many elite universities, which previously defined themselves as Christian institutions and even had Protestant denominational affiliations. The new intellectual culture forged by Jews and liberal Protestants gradually turned universities into temples of "established nonbelief," to use historian George Marsden's phrase, and spread beyond them to help forge a civic culture of religious tolerance.[8]

In talking about these sorts of changes, the words, and to some extent, the concepts have shifted over time and still differ between the United States and the other countries we are considering. In the past, "assimilation" was the central idea, promoted by theorizing about the European immigrant-group experience in the United States. This idea has made a comeback there as a way to think about immigration-related changes, refurbished by purging the concept of its past, unsavory ethnocentric associations and by bringing it up to date for the twenty-first century.[9] In Canada and in most of Western Europe, "integration" has become the main way to talk about immigrant-group inclusion. Its adoption reflects in many quarters an opposition to the "assimilation" concept and its presumed assumption (false, in our view) of one-way cultural change.

How different are these ideas really? The theorizing about assimilation was inspired by the U.S. experience with immigration in the nineteenth and early twentieth centuries. It especially addresses the processes by which members of originally low-status and/or ethnoracially excluded groups, such as southern Italians and Russian Jews at that time, were able to enter the societal mainstream and attain life chances on a par with those of members of the dominant group. Assimilation theory posits that in general there is a relationship between cultural and social assimilation, on the one hand, and drawing close to the mainstream and the life chances of the native majority, on the other. In its latest version, though, it does not presume there is a specific sequence among these dimensions. Rather, there is typically a mutual interaction, as individuals and families are motivated to undertake various forms of assimilation by the attraction of greater opportunities in the mainstream; and achieving social mobility through mainstream institutions often entails constraints that accelerate some forms of assimilation (in language and in speech patterns, for example). Because assimilation envisions that majority and minority group differences may attenuate over time, it also includes the possibility that the social distinctions involved—or in other terms, the boundaries that separate groups—may weaken, eventually reaching the point where they hold little relevance for the everyday life of most "group" members.[10]

The integration concept, by comparison, is agnostic about cultural and social change. Many scholars who use the term "integration" reject the relevance of the cultural and social dimensions of assimilation and view the assimilation concept as questioning or devaluing the autonomy of immigrant families to decide on important sociocultural aspects of their lives. Dutch researchers Hans Vermeulen and Rinus Penninx observe that the term "integration" was introduced into the discourse of several European countries in order to replace assimilation and "to indicate a greater degree of tolerance and respect for ethnocultural differences."[11]

Assimilation, it must be pointed out, does not necessarily produce cultural homogeneity. The mainstream can expand to take in elements of immigrant-group cultures, and so encompass cultural difference, at least to some degree. There is perhaps no better example than the inclusion of immigrant religions in the mid-twentieth-century United States, an example that is all the more pertinent because religion is seen as the foundation of salient immigrant/native divisions in Western Europe today. In the early twentieth century, when Jewish and Catholic immigrants from southern and eastern Europe were landing in American ports in unprecedented numbers, the U.S. mainstream was defined as "Christian," a term opposed to Roman Catholicism as well as non-Christian religions. Non-Protestants were seen as outsiders, and the boundary that excluded them was defended by such actions as restrictions on the admission of Jews to elite universities, where privilege was minted, and by the mass mobilization of white Protestants to defeat the Catholic presidential candidate, Al Smith, in the election of 1928.[12] Yet, in the end, the mainstream expanded and was redefined as "Judeo-Christian," an expansion that accompanied post–World War II mass assimilation. To be sure, the struggle for inclusion was not a seamless process, but a product of contestation and conflict—even as late as 1960, the campaign of John F. Kennedy for president, the watershed event for Catholic inclusion, brought forth significant Protestant opposition. Moreover, during the twentieth century Judaism and Catholicism in the United States underwent changes that made them resemble American Protestant models more. But Jews and Catholics did not become carbon copies of Protestants. The crucial point is that the once salient boundaries separating them from Protestants faded while, at the same time, they retained distinctive religious identities, beliefs, and practices. The end result was the incorporation of the children and grandchildren of Irish and southern and eastern European immigrants into a "remade" American mainstream.

What is apparent is that there is considerable overlap between the assimilation and integration concepts, and both apply to our major concern in this book: the extent to which immigrants, and especially their children, are able to participate in key mainstream institutions in ways that position them to advance socially and materially. "Parity" with members of the native majority is too strong a standard to use given the historic recency of the large immigration streams coming to Western Europe, the United States, and Canada. An additional issue in assessing the social and economic position of immigrant minority groups is that large proportions of adult members are first-generation immigrants, and the second generation is still concentrated in youthful ages. The relevant question is whether specific groups such as North Africans in France or Mexicans in the United States appear to be blocked from social and economic advancement or, alternatively, seem to be on a promising trajectory.

While either concept might be applied to this question, we will speak mainly of "integration." We choose this word in recognition of its greater acceptability on the international scene; we want to avoid the impression that an analysis by two Americans is conducted solely from a U.S. perspective and will inevitably vindicate a U.S. model of incorporating immigrant groups (it will not). At the same time, we will take up some topics that are generally considered under the heading of "assimilation"—intermarriage, for example, as an indicator of weakening boundaries and decreasing differences between social groups. That concept rightly applies in those cases.

GRAND NARRATIVES AND SCHOLARLY CONTROVERSIES

In examining the integration of immigrants and their children, our analysis raises questions about a number of "grand narratives" or overarching ideas, which attempt to provide all-encompassing explanations for cross-national differences and similarities; these ideas loom large in transatlantic comparisons and, in some cases, have been widely assumed true by the general public.

The ideas are not always explicit about the mechanisms that are presumed to foster integration. But beneath the surface, two sorts of general mechanisms can be discerned: those that enhance the access of immigrants and their children to valuable social resources, such as income or education, and promote greater equality between immigrant and native groups; and those that enlarge the circle of membership in the national community, helping immigrants and the second generation to avoid marginalization as "them," in opposition to "us" of the majority group. The mix between these two sorts of mechanisms varies in the different narratives, though not always in an obvious or clear way.

National Models   One grand narrative that is widely influential concerns models, ideologies, or public philosophies of immigrant integration that are rooted in national cultural and historical traditions. The emergence of national models in the literature on immigration can be traced back to scholarly accounts in the 1990s seeking to explain why different European countries developed distinctive integration policies and conceptions of citizenship. Rogers Brubaker's comparison of French and German citizenship regimes and Adrian Favell's of the role of national philosophies of integration in shaping policy frameworks in France and Britain provided the groundwork for subsequent analyses of national models and their impact. In France, the emphasis has been on the Republican model and its strongly assimilationist principles; in Canada, on multiculturalism, with its stress on the legal and political accommodation of ethnic diversity; and in Germany, on what is often described as the ethnocultural conception of nationhood.[13] Not every one of the six countries we consider fits neatly into such schemes, but in each some key relevant themes can be identified. The United States is sometimes characterized as de facto multiculturalist because it lacks laws and policies that directly promote and shape assimilation and tolerates multiple languages (though their survival times are often short) as well as many other manifestations of cultural origins, although it also sometimes is characterized as assimilationist.[14]

One argument is that these national models determine how immigrants become part of their new societies, to a large extent because the models not only shape the willingness of nation-states to acknowledge immigrants as ethnic minorities with distinct needs and cultural rights, but also influence policies and political decisions that have wide-ranging effects. In this light, for example,

German laws for citizenship, which until 2000 denied birthright citizenship to the children born on German soil to most immigrant parents (so-called *jus sanguinis*, based on parental citizenship rather than birthplace), have been seen as a reflection of its ethnocultural model, while the French insistence on assimilation to French culture and discomfort with openly religious practices such as the Islamic headscarf are viewed as a reflection of its paradigmatic approach. Whether labeled a "public philosophy, a policy paradigm . . . or a national cultural idiom," the concepts "attempt to show how social reality is structured by pre-existing ideas about a nation's self-understanding, and how such ideas frame at once social interactions, institutional arrangements, [and] policy outcomes."[15]

Among the many questions is whether the assumptions in the scholarly literature about the national models of integration are accurate. There is disagreement, for example, about whether the Dutch actually had a multicultural model in the late twentieth century and if, and how much, the British have moved away from multiculturalism to an emphasis on cultural assimilation to British values.[16] Critiques of the "national model approach" point out as well that national models of integration are not fixed, but change over time, often in quite dramatic ways.

A key issue on both sides of the Atlantic is the relative importance of models of integration as compared to institutional arrangements and structures in explaining cross-national differences in immigrant integration. Indeed, the models' connections to public policy and social, political, and institutional practices are often limited and contradictory. State-supported programs, for example, may develop in response to on-the-ground political, economic, and social realities that contradict or have nothing to do with the models.[17] Yet in the end, the basic issue is not whether national models or ideologies of integration exist—they do, at the very least in public discourse—but how, and to what degree, they influence the range of opportunities available to immigrant minorities and their ability to participate and feel included in mainstream institutions.

Political Economy   Another grand narrative views the nature of a country's political economy as fundamental. This approach has its origins in typologies analyzing the character and role of different political economy regimes in advanced Western societies, specifically institutional variations in the regulation of the labor market and the provision of social welfare by the state.[18] The typologies developed to distinguish these variations have been elaborated in different ways by different authors, with the classification of Gøsta Esping-Andersen describing social welfare regimes as liberal, corporatist-statist, or social democratic as the most seminal. Drawing on the classification developed by Jonas Pontusson, we employ a simplified variant that divides the countries in our analysis into two groups: the United States, Canada, and Britain as liberal market economies in contrast to the German, French, and Dutch social market economies or social welfare states. In the latter, the economy is more heavily regulated by the state, which in addition provides workers with greater social protection against the vagaries of the labor market in the form of government benefits. To give one example, with respect to the protection of workers against dismissal—reflected in mandated procedures employers must follow and severance pay they must provide—France, Germany, and the Netherlands are clustered at the high end, while Britain, Canada, and the United States anchor the low end, according to OECD rankings.[19]

The benefits of social welfare regimes have been widely noted in the social science literature as protecting immigrant families from a fall into poverty and ensuring that they have the financial means to live decent lives; in the liberal market economies, many immigrants are forced to choose bad jobs over unemployment, yet still may not earn enough to lift their families out of poverty, thereby affecting their own and their children's prospects. At the same time, it could be argued that employment in liberal market economies, even at the low end of the labor market, promotes some degree of integration for immigrants and may provide possibilities for developing potentially useful social networks and additional skills.

At root, the central question is whether the nature of the political economy is as paramount as this grand idea assumes. Is the liberal market/social market economy distinction able, for example, to explain differences in immigrant employment and poverty rates among the six countries and, equally important, in noneconomic domains such as immigrant residential patterns and second-generation educational achievements?

Settler Societies Then there is a perspective prominent in cross-national comparisons of immigration that emphasizes the position of the United States and Canada as settler societies, with deep histories of immigration, distinct from the Old World societies of Europe. The underlying assumption is that the settler societies are more successful in integrating contemporary immigrants and their children because immigration has been an essential element in their establishment and development. In Canada and the United States, large-scale immigration played a decisive role in the conquest and peopling of sparsely occupied territories; as nations, they were founded, populated, and built by immigrants (including hundreds of thousands of forced immigrants, African slaves, in the United States). The result is that immigration is a fundamental part of the origin myth, historical consciousness, and national identity in both countries.

In Western Europe, by contrast, mass immigration did not occur until after nation-states had been in place for some time. European states were mainly formed through disputes over borders or consolidation of population groups who had lived in a particular region for centuries, not by new arrivals who displaced and almost wiped out an indigenous population. Even though migrations across borders, such as the Huguenot flight from Catholic France to England, Prussia, and the Dutch Republic in the sixteenth century, and rural to urban movement to nearby countries in the 1800s, played an unmistakable role in European history, the main international migration experience of the eighteenth and nineteenth centuries was one of emigration, chiefly to the Americas, north and south, by tens of millions of Europeans. As a result, it has been argued, immigration (especially from other continents) has not been a core part of European identity the way it has been in North America, or of European countries' past nation-building processes.[20] The implication is that the settler societies will thus extend a warmer welcome to immigrants and be more confident about their integration—and more comfortable about bringing immigrants and their children into the national fold.

How much does the settler/nonsettler society difference matter to the success of integration? Are there ways in which European countries differ as contexts of reception from the United States and Canada because they lack a self-conscious immigration story? Whatever their histories, all the countries in our study are *now* societies with substantial proportions of first- and second-generation immigrants: to what extent does this shared present reality overshadow their different settlement pasts? Moreover, an overemphasis on the position of the United States and Canada as settler societies minimizes the role of other aspects of their histories in shaping national ideologies, identities, and discourses and can lead to disregarding differences between the two countries that have significant consequences for integration. Stressing the advantages of the settler societies can also lead to overlooking ways in which they may be less successful than European countries in providing opportunities for immigrants and their children.

American Exceptionalism   This leads to another "grand" idea—U.S. exceptionalism—about which much has been written, particularly in terms of the differences between the United States and Western Europe. One common popular claim is that the United States has been an exceptionally—some would say, uniquely—open society, welcoming immigrants and quickly investing them with membership rights, including access to America's historically broad escalator of mobility into the middle class. But how exceptional really is the United States in incorporating immigrants? More fundamentally, is the notion of American exceptionalism a productive way to think about transatlantic comparisons of immigrant minorities?

American exceptionalism has a long history in American social theory and historical writings. On one side, writings about it often have a congratulatory tone, emphasizing that the United States is exceptional among nations in its early democracy and republican tradition, its frontier spirit and mobility opportunities, and in picking and choosing the best of its many European legacies (though, we must point out, recent research demonstrates that social mobility in the United States now lags behind the levels in most economically advanced societies[21]). On the other side, many liberal American social scientists have adopted a critical approach—what John Torpey calls the "bad exceptionalism thesis"—which sees the United States as distinctively harsh and ungenerous, lacking the more robust welfare-state arrangements that have been characteristic of Western European countries and that provide economic and social protections for their populations.[22] Also, there is the sordid history of slavery and legal segregation on its home soil—a "bad" feature of the United States that stands out from Europe, and that has surprisingly complex effects for immigrants in the United States today.

Clearly, there are ways that the United States is unique as an immigrant society, and we will point to them throughout this book. The problem, though, is that the "exceptionalist" framework ignores or downplays similarities between the United States and European countries, to say nothing of Canada. To put it another way, this idea has a tendency to overemphasize or blow out of proportion U.S.-Europe differences, not unlike what Sigmund Freud famously characterized as the "narcissism of small differences."

In any case, as Aristide Zolberg points out, there are "many exceptionalisms," indeed as many "exceptionalisms" as there are countries of immigration.[23] Our aim, as we have said, is to systematically analyze cross-national commonalities and variations in search of factors that seem fruitful for integration. This gets us away from either demonizing or celebrating the United States. Either would be wrong—and too simple. The key questions are not just what is distinct, or exceptional, about immigrant integration in the United States, but also what is particular to Canada and each of the four European countries in our study. Moreover, what are the similarities or parallels in the integration process in the United States and elsewhere?

Convergence The final grand idea or narrative—stressing convergence—shifts the ground to emphasize the erasure or decline of differences among nations rather than ways they stand out from each other. A major topic in scholarly discussions is whether, and to what degree, we are witnessing a convergence process that undercuts national differences in the responses to and effects of immigration in Europe and North America.

The basic gist of convergence approaches is that Western Europe and North America are becoming more similar with regard to state policies concerning immigrants, especially policies toward citizenship, cultural practices, and social welfare benefits.[24] In explaining this growing convergence, the emphasis is on common domestic and international pressures and societal structural features as well as on mutual borrowing or emulation. Convergence theorists point to the basic principles of liberal democracies in the context of mass immigration; the emergence, particularly within Europe in light of the European

Union's increasingly important role, of transnational and postnational norms, laws, and rules undermining or diminishing the significance of nation-states; and the need to deal with similar sets of problems arising from the challenges of integrating the growing number of immigrants and their children. The recent period of mass immigration coincides with the rise of new globalizing forces. As one scholar puts it, modern-day transportation and telecommunications, among other changes, have led to "convergent modes of social and cultural transformation associated with the globalizing of cultural forms."[25]

But how extensive and significant is convergence in government policies and practices in bringing the countries of Europe and North America closer together? Does it make more analytic sense to speak of *relative* convergence given that marked national differences remain? After all, we are not yet living in a postnational world; it is too early to declare the end of historically rooted national distinctions.[26] Should we give up the quest for convergence altogether because nations may converge in some ways and diverge in others, given the "ramshackle, multifaceted, loosely connected sets of regulatory rules, institutions, and practices in various domains of society" that affect immigrant incorporation—so that it is impossible to speak of an overall convergence trend or process?[27] School systems in different countries, to take one example, are notoriously resistant to change and are rooted in educational institutions and traditions that often predate large-scale immigration. How would the notion of convergence apply to them?

As this review of analytic perspectives indicates, our focus is mainly on the national rather than the local plane. It is not that we fail to recognize the importance of local contexts, such as cities, for the integration process.[28] Anyone who has lived in New York City, as we have done, has to recognize that it is a very different location for immigrants and their children, than is, say, Houston. In fact, one of us has written extensively on this topic.[29] However, the big ideas about how integration may vary across contexts are pitched at the national level, and there is considerable work to be done in comparing national contexts. This book is the proof.

THE ULTIMATE STAKES

Immigration is quite literally changing the face of the West. The rich societies of North America and Western Europe are facing a transition of enormous consequence during the coming quarter century as a result of irreversible demographic changes wrought by immigration, combined with the aging of their native majority populations. This looming shift can be described as a "diversity transition" because the adult population will come to include fewer individuals from the native majority and more from immigrant homes. Diversity will be increasingly a matter of second-, and even third-, generation individuals who have grown up and been educated in these societies and can claim insider status, although given low overall fertility rates (especially in parts of Western Europe) and aging populations, pressures for continued inflows of first-generation immigrants will also be strong. In looking ahead, it is clear that the economic, cultural, and social vitality of West European, American, and Canadian societies will be affected by their ability to integrate young adults of immigrant origins and draw on their talents.

This transition will be deeply felt in the group of active-age adults and therefore in the labor market, civic institutions, and the polity. It will be accelerated by a phenomenon that was universal in Western societies at the end of World War II: the baby boom. The baby boomers, who in the United States in 2014 were between the ages of 50 and 68, will be retiring during the next several decades. This massive group is on average well educated and includes the first cohorts to experience mass higher education; and the baby boomers are well positioned in the labor market, occupying a disproportionate share of the most skilled and best-paying jobs.[30] The question that will have to be faced on both sides of the Atlantic is who will replace them? The young adults coming of age in the period ahead will include fewer members of the native majority and many more individuals from immigrant or other minority backgrounds. Unless these young people are successfully integrated into the larger society, they will not be able to effectively compete for the better positions being vacated by the baby boomers.

The prospect of the demographic transition sharpens the edge of some of the most important questions about integration. How will this transition, and the replacement process it entails, affect opportunities for immigrants and their children as well as their inclusion and acceptance in the mainstream society? If, as we have said, a major challenge is how to integrate the children (and, in some cases, the grandchildren) of the immigrants so they can participate in the labor force and other institutions on a par with natives, we have to ask how successful the societies of North America and Western Europe have been in pursuing integration. This question is all the more freighted with significance because large numbers of immigrant-origin children in most Western countries face substantial disadvantages in reaching educational parity with children from native backgrounds, given not only the limited education of immigrant parents but also the stigmatization they experience owing to their national origin, phenotypic appearance, or religion.

Quite obviously these questions are as much about the societies themselves as they are about the immigrant minorities. We do not, of course, claim powers of prognostication about outcomes that cannot be known for decades. Still, the chapters that follow provide clues about the impact of sustained immigration and growing diversity on the countries in our study in the years to come. Are these societies on their way to successful integration of immigrants and, even more importantly, the second generation? Will they thereby avoid sharp divisions along ethnic, racial, and religious lines in the opportunities for social mobility and personal development open to young people from different backgrounds? Or, alternatively, are social cleavages opening up between the native population and some of the immigrant-origin groups? Such cleavages, which can be reflected in unequal opportunities, segregation by residence, or other indicators of limited social contacts, would suggest the emergence, or in some cases the expansion, of permanently disadvantaged minority groups.

These are the ultimate stakes.

PLAN OF THE BOOK

The first step in understanding the challenges of diversity is to appreciate how Western European and North American countries became so diverse in the first place and who the new groups are. We thus begin, in chapter 2, by exploring the role of post–World II immigration laws and policies of the six countries in giving rise to the mix of new social groups on their social landscapes. We organize the discussion mainly in terms of types of immigrants who have arrived, in varying number and proportion: labor immigrations, high human-capital immigrations, postcolonial migrations, and refugee and asylum inflows; and we consider the role of subsequent family reunification. We also examine the challenges of controlling immigration and how open (or closed) the six countries are to continued arrivals from abroad. In addition, the chapter sketches the demographic impacts of immigration, revealing the rapidly increasing diversity of working-age populations found throughout the wealthy West.

The next two chapters focus on domains, economic and residential, that immigrants must deal with early on in the settlement process, although these beginnings can have long-term, even intergenerational, consequences for integration. Chapter 3 looks at the economic situations of the immigrants. They have uprooted themselves in the search for better economic prospects, but profound changes in the economic structures of the rich societies of the West in recent years raise serious doubts about whether their aspirations will be fulfilled and therefore about the starting point for the next generation. This chapter explores the implications of growing labor market inequality and precarious work for the economic incorporation of immigrants, including rates of labor force participation, unemployment, and risks of poverty. The emphasis is on how immigrants are doing compared to natives in the countries where they live, with the emphasis—as in all the chapters—on low-status immigrants.

Chapter 4 turns to the residential contexts of immigrant families, which also affect the starting point for the second generation. Fears that immigrants and their children will end up living in "parallel societies" like the black ghettoes of American cities are vastly overblown. Nevertheless, neighborhoods of immigrant concentration, at least for low-status groups, may create marked disadvantages. We examine the actual extent, and consequences, of residential segregation, also looking at the role of public policies in shaping these patterns. Neighborhoods are often the places where immigrant minorities and native majorities have initial contacts and thus where the impacts of immigration on the mainstream society are particularly salient. In this vein, we consider the emergence of "super-diverse" neighborhoods.

The following two chapters consider two fundamental social divisions, race and religion, that could affect the ability of some immigrant-origin groups to eventually achieve full integration. Chapter 5 puts the spotlight on race, with a stress on the special position of the United States. While color-coded race is a source of stigma in Canada and Western Europe, it is a more severe barrier in the United States, especially for immigrants of African ancestry and their children, owing to the legacy of slavery, legal segregation, and ghettoization. Yet, the paradox of racial dynamics in the United States is that they have also had some positive consequences for immigrants there, who are overwhelmingly people of color from Latin America, Asia, and the Caribbean. The heritage of the U.S. civil rights movement and legislation of the 1960s, as well as the sheer presence and size of the native black population have provided immigrants in the United States with certain advantages that they lack in Europe and Canada.

If racial divisions are a defining characteristic of the United States, religious cleavages seem their nearest equivalent in Western Europe. Religion dominates discussions about immigrant integration there, and the core issues concern Islam. Anti-Islam sentiment, of course, is hardly absent in North America, but religion is not the kind of bright boundary between immigrants and native-born residents that it is in Western Europe. Chapter 6 describes how immigrant religion generally has become a more significant social divide, a greater challenge to integration, and a more common source of conflict with mainstream institutions and practices in Western Europe than in the United States (with Canada positioned between the two). We analyze the reasons for this difference between the two sides of the Atlantic, and also consider possible changes in the future that may make Islam less of a barrier for immigrant-origin populations in Europe, and blur some of the distinctions among the six countries found today.

In the subsequent three chapters we investigate domains involving long-term integration, and thus processes that can span the generations or primarily affect the second generation. Chapter 7 deals with the political integration of immigrant groups. Entry into the inner precincts of power is a paramount indicator of the overall inclusion of newcomer groups. Our focus is on the ability of politicians from immigrant backgrounds to be elected to office, which we argue is the gold standard for political inclusion, bringing rewards of societal power and a voice in political decisions. We provide data on the success of immigrant-origin groups in winning positions in local, regional, and national legislatures in the six countries of our study; probe the factors that explain the differences in electoral representation; and consider whether, and to what degree, convergences in national laws and policies have reduced the importance of national differences in political integration and may continue to do so in the future.

In chapter 8 we zero in on the group that is the key to the future, the second generation. Educating the children of immigrants is one of the greatest challenges facing the countries of Western Europe and North America today. The progress of these children has implications for their own and their families' futures, and, on a wider canvas, for the labor forces in the countries where they live. This chapter addresses such critical questions as: To what extent do educational systems reproduce inequalities between native and immigrant-origin students? What kinds of opportunities do schools provide, especially for immigrant children from disadvantaged backgrounds? And, when it comes to the adult world of work, how far do these opportunities allow the children of immigrants to go?

Chapter 9 takes the analysis of the second generation further by examining a subjective topic: feelings of belonging. At bottom the issue is the extent to which the children of immigrants feel truly at home in the societies where they are living, and whether they are seen by others as perennial outsiders. In exploring identities, our key questions are how, and to what degree, a national identity is extended to those of immigrant background. A related subject concerns intermarriage or—more broadly, since family partnerships are increasingly formed without marriage ceremonies—mixed unions. We look at the acceptability of the descendants of new immigrants by dominant majority groups through an analysis of mixed unions, examining both the frequency and consequences of these most intimate of relations.

The concluding chapter has three main goals. The first is to sum up the lessons learned from the comparisons in the preceding chapters and to assess how immigrants and their children are likely to fare in the different countries in the context of the impending demographic transition of the next several decades. The second goal is to consider the ideas and perspectives raised previously—what we have called the "grand narratives"—in light of the evidence provided throughout the book. Finally, we turn to policy implications of our study, evaluating remedies commonly suggested by others, and putting forward some of our own, which may help reduce the barriers immigrant-origin groups encounter and ease their struggles for inclusion on both sides of the Atlantic. These are issues of signal importance since the future of these societies will depend, to a large degree, on how well they manage the integration of immigration-driven ethnic, racial, and religious diversity.

CHAPTER 2

WHO ARE THE IMMIGRANTS?

The Genesis of the New Diversity

At the beginning of the twenty-first century, the rich countries of Western Europe and North America are immigration societies, visibly and irrevocably altered by decades of inflows from abroad. In 2012 the United States was home to about 40 million immigrants—the largest foreign-born population in the world—comprising 13 percent of the population (see table 2.1). Canada can boast of an even higher population share of immigrants, who amount to approximately 20 percent of Canadians, though their absolute number is much smaller: 6.8 million in 2011. Both countries continue to receive many newcomers every year, adding 3 to 6 percent directly to their populations over a decade. The European countries are often seen as more ambivalent about immigration, but they, too, are expanding demographically as a result of it (though France and Germany are doing so slowly). The new arrivals join what have become substantial established migrant communities, with the foreign born in Britain, France, Germany, and the Netherlands accounting for between 8 and 13 percent of the population.

Understanding the integration prospects of these immigrants and their children requires a fuller appreciation of who they are. Immigrant groups are not all the same when it comes to integration. Some, because of their ethnic resemblance to the natives of the receiving society or the educational and professional status of their members, are scarcely visible and easily absorbed into the mainstream. Others, because of racial, ethnic and/or religious differences from the native majority and low levels of human capital, pose major challenges to integration and may be at risk of developing into permanent minorities, separated from the mainstream by durable disadvantages. In the United States, the thirty thousand or so British and Canadians who immigrate each year are barely noticed, whereas the thirty to fifty thousand Dominicans—one could pick any of a number of groups from Latin America and the Caribbean—stand

Table 2.1. Basic Immigration Data (ca. 2009–14)

	Population (1000s)	Immigrant % of population	% ethnoracially distinct immigrants[1]	Leading countries among foreign born	Net immigration rate
North America					
Canada	35,345	20.6	60.2	UK China India	5.66
US	313,874	13.0	81.4	Mexico China India	2.45
Western Europe					
France	65,821	8.5	56.9	Algeria Morocco Portugal	1.09
Germany	80,511	12.9	37.8	former USSR Turkey Poland	1.06
Great Britain[2]	61,881	12.4	60.1	India Poland Pakistan	2.56
Netherlands	16,849	10.7	60.6	Turkey Surinam Morocco	1.97

[1] Immigrants from the countries of Africa, Asia, the Caribbean, and Latin America.

[2] Here and elsewhere in the book, we generally refer to Britain or Great Britain (officially, England, Wales, and Scotland) but use England and Wales or the UK (Great Britain plus Northern Ireland) when these terms are used in reporting the data we rely on.

Sources:

Canada: Statistics Canada website; National Household Survey (2013).

US: Census Bureau website; 2012 American Community Survey data; Pew Research Center (2013).

France (definition of immigrants conforms to the official French definition, excluding those born abroad who were French citizens at birth and thus not counting the *pieds noirs* from Algeria): INSEE website.

Germany: Statistisches Bundesamt (2010).

Great Britain: Office for National Statistics website.

Netherlands: Statistics Netherlands website.

Net immigration rates from Migration Information Source website for 2014.

out as distinct on the American scene. Across the Atlantic, the intra-European migrations enabled by the rules of the European Union generally are not regarded as being as problematic as the flows from countries such as Morocco and Turkey.

THE IMMIGRATION SYSTEM AND THE IMMIGRANT MIX

Central to determining who the immigrants are in any country is its immigration system, the topic of concern for much of this chapter. By the term "immigration system," we refer to the post–World War II immigration laws and policies of the six countries in our study, which have given rise to the mix of new groups and to their initial position in national communities. Of course, when we say that the immigration system is central to shaping immigrant inflows in different places, we do not mean to suggest that other factors are of no consequence. In every receiving country, a broad range of factors is involved, as the pages that follow indicate. These include geographical proximity to a major sending country, the case of the U.S. border with Mexico being perhaps the most dramatic; the history of military, political (and, importantly, colonial and neocolonial) relations between the countries of origin and destination; and the push of economic and political conditions at one end of the migration chain and the pull of labor demands at the other. Our emphasis, however, is on immigration laws and policies, which have played an especially important role in creating the distinctive mix of immigrants in North America and Europe in the past six decades, and thus provide a useful framework for our discussion.

The key word here is "mix," for nowhere has the immigration system created a uniform flow of newcomers, consistent in their characteristics and prospects for integration. A common observation is that immigration tends to be "bimodal," including low-status groups whose members take jobs at the very bottom of the economic ladder, as well as groups with high levels of educational and professional qualifications whose members often can insert themselves at or near the top of the labor market. But the term "bimodal" fails to grasp the typical complexity of immigration streams. Immigration laws and policies generally serve multiple purposes—for example, to bring in low-wage workers who will occupy positions in the labor force that natives of the society are reluctant to take; to address some of the dilemmas of decolonization by allowing those with close ties to the colonial power to migrate to what they see as the homeland; and to contribute to the resolution of refugee crises by taking in a portion of those who have been displaced. These purposes may overlap in complex ways and evolve over time.

This is not to say that states can entirely control the movements of people. The intent of immigration law is one thing; how the letter of the law has been used by potential migrants, often desperate to reach a country in Western Europe or North America where they will have the chance to improve their economic fortunes, may be something quite different. As the Swiss writer Max Frisch famously wrote, "We called for labor, and human beings came." For instance, family-reunification provisions of immigration law in Europe have given rise to marriage markets in which the children of immigrants, possessing the legal rights of permanent residents or citizens, sponsor the immigration of spouses from their parents' home villages. High percentages of the second generations of some groups, such as the Turks, have found marital partners in the home country rather than in the native majority or even among the coethnics they have grown up with in European cities. While some European countries have tried—with some success—to find ways to narrow this opening for new immigrants, there are obvious humanitarian limits to the degree to which they can restrict the rights of citizens to bring close family members to live with them, especially marital partners who happen to be from other countries.

In reflecting on the implications of immigration systems for the potential integration of the groups they introduce, it is helpful to think in terms of types of immigration, such as labor and refugee immigrations, for broadly speaking their relationships to integration prospects are distinct. Organizing the discussion according to types also helps to bring out the comparative aspects of immigration systems, for different countries have often gone about creating a portal for a particular type in different ways, with potentially divergent implications for future integration. In what follows, then, after a brief overview of the unfolding of immigration in Western Europe and North America, we discuss labor immigrations, high human-capital immigrations, postcolonial migrations, refugee inflows, and family reunification.

THE FOUNDATIONS OF POSTWAR IMMIGRATION SYSTEMS

WESTERN EUROPE

In Europe, the massive waves of immigrants began arriving soon after the end of World War II. Britain, France, Germany, and the Netherlands all needed to rebuild damaged infrastructures and economies, and yet did not have enough workers owing to the massive casualties from the war. In Britain, a superintendent in a Midlands foundry described the great labor scarcity of the 1950s: "The big influx of labour began in 1954. At this time you couldn't get an armless, legless man never mind an able-bodied one."[1]

One solution adopted in many European countries was to bring in "guestworkers," who were expected to come without their families, work for predetermined periods, and then return home. The German program, exemplary in a number of respects, was based on binational agreements, which began in 1955 with Italy and were quickly extended throughout the northern Mediterranean. Turks soon became the largest guestworker group.[2] The guestworkers typically took jobs at the bottom rungs of the labor market, in such industries as mining, manufacturing, and the building trades. The numbers were enormous. The arrival of the millionth guestworker—as it happens, a 38-year-old carpenter from a Portuguese village—was celebrated with great fanfare in 1964 at the Cologne train station. "Without the additional work of foreigners," the representative of the German Employers' Association said from the podium, "our economic development in recent years would be unthinkable."[3] Altogether, the number of foreign workers in the Federal Republic of Germany rose from ninety-five thousand in 1956 to 2.6 million in 1973.[4]

France and the Netherlands also turned to guestworkers to deal with labor shortages. Throughout the 1960s the Dutch government signed labor agreements and acted as a mediator in recruitment, first looking to Italy, Spain, and Portugal, and later, in the mid- and late-1960s, to Turkey, Morocco, and Yugoslavia. France established the National Immigration Office (ONI) as early as 1945 to organize the recruitment of workers and, in some cases their families, from southern Europe—mainly Italy, and then Spain and Portugal—and to place them in various sectors of the French economy. In effect, the ONI became a clearinghouse for employers, who went to sending countries to find the labor they needed, brought the workers to France, and integrated them into the workforce. By the early 1970s, some 570,000 Spanish, 812,000 Portuguese, and 572,000 Italian migrants were living in France.[5]

The guestworker period came to an abrupt end in the early 1970s. The shock of rising oil prices after the OPEC oil embargo in 1973 followed by recession and growing unemployment led to a drastic change in immigration policy and patterns virtually everywhere in Europe. Germany shut off guestworker recruitment. The Netherlands did not formally declare a halt to labor immigration, but recruitment of workers came to a virtual standstill. France sought to ban the entry of dependents as well as workers and offered repatriation allowances to workers who would go home.[6]

In several European countries, the labor pool was augmented also by colonial and postcolonial migrations, often spurred by the turmoil associated with decolonization in Africa, Asia, and the Caribbean. Britain depended heavily on immigration from colonies such as Jamaica and former colonies such as India to meet labor needs in the immediate post–World War II period; Ireland, long ruled by the English and a major source of migrants, continued to supply large numbers of workers in the 1950s and 1960s, several decades after independence. France took in more than a million North Africans—Algerians, Moroccans, and Tunisians—by the early 1980s.[7] The greatest number came from Algeria, many in a wave of repatriates in 1962, at the end of the war for independence, and others as citizens of the newly independent state who were taking advantage of quotas established by an accord between the two countries. The former colonial powers soon attempted to limit these inflows, however. Britain began this process with 1962 legislation that restricted the entry of Commonwealth citizens from the former colonies. In 1972 a new agreement between Algiers and Paris reduced the inflow from Algeria.

However much Western European countries may have wished to seal their borders, they did not entirely shut the door on these immigrations. Family reunification subsequently became—and remains—a dominant mode by which new immigrants from outside Europe gain entry. Indeed, the closing down of guestworker programs accelerated the process of family reunification, as many migrants decided against returning home. In Germany, for example, the number of Turkish citizens rose by 70 percent in the decade following 1973.[8] Immigrants from former colonies also continued to arrive in Europe as a result of family reunification, often achieved through marriage to a compatriot with European citizenship or at least permanent resident rights.

Moreover, the European countries remained open to intra-European migrants through their membership in what was initially the European Economic Community (EEC) and later the European Union (EU). The mobility of workers had been guaranteed in the 1957 Treaty of Rome that founded the EEC, and three of the countries in our study—France, Germany, and the Netherlands— were original members. (The United Kingdom joined in 1973.) This initial mobility guarantee mainly benefited citizens of Italy, a fourth member, who were numerous as guestworkers in northern Europe.[9] As the initial EEC group expanded over time, other Europeans came to enjoy the guarantee of free mobility, which allowed them to settle and work in another member country and to travel back and forth without hindrance between it and their home countries. Thus, in 1986, Spain and Portugal, which had already supplied large labor migrations to France, came on board.

In recent years, the situation with respect to intra-EU labor migration has been changed fundamentally by the accession to membership (in 2004 and 2007) of ten Eastern European countries, including Poland and Romania, the sources of many recent migrants to Western Europe. The hope has been, at least at the governmental level, that future labor needs can be met by the labor surpluses of Eastern European populations. This hope is poised against the concern in many countries that Turkish entry into the EU would allow a flood of Turkish Muslims into Western Europe. Sentiments against Turkey's membership are particularly strong in countries with large Turkish immigrant populations, including France, Germany, and the Netherlands. How long Eastern European countries will continue to supply large numbers of migrants to Western Europe is, however, an open question that will affect future needs to recruit from farther afield.

Oddly, despite the expectations of long-term labor flows from Eastern Europe, most EU members, including France, Germany, and the Netherlands, took an initially wary stance toward migrations originating in the new member states. In a shift from the rules that governed mobility between older member states, individual countries were allowed to postpone the guarantee of mobility for citizens of the Eastern European members for a transition period lasting as long as seven years. Germany, with a long and conflicted history of labor migrations by Poles, took the hardest line, invoking in 2009 a clause allowing two more years postponement in case of "serious labour-market disturbances."

However, as of 2011, Poles and most other Eastern Europeans have obtained the guaranteed access to Germany.[10]

Britain was an exception to this reluctance. Between 2004 and 2006, around half a million people from the eight Eastern European countries that joined the EU in 2004 registered to work in Britain, the majority of them from Poland. The "Polish plumber" became a symbol for the Eastern European influx and for the threat it presumably posed to wages and working conditions in affluent Western Europe. Because, however, of downturns in the British economy, combined with improving prospects for some Eastern Europeans at home, many did not settle. Nevertheless, by 2011 the census counted close to 580,000 Polish-born residents in England and Wales, a tenfold increase from a decade earlier.[11]

NORTH AMERICA

The United States also operated a temporary worker program in the immediate post–World War II period. The Bracero program, which brought in Mexican agricultural workers, had begun during the war as a way of replacing the men taken from the fields by military service, but it continued until 1964. It is often seen as a prelude to the much more open immigration period that began in 1965, as it gave more than four million Mexican workers a taste of life in "El Norte" and contacts with U.S. employers. Permanent Mexican immigration began to grow in the early 1960s, as the Bracero program was coming to an end.[12]

For the United States, the primary portal for the legal entry of migrants was created by the watershed Immigration and Nationality Act of 1965, which, despite predictions of the legislators who supported the law, ushered in a new era of immigration. The law brought an end to a system that, since the 1920s, had been based on ethnoracial exclusions and on preferences biased in favor of immigrants from northwestern Europe: it eliminated the severe racial bar against Asian immigration and the national-origins quotas that limited immigration from many other parts of the world. The law was not the only cause of the change in quantity and characteristics of immigrants in the late twentieth century: immigration from Mexico and elsewhere in the Americas began surging during the 1950s and early 1960s. But with the 1965 act, as Richard Alba and Victor Nee have noted, "the United States was in effect declaring that it was prepared to accept newcomers from all over the world."[13]

The act put in place the framework for the immigration system that exists today, although there have been numerous modifications along the way. The law set an annual maximum, originally fixed at twenty thousand immigrants per country for the Eastern Hemisphere (extended to the Americas in the Immigration Act of 1976). Although the per-country limits have been increased, these immigration slots continue to be allocated by way of ranked "preferences," roughly 70 percent of them awarded on the basis of family connections to U.S. citizens and permanent residents. A minority (20 percent) are awarded on the basis of labor-market qualifications. The numerical caps are not absolute, however. The 1965 law provided for additional categories—the parents, spouses, and minor children of U.S. citizens—who were exempt from the per-country limits. These immigrants have contributed to the soaring of legal immigration since 1965.[14]

And soar it has. The 1965 act is often held up as an example of the unintended consequences of public policy. Thinking that the family-reunification emphasis in the law would favor the admission of the relatives of Americans of the last large wave of European immigrants, the law's authors did not anticipate a large increase in admissions. Perhaps, as Aristide Zolberg has noted, they were disingenuous or merely lacked an understanding of global migration dynamics. Whatever their intentions, the fact is that legal admissions increased by half in a decade, from 3.3 million during the 1960s to 4.5 million during the 1970s.[15]

It was not only the numbers that changed. So did the source countries. The United States has turned once again into a nation of immigrants—one that more and more draws from all over the globe. Until the middle of the twentieth century, the great majority of immigrants were from Europe and Canada. As of 1960, more than 80 percent of the foreign born residing in the United States had come from these regions. By the 1980s, only 13 percent of legal immigrants each year were from Canada or Europe, and more than four-fifths came from Asia, Latin America, and the Caribbean, with Africa joining the mix in the 1990s. Altogether, between 1968 and 2000, Asia was the source of slightly more than a third of all legal immigrants to the United States, while the Caribbean, Central and South America contributed nearly a quarter. Yet, despite all of this diversity, neighboring Mexico stands out as the major source country, accounting for a remarkable 29 percent of all immigrants living in the United States in 2010. No other single country accounted for more than 5 percent.[16]

Legislation since the 1965 act, such as the Immigration Act of 1990, has expanded the legal influx, not restricted it. The United States has so far refused opportunities to cut back the immigrant flow, even when it became clear that the 1965 act encouraged unanticipated sources. After the attacks of September 11th, for example, the country's relatively generous immigration policy was not reversed, though the immigration from largely Muslim societies came under much greater scrutiny.[17] The allure of cheap and mobile labor in a society with highly flexible labor markets has always stood as a pillar supporting expansive immigration policies. Business interests have combined with unlikely political allies—ethnic and civil rights groups, religious bodies, and immigrants' rights organizations—to promote expanded immigration as well as porous borders and lax enforcement.[18]

Even an attempt to curb unauthorized immigration, the Immigration Reform and Control Act of 1986 (IRCA), was responsible for a huge expansion in legal admissions. It ended up legalizing nearly three million people, most of them Mexicans. Unauthorized residents who had entered the United States before 1982 were eligible for amnesty, and a special legalization program was extended to agricultural workers, many of whom came later. Given the emphasis on family reunification in U.S. immigration law, the effects of IRCA exceed the initial legalizations. As one account sums it up, "Altogether, the legalization program created a pool of some three million permanent residents and prospective citizens, who would eventually stimulate more immigration by way of family reunion."[19]

Canada has pursued a more selective immigration policy than either the United States or Western European countries, installing in 1967 a points system that favored highly skilled immigration. Prior to then, the results of immigrant selection were not all that different in Canada and the United States. Postwar immigration policy initially favored immigrants from Britain, the United States, and European countries. Between 1946 and 1967, 82 percent of immigrants admitted to Canada were from Europe, 29 percent of them British. In the 1950s, as preferred sources of immigrants in the British Isles dried up, southern Europe, which had long exported labor migrants, became a major source; the number of Italians climbed into the hundreds of thousands, and by 1960 Italian immigration had overtaken that from Great Britain.[20]

Like the United States, Canada opened the gates in the 1960s to new sources. By 1970 a dramatic shift had occurred, away from Europe altogether as the vestiges of racial and ethnic discrimination were eliminated from immigration regulations and procedures.[21] The changes in immigration policy, it has been argued, were a response not only to a shrinking supply of immigrants from Europe but also to the 1965 changes in U.S. immigration law, which increased the southern neighbor's attractiveness to skilled migrants, for whom international demand was rising.[22] Canada has not only long faced competition for immigrants from the United States but has also lost many whom it accepts, those who view Canada as a way station to greener pastures south of the border—a phenomenon one observer calls the "churning problem."[23]

Whatever the reason for Canada's change in immigration policy, there is no question about the consequences, particularly the shift of major sources away from Europe. Whereas Asians were only 4 percent of Canada's immigrants between 1946 and 1967, they were a whopping 54 percent of the 3.8 million admitted to Canada as permanent residents between 1979 and 2000 and about 60 percent between 2001 and 2010, with especially large numbers from China, India, and the Philippines.[24] Since 1970 there have also been substantial entries from the Caribbean, Africa, and the Middle East.

Unlike that of the United States, Canada's Latin American population is small, and Mexico is barely represented among its immigrants. Between 2001 and 2010, around twenty-seven thousand Mexicans were admitted as permanent residents, only 1 percent of the total number. Several thousand—seven thousand in 1998 and eighteen thousand in 2007—also entered yearly on a temporary basis, as part of a seasonal agricultural worker program.[25] Obviously, Canada does not share a border with Mexico, which helps explain these low numbers. But something else is going on, as well. Canada's very selective, indeed highly restrictive, immigration policies favor the well educated and make it hard for those with low levels of education and skills to enter as permanent residents ("landed immigrants" in common Canadian parlance). By comparison, the United States still looks like a haven for "the huddled masses."

MAJOR TYPES OF IMMIGRATION

LABOR MIGRATIONS

The postwar immigration systems were designed in significant part to import workers, especially to fill manual-labor and service jobs on the lower rungs of the labor market. Of the major types of immigration, such labor migrations are the most consequential for integration challenges. Many of the groups that are viewed by natives as "low status" and that generally have the most problematic prospects in their new societies, such as Mexicans and Central Americans in the United States and Turks in Germany and the Netherlands, originated in labor migrations. These migrations have several characteristics that are connected to this problematic status: they are typically large in size; they originate in the countries of the global South, and thus the migrants usually differ quite visibly from natives in race, ethnicity, and/or religion; their educational levels are well below the norms of the native population; and the jobs the immigrants take are typically lower in status than those most natives would consider doing themselves.

In addition, many labor migrations were initially conceived by the natives and government of the host country as temporary sojourns by workers who would eventually return home, and they only slowly mutated into permanent settlement by immigrants who decided that life in the new society, however humble, was preferable to that awaiting them in their home communities. This was certainly the case for many guestworker migrants in Western Europe who came from Turkey and North Africa. Even though guestworker recruitment ended in the early 1970s and countries such as France and Germany made serious attempts to encourage return migration, many immigrant families chose to stay and found ways to bring in relatives, thereby expanding their communities. As noted earlier, transnational marriage markets pair many members of the second generation with partners who come from the hometowns and villages of their parents, thus perpetuating a strong first-generation presence in numerous multigeneration families and communities.

Family-reunification provisions in U.S. immigration law are also responsible for the entry of a great many workers who seek low-paying jobs, in such areas as service, construction, and agriculture. As of 2010, nearly a third of adult immigrants had not completed secondary school, compared to 11 percent of the native born.[26] In the main, these immigrants cannot qualify to come to the U.S. except through family ties to permanent residents or citizens. For immigrants with such low levels of education, there is little alternative to the jobs at the bottom of the labor market.

Furthermore, undocumented migration adds many low-wage workers to the U.S. workforce. The undocumented come mostly from Mexico and Central America, and before 1986, many of these migrants were involved in circular migration patterns that saw them return to their home countries after relatively short-term earning seasons in the United States. However, the increasing enforcement of the border by the United States made it more difficult to continue these patterns and induced many to remain in el Norte and bring their families to join them. The consequence has been a growing population of settled individuals who nonetheless lack the legal rights to reside and work, estimated at 11.7 million in 2012. Even the Great Recession that started in 2007 did not pare this number very much. For the members of this population, the challenges of integration are insoluble without changes to American law. Even for their U.S.-born children, who possess birthright citizenship, the challenges are immense.[27]

POSTCOLONIAL IMMIGRATION

In Western Europe, another source of labor migrants has been colonies or former colonies. These migrants have been of great significance for Britain, the Netherlands, and France, in particular. Migrants from colonies have often had privileged access to the metropole, even after their homelands' independence, at least for a time. In fact, migration has frequently been spurred by the struggles for independence and subsequent upheavals, leading us to describe this type of migration as mainly "postcolonial."

Postcolonial migrations are often heterogeneous. That is, many have included a privileged stratum of Europeans whose families may have resided in the colonial setting for several generations but now are returning to the metropole because they expect their status in the former colony to deteriorate after independence; along with these Europeans may come members of the non-European population, whose position in the post-independence society will have been compromised by their close ties to, and cooperation with, the former European rulers. Finally, there is a stream of workers from the non-European

gender dynamics ?

group, nearly always the largest segment of migrants, who typically are citizens of the new nation but are taking advantage of the tie that binds the former colony to the metropole in order to immigrate for economic reasons.

The fates of these different components of a postcolonial immigration are usually quite different. The returning Europeans, though they have lost status, can generally melt into the mainstream of the metropole. Certainly, this happened to the nearly one million *pieds noirs* who arrived in France as Algeria gained independence in 1962. The situations of the other postcolonial migrants can be more problematic, sometimes even more difficult than that of other labor immigrations from the global South. The reason is that, as the formerly ruled, they are generally subject to stereotypes and prejudices that originated in the colonial era but live on past its end.[28]

The postwar labor immigration to Britain has had a pronounced colonial and postcolonial flavor. Large-scale migration from the West Indies, India, and Pakistan began in the early 1950s and lasted for over a decade. In 1951, Britain was home to 15,300 immigrants from the West Indies, 5,000 from Pakistan, and 30,800 from India; in 1966, the numbers had mushroomed to, respectively, 267,000, 67,700, and 163,600. The empire had indeed struck back, and the British government responded to hostile public opinion against nonwhite Commonwealth immigrants by striking in turn and ending its liberal immigration regime. By the early 1960s, Britain had eliminated its open-door policy with regard to the Commonwealth and became increasingly restrictionist, introducing an entry voucher ssystem to control the nonwhite influx. The 1971 Immigration Act definitively ended the right of citizens of independent Commonwealth countries to settle in Britain.[29]

The Netherlands drew people from its East Indian colonies as well as from Suriname and the Netherlands Antilles. Between 1945 and the early 1960s, up to three hundred thousand repatriates from the former Dutch East Indies (now Indonesia) settled in the Netherlands. After Indonesia became independent in 1949, all Dutch citizens living there (European and Indo-Dutch) could retain their Dutch citizenship; and the great majority of them headed for the Netherlands. A huge influx from Suriname (the former colony of Dutch Guiana) occurred in the years before and following independence in 1975, with roughly a third of the new country's population moving to the Netherlands by the early 1980s. Before independence, Surinamese had the right of free entry to the Netherlands; afterward, the Dutch allowed "open admission" for five years. By 1982 about 182,000 people of Surinamese origin lived in the Netherlands; by 2012, with a growing second generation, the number had nearly doubled. Because the Netherlands Antilles and Aruba are part of the Kingdom of the Netherlands and its residents have Dutch nationality, migration to the Netherlands has been unrestricted. It took off in the 1990s owing to declines in the islands' economies, reaching annual levels of around ten thousand. As of 2012 the first- and second-generation Antillean population in the Netherlands was 144,000.[30]

France also has taken in large migrations from former colonies. By 1970 there were over 600,000 Algerians, 140,000 Moroccans, and 90,000 Tunisians in France. Many immigrants also have come from former West African colonies such as Senegal, Mali, and Mauritania. Some arrived before independence: during World War I, for example, Algerian workers were recruited to replace men who had been mobilized for the war. Others came later through preferential migration arrangements that arose from the process of decolonization. After the Algerian War of Independence with France (1954–62), there was a sharp rise in immigration, made possible by the Evian Accords that sealed the war's end. According to the agreement, Algerians were free to move between Algeria and France—a policy motivated partly by the French demand for labor as well as interest in Saharan oil reserves. (Mobility was constrained within a decade.) Migrants also have come from the overseas departments and territories such as Guadeloupe, Martinique, and Réunion. Because they are French citizens, there are few migration statistics on this population, but a recent estimate puts their number among 15- to 50-year-olds residing in metropolitan France at 235,000.[31]

HIGH-SKILLED IMMIGRATION

All of the rich countries welcome high-skilled immigration, though their policies to encourage it and the success of these policies vary enormously. In an era of high-technology goods and services, foreign scientists, computer programmers, and engineers, among others, are widely seen as helping to meet the needs of a global economy.[32] The focus on high-skilled immigration reflects a widely shared vision of the near future—a future characterized by intensifying economic competition on a global scale, stoked by the ascendancy of new economic dynamos such as China and India, so that the wealthy societies of North America and Western Europe can no longer take their previous economic predominance for granted.

Of the countries we are considering, Canada stands out for the selectivity of its immigration. At the heart of its immigration system has been a points scheme, introduced in 1967, favoring highly skilled immigrants by assigning points among other things for education and accepting those with high scores. Over the years, the selection standards were raised, with increased importance to occupational qualifications as compared to age and "personal suitability." In 2011 the required number of points was sixty-seven. In addition to education and work experience (a maximum of forty-six points), aspiring immigrants got high points for command of English or French (a maximum of twenty-four points) and for arranged employment in Canada (a maximum of ten points). To encourage those with financial capital and business skills, Canada set up a program in 1978 to admit "business immigrants," who included entrepreneurs, investors, and the self-employed; they numbered ten thousand in 2007 or 4.3 percent of all immigrants.[33]

Altogether, "economic immigrants" represented more than six out of ten of all permanent residents admitted to Canada in 2011 and 2012. (This compares to 14 percent of lawful permanent residents admitted to the United States in 2012 through an employment-based preference.) Canada admits far fewer immigrants on the basis of family ties than does the United States. Because of the points system, the Canadian foreign born hold a clear advantage over natives in terms of university credentials: for example, at the upper end of the educational spectrum, about half of all recent immigrants hold a university degree, compared to only about a fifth of the Canadian born. Over time, the credentials of immigrants have been improving, although the gap separating them from natives has been shrinking because of a continued rise in overall levels of education in Canada.[34]

It is open to question whether the Canadian economy has benefited commensurately from the success of its immigration policies in recruiting immigrants who bring relatively high levels of skills and education with them. Many immigrants, perhaps especially those belonging to what Canadians label as "visible minorities," appear to have taken jobs well below their skills and credentials. The stereotype of the immigrant taxi driver with a Ph.D. is widespread and rooted in reality. The problem of "brain waste" may well have contributed to recent changes in admission requirements. In 2015, Canada introduced a new "Express Entry" system that has increased the weight given to employment offers for people applying to become permanent residents.[35]

The United States, as already noted, has portals in its immigration system for the entry of immigrants with valued educational credentials and/or occupational qualifications, but such economic immigrants make up a much smaller part of the overall immigration flow than they do in Canada. Still, the U.S. immigration flow is bimodal and includes a sizable group of the highly educated, along with a large group of low-skill workers. In 2010 slightly more than a quarter of the foreign born possessed at least a bachelor's degree (some of whom came as students and earned degrees at American universities). However, because of the overall higher levels of post-secondary education in the United States, the foreign born were not ahead of natives in this respect, but more or less tied with them.

The United States also admits the highly educated as temporary workers. This can occur through any of multiple visa categories, but the most important is the H-1B program. This program, which as of 2012 was awarding about 85,000 new visas a year, allows employers to bring in foreign workers with the equivalent of a bachelor's degree or more for up to six years to perform so-called "specialty occupations," basically, highly skilled jobs in technical fields. (The computer software company Microsoft is one of the major employers of H-1B migrants.) According to one estimate, 60 percent of these workers will end up staying in the United States permanently and bring in an average of one dependent each.[36]

Intra-European migration provides highly skilled workers to some Western European countries, including all of those in our study. According to a survey of EU citizens who have migrated, young professionals constitute a major component of the flow between EU countries.[37] However, the extent of these migrations should not be exaggerated. In 2011, 16.5 million EU citizens were living in another EU country, a small fraction of the total EU population of more than 500 million.[38]

Many European countries recognize that they need to do more to bring in highly skilled immigrants, including those from outside the EU. Official views have become somewhat more "migration-friendly" in many countries. There has been a trend to make some immigration easier, although generally only for limited quotas, often of highly skilled people, in sectors with labor shortages.[39] Official government reports have also changed their tune. A 2001 German government report stated that Germany would need to rely on labor migration to fill many skilled and less-skilled jobs in the future.

Some European countries are erecting temporary worker programs not unlike the U.S. H-1B program. In the hope of fostering a selective immigration (*immigration choisie*), a 2006 French law created "skills and talents" visas, valid for three years, to assist employers in economic sectors and regions of France "characterized by recruitment difficulties" to find needed workers. The law also sought to encourage foreign students to remain in France after their studies in order to gain a "first professional experience." In 2000, Germany tried the equivalent, creating a so-called "green card" that allowed migrants in technology fields to work in Germany for a period of up to five years. The more recently instituted EU Blue Card enables very highly skilled and educated temporary migrants to apply for permanent residence after about two or three years. However, not all developments point in this direction as the United Kingdom began to tighten requirements for highly skilled workers from outside the EU around 2009, in an effort to safeguard jobs for British citizens in tough economic times.[40]

REFUGEES AND ASYLUM SEEKERS

The rich countries recognize that they have a responsibility to assist people who have been forced to flee their countries of origin because of imminent threat. A refugee, according to a 1951 UN convention, which is widely recognized in the international community, is someone who cannot or will not return to his or her country of origin because of "a well-founded fear of persecution on account of race, religion, nationality, membership in a particular social group, or political opinion." Asylum seekers are generally defined as individuals who have migrated to another country in the hope of being recognized as refugees there.[41] As a general rule, refugee and asylum-seeker flows are different in their characteristics from economically motivated ones—for one thing, they tend to contain smaller numbers of economically active young adults. Those in flight are usually not prepared to enter the labor market of the receiving society, and thus they require economic and other assistance, perhaps for an extended period of adjustment.

These categories represent major legal routes to settlement in the countries of North America and Western Europe, though the recognition of refugee status by governments frequently involves political calculations of national self-interest. U.S. refugee policy, which governs the admission of displaced persons who are still abroad, bears out these points. The government has "repeatedly invoked foreign and security policy imperatives to initiate much larger refugee programs" than the fifty thousand provided for by the Refugee Act of 1980. Major sources of refugees have included "Cuba in the wake of the Castro revolution; the Soviet Union, which allowed Jews to leave as a condition for détente and access to U.S. trade; Indochina, in the wake of the Vietnam War."[42] During the 1970s the number of refugees and asylees granted lawful permanent resident status in the United States was over fifty thousand annually, rising to about one hundred thousand during the 1980s and well over one hundred thousand per year in the 1990s, when large numbers arrived from the former Soviet Union. Security concerns after September 11th slowed down the flow, although it began to pick up again after a couple of years, with more than seventy thousand admitted as refugees and more than twenty thousand granted asylum in 2010, Iraqis the largest group among them.[43] Given the family reunion emphasis in U.S. immigration law, refugee flows have tended to become the seeds of subsequent immigration quite apart from the conditions that promoted the initial refugee movement.

Canada and Western Europe have received large numbers of asylum seekers, particularly since the end of the 1980s, from Africa, Asia, the Middle East, Latin America, Eastern Europe, and the former Soviet Union. The numbers in Western Europe were especially high in the 1990s, declined to lower levels during the early 2000s, and had grown again by the start of the next decade. Germany received a peak of 438,000 asylum seekers in 1992 following the civil war in Yugoslavia, but the numbers fell subsequently, though they rose to about 110,000 in 2013, making Germany the largest recipient of new asylum claims among the world's industrialized countries in that year. [44] In France, the Netherlands, and the United Kingdom, the number of asylum claims has also risen in recent years.

Whatever the number of asylum applications, the large majority of them have been denied—in 2011, the rejection rate in France was 86 percent, in Germany 80 percent, in the United Kingdom 65 percent, and in the Netherlands 55 percent. (Canada's system is more favorable to applicants, with acceptance rates generally in the 40–45 percent range.) Asylum applicants whose claims are denied are rarely deported owing to legal, financial, and moral constraints on states, and they often end up staying and working illegally. This is one reason for the more rigorous attempts to cut back the numbers who enter in the first place.[45] To the extent that the hardening of asylum policies has made it tougher to use this "side door" to enter Western Europe, it seems to have encouraged entry through the "backdoor," that is, through illegal and clandestine means.

Since the end of World War II, immigration to Germany has been bolstered by flows that bear some resemblance to refugee flows but have a special character because of their ethnic selectivity—individuals of putative German stock coming from Eastern Europe or the former Soviet Union. The first such flow took place at the end of the war, when millions of ethnic Germans were expelled, often violently, from countries in Eastern Europe where their families often had resided for generations. These expellees (*die Vertriebene*, in the German political lexicon), about twelve million in total, were mostly accepted in the western part of then-divided Germany, where they became fairly rapidly integrated. During the period of the two Germanys, West Germany had a standing policy of accepting anyone fleeing from the eastern side, though the numbers involved dwindled after the construction of the Berlin Wall in 1961.[46]

Germany also accepted many ethnic Germans coming from further east, on the principle that their German heritage was a liability in their home societies and their culture endangered. From 1950 to 1988, 1.4 million ethnic Germans or *Aussiedler*, who had the right to enter Germany and claim citizenship, moved to Germany, most coming from Poland and Romania; in the 1990s about 2.6 million arrived, virtually all from the former Soviet Union. Despite the principle of free admission to people of German ancestry coming from former communist countries, the German government made it more difficult for ethnic Germans to enter after 1990, introducing an annual quota of 220,000 a year and, in 1996, adding a language test.[47]

FAMILY REUNIFICATION

Each of our countries allows immigration on the grounds of close kinship ties, and in each family-reunification immigration accounts for a substantial fraction of yearly legal entries, from around one quarter in Canada to two-thirds or so in the United States. In general, family reunification contributes to each of the different immigration streams we have discussed, but its role is most important for potential immigrants who cannot qualify for entry under another provision. In this respect, it has been especially critical for the maintenance of low-wage labor migration and for the groups we have labeled as "low status."

Family-reunification immigration has strong justification in international law and treaties and in human rights considerations. The European Union, for example, issued in 2003 a Family Reunion Directive to protect the family rights of immigrants from outside the EU. Despite the universal acceptance of family reunification in principle, the provisions determining who may sponsor which family members under what conditions are far from uniform across our six countries. These provisions are most generous in North America, where they allow the entry of some relatives who are not part of the nuclear family, such as, in the U.S. case, the adult brothers and sisters of U.S. citizens.

In general, European countries are more restrictive, and their laws are most open to the immigration of spouses and children. However, the impacts of such family immigration have been the subject of much debate. This story begins in the mid-1970s when Western European governments declared an end to open immigration, and a gap between policy goals and actual practice soon became evident. Immigration levels did not decline as drastically as expected, according to Martin Schain, "even after the strong declaration of 'zero' immigration policies at the governmental level. Although the main objectives of policy have not changed over a 25-year period, large numbers of legal immigrants—workers, as well as family members through family reunification—have been admitted to all European countries."[48]

The attempts to reduce immigration to zero appear to have ended up encouraging international marriage as a backdoor to entry, at least for some groups; and this phenomenon has become a major source of contention in Europe. Because family ties offer a pathway to legal settlement, they became, as one account notes, a "main anchoring point for migration plans and ambitions. In Pakistan, for example, young men pin their hopes of social advancement on going to England by marrying a relative there."[49]

There have, in fact, been frequent marriages in the second generation with partners imported from the home country. The pattern is especially prominent for groups from countries where arranged marriages are common, often to cousins or more distant relatives. In Germany, about a third of second-generation Turkish men and a quarter of second-generation Turkish women who married between 1976 and 2004 had a partner who came from Turkey either in the year of the marriage or later. In the Netherlands, 50–60 percent of the marriages entered into by second-generation Turks and Moroccans between 1999 and 2001 were "migration marriages," although the rates had declined by 2010 to 16 percent among Dutch-born Turks and 10 percent among Dutch-born Moroccans, partly due to stricter government rules.[50]

The high proportion of migration or transnational marriages, especially among Muslim groups, has generated at times fierce debate in several European countries. Many Europeans react very negatively to arranged marriages, which bring young adults to join partners they may never have met before. There is, in addition, concern that these marriages are impeding the integration of the Turkish, North African, and Pakistani second generation by importing partners steeped in homeland cultural and religious practices. As one might expect, migration marriages have been less common among immigrant groups lacking a cultural pattern of arranged marriages, the Afro-Surinamese in the Netherlands being a case in point.[51]

Yet the great difficulty of immigrating to most European countries seems essential to explaining the remarkable number of second-generation migration marriages. For non-European groups, often the only legal entry ticket for young people is through marriage. Furthermore, the absence of continuing immigration from many countries means that there are few newly arrived young immigrants available as marriage partners.

The practice of transnational marriage has persisted, although its scale seems to be declining. Several European governments have made efforts since 2000 to prevent or limit the migration of homeland spouses by, for example, raising the age requirement for the partners or mandating mainstream language proficiency for the arriving spouse. This has been a difficult matter to legislate because family reunion is recognized in Europe as a human right, and in many countries court decisions have played a role in preserving access rights for family members of settled immigrants.[52]

While family networks fuel immigration to the United States, transnational marriages are much less common among the second generation there. (South Asians, notably Indians, are something of an exception.) This is despite the right that members of the second generation, as U.S. citizens, have to bring in spouses fairly easily, without being subject to any numerical limitation. The lower proportion of transnational marriages in the United States partly has to do with cultural and religious patterns among immigrants, the vast majority of them from countries lacking a tradition of arranged marriages. But also, given the more liberal immigration laws in the United States, there are other legal means of entry, as well as more available partners from the immigrant and second generations to choose from, and so less need to look to the home country for spouses. Similar observations apply to Canada.

THE CHALLENGES OF CONTROLLING IMMIGRATION

It is a fundamental principle that all states want to control the flows of people coming across their borders to live and work. But for countries that have become hosts to large immigrant populations, control usually becomes elusive, as legally settled immigrants find innovative ways to bring in family members and clandestine immigrants can hide in immigrant communities and networks to escape official scrutiny.

Unauthorized immigration, that is, the entry and, in many cases, settlement of migrants who lack the legal right to reside in a country, constitutes the ultimate challenge to the state's control over newcomers. In the United States, unauthorized immigration rose to astonishing levels in the early 2000s, certainly to numbers much larger than in Western European countries. As of 2012 the number of the unauthorized was estimated at 11.7 million, up from an estimated 3.5 million in 1990.[53] In a nation with a population of 313 million at the time, this means that one out of every twenty-seven residents lacked the legal rights to reside and work. To put it another way, unauthorized migrants constituted almost 30 percent of all immigrants of any kind in the United States in 2012. Partly owing to the sheer enormity of these numbers, the question of how—and, indeed, whether—to allow current unauthorized immigrants to gain legal status has been the subject of heated debate in the U.S. Congress and the media.

Most unauthorized immigrants have entered at the U.S-Mexico border while the rest have arrived legally and overstayed a visa. The overwhelming majority are Mexicans (the next largest national-origin group, Salvadorans, is about one-tenth as large). The predominance of Mexicans has colored debates about unauthorized immigration and produced a denigrating stereotype of the group as heavily illegal. As of 2012 slightly more than half of the 11.6 million Mexican immigrants in the United States were estimated to be unauthorized.[54]

In fact, unauthorized immigration from south of the border has a long history of coming, as it were, through the "backdoor." Zolberg writes of a hybrid regulatory system that long combined barriers to Mexican legal immigration with a laissez-faire approach to the movement of unauthorized labor. He argues that this system should not be viewed as a case of policy failure but rather of a "purposefully weak regulatory system that allows a relatively stable informal 'guest worker' program to stay in place in keeping with the clearly expressed preferences of powerful regional economic entrepreneurs, whose interests have come to be assumed as an obligation of the American state."[55] In the early twentieth century, the legal barriers involved strict enforcement of the literacy test and the LPC ("paupers or persons likely to become a public charge") clause. The present legal barriers stem from the imposition in 1976 of the same small quota of green cards for Mexico that is allotted to any other country—Jamaica, say—despite its large size and immediate proximity to the United States. At the same time, for most of the twentieth century, enforcement was lax at the border and in the workplace, owing to entrenched economic and political interests as well as a poorly funded, overburdened, and compromised immigration bureaucracy.[56]

Since 2000 the dramatic rise in the size of the unauthorized Mexican population has led to a renewed, and intensified, focus on this flow. Paradoxically, the increase is partly due to beefed-up border enforcement. By making reentry more difficult, dangerous, and expensive, increased border enforcement has ended up lengthening stays in the United States; Mexican workers who, in the past, would have returned to Mexico in the winter have been settling in the United States and sending for their families. Also responsible for the growth in numbers have been weaknesses of the Mexican economy and fear of the violence of organized crime. Further, the North American Free Trade Agreement (NAFTA), which became effective in 1994, may have played a role. NAFTA not only required Mexico to relinquish protectionist agricultural policies that had allowed small farmers to remain on their land, but also stimulated the expansion of transborder economic linkages, including truck traffic, which facilitate undocumented entry.[57]

What about Canada? Canada does not have the same problems with undocumented immigration as the United States, and the numbers are much lower; in the absence of credible tallies, scholars cite media reports of between 200,000 and 400,000. Jeffrey Reitz speaks of "the relative absence of illegal immigration in Canada due to its geographic location."[58] Canada lacks a land border with a country where wages are much lower, and one scholar observes that the United States provides a "natural buffer to absorb unauthorized migrants [from Mexico] who might otherwise come to Canada."[59]

In Western Europe, the restrictions on legal immigration from outside the European Union have led many would-be immigrants to try other, illegal, ways to enter and work. Smuggling and human trafficking syndicates have received a great deal of media attention, particularly when their actions result in tragedy, such as the death of fifty-eight Chinese migrants in a cross-channel truck going to England in 2000. This is only one part of the unauthorized migration story. Some enter legally with tourist visas or as students and remain after their visas expire. Others enter using false documents or fail to leave after their asylum claims have been denied. Estimates of the number of irregular or unauthorized immigrants vary widely, with experts putting the total number among the twenty-seven European Union member states somewhere between 1.9 and 3.8 million in 2008. In Germany, estimates of the undocumented population for that same year ranged from 196,000 to 457,000; in Britain, from around 417,000 to 863,000. In France, the number of *sans papiers* has been estimated at 178,000 to 400,000.[60] The numbers are much smaller than in the United States, in part because many major European countries have much tighter internal controls— for example, requiring the regular presentation of identity documents—than the United States does.

THE DEMOGRAPHIC IMPACTS

Immigration is having a profound impact on the populations of the wealthy societies of the West. Everywhere, populations are becoming more diverse, as increasing shares of young adults and children come from recent immigrant backgrounds and often belong to groups that are ethnoracially distinct from the native majority. This diversity means, for example, that in many large European and North American cities one now hears languages from all over the world—in the New York City borough of Queens, more than 150 languages are

Table 2.2. Demographic Impacts of Immigrant-Origin Populations

	North America		Western Europe			
	Canada	US	France	Germany	Great Britain	Netherlands
% second generation in population	17.4	11.6	10.2	6.2	5.9	10.4
% second generation ethnoracially distinct	29.8	65.3	56.7	45.3	39.6	50.2
% all children who are children of immigrants	32.6	22.1	17.3	25.5	16.3	22.3
Ratio of middle-aged group (individuals aged 40–59) to children (0- to 19-year-olds)	1.28	1.03	1.10	1.69	1.13	1.26

Sources:

Canada: Statistics Canada website; Boyd and Worts (2016), children 0–14 years old; National Household Survey (2013).

US: Census Bureau website; Dixon (2006); Innocenti Insight (2009); Pew Research Center (2013).

France: INSEE website; Breuil-Genier et al. (2011); Innocenti Insight (2009).

Germany: Statistiches Bundesamt website; Statistisches Bundesamt (2010); Innocenti Insight (2009).

Great Britain: Office for National Statistics website; second-generation data thanks to Yaojun Li from Labor Force Survey (limited to ages 16+); Innocenti Insight (2009).

Netherlands: Statistics Netherlands website.

spoken—and that the stereotypical "look" of different nationalities—say, of the Dutch in Amsterdam or Germans in Berlin—is contradicted visibly by the wide range of appearances seen on many city streets. Needless to say, the ideas that members of the native majority have about their society and its people have often not caught up to these fast-evolving realities.

A simple measure of immigration-driven diversity is the percentage of the population belonging to the first and second generations, in other words, the immigrants and their children. As the data in tables 2.1 and 2.2 show, this percentage is generally on the order of 20 percent, a fifth of the population, though there is substantial variation from one country to another. In Canada, where the immigrants themselves make up about a fifth of the population, the first and second generations combined amount to almost 40 percent. At the other end of the spectrum, immigrants are 12 percent of Great Britain's population, but the second generation is relatively small: together, the two generations amount to just 18 percent of British residents. (The totals for France and Germany are not much different.)

These percentages would all look higher if we confined the calculations to youth and the working-age population, because the elderly in all the rich societies belong overwhelmingly to the native group. Individuals of immigrant origin become more common as we move down the age scale, a gradient that points in the direction of growing diversity in the future. A sixth of all children in France and Great Britain come from immigrant homes, whereas a quarter, or nearly a quarter, come from such families in Germany, the Netherlands, and the United States. In Canada, the fraction rises to a third. Recent data on births in some countries indicate that the share of immigrant-origin children in the total child population continues to rise. For example, according to the United Kingdom's Office of National Statistics, one quarter of 2010 births in England and Wales were to immigrant mothers.[61]

Immigrants from Africa, Asia, the Middle East, the Caribbean, and Latin America, along with their descendants, play a varying role in the immigrant-origin populations of these six countries; but everywhere it is substantial. These are the immigrant groups whose members differ most from native majorities in racial appearance, religion, and, fairly often though not always, in the educational level they bring from their home societies. They present the greatest challenge to integration in the long term—if all of these groups are not "low status" in the sense of rank in the socioeconomic hierarchy, they are all nevertheless marginal to the native mainstreams of their host societies. In France, the Netherlands, and the United States, the majority of the immigrant and the second generations have origins in these regions of the globe. It is notably lower, less than the majority, in Germany. (In Canada and the United Kingdom, the picture is more mixed: the immigrant generation is dominated by nonwhites, but the second generation is still largely white. In Canada, this disparity reflects the lingering influence of earlier European immigration on the older part of the second generation.)

Despite this variation, the future of all these countries is bound up with their ability to integrate the new groups. In the next several decades, the adult group in the active ages, which makes up the bulk of the workforce and of the participants in other key institutions, will undergo transitions to much greater diversity as the children of today mature and the post–World War II baby boomers retire.

Some specifics are helpful to indicate more precisely the magnitude of the shifts ahead. The United States presents one version of this transition; and the U.S. data are especially helpful because we can rely on a carefully prepared 2012 population projection carried out by the U.S. Census Bureau.[62] The projection for two decades from now, for 2035, along with recent data, for 2010, are displayed in figure 2.1 in the form of age pyramids, which we have simplified to show just the distinction between the majority population, whites who are not Hispanic, and minorities, or everyone else. In contrast to much of Western Europe, the youthful population of the United States is expected to grow, not stagnate or shrink; but its composition is changing, and will continue to change, quite dramatically. In particular, the portion coming from the white majority is already reduced considerably from its numbers in the outgoing baby-boom

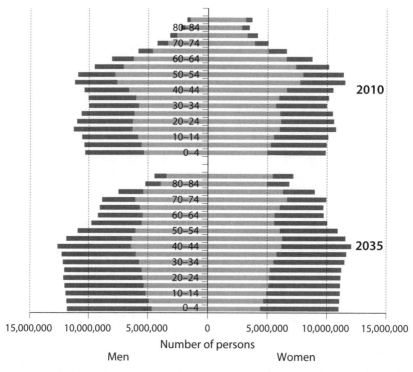

Figure 2.1. U.S. population, 2010 and 2035. *Notes*: Non-Hispanic whites are shown by the inner portions of the bars, everyone else by the outer portions. *Sources*: The 2010 data come from the decennial census; the 2035 projections from the Census Bureau's 2012 population projections.

group (compare the length of the non-Hispanic white fractions of the bars for ages forty-five to fifty-four in 2010 to their equivalents in younger groups). Barring a large-scale assimilation of minorities into the white population, something that is possible but unlikely in the near future, there will not be as many whites as there were in the baby boom.[63] As the numbers of the majority shrink, those from minority groups will grow, and this is happening already. The group of young children is now divided about 50:50 between non-Hispanic whites and everyone else. By 2035, it is highly likely—again barring large-scale assimilation into the white category—that minorities will outnumber whites among the population under the age of forty. Since the African American population is not expected to increase its relative share by much, predominant among these minority young adults and children will be the second and third generations issuing from the immigrants of recent decades, especially those from Latin America. The ramifications of this demographic shift are obviously enormous.

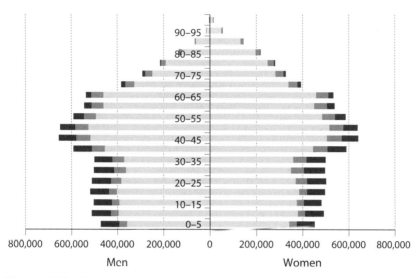

Figure 2.2. Dutch population pyramid, 2010. *Notes:* Innermost portion=native Dutch; intermediate=1st and 2nd generation of Western origins; outermost=1st and 2nd generation of non-Western origins. *Source:* Statistics Netherlands.

The Netherlands, fairly typical for Northern European countries (Germany presents a more extreme case), illustrates a different version of this transition. In this case, we lack a population projection that distinguishes between the native- and immigrant-origin groups, but much of the near-term demographic future can be read from the population pyramid for 2010, displayed in figure 2.2.[64]

Understandably, the baby boom took longer to develop in war-devastated continental Europe and lasted into the 1970s, so that the youngest baby boomers were in their late thirties in 2010. However, fertility has been low in the Netherlands since the baby boom, and the result is seen in the reduced sizes of young cohorts by comparison with their elders. (As table 2.2 shows, individuals of middle age, in their 40s and 50s, outnumber children by 26 percent.) As the baby boomers retire, a process that could take three decades, there will not be as many young people aging into the active years to fully replace them (unless the Netherlands accepts far more immigrants in the future than it does now). The country will depend critically on the qualifications of these relatively scarce youth. Increasingly, they come from immigrant backgrounds: among the young children of 2010, the fraction reached almost 25 percent; and, as a consequence of future immigration, this proportion is likely to rise by the time these youngsters reach working age.

Some other countries, notably France and Great Britain, lie between the future scenarios implied by the population pyramids for the Netherlands and the

United States. Overall, the demographic situation in the wealthy countries suggests their need for continued immigration, including individuals who can fit into the higher-skilled portions of the workforce. This need may not manifest itself immediately; in general, the largest portion of the baby boom was born in the 1960s and, in some countries, in the early 1970s; as of 2015, say, many of its workers are still in their 40s and early 50s. But as they age and become less productive, their skills more out of date, the demand for immigrants will announce itself. As we noted earlier, some countries have been experimenting with policies to attract more highly skilled workers, though their success remains unclear. In the future, as the international competition for high-skilled immigrants intensifies, not all of the wealthy countries will be successful in attracting them in sufficient numbers.

CONCLUSION

In one fundamental sense, the immigration regimes of European countries, the United States, and Canada are very much alike. All are restrictive in that they set limits on the numbers and type of people who can settle as permanent residents. These regimes prevail, Zolberg argues, because they constitute "a sine qua non for maintaining the Westphalian international state system, as well as the privileged position of the core states amid highly unequal conditions. . . . In effect, borders prevent labor from commanding the same price everywhere and also prevent people from the poorer countries from gaining access to the bundles of 'public goods' dispensed by the more affluent states."[65]

These regimes are also alike in that each now implies a recognition of the need for continued immigration in the future, for reasons that have to do with the demand for more labor, including highly skilled labor, to bolster the native supply and for more young people to contribute to the support of aging societies in the face of declining worker-retiree ratios. In some Western European countries, such as Germany, below-replacement birthrates over long periods of time have created "demographic time bombs" that will lead to population decline, along with aging, without immigration. In Western Europe, the recognition of the need for ongoing immigration is implicated in the guarantees of free mobility that apply to Eastern European countries like Poland that have been accepted as EU members. In North America, it is apparent in immigration regimes that accept newcomers from all over the globe.

There are, however, important transatlantic differences, and they lend some support to the common perception that Canada and the United States are more welcoming of immigration. Western European countries continue to be wary about immigration from outside of Europe. Their wariness is reflected in their attempts to make migration through marriages to the second generation more difficult, as well as in immigration laws that constrain economic migration from the global South, keeping its numbers modest while seeking to select high human-capital immigrants.

One factor behind these restrictions has to do with the combination of generous welfare states and highly regulated economies in continental Europe. Relevant here is what some call an insider-outsider cleavage, with immigrants displaying relatively high rates of unemployment and low rates of labor force participation and being resented for taking advantage of liberal welfare-state provisions—thereby offering opponents of immigration a further incentive to shut off the entry of new arrivals.[66]

In North America above the Rio Grande, immigration is seen as very much a part of the national identity. Canada continues to have an expansionist immigration policy, which aims to increase the Canadian population. Between 2000 and 2012, Canada admitted from 220,000 to 280,000 immigrants per year. By U.S. standards the absolute numbers seem small, but they need to be viewed in relation to the size of Canada's population, thirty-five million in 2014 compared to more than three hundred million in the United States. The share of the foreign born in the Canadian population, at 21 percent in table 2.1, is substantially higher than in any of the other countries considered here.

For its part, the United States has recognized a million or more foreigners as legal immigrants in all but three years between 2000 and 2012, with high levels of legal immigration supported by groups on the political left and right, including major corporations as well as labor unions and ethnic lobbies. Since 1990 the United States also has had a flow of unauthorized migrants that exceeds anything found in Europe or Canada. U.S. immigration policy is in a fundamental way more generous than that of Canada or the Western European countries. Canada, as we have stressed, has structured its policies to restrict the entry of the low skilled, and this tilts its recent immigration sources strongly in the direction of Asia. The United States accepts a considerably more diverse immigration, with large numbers coming from elsewhere in the Americas as well as Asia, and with a growing presence of African immigrants.

The demographic impacts of immigration will continue to be felt, regardless of the future level of immigration. A transition to diversity is underway everywhere in the West, as large, post–World War II baby-boom cohorts, disproportionately coming from long-established native groups, exit from the active ages during the next several decades and are replaced by young cohorts containing many more immigrants and children of immigrants. Because in general the baby-boom groups are large relative to the child population, the rich societies of North America and Western Europe will depend on the successful integration of many immigrant-origin young people to replace adequately the losses of workers, the highly skilled among them, that are associated with the retirement of baby boomers.

These societies will probably also seek to enhance their recruitment of high-skilled immigrants, some of whom may come to European and North American universities to complete their training and stay on afterward, and some of whom may migrate after finishing their educations in their home countries. Much of course depends on the state of Western European and North American economies in terms of shaping job opportunities. Yet the likelihood is that with declining numbers of the native majority, who have long constituted the main pool of recruitment for the top tiers of the labor market, the pressures will increase to find new sources of talent in order to maintain societal positions in a world of intensifying competition on a global scale.

CHAPTER 3

ECONOMIC WELL-BEING

Most immigrants come to the rich societies of the West with the hope of dramatically improving their economic prospects. That economic motivations are paramount is shown by the high volume of immigrant moves from low-income to high-income societies. Apart from migrants returning home and elderly citizens of rich countries seeking cheaper (and warmer) places to live, little movement takes place in the other direction.

The aspiration for economic gain explains the "immigrant bargain"—the initial willingness to accept low-level jobs, such as cleaning floors, in exchange for the possibility of future advances, even when immigrants arrive with educational and professional qualifications that brought significant status in their home societies. Immigrants expect to work hard but to see their economic position improve over time. Even more, many hope that their children can reach economic heights that they themselves cannot and that would have been impossible in their societies of origin.[1]

Yet, at the beginning of the twenty-first century, the terms of the immigrant bargain may be changing in ways that could disappoint these aspirations. The profound alterations to the economic structures of the rich societies at the end of the twentieth and the beginning of the twenty-first centuries raise doubts about the degree to which immigrants and their children will gain from their move. One prominent trend is the growth of economic inequality—greater differences between the affluent and the less fortunate in terms of income and wealth. This trend is most apparent in the United States and some other so-called liberal market economies (such as Great Britain), but it is occurring elsewhere as well, in such social democratic welfare states as Norway and Sweden.[2] The growth of income and earnings inequalities implies that those at the bottom of the economic ladder, a group that includes many immigrants, face a longer climb than before to reach the middle class.

A related trend in most rich societies is the expansion of the low-wage sectors of the workforce. This trend, too, is not limited to the liberal market economies but includes countries such as Germany, a self-conscious social market economy (*Sozialmarktwirtschaft*) where the state is supposed to play a greater role in smoothing out the frictions of the marketplace. Along with low-wage jobs have come other labor-force developments associated with more marginal forms of employment, such as the expansion of part-time work and short-term jobs. As one might expect, immigrants are overrepresented in the low-wage sector.[3]

These trends are already affecting the countries in our study in different ways partly because of their institutional variations in regulation of the labor market and in social-welfare provision. In these respects, the six countries divide evenly, between one set of three—Canada, Great Britain, and the United States—where the pressure of the regulatory hand on employers is light and the net of social welfare safeguarding individuals with inadequate or no labor-market earnings is not sturdy; and the other set of three—France, Germany, and the Netherlands—where greater levels of protection are afforded workers and social-welfare support is more robust. This distinction is at play in a familiar pair of linked assertions: on the one hand, that immigrants are more likely to be in the labor force in the United States, and less likely to be unemployed, than in continental Western Europe; and on the other, that immigrant minorities in Europe have access to more generous social welfare provisions than are available in the United States. The less-regulated U.S. economy, it has been argued, has provided jobs for immigrant minorities who, because of weak state protection, often have no alternative but to take low-end, low-paying work that may still leave them in poverty. These assertions are not wrong; indeed they are an important part of the story. But they simplify, and indeed somewhat distort, the way immigrants have fared in the labor markets in Western Europe and North America; they also downplay some surprising transatlantic similarities as well as some unexpected differences.

In what follows we explore the growing labor-market inequality in the societies in our study and the implications for the economic incorporation of immigrants, whose position determines the starting point for the second generation. We look at such indicators as rates of labor-force participation, unemployment, and poverty risk. In line with our emphasis throughout the book, we focus on low-status immigrants and the disadvantages that they confront. Our concern is with how the first generation is faring in the economy compared to the natives of the countries where they live. The analysis is, inevitably, a complex one, for there are features peculiar to each country that need to be considered. We are not so much looking to identify overall "winners" or "losers" as to better understand underlying patterns and trends, as well as specific characteristics in each country, that affect immigrants' ability to improve their economic position and the chances for their children and that, for some less fortunate, lead to economic marginality. Ultimately, the central question is the viability of the immigrant bargain in the twenty-first century.

GROWING LABOR-MARKET INEQUALITY

Throughout the rich societies, the winds of globalization have brought about changes in labor markets that, on the whole, have weakened the position of workers on the lower rungs, as employers facing the pressures of international competition have sought to reduce labor costs. "Precarious" work and "low-wage" labor are some of the characterizations that depict these changes.[4] The phrase "precarious employment" is intended to signal that the stable work careers—often with a single employer and featuring a steady rise in real wages over time—common during the several decades of prosperity after World War II are much less attainable today, especially for workers with limited human capital, such as those without university credentials.[5] "Low-wage" work identifies a labor-market trend that is general to many rich societies, as increasing numbers of workers, especially those with low human capital, labor for very low wages.

Precarious work means that many workers' connections to their employers have become tenuous, so that their work careers entail considerable instability and difficulties in achieving earnings gains and job promotions. A great risk is not being able to escape the trap of precarious work and thus facing a lifetime of job insecurity and an absence of career ladders. The sociologist Arne Kalleberg points to a number of labor-market developments at the end of the twentieth century that have contributed to the growing prominence of precarious employment, among them, part-time work, temporary agency jobs, and independent contracting.[6] Such arrangements offer employers much greater flexibility in meeting demand for their products and services, as they can take on additional workers when needed and shed them when they are not. For workers, the arrangements have decided drawbacks because they involve considerable churning in work careers, as individuals move laterally from one employer to another with reduced prospects of climbing upward. In the United States, the workers in precarious forms of employment also fail to gain the benefits—decent health insurance and contributions to pensions—that more advantaged workers obtain from employment.

Then there is the growth of low-wage jobs, which are defined in one international study as jobs with hourly pay less than two-thirds of the median hourly pay in a labor market. For our purposes, this is a convenient way to measure complex labor-market changes, since, as it happens, this extensive study covers all of our countries save Canada.[7] There is moreover an overlap in the categories of low-wage and precarious work, since many precarious forms of work entail low wages—for example, part-time workers are more likely to receive low-wages than full-time workers do. The study shows that low-wage labor is common and/or expanding in four of our countries (Britain, Germany, the Netherlands, and the United States); France is the exception.

Table 3.1. Political Economies of Major Countries of North America and Western Europe

	Size of low-wage sector (2003–5)[1]	Employment-population ratio[2] (2007)	OECD Employment Protection Index[3]	Public social expenditures, % of GDP (2007)[4]
Canada	No data	74	1.5	17
US	25	72	1.2	16
France	11	64	2.8	30
Germany	23	69	3.0	25
UK	22	72	1.6	20
Netherlands	18	74	2.9	21

[1] Gautié and Schmitt (2010).
[2] OECD (2013a).
[3] OECD (2013b).
[4] OECD (2013c).

Low-wage labor is most common in the United States, where 25 percent of workers, including part-timers, earn low wages.[8] (See table 3.1.) This fraction has remained quite steady since the 1970s. If the leading position of United States in this respect seems unsurprising, this is because the United States is often viewed as the epitome of a liberal market economy, where the state's regulation of employers is loose and firms are relatively free to fire employees as well as to set the conditions under which they work. In the United States as well, the unionized sector of the labor force has declined dramatically since the 1970s and represented only 11 percent of the workforce in 2012, slipping from 20 percent as recently as 1983,[9] with the public sector so far holding out as the bastion of union solidarity despite coming under attack in some places (such as Wisconsin, where public employees' collective bargaining rights were curtailed in 2011).

However, some other countries are catching up in the expansion of low-wage work. In a confounding of conventional expectations, this is true of Germany, which in the early 2000s came in second place, with 23 percent of workers in low-wage jobs. While Germany is often thought of as a country where the state and unions play a much greater role in wage settlements than in a liberal market economy like that of the United States, some recent developments, like the greater use of temporary agency workers and also of "posted" workers (often temporary immigrants, who come from other EU countries and work under the conditions prevailing in their home labor markets), have contributed to a sharp rise in the prevalence of low-wage work. Low-wage work is also widespread in the United Kingdom, another liberal market economy, where it characterizes about 22 percent of all workers. And it has increased sharply in the Netherlands, where 18 percent of all workers are involved.

France is the great exception, where low-wage workers make up just 11 percent of the workforce. This exceptional status stems from the role of the state and unions in establishing labor-market conditions. In particular, the state has set a statutory minimum wage (the so-called SMIC, the *salaire minimum interprofessionnel de croissance*) that is relatively high and hence protects workers at the bottom of the wage scale. In addition, France gives an unusual degree of influence to unions in setting wages, even though the proportion of all workers who belong to them is low, on par with the United States. The negotiated wage settlements between French unions and employers are extended to cover most workers in the labor market, even those who are not union members.[10]

However, there can be a price to be paid for protecting the wages of low-skilled workers from slipping, and it lies in job creation. France stands out among the countries we are examining for its persistently low employment-population ratio—in other words, a relatively low proportion of working-age adults (counted as persons fifteen to sixty-four years old) hold jobs. In France in 2007, the figure was 64 percent, while in the Netherlands, the United Kingdom, and the United States, it was above 70 percent (table 3.1). This ratio in France has been low for a number of years.[11] Contributing to the relatively weak job creation in France are the state-mandated protections for employees, which make it very difficult for employers to shed unwanted workers; firms are consequently cautious about adding new employees. Relatively weak job creation affects young workers especially, and in France, the employment-population ratio is particularly low for them.

A major question is whether such national differences can be grasped by the distinction between social market and liberal market economies.[12] Two characteristics of the state labor-market relationship can be seen as defining: the extent to which the state protects workers from arbitrary actions by employers such as dismissal; this is much higher in some rich economies than in others, as shown by the OECD's Employment Protection Index in table 3.1. The other key characteristic involves "social protection."[13] This refers to the degree to which the state compensates individuals and households for the imperfections of the labor market, through such measures as unemployment insurance and income supports. These measures are more extensive and more generous in some countries than in others and are indexed in the aggregate by the OECD data in table 3.1 on the percent of GDP devoted to social expenditures by the state (in 2007, a year deliberately chosen to come just before the economic crisis hit and social expenditures rose as a result).

The countries we are considering, as we suggested, divide evenly between the two categories: France, Germany, and the Netherlands are social market economies, while Canada, Great Britain, and the United States are in the liberal market economy category. The three continental European countries offer considerably more protection to workers from dismissal than do the English-speaking, liberal market economies. There is some blurring of the boundary between the social and liberal market categories when it comes to public social expenditure, however, reflecting a decline in the generosity of welfare-state benefits in some social market economies, especially the Netherlands.[14] France and Germany[15] devote substantially higher percentages of their GDPs to social expenditures than do the other four, and Canada and the United States occupy the bottom on this measure. Britain and the Netherlands are nearly tied in the middle, though the Netherlands was decidedly more generous in the recent past, a fact that is relevant to us because the great majority of Dutch guestworkers who arrived in the mid-twentieth century experienced a more generous welfare state during their work lives.

The United States stands out, we should note, for the consistency of its fit to the liberal market economy model, including having the lowest score on the Employment Protection Index in table 3.1 and more limited social welfare benefits. It also has a low unionization rate (less than half the rates for Canada and Britain). Noteworthy is that, even with the implementation of the Obama administration's Affordable Care Act, the United States will still lack a universal and comprehensive national health insurance program, which all other rich democracies of the world provide. In terms of a number of other social-welfare provisions, it also lags behind the other countries in our study in having, for example, a smaller social housing sector and no legal minimum standard for vacation time or national law ensuring maternity pay.[16]

However, the stereotypic notion that a liberal market economy like that of the United States offers jobs to virtually all who want them, even if sometimes at low pay, has been belied by early twenty-first-century developments. The employment-population ratio has been falling in the United States since 2000, a decline accelerated by the Great Recession. As of 2012, the ratio had slipped to 67 percent—still above the French one, but well below those in the other countries in our study, including the two other social market economies, Germany (73 percent) and the Netherlands (75 percent). Moreover, the ratio for a key group of workers, one closely tracked by economists, those of "prime" working age (twenty-five to fifty-four), is now lower in the United States, at 76 percent, than in France, at 81 percent.[17]

The liberal market/social market economy distinction also does not consistently capture differences among countries in the growth of their low-wage sectors. The rise of low-wage labor cuts across the division between the two types of economies, despite the more powerful role of labor unions, greater regulation, and more generous social protections by the state in the social market economies. Two of the three social market economies in our study have been unable to avoid the trend to an expanded role for low-wage labor that has been set in motion and sustained by heightened economic competition on a global scale.

IMPLICATIONS FOR IMMIGRANT INCORPORATION:
PRECARIOUS EMPLOYMENT

The developments in the labor markets of the rich societies would seem to go hand in hand with immigration in the sense that immigrants could provide a disproportionate share of the workers in the growing numbers of precarious low-wage jobs. Immigrants, it turns out, do have a greater chance of participating in the labor market in countries where low-skilled jobs make up a larger share of the workforce.[18] The industrial sectors where low wages and precarious employment are prevalent include several where immigrant workers tend to be concentrated, such as hotels and restaurants, retail trade, personal services, and agriculture. Of course, immigrants are not the only categories of workers overrepresented in low-wage jobs: youth and women are found there, too.[19] However, in the case of youth, low-wage work often represents a temporary situation, reflecting their lack of work experience. For immigrants (and women) the low-wage situation can be more enduring and may leave them and their families in poverty.

This is not to say that all immigrants are at risk of ending up in marginal sectors of the labor market. The immigrants coming to the rich societies differ considerably in their levels of human capital; in this respect, they are very different from the classical image derived from earlier eras of immigration (to Canada and the United States, for example) of an impoverished peasantry with skills of limited use in an advanced economy. Today, the streams to many countries include a highly educated stratum of individuals seeking high-status professional, technical, and managerial jobs. In the United States, for example, many immigrants have not gone beyond the ninth or tenth grade, but about a quarter have college and university degrees—almost equal to the proportion in the native population. Since it is well known that immigrants' human capital tends not to receive full recognition in the labor market, highly skilled immigrants often overcome this difficulty by earning university credentials in the new society.[20]

Those in some immigrant groups, however, are at high risk of ending up in precarious work and low-wage jobs—for instance, Mexicans, Central Americans, and Dominicans in the United States; Pakistanis and Bangladeshis in Great Britain; North Africans in France; and Turks in several countries. In general, immigrants in these and other low human-capital groups bring levels of educational attainment well below the norm for the native population, and initially they have little familiarity with the host-country language. In the United

States, many of these immigrants are also handicapped by lack of legal status. Hence, their options in the host society labor market are extremely limited at the outset, although, as data on changes in earnings indicate, they often experience some economic mobility over time.[21]

Another factor affecting immigrants' employment prospects is their frequent exclusion from a highly protected sector in all the rich societies, namely, public employment, whether at the national, regional, or local levels. In the average OECD country, 15 percent of the workforce is employed by government.[22] In general, government employees have stable work careers, in positions that, if not always well paid, typically offer generous benefits in such terms as vacation time and retirement pensions. Studies routinely show that minorities enjoy greater parity with the majority population in the public sector, but a good many government jobs require citizenship, and this eliminates many immigrant applications.[23] Even immigrants who naturalize do so in many cases at a point in their lives when it is too late to start a new career as a police officer, say.

At the other end of the labor market, immigrants are often forced into irregular or informal forms of work, that is, jobs that are "off the books" or evade in other ways the protective regulations of the state.[24] Such jobs may involve pay below the legal minimum wage and lack health, pension, and other benefits. It goes without saying that these jobs afford no security. Indeed, they may last as short as a day, as is the case in the United States for Latino day laborers, who congregate at particular traffic intersections in the hope that they can be hired for a few hours in landscaping or construction. Such irregular work is not just a feature of the liberal market economies. In Germany, for instance, it is designated as *Schwarzarbeit* ("black work") and, according to one authoritative study, "the informal are often the only jobs which low skilled unemployed persons can find," whether they are undocumented migrants or legally resident Turks.[25] For obvious reasons, we lack credible data on the exposure of immigrants to irregular work.

If immigrants from low-status groups are being channeled into precarious employment, we would expect to see differences between them and natives in the risks of separation from the labor force and in unemployment. And by and large, in table 3.2, we do.[26] (The data are consistent with conventional definitions: the "labor force participation rate" refers to that portion of the working-age population who are in the labor market at a specific moment, that is to say, either employed or seeking employment; the "unemployment rate" refers to that part of the labor force that does not have a job, in other words, the ratio of the unemployed to the sum of the employed and unemployed.) The data document, for the most part, the differences to be expected from a greater concentration of low-status immigrants in precarious employment, with one exception—the United States, which requires special consideration because of its particularly thin and therefore unforgiving welfare net.

Table 3.2. Labor-Force Participation and Unemployment of Low-Status Immigrants

		Labor force		Unemployment	
		Natives	Immigrants	Native	Immigrants
	Men				
Canada	2006, visible-minority immigrants, ages 15+	74	69	8	6
France	2008, outside-EU immi-	95	91	5	13
Germany	grants, ages 25–54	94	90	6	15
Netherlands		96	86	1	4
UK		92	89	4	7
US	2006–8, Hispanic immi-grants, ages 25–54	88	92	5	4
	Women				
Canada	2006, visible-minority immigrants, ages 15+	62	56	7	8
France	2008, outside-EU immi-	85	66	6	15
Germany	grants, ages 25–54	84	62	6	14
Netherlands		85	64	2	6
UK		80	63	4	7
US	2006–8, Hispanic immi-grants, ages 25–54	77	63	5	8

Notes: EU data from Eurostat (2011); Canadian data from Statistics Canada website; Hispanic immigrant data from the 2006–8 American Community Survey, tabulations by Guillermo Yrizar-Barbosa.

First, however, consider Europe. The best available data, compiled by Euro-stat, the European Union statistical agency, are not broken down by immi-grants' country or region of origin, but instead use a broad category of immi-grants from outside the European Union. Admittedly, not all of these immigrants belong to low-status groups, but the non-EU immigrant category does capture the groups that are ethnoracially (including religiously) different from the European majority, and the low-status groups are a subset of these. The comparison category, "natives," includes all born in the country, regardless of ethnoracial background.

The key pattern is that immigrants from outside the EU are both less likely than natives to be attached to the labor market and more likely to suffer unem-ployment when they are.[27] For example, in the Netherlands, according to table 3.2, immigrant men from non-EU countries had a labor-force participation rate in 2008 of 86 percent compared to 96 percent for men of native Dutch background; the unemployment rate for non-EU immigrant men at the time was 4 percent, but just 1 percent for native men. Age is not a factor in these differences, because the data are restricted to natives and immigrants of prime working age, twenty-five to fifty-four years old. The non-EU immigrants' risk of unemployment is quite high in France and Germany and more moderate in the Netherlands and United Kingdom; the immigrant/native differentials in unemployment are very similar for men and women.

The immigrant/native labor force–participation gap, however, is substantially larger for women than for men, indicating that the precarious nature of immigrant employment is not the only factor behind the gap. Whether native or immigrant, women are generally less likely than men to be in the labor force. However, as table 3.2 shows, the gender differences are modest for native women, and more substantial for immigrant women, especially in Western Europe. Cultural factors appear to play a role in lowering the labor force participation of some immigrant women. In all the European countries we are examining, Muslims figure prominently in the immigrant population, and norms about married women's family responsibilities are likely to keep some Muslim immigrant women from working outside the home.[28] In addition, many non-European immigrants come from countries where women's involvement in the workforce is relatively low, and immigrant women from these countries often expect to stay home, especially if they have young children. Of course, these factors do not explain why unemployment among those in the labor force is consistently higher for immigrant than native women—a pattern that does strongly hint at the precariousness of jobs.

The employment differences between immigrants and natives look rather different in the North American liberal market economies. In the case of Canada, the overall labor force–participation rates are low because of the wider age range included in the data (fifteen years or older in table 3.2); also in Canada, immigrants are those in groups classified as visible minorities, a category that, like non-EU immigrants in Western Europe, encompasses some groups that would not be considered low in status. As in Europe, it is the case in Canada that natives have moderately higher labor force–participation rates than visible-minority immigrants, but with no difference in this respect between men and women. There is little or no native advantage in Canada, however, when it comes to the risk of unemployment. In the United States, the data are for immigrants from Latin America, a broad category that on average reflects the situations of low-status groups. Nevertheless, the male immigrants have slightly higher labor force–attachment than do their native-born counterparts; and there is hardly any difference in unemployment. Female immigrants are less likely than natives to be in the labor market, and they have somewhat greater unemployment rates when they are; but these differences are generally smaller than in Europe. Note, however, that the U.S. data are from 2006–8 and subsequently, because of the recession, the unemployment rate of Hispanic immigrants went up sharply, to 8 percent, and clearly exceeded unemployment among white workers.[29]

A closer examination suggests a role for the political-economic framework in native-immigrant employment differences. The two countries with the highest native-immigrant unemployment gaps, France and Germany, also rank among the top OECD countries in terms of employment protection legislation (the Netherlands ranks near the top as well). A high level of employment protection, which presumably makes employers hesitant about adding new workers, tends to increase the advantages of native workers, who are probably easier for employers to evaluate.[30] In Germany, for instance, the immigrant-native gaps in unemployment are longstanding and appear even among the guest-worker groups, who came there in large numbers starting in the 1950s after having been recruited as workers in the first place.[31] The extreme case is that of Turkish men, whose unemployment rate in the mid-1990s was 19 percent, at a time when it was just 6 percent for native German men. Unemployment has been even higher among some of the newer immigrant groups, such as Eastern Europeans and Middle Easterners. Similar patterns are evident for female immigrants, though the overall Turkish disadvantage seems enhanced because many Turkish women are not economically active.

In general, the risks of precarious labor force–attachment are concentrated among immigrants from certain groups in European countries; their unemployment rates at times have been astonishingly high. Even in the liberal market economy of Great Britain, where the native/immigrant differences in table 3.2 are relatively small, so-called New Commonwealth immigrants (from Commonwealth countries other than Australia and Canada, like India and Pakistan) and those from the Middle East experience higher employment instability than native white workers. Pakistanis and Bangladeshis in particular are more likely both to be out of the labor market and to be unemployed.[32] The unemployment rate for the men in these groups in the 1990s was 26 percent, at a time when it was 9 percent for native British men. The gap could not be counterbalanced by women's employment because relatively few Pakistani and Bangladeshi women were economically active. In the Netherlands, the most disadvantaged groups are the Moroccans and Turks. In the 1990s the unemployment rate for first-generation Moroccan and Turkish men was above 30 percent, four times higher than that for native Dutch men.[33] The women from these groups are, for the most part, not economically active. In France, the risk of unemployment is especially high for several immigrant groups, including North Africans (Maghrebins), sub-Saharan Africans, and Turks.[34]

In some countries, notably France and the Netherlands, the employment picture for immigrants from some groups suffered during the late twentieth century as a consequence of economic restructuring, as the industries that initially drew heavily on immigrant labor were downsized. In the Netherlands in the 1980s, the economy shifted into a service-oriented postindustrial mode, and "labor-intensive forms of industrial production" declined.[35] Moroccans and Turks had been recruited to work in such sectors as coal mining, shipbuilding, and textiles, which then underwent shrinkage.[36] The shift threw many immigrant workers out of their jobs. Their unemployment rate soared, and many left the labor market altogether and relied for financial support on the Dutch national insurance program for disabled workers. A similar phenomenon took place in France during the 1970s and 1980s, as first-generation Maghrebin workers were forced into unemployment or early retirement by industrial restructuring that eliminated their jobs.[37]

Lack of employment should in principle be less prevalent among immigrant workers in the liberal market economies, and the North American case seems to bear this out. In the United States, in particular, levels of employment for male immigrants are quite high. Mexicans, often typed as one of the most disadvantaged of U.S. immigrant groups, are among the most likely to be working: almost 90 percent of working-age Mexican immigrant men were employed around the turn of the twenty-first century. Dominican and black immigrants are more likely than others to be affected by detachment from the labor force and unemployment, although their rates of employment—which around 2000 were in the 70–80 percent range for men—look favorable beside some of those in Western Europe. In Canada, African immigrants appear to be the most disadvantaged but, again, their employment rate—60 percent among working-age men in 2001—is no worse than that of some groups in Europe.[38]

This does not mean that the higher labor-market attachment of immigrants in the liberal market economies can be taken for granted. Certainly, the onset of the Great Recession in the United States led to a sharp rise in Hispanic immigrant unemployment, bringing it above the rate for whites, as Hispanic immigrants were especially hard hit by job losses in the construction and hospitality industries. And new immigrants to Canada have been experiencing declining employment rates for some time.[39]

Moreover, there may be some degree of illusion to the more favorable employment situation of immigrants in the North American liberal market economies. This is especially true of the United States. Limited social protections, such as means-tested income assistance or social welfare, for the nonemployed in liberal market economies can lead some immigrants who cannot support themselves through employment to return home. In the United States, lack of employment is exacerbated for recent legal immigrants, since a 1996 federal law (the Personal Responsibility and Work Opportunity Reconciliation Act) limits immigrants' ability to receive many forms of cash assistance during their first five years of U.S. residence; in the case of undocumented immigrants, access to social welfare programs is far more restricted, although their U.S-born children are eligible for assistance.[40] This impact has been measured to some extent, for we know that there has long been a back-and-forth flow of Mexican immigrants in response to U.S. labor-market conditions, even if circular migration has diminished in recent years.[41] Thus, some of the difference between liberal market economies and other immigration countries may be due to a difference in the likelihood of returning home when facing inadequate employment opportunities.

However, by the same token, the immigrants who remain and are employed in the United States are to some degree integrated into American society through work. This observation acknowledges the opportunities opened up by paid employment, which often involves regular interactions with non-coethnics along with the possibilities to develop potentially useful social networks and additional skills. An alternative perspective is that the European immigrants who are unemployed long term or have retired early are economically integrated to the extent that social welfare generally provides them with incomes sufficient to keep their families out of poverty. Still, the lack of employment implies less social capital in the receiving society, and the negative consequences can be seen in the employment difficulties sometimes faced by the children of these immigrants. Indeed, a comparison of non-university educated second-generation Mexicans in Dallas and North Africans in the Parisian suburbs found that young Mexicans could rely on family networks to find jobs to a degree that was not true of their North African counterparts.[42]

LOW-WAGE WORK: THE EVIDENCE

If there is substantial evidence that many low-status immigrants are in precarious employment situations, what about low-wage work? Once again, the evidence points to a high concentration in the least favored parts of the labor market. The data on occupations, income, and risk of poverty underscore the decided disadvantages for low-status immigrants, even in the social market economies.

Occupational data indicate that, in many countries, immigrants of low-status origins are much more likely than natives to wind up on the lowest tiers of the labor market. In the Netherlands, more than 60 percent of employed Turkish and Moroccan men are in the semi- and unskilled manual labor category, and most of the rest are skilled manual workers. Few, in other words, have risen into the white-collar ranks. The picture is similar for the guestworker groups in Germany, such as the Italians and Turks. In France in 2003, male immigrants from North Africa were three times more likely than natives to hold semi- or unskilled manual jobs. More than a third of these immigrants held such jobs, and 80 percent were in some sort of manual job.[43]

In the United States, which leads the way in terms of the size of its low-wage sector, immigrant Hispanics, both men and women, are plainly concentrated in low-skilled occupations. In 2008, according to a Pew Hispanic Center analy-

Table 3.3. Hispanic Immigrant Concentration (Percentages) in U.S. Low-Wage Occupations, 2008

	Hispanic immigrants	Non-Hispanic whites
Food preparation and serving	9.6	5.3
Cleaning and maintenance	13.2	3.1
Personal care and services	3.3	3.3
Agriculture	4.0	0.6
Production	12.0	5.7
Transportation	9.6	5.7
SUBTOTAL (%)	51.7	23.7
All other occupations	48.3	76.3

Source: Velasco and Dokterman (2010)

sis, slightly more than half of Hispanic immigrant workers were found in just a few occupational groups, which are typically dominated by low-skilled and poorly remunerated jobs: food preparation, building cleaning and maintenance, personal services, agriculture, production, and transportation (see table 3.3).[44] Only 24 percent of white workers were in these categories, so that the Hispanic immigrant disproportion was more than 2-to-1.

The table obscures one well-documented concentration: the outsized role of immigrant women, many from Latin America, in domestic work and especially in caring for the children of middle-class U.S. natives. Much of this work takes place in middle-class homes, where many immigrant women serve as live-in help, which can mean that they are on call twenty-four hours a day. At its worst, this type of work can approximate a form of ethnoracially marked servitude, where the individuality of the worker receives little or no recognition. Immigrant women typically receive low pay for domestic work, especially given the hours involved.[45]

The Hispanic concentration in low-skilled jobs has a lot to do with relatively low educational attainment. In 2008 over half of the Latin American foreign born had not completed high school and more than a third had not gone beyond the eighth grade. But it is more than this. A great deal of evidence demonstrates that immigrants experience difficulty in gaining labor-market recognition for their human capital, such as premigration work experience and educational credentials, especially when earned in the home society.[46] Immigrants also face disadvantages in the receiving-society labor market owing to another human-capital factor: proficiency in the mainstream language, which is typically limited in their case, unless they come from a country where that language is widespread (English in India, for example) or they have immigrated at a young age (in which case they could be said to belong to the 1.5, rather than the first, generation). All of these handicaps are exacerbated when immigrants are "unauthorized," that is, lack the legal rights to live and work in the country of reception.

The disadvantages immigrants confront in Canada are revealing since it is a society that specifically targets highly educated, skilled immigrants for admission. Even though the educational levels of Canadian immigrants have been rising in recent years, their position in the labor market has been weakening. Not only have newly arrived immigrants had difficulties finding employment—in 2006 the unemployment rate of those arriving during the previous five years reached 12 percent, over three times the rate of the Canadian-born—but when employed their occupations are often not commensurate with their educational credentials.[47] Between 1996 and 2006, the proportion of recently arrived immigrants with university degrees working in low-skilled occupations increased relative to their Canadian-born counterparts. What has been called the taxi driver syndrome—immigrant professionals winding up in jobs far below their educational qualifications—is all too common. Among the small number of occupations in which the majority of immigrants are employed, according to Statistics Canada, are "restaurant and food-service managers, taxi and limousine drivers and chauffeurs, truck drivers, security guards and related occupations and janitors, caretakers and building superintendents."[48] To add to their difficulties, immigrants' earnings in these jobs are lower than those of their native Canadian colleagues. This situation has been characterized as an "underutilization of immigrants' skills."

Jeffrey Reitz argues that the devaluation of immigrants' educational credentials in the Canadian labor market has been growing in recent decades for several reasons. One is that larger numbers of natives are acquiring university credentials, and employers prefer them to immigrants. Another is that visible minority immigrants, who dominate the immigrant stream, appear to suffer from racial discrimination. The main evidence is that a substantial portion of the decline of immigrants' wages in Canada occurred at the historical moment when a shift in immigrant origins from European to non-European sources took place.[49]

Wherever they move, one way that educated immigrants can hope to avoid the labor-market discounting of their credentials is to arrive as students and earn their final degrees in the receiving society. Though this does not guarantee a job that corresponds with educational achievements—among other things, educated immigrants can still be held back by imperfect oral proficiency in the mainstream language—immigrants who earn degrees in the receiving society do substantially better than those who have only credentials earned in their home society.[50] This mechanism no doubt partly accounts for the large number of Asian immigrants who hold jobs in the higher tiers of the U.S. labor market. Examining changes in the top 10 percent of the labor market, that is to say, the best remunerated occupations, Alba finds that among young workers Asian immigrants have taken more than 10 percent of these good jobs.[51]

Table 3.4. Median Household Income and Risk of Poverty, 25–54-year-olds, 2007 (US) and 2008 (Europe)

| | Equalized disposable household income | | | Risk of poverty | |
	Natives	Immigrants from outside the EU	Ratio, immigrant to native income	Natives	Immigrants from outside the EU
France	18,574€	13,893€	.75	14	40
Germany	19,839	15,066	.76	19	33
Netherlands	20,788	17,931	.86	13	25
UK	21,275	18,496	.87	18	29
		Hispanic immigrants			Hispanic immigrants
US	$31,050	$17,746	.57	17	43

Notes: Household income figures are for "median annual equalized disposable household income" (Eurostat, 2011); for the US, the data are calculated from the 2008 Annual Social and Economic Supplement of the Current Population Survey, in which income is measured for the prior year. Poverty is indicated by a measure entitled "the risk of poverty or social exclusion," whose threshold is calculated as 60 percent of national median income (Eurostat 2012a).

Income data, shown in table 3.4, sustain the picture of the economic marginality of many immigrants on both sides of the Atlantic. The data come in two parts. One is based on "equalized disposable" household income. These income calculations involve estimates of after-tax, post-social transfer income adjusted for household size. The other entails the "risk of poverty or social exclusion" (not official poverty itself); this risk is registered when an individual is part of a household whose equalized disposable income is below 60 percent of the national median.[52] The data are for adults in the prime working ages (twenty-five to fifty-four years), when presumably economic activity is at its peak.

The household income comparisons show that the incomes of immigrants from low-status groups are significantly lower than those of natives everywhere, but that the liberal market/social market economy contrast does not correspond with the size of these differences. The income gaps between low-status groups and natives are greatest in the United States, one of the liberal market economies. But they are next greatest in two of the social market economies, France and Germany. In the United States, immigrant Hispanics live in households with incomes that are on average not even 60 percent of those of the households of U.S.-born Americans. In France and Germany, the gaps are much smaller, but still the households of immigrants from non-European Union countries have incomes that are only three-quarters of those of native households. The gaps in household income are smallest in the Netherlands and the United Kingdom, one a social market economy and one a liberal market economy. The correspondence in Europe between the data on household income and on unemployment (in table 3.2) hints that the lower unemployment rates of non-European immigrants in the Netherlands and the United Kingdom in 2008 are implicated in the smaller household income gaps in these two countries.

The risk of poverty provides another angle of vision on the economic situations of immigrants: in general, it is quite high (table 3.4). The extreme cases are in the United States and France; in the first case, the immigrant risk is highest in an absolute sense, at 43 percent; in the second, where it is 40 percent, it is highest in a relative sense, at nearly three times the level for natives. The countries with the lowest risks of poverty are also a mix from the liberal market and social welfare categories. The lowest absolute risk is found in the Netherlands, but the lowest risk for immigrants relative to natives occurs in the United Kingdom.

Overall, the income and risk-of-poverty data confirm the economic marginality of immigrants from low-status groups. However, there are important variations within this picture, and they suggest that no single formula can account for immigrant economic well-being, or the lack of it. Precarious work, which implies spells of un- and underemployment, and low-wage work are both part of the picture, but their combined roles are variable across national contexts. As long as wages are not extremely low, employment, rather than generous welfare benefits, appears to be the critical factor behind well-being. That is, the European countries, France and Germany, where the relative income situation of immigrants is the weakest, are also those where immigrant unemployment is the highest (in table 3.2); yet these are also the countries in our study with the most robust welfare states. The United States, where the economic situation of many immigrants is also parlous, has high employment rates but also the largest low-wage sector, where many immigrants are employed, combined with a threadbare welfare net. (The relatively low household incomes of Latin American immigrant households in table 3.4 are a sign, if one is needed, that wages are indeed quite low for many immigrants, since many of these households contain multiple earners.) There are different national pathways, it seems, to high rates of economic marginality among immigrants.

SMALL-BUSINESS OWNERSHIP

An alternative for immigrants seeking to avoid economic marginality is to set up shop. On both sides of the Atlantic, immigrant small businesses have added vitality to urban economies, providing an array of goods and services on which those in immigrant communities, and many in the majority population, have come to depend. In many American cities, for example, residents rely on stores run by immigrants from Korea or other countries for fresh fruit and vegetables and for dry cleaning; in Britain, "going out for a curry" at a South Asian restaurant has become a part of mainstream social and cultural life.[53] In starting small businesses, immigrants create their own jobs—and often jobs for relatives, friends, and other coethnics as well. For some immigrants, small-business ownership offers an escape hatch from condemnation to the bottom of the employment ladder, but its importance as an economic strategy for success should not be overdrawn. Small-business ownership does not provide a general solution to the handicaps facing large segments of the broader immigrant population in the labor market.

Immigrant small business, for one thing, is not generally a pathway to wealth. In many, probably most, cases, the businesses are modest ventures, such as grocery stores and restaurants, often catering to the special tastes and needs of the ethnic market. They range from Turkish bakeries and kebab outlets in the Netherlands and Germany to North African small retail stores in France and South Asian confectioners and newsagent shops in Britain.[54]

Whatever their clientele, immigrant small-business owners, especially those in low-status groups, tend to gravitate to enterprises where startup costs are low, little or no specific education is required, and costs are reduced by relying on family members or people in their own social networks.[55] In France and Germany in particular, government regulations limit the access of immigrants from outside the EU to self-employment in certain sectors and, more generally, create bureaucratic hurdles to business creation. To set up a hairdressing business in France in 2006, for example, it was necessary to have a professional diploma or proof of three years working experience in the field, a compulsory four-day training in business management costing 200 euros, and registry with the Chamber of Crafts costing about another 116 euros. Germany generally confronts prospective business proprietors with an elaborate maze of approvals and bureaucratic checklists, which is difficult for foreigners to navigate; in addition, specialized training and certification are required for some kinds of business (for example, crafts and insurance), and non-EU immigrants must possess the right kind of residence permit.[56]

Small businesses are a mixed blessing for owners. On one side, they provide an alternative to low-level menial jobs—or sometimes no job at all—for immigrants struggling with disadvantages and discrimination in the mainstream labor market. The autonomy that comes with being your own boss is appealing. Some research shows that immigrant self-employment provides an earnings advantage over other forms of employment, although this is a debated topic. What is not in dispute is that small business has downsides: immigrant owners tend to put in long hours of hard work, profits are often low, and the failure rate is high. Studies in the Netherlands have found that a quarter of immigrant businesses did not survive the first year, and after ten years only one out of five was still in existence; in France, 60 percent of non-EU immigrant businesses created in 2002 were gone five years later.[57]

Moreover, despite the outpouring of scholarly literature on immigrant entrepreneurs, generally speaking, only a relatively small minority of immigrants are actually engaged in running small businesses; this is not, in other words, a way out for the majority of a group.[58] Overall, the self-employed were a tenth to a fifth of the total immigrant workforce in the six countries in our study in 2007—around 10–11 percent in France, Germany, the Netherlands, and the United States, and somewhat higher in Canada (18 percent) and Britain (13 percent).[59] Among the most disadvantaged of the major immigrant groups, usually even a smaller proportion operates a small business. In the United States, although immigrants on the whole are slightly more likely than the native born to own a small business, Mexican immigrants have one of the lowest rates of small-business ownership, at least in part because a significant share (more than half) lack legal status. Despite the visibility of the Turkish small-business sector in Germany, Turks are underrepresented in small business, as is the case for Moroccans as well as Turks in the Netherlands.[60] Notable exceptions are Pakistani and Bangladeshi immigrant men in Britain, who have unusually high self-employment rates.[61]

Why business ownership is more common among some immigrant groups than others reflects a combination of factors, including skills, language, business experiences, family and kinship patterns, and legal status. The ability to raise the capital necessary to get a business started is obviously important, and prior experience—the preparation for running a successful business—sometimes plays a role. Network processes are also critical, as there is considerable evidence that new immigrants learn how to run a business through employment with, and assistance from, their conationals who have preceded them.[62]

Members of some immigrant groups with low average levels of education gravitate in substantial numbers to small business as an economic strategy, Bangladeshi men being a prime example. Yet it is also the case that groups with high average levels of education sometimes resort to small-business ownership because of their weak position in the labor market, owing to lack of facility in the receiving country language, inability to meet licensing requirements, and lack of networks to the mainstream economy. Most famously, this is true of Koreans in the United States, who have specialized in such businesses as greengrocers, dry cleaners, and nail salons. Although many Koreans arrived in the United States with high levels of education, they experienced blocked mobility because their credentials were not recognized and they did not speak English well, or at all. Small business, though risky, grueling, and with low profit margins, was a better bet than low-level service or factory jobs, and a variety of ethnic and class resources gave them a leg up in setting up enterprises. Family members, also with limited employment opportunities, were often on hand to work in the business; the patriarchal structure of Korean families helped to bring the unpaid labor of wives into the store. Some Koreans, moreover, arrived with financial capital, had family members who could supply loans, or obtained funds through rotating credit associations in the community. Once the first wave of Koreans became involved in small business, others followed: a dense web of trade associations, churches, and friendship and kinship ties in the Korean community provided help with business information, loans, and staffing problems.[63]

The Korean second generation, educated in the United States and without language and other liabilities their parents suffered, has tended to shun the small-business path, instead entering the mainstream economy, often in professional jobs. A falloff in small-business ownership in the second generation is not universal, however. Indeed, sometimes the second generation is even better represented in small business than the first, as among Turkish and Moroccan second-generation men in the Netherlands and Maghrebin men in France. However, even in these second-generation groups the proportions in small business still are very low—for example, about 10 percent of Maghrebin second-generation men in France, and only 3 to 4 percent of second-generation Turkish and Moroccan men in the Netherlands and Turkish men in Germany.[64] This brings us back to our main point. As among first-generation immigrants, small business ends up being an answer for only a small minority of the second generation as a way to overcome barriers in the world of work.

CONCLUSION

One of the most consistent aspects of immigration concerns the disadvantages of immigrants in the labor markets of rich societies. Immigrants come because of the allure of jobs that pay better than those at home, and this backward-looking comparison helps to sustain them in situations where they often enough occupy the bottom. Nevertheless, the "immigrant bargain," whereby immigrants are willing to work hard at low-status jobs in return for the chance to gain economically and see their children do well, seems at risk. Changes in the economic structures of the receiving societies—growing inequality of income and the proliferation of precarious and low-paid jobs—hit them hard. The disadvantages of low-status immigrants loom large in both liberal market and social market societies, suggesting that these patterns are widespread and difficult to avoid.

The problem of securing stable employment is one expression of these difficulties. Immigrants typically find work during the early phases of settlement, or they would not be able or motivated to stay on. This attachment to the labor market does not always last. In Western Europe, immigrants are generally more likely than natives to be unemployed, and in some places their ranks include many discouraged workers who have dropped out of the labor market altogether. This appears to have been the fate of many guestworkers who took jobs in declining industries; the relatively generous social-welfare nets in countries such as Germany and the Netherlands at the time allowed them to remain in Europe after they lost their footholds in the labor market. For those immigrants who lose their jobs in the United States, the consummate liberal market society, it can be difficult to remain because of its weak welfare supports and the limited access of noncitizen immigrants to such aid. Yet, as we have also argued, there can be positive sides to being employed, even in low-level jobs, in that it promotes some degree of integration into the new society.

The incomes of many immigrant families are low, exposing them to economic marginality, even poverty. Average incomes tend to be lower for low-status immigrant families than for native ones, but the degree of inequality is variable, not as great in Great Britain and the Netherlands as in France, Germany, and the United States (we lack the data for Canada for this comparison). However, the concentration of immigrant families on the very bottom tiers of the income scale is more severe than average household income data convey. For immigrants from outside the EU in the Western European countries, the risk of falling to the bottom is everywhere more than 50 percent higher than it is for native families; and it is close to three times as great in France. What seems clear is that the liberal/social market economy division, which is so prominent in the academic discussion, is not always relevant, or correct, for an understanding of the dynamics of labor market incorporation for low-status immigrants.

One might object that the statistical data yield a bleaker picture of the immigrant economic situation than is justified. After all, most immigrants have the option of returning to their home countries if they find their situations unacceptable; that so many have chosen to stay suggests that they find life near the bottom of a wealthy society preferable to that in their places of origin. There is a truth to this observation, but it overlooks the importance of the first generation's economic position for the start that the second generation receives. The data on poverty indicate that many children of immigrants, for whom the option of returning to the home countries of their parents is illusory, are starting at or near the bottom of the wealthy societies. The fragility of the immigrant bargain in the early twenty-first century is likely to continue, then, to have reverberations for the second generation.

CHAPTER 4

LIVING SITUATIONS

How Segregated? How Unequal?

Immigrant neighborhoods are common sights in the cities and suburbs of rich societies. Flushing in the New York City borough of Queens, Belleville in Paris, Tower Hamlets in London, and Kreuzberg in Berlin are a few of the better-known examples. For many natives, these areas seem to be worlds apart, where they hear incomprehensible languages and are confronted by unfamiliar sights and smells. For the more adventuresome, they offer opportunities to experience the sensations of a foreign land and culture without going far from home.

Lately, a darker vision of these neighborhoods has taken hold. A specter haunts many native-born citizens and policymakers: the "parallel society," where immigrants and their children live isolated from the mainstream.[1] Immigrant neighborhoods—and the more abstract phenomenon of residential segregation—have become flashpoints for this anxiety. Simply by existing as areas where immigrants can carry on a life in their homeland tongues and among relatives and coethnics, the neighborhoods seem to challenge the goal of integration. For the children growing up in these areas, the possibility looms that they will end up living, and even preferring, a life without much mainstream involvement. In Europe, the concerns have gathered in intensity as multiculturalism has suffered a loss of confidence and been subjected to a barrage of public criticism.[2]

A more extreme worry is of ghettoes. The term "ghetto" originated in the context of enforced Jewish segregation in late medieval Europe, but it is now a reference to poor African American areas in cities like Chicago. It hovers over the discussion of immigrant neighborhoods on both sides of the Atlantic. The ghetto is equated with an ethnoracially homogeneous area, in which the great majority of a group is confined. It is, in addition, an impoverished neighborhood in two senses: a large number of its residents are in dire economic need and cut off from the world of regular employment; and its provision of basic communal institutions, such as supermarkets, banks, and safe play areas for youngsters, is inadequate.[3] The ghetto invokes the nightmare of large groups permanently divorced from the mainstream and unable economically to sustain a decent existence by themselves. In Great Britain, Trevor Phillips, then head of the Commission for Racial Equality, invoked this nightmare in 2005 when he controversially declared in a speech that Britain was "sleepwalking to segregation" and invoked the Chicago ghetto as the endpoint of this process.[4]

These fears are greatly exaggerated, as this chapter's examination of the actual extent, and consequences, of residential segregation in the six countries in our study makes clear. Getting the benchmark right is critical: As a general rule, the African American ghetto is not an appropriate standard in an immigration context. The relevant issue turns out to be the degree and nature of immigrant-group residential segregation in Europe and Canada compared to that of the United States. In all six countries, including the United States (with the major exception of immigrants of African ancestry), immigrants and their children are generally much less residentially segregated from the native majority than are African Americans.

There is much variation in the residential circumstances of immigrant origin groups across countries and groups (as well as within groups). Nevertheless, in Western Europe, where governments tend to be more active in creating policies to encourage neighborhood mixing of ethnic groups and social classes, areas of immigrant concentration are less homogeneous than in North America, especially the United States. The neighborhoods on both sides of the Atlantic where low-status immigrants cluster are, by and large, inferior to those of the native majority. But the disadvantages seem greater in the United States because of the high degree of income and wealth inequality there as well as less active government support for policies mitigating place-based inequalities. At the same time, there is a noteworthy new development in the United States and elsewhere: the emergence of "super-diverse" neighborhoods that bring together a multiplicity of ethnic groups as well as a significant number of the native majority.

Ultimately, we need to ask whether immigrant neighborhoods are way stations to integration or intensifiers of disadvantage. The term "way stations" implies that immigrant families reside upon arrival in areas of immigrant concentration but eventually, perhaps in the next generation, move on; "intensifiers" concentrate serious disadvantages for immigrant families, hinder the mobility prospects of the second generation, and residence in them is often long term. Fears about neighborhoods of disadvantage may be warranted in some cases, such as the barrios housing poor, undocumented Latin American immigrants in the United States. However, on the whole, they are not. For many immigrant families in Western Europe and North America (including those of U.S. Latinos) the immigrant neighborhood is probably a way station, as they leave the ethnic enclave for other areas when they have the economic resources and mainstream language skills to do so. An important question is how much improvement such a move brings, for the new neighborhoods may still lag behind those of the native majority in various services and amenities.

IDEAS AND QUESTIONS

The reasons why many newly arriving immigrants settle, at least for a time, in neighborhoods where conationals are concentrated are easy to discern. The newcomers lack familiarity with the receiving society and, without assistance, might have difficulty meeting their daily needs for shelter, sustenance, and some degree of comfortable social interaction. In most cases, they are not able to speak the language of the natives well, and so are rarely able to navigate the labor and housing markets on their own. Consequently, the predominant pattern is for new arrivals to seek out areas where they can find kin and other social intimates on whom they can rely for initial support. This usually means they move to immigrant enclaves, where there are many others like themselves, their mother tongue is in common usage, and the stores and institutions (such as churches, synagogues, and mosques) are culturally familiar.[5]

One fundamental question concerns the degree to which immigrants' residential situations change over time. This is linked to several others: How homogeneous are the neighborhoods where they live, and with what other groups do they share them? What is the "quality" of the neighborhoods? "Quality" refers to aspects of residential areas affecting how well residents live (for example, the cleanliness and safety of streets) as well as their long-term life chances (such as the education their children receive in schools).

One way of thinking about residential change comes from the theory of assimilation, formulated specifically as a model of "spatial assimilation."[6] A premise of the model is that the initial areas in which immigrants settle have undesirable features, such as overcrowded, run-down housing and unsafe streets. There is thus an incentive for immigrant families to look for better residential locations as their financial situation improves and their acculturation progresses, enabling them to better maneuver within the housing market. Since more desirable residential situations are mostly found in areas where the native majority predominates, many immigrant families are motivated to leave ethnic enclaves, according to this logic. The presumption is that the immigrants do not face high barriers of discrimination in other neighborhoods, which might deter any attempt to leave the immigrant enclave.

This presumption may not be true, as a second approach to residential change emphasizes. Members of immigrant minorities may not be able to participate fully in the mainstream housing market. Instead, they may find their options confined to less-attractive residential situations in a hierarchy of places, where the native majority monopolizes and defends the best residential environments.[7] Even if the options for immigrant families include improvements over immigrant areas, the neighborhoods available to them may fall short in a variety of ways, from the condition of housing to the quality of schools and stores, as compared to those in neighborhoods where members of the majority population reside. According to this perspective, then, immigrant minorities not only remain permanently segregated from the native majority population, but are more or less confined to neighborhoods of lower quality, which create disadvantages for the families living in them.

A third way of thinking about the evolution of immigrants' residential situations turns the idea of immigrant-enclave disadvantage on its head by assuming that immigrant areas may have positive attributes that compensate for their deficits. Quite some time ago, Canadian sociologist Raymond Breton observed that the institutional infrastructure of immigrant communities could, if it was sufficiently "complete," act as an attractive force bonding the immigrants socially and culturally.[8] As recent studies of Asian immigrant communities in the United States have noted, these institutions can include cultural and educational organizations that provide after-school instruction for children—in the homeland language or the intricacies of the SAT test for college-bound youngsters—and thus promote academic achievement.[9] The idea of "social capital" has been invoked as the basis for another possible advantage of immigrant communities. That is, immigrants are thought to find helpful connections through immigrant communities, connections that may lead to jobs or information about the school system that will help their children. Some immigrant communities have been found to house substantial ethnic subeconomies. Under the right circumstances—Cuban Miami is often cited—a subeconomy may develop to the point that it affords employment opportunities to immigrants, and perhaps even the second generation, on a par with those in the mainstream economy.[10]

The longer-term benefits of living in coethnic concentrations have been invoked by a residential pattern among Asian groups in North America, which is often described as an "ethnoburb."[11] Ethnoburbs are concentrations of socioeconomically well-off coethnic immigrant families in advantaged suburbs, where the immigrants frequently mix with native families of similar status. Because such neighborhoods offer immigrants access to good housing—typically, owner-occupied, single-family homes—and amenities such as excellent schools, they do not create a strong incentive to move elsewhere. And when the concentration of an ethnic group is sizable enough, these neighborhoods can accommodate a corresponding business sector that caters to immigrants' needs. Cupertino, California, an affluent Silicon Valley city of sixty thousand, home to many Chinese and Indian families, who together with other Asians make up 60 percent of the population, is an example.[12] Even though such high-human-capital Asian immigrant families are distant from the low-status immigrant groups who form the main focus of this book, we consider ethnoburbs and similar residential contexts in our discussion because they are an essential element in the overall picture of immigrant settlement and help to put in perspective the situations of many low-status groups.

Attempts to adjudicate empirically among these three perspectives may produce a misleading picture of immigrant settlement. Reality may be too complex to be grasped adequately by any of the ideas. Instead, it is preferable to pose a series of questions that these perspectives suggest: Where do immigrants live—in enclaves or elsewhere? What sort of neighborhoods do they live in—good or bad? What consequences do their residential circumstances have for immigrants and their children? How able are they to move to improve their living situation? In the United States, and increasingly now in other immigration societies, an immense literature has arisen in which immigrant settlement patterns have been studied under the magnifying glass that focuses on segregation from the mainstream. That literature tells us with great precision where and to what extent immigrants concentrate, but sometimes provides only indirect hints about the answers to these other questions. We will try to tease them out as we go along.

REGIONAL CONCENTRATION

Any consideration of these questions should start with the fact that immigrant groups almost never spread uniformly throughout the country that is receiving them. They cluster in particular locations as the latest arrivals head for places where there are preexisting immigrant concentrations. Moreover, new arrivals often tend to stay in or near these landing places or, if they move, to go where significant numbers of other immigrants are present.

Consequently, a national map that highlights immigrant concentrations typically reveals a few places that show up brightly; the rest of the country is largely dark. Still, there are noteworthy cross-national differences. In some countries, like France, the degree of immigrant regional concentration is extreme, while in others—and here the United States stands out because of the spread of immigrant groups to what are being called "new destinations"[13]—it is weaker. One French city and its suburbs stand out above all other areas in terms of immigrant residence, and in general the foreign born in France are concentrated in just a few places. The Parisian region forms the immigrant lodestar, where about 40 percent of all the nation's immigrants reside. Another 20 percent are located in the regions around Lyon and Marseille.[14] By contrast, as of 2010, the Los Angeles and New York City metropolitan areas, which were home, by a big margin, to the largest numbers of immigrants in the United States, contained just a quarter of the foreign-born total.

The French degree of concentration is approximated in some other countries. For example, immigrants are as highly concentrated in Canada. The three "gateway cities"—Toronto, Montreal, and Vancouver—house more than 60 percent of all the nation's immigrants, while being home to about 30 percent of all Canadians.[15] Toronto is especially prominent as an immigrant destination, with nearly 40 percent of all the country's immigrants (as of 2011). A broadly similar picture obtains for the Netherlands, where the non-Western immigrant groups are highly concentrated in the four largest cities—Amsterdam, Rotterdam, the Hague, and Utrecht. In Great Britain, concentration has been very high in the recent past, but immigrants are now spreading out from four regions of initial concentration: Greater London, Greater Manchester, and the metropolitan counties of the West Midlands and West Yorkshire. Yet the London region by itself still stands apart from all others: according to the 2011 census, it contained 40 percent of the country's foreign born.[16]

In terms of the geographic concentration of immigrants, Germany is the least concentrated of all. The highest numbers of immigrants are found in the three largest cities—Berlin, Hamburg, and Munich—but they house only a modest fraction of the total immigrant population, around 15 percent.[17] The reason for this dispersion lies in the original geographic distribution of the guestworkers, who came mainly during the 1950s and 1960s. Their immigration was "directed" because they arrived linked to particular employers, and they and their children have mostly remained in or near their places of original settlement. In terms of their rootedness in place, they resemble other Germans, who are also more reluctant than are Americans to pull up stakes and move.

THE SEGREGATION OF IMMIGRANT POPULATIONS

Although immigrants tend to concentrate in particular neighborhoods that are readily recognizable, researchers generally have focused less on identifying these neighborhoods than on measuring the extent of segregation, or separation, of immigrants and their children from the native population. Because this vein of research is both technical and critical to answering questions about immigrant settlement patterns, we need a brief interlude to introduce its main statistical tools.

MEASURING SEGREGATION

Measuring segregation requires that a large area like a city be divided up into spatial subunits, which ideally should be small in size: in the United States, for example, these units are typically so-called census tracts, which usually range in size from four thousand to eight thousand residents; in Great Britain, they often are wards, which in the case of London had an average population of around 11,000 in 2001.[18] For the analysis of segregation in Paris, however, some studies have used the eighty *quartiers* of the city, which are divisions of the *arrondissements*; the average population size of quartiers is more than twenty-five thousand, much larger than are census tracts.[19] The larger the size of the spatial unit, the more likely it is to encompass multiple neighborhoods and therefore to be heterogeneous; this obviously reduces the ability to measure relative homogeneity.

The primary statistical tool for identifying segregation, called the "index of dissimilarity," measures the "unevenness" of the immigrant distribution over an area like a city in comparison to that of some standard population, constituted, say, by natives. Ranging from 0, or no segregation, to a total segregation score of 100 (or 1, depending on how it is scaled), its value refers to the percentage (or proportion) of the immigrant minority that would have to move in order to match the residential distribution of the reference population. Rules of thumb exist for characterizing the magnitude of the index—thus, values under 30 are viewed as indicating low segregation, and values over 60 high segregation. Some of the highest values found have been for blacks compared to whites in U.S. cities and metropolitan regions. In 2010, for instance, the black-white index of dissimilarity for the Chicago metropolitan area, often cited as the paragon of ghettoization, was 76, an extremely high value; in 1980 the index was even higher at 89, a value close to complete segregation.[20]

The index of dissimilarity represents an abstract definition of segregation, one that is, in an important sense, independent of any individual's experience of it. Another type of segregation measure—the "exposure" index—is more clearly linked to the experience of living in segregated neighborhoods. It directly reflects the ethnoracial composition of the neighborhoods in which members of an immigrant minority reside. The index estimates the percentage of a second group—native-born whites, say—among the residents of the neighborhood of the average minority-group member. When the second group is the minority itself, then this measure is called the "isolation" index, and its value is the percentage of the immigrant minority in the neighborhood of the average group member. The isolation index thus indicates the degree of homogeneity in a group's neighborhoods. For the Chicago region the isolation index in 2010 for blacks was 67, indicating that the average black lived in a neighborhood two-thirds of whose residents were also black. This is a high degree of homogeneity, but one that has fallen substantially in just a few decades (from 84 in 1980). It is compatible with the existence of some virtually all-black neighborhoods, like some parts of the south side of Chicago, but it indicates also that many blacks now live in neighborhoods with nonblacks.[21]

IMMIGRANT-GROUP CONCENTRATIONS
IN THE UNITED STATES

The residential segregation of African Americans represents a much-invoked standard in the literature on immigrant settlement. Their extreme segregation, whose image looms over the research on immigrant settlement, has been a prominent feature of the urban scene since the mid-twentieth century. In cities like Chicago, African Americans have confronted *hypersegregation*, a situation in which the great majority live in large, ethnoracially homogenous areas, where they are unlikely to come into regular contact with members of other groups, other than in highly choreographed unequal interactions.[22] Prompted by the image of the African American ghetto, researchers have focused a great deal of attention on the residential concentration of immigrant minorities in the U.S. Hence, we know a lot about this part of the American landscape, and it is useful to start with a sketch of it, to create a sort of template for evaluating immigrant settlement patterns elsewhere.

During the third quarter of the twentieth century, the index of dissimilarity for blacks (in relation to whites) in some American cities and metropolitan areas lodged in the 80–90 range, reaching what is probably a practical limit for segregation where it is not rigidly enforced by law. Since then, black-white segregation has declined virtually everywhere, although it remains very high in places like Chicago and New York City. There is a Hispanic analogue to this segregation, in the border regions, especially in Texas, where Latino settlement patterns date back to the nineteenth century and the incorporation of Mexican communities into the United States resulted from conquest. In metropolitan areas like Laredo and Brownsville, Mexican Americans are concentrated in barrios where 90 percent or more of their neighbors are coethnics. These barrios are home to some families that have lived in the United States for generations.[23]

Immigrant-origin groups, or in other words, immigrants and their descendants, are not so concentrated on the whole, but that does not mean that their residential contexts raise no concerns. If we use broad ethnoracial categories (the categories that predominate in the U.S. segregation literature), Hispanic residential concentration stands out. The average index of dissimilarity for Hispanics in relation to whites (non-Hispanic whites, to be precise)—this is the standard comparison—stood at 48 for all U.S. metropolitan regions in 2010, down from 51 a decade earlier. As a point of reference, the equivalent average index value for black Americans was 59 in that year, having declined from 64 in 2000.[24] So, by this measure, Hispanic segregation is less than that of blacks, even though the latter has declined considerably over several decades. Remarkably, Hispanic segregation has also declined during the first decade of the twenty-first century, despite a high level of immigration from Latin America.

Nevertheless, the lower segregation of Hispanics by one common measure still allows for a great deal of residential concentration. This becomes visible through another measure, the index of isolation. According to it, the average Hispanic in the nation lives in a neighborhood (that is, census tract) where 46 percent of the residents are also Hispanic. The index of isolation has been rising for Hispanics, partly as a function of the overall growth of the Hispanic population.

Segregation among Hispanics tends to be higher where there are large numbers of Hispanics and recently arrived immigrants. Because new immigrants tend to head for existing immigrant concentrations, the large inflows from Latin America generally have been strengthening Hispanic neighborhoods and increasing the apparent extent of segregation. Hispanic segregation is also sustained by large numbers of undocumented immigrants, whose compromised legal status hinders their departure from the protection of enclaves.[25] Yet the stability, and even small decline during the oughts decade, in average segregation as measured by the dissimilarity index implies that there is also significant outflow from these neighborhoods, presumably by Hispanics who have been living in the United States for some time and who are seeking to improve their residential situation.

Los Angeles and New York, the two metropolitan regions with the largest numbers of Hispanics and also foreign-born Hispanics, ranked first and second in the extent of Hispanic segregation in 2010.[26] Their dissimilarity index values above 60 also place them very high in an international comparison (see figure 4.1). These two regions differed greatly in the national-origin composition of their Hispanic populations: Mexicans and Salvadorans dominate in Los Angeles; Caribbean-origin Hispanics, including Puerto Ricans, not an immigrant-origin population in a strict sense, have been the most prevalent in the New York region. Apparently, then, segregation among Hispanics is not so dependent on where, precisely, they come from.

In the big gateway regions, Hispanics often live in highly homogeneous neighborhoods, where most of their neighbors are also Hispanic. This is indicated by the values of the isolation index (figure 4.2), which in 2010 was 65 in Los Angeles and 76 in Miami. Hispanic neighborhoods usually achieve these high concentrations by mixing Latinos of different national origins. One example is the Pico-Union area of Los Angeles (78 percent Hispanic in 2000), where Mexicans and Central Americans live together.[27] The extent of Hispanic segregation trails off significantly in regions where the Hispanic population is more modest in size. For example, in the Washington, D.C., area, an area of emerging Hispanic settlement, the index of dissimilarity value was 48 in 2010, in the moderate range. In Las Vegas, likewise an area of emerging Hispanic settlement, it was 42.[28]

Some regions where the Hispanic population is small in size and segregation is modest are so-called "new destination" areas, many in the southern U.S., in places that have not received many new immigrants since before the nineteenth century.[29] Thus, in the Atlanta region, where after a rapid rise in their numbers, Hispanics have now reached 10 percent of the population, the dissimilarity index between whites and Hispanics is 49, almost exactly at the national average value for Hispanic segregation. In the Orlando area, where the Hispanic population has grown twenty-fold since 1980 and now amounts to a quarter of all residents, the value of the index is 40, and in the region around

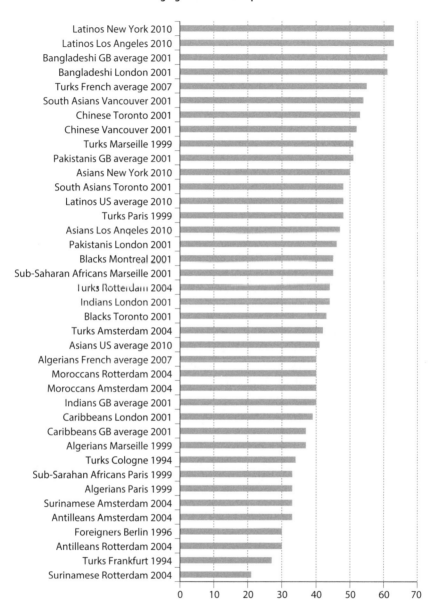

Figure 4.1. Immigrant group segregation in selected major metropolises, index of dissimilarity values. *Sources*: Friedrichs (2008), Hou (2006), Logan and Stults (2011), Musterd and Ostendorf (2009), Peach (2009), Préteceille (2009), Safi (2009), Pan Ké Shon and Verdugo (2014).

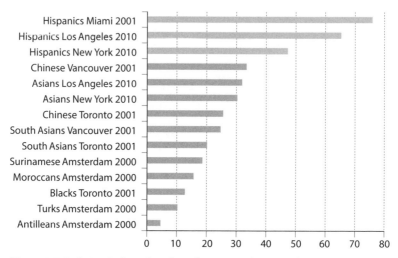

Figure 4.2. Isolation Indices for selected groups and metropolitan regions. *Note*: Isolation indices are available for fewer groups and metropolitan regions than the index of dissimilarity. *Sources*: Hou (2006), Logan (2006), Logan and Stults (2011).

Raleigh, North Carolina, where Hispanics are 10 percent of the 2010 population, it is 37. It remains to be seen how much segregation will increase in newer destinations as their Hispanic populations grow; almost certainly, it will increase some.

For the many Hispanics living outside of neighborhoods where Latin Americans predominate, the question arises of who their non-Hispanic neighbors are. In gross statistical terms, non-Hispanic whites or Anglos, the members of America's ethnoracial majority, are most numerous among these neighbors. In 2010 the index of Hispanic exposure to Anglos was about 35, indicating that the average Hispanic lived in a neighborhood where whites were more than a third of residents; by comparison, non-Hispanic blacks comprised 11 percent and Asians 7 percent. Moreover, the prevalence of whites among the neighbors rises with Hispanic family income: as Hispanic families improve their economic situations and move into better neighborhoods, they live with larger numbers of the white majority population.[30]

Nevertheless, Hispanics also live with African Americans in some of the most destitute areas of American cities and suburbs. The southern Bronx, still an icon of such areas, is home to more than one million residents, where poverty—at a rate of 36 percent in 2010—is rampant. Ninety percent of residents are black or Hispanic, with Hispanics the numerically dominant population—a mix of Puerto Ricans and many Latin American immigrant families, chiefly Dominicans and Mexicans. While the South Bronx was never an African American ghetto, there is evidence that elsewhere many Latin American immigrants are moving into former African American ghetto neighborhoods. For instance, a study of the small cities of New York's Hudson Valley shows that recent immigrants from Latin America find housing in dilapidated inner-city neighborhoods that they share with poor African Americans.[31]

Asians are generally less segregated than Hispanics and much less likely to reside with large numbers of coethnics, though such neighborhoods do exist, as the well-known Chinatowns of New York and San Francisco illustrate. Partly, this greater integration results from the many human-capital immigrants coming from Asia. Since, moreover, the various Asian groups do not share a language as Latin American groups do, there is less incentive to mix in neighborhoods that amalgamate different groups such as Chinese and Indians.

The highest 2010 value for the index of dissimilarity between Asians and whites, 54 in the Edison, New Jersey, region, is not much higher than the average value for Hispanics. In many regions with large numbers of Asian immigrants, the index value is much more modest—37, for instance, in the Washington, D.C., region and just 33 in Seattle. Moreover, the isolation index demonstrates that the average Asian in virtually all regions resides in a diverse neighborhood, in which Asians constitute a minority. Apart from a few exceptional regions with heavily Asian neighborhoods such as Honolulu, San Francisco, and San Jose, California, the isolation index values are quite low for Asians, with most under 20; values above 40 are rare.[32]

The relatively high incomes of many Asian families often translate into residence in well-off suburban communities, ethnoburbs. These communities are often dominated numerically by whites, though some like Monterey Park, outside of Los Angeles, have Asian majorities. The residential mixing with whites does not mean that Asians are necessarily attempting to immerse themselves in the white mainstream. Frequently, the affluent neighborhoods in which Asians live have a significant presence of coethnics, even if it is a minority one. For example, Bergen County, New Jersey, just across the George Washington Bridge from New York City, is home to many Korean families. In 2010, Koreans and other Asians made up about 15 percent of the county, more than 60 percent of whose residents were whites. Even in Bergen County's Fort Lee, which features many signs in Korean that greet the tens of thousands of drivers who pass by every day, Asians were 38 percent of residents in 2010, while whites were 47 percent.[33]

The Asian pattern frequently comes close to what has been described as the "ethnic community" model, as distinguished from the "immigrant enclave."[34] While the immigrant enclave tends to be established in less desirable residential settings and hence spurs socially mobile families to leave, the ethnic community is often found in high-status settings, where many members of the white majority also live. Both patterns arise in part from the desires of immigrants to live near others who are like themselves, but the ethnic community may be more stable because it provides access to neighborhood-based resources and amenities like good schools that are superior to those in immigrant enclaves. Bergen County, New Jersey, for example, is one of the most affluent counties in the United States. At the same time, the ethnic community pattern also implies more possibility of interaction with white Americans, especially for the children of the immigrants who attend mixed schools.

Given the realities of race in the United States (see chapter 5), it is not surprising that immigrants of African ancestry, from the Caribbean as well as Africa, stand out as highly segregated, whether segregation is calculated in terms of the index of dissimilarity or isolation. In the ten metropolitan areas with the largest Afro-Caribbean populations in 2000, the index of dissimilarity between Afro-Caribbeans and whites ranged from 57 (in Fort Lauderdale) to 83 in (New York City). Afro-Caribbean neighborhoods overlap substantially with those of African Americans. Exposure to African Americans is generally lower for the African born, but segregation from whites is in much the same high range.[35]

Finally, we need to bring the white majority into this picture. Those who write about residential segregation often complain that the frequently extreme segregation of the ethnoracial majority is not viewed as problematic; only the segregation of minority groups is. Yet, though whites in the United States do succeed sometimes in segregating themselves—for example, by living in gated communities—immigration has had a large impact on diversifying the communities where they live. The average white now lives in a neighborhood that is 75 percent white (down from 88 percent in 1980).[36] In other words, one in four neighbors belongs to a minority group. In such a neighborhood, the increasing ethnoracial diversity of American society, largely a result of the post-1965 immigration, is unavoidable, if only because of the visual diversity encountered on the street or in public places.

SEGREGATION IN CANADA

Of the other countries we are considering, Canada would seem the most likely candidate for similarity to the United States. The housing market in Canada looks very much like that in its neighbor to the south and is quite different from that in most Western European countries. It is dominated by owner-occupied residences, very much as in the United States; and the social housing sector, subsidized by the state, is small.[37] Moreover, because of the large immigration flows into a few Canadian metropolitan areas in recent decades, the ethnoracial composition of neighborhoods in key metropolitan regions such as Toronto and Vancouver has been changing rapidly. This reduces the possibility for immigrants and their children to live with whites. Of course, something similar has been happening in U.S. cities and regions that are becoming "majority-minority" areas, such as Los Angeles.[38]

There are, however, some key differences between the two countries that bear on residential patterns. One, already mentioned, is the high degree of concentration of the immigrant-origin population in just three gateway metropolitan areas: Toronto, Vancouver, and Montreal.[39] There are few Latin Americans north of the U.S.-Canada border, and Asians make up a much larger share of immigrants there. In addition, the black population is much smaller and is made up of immigrants and their children. There are no large black ghettoes in Canadian cities, as there are in the United States.

The rapidly growing Asian fraction of the Canadian population—the three main groups, South Asians, Chinese, and Filipinos, made up about 11 percent of the population in 2011—is concentrated in a few metropolitan regions, making for a sizable number of neighborhoods where Asians are in the plurality or majority.[40] Asians have generally not been treated as a single group for purposes of measuring segregation in Canada, in contrast to the general practice in the United States. Across the main Canadian metropolitan areas, the values of the index of dissimilarity for the major Asian groups in relation to white groups generally hover around 50, which is similar to the average index value for Hispanics in the United States.[41]

The Chinese in Canada are especially likely to live in neighborhoods where they are a prominent, even dominant, presence. Isolation indices for the Chinese in Toronto and Vancouver, the regions of their greatest concentration, indicate for 2001 that the average Chinese individual resided in a neighborhood whose residents were, respectively, a quarter and a third other Chinese (see figure 4.2). Sizable numbers of residents of such neighborhoods were other racial minorities, presumably mostly other Asians given the composition of Canada's urban minorities, so that a minority of residents were whites.[42] Chinese immigrants tend to move quickly to become homeowners; but even after long residence in Canada, the Chinese in Toronto live in neighborhoods with sizable numbers of coethnics. In contrast, black and South Asian immigrants tend over time to move away from neighborhoods with a strong coethnic presence.[43]

The neighborhoods of Asian immigrant concentration are not as disadvantaged as the neighborhoods of comparable immigrant concentration in the United States, which mostly are dominated by Latin Americans. One exception concerns the Bangladeshis of Toronto, a recently arrived group, who are concentrated in a few areas, such as Victoria Park, a high-rise complex in east Toronto that housed other immigrant groups before the Bangladeshis arrived. The average income of the area is well below that for the city as a whole.[44]

Blacks in Canada, a collection of immigrant-origin groups of recent vintage, are much less segregated than American blacks and even less segregated on the whole than Canadian Asians are (see figure 4.1). One study found no black majority urban neighborhoods among the four thousand analyzed, a situation that presents a strong contrast to that in the United States. The most segregated immigrant-origin group in Canada, it appears, is the Vietnamese, who, like the Vietnamese in the United States, are made up largely of refugees who arrived after the end of the Vietnam War.[45] Their greater segregation probably reflects the impact of their original settlement clusters, created by the assistance of Canadian sponsors. Nevertheless, it is unclear from the state of published residential data for Canada whether there are any majority Vietnamese neighborhoods.

SEGREGATION IN WESTERN EUROPE

Patterns of immigrant-group segregation in Western Europe generally look even less like those in the United States. In particular, the immigrant neighborhoods there tend to be more mixed, less dominated by immigrant and second-generation families. One reason is undoubtedly the greater housing role played by the state in European countries by comparison with North America, especially the United States. State-subsidized social housing accounts for substantial proportions of all housing units in some European countries. Although social housing is not guaranteed to be a force for desegregation—as witnessed in U.S. public housing—where the state pursues policies of social mixing in communities and uses social housing as a tool to further this goal, some mitigation of segregation seems likely.[46]

The European nation that might seem to offer the strongest analogy to the United States is Britain. While the percentage of ethnoracial minorities in Britain is much lower than in the United States, amounting to 13 percent in the 2011 U.K. Census, they are more highly concentrated regionally than is the case across the pond. Hence, those urban areas with large minority populations, such as London and Manchester, possess the population base for extensive and concentrated minority neighborhoods. Moreover, Britain has a sizable African-descent population, although one that has arisen from postwar immigration from former colonies, unlike in the United States, where immigrants and their descendants amount to just a small part of the overall black population. Perhaps it should not come as a surprise, then, that some British observers have feared the development of U.S.-style ghettoes.[47]

All of the scholars who have looked systematically at the question of ethnic and racial segregation in Britain have rejected emphatically the notion that minority ghettoes are developing in British cities. What they have found is patterns of residential segregation that at first blush, by the standards of the index of dissimilarity, seem much like those of Hispanic and Asian groups in the United States.[48] As in Canada, the most segregated groups in Britain originate in Asia, especially in Bangladesh and Pakistan—for example, as figure 4.1 shows, the index of dissimilarity for Bangladeshis averaged about 61 in the main cities of ethnic-minority concentration in 2001. The groups of African descent, in particular the large Afro-Caribbean population, are only moderately segregated. The average index for black Caribbeans in 2001 was just 37 and had declined over the preceding decade.[49]

In Britain, immigrant neighborhoods are, on the whole, less homogeneous than those in the United States. Admittedly, the smaller ethnoracial minority population in Britain may reduce the likelihood of large, fairly homogeneous areas such as are found in some U.S. metropolitan regions—but, as the sizable minority population of London underscores (40 percent in 2011), the difference cannot be entirely reduced to scale. Insofar as there are areas of minority homogeneity, they tend to be small and are often in industrial cities, rather than in London.[50]

Indians are the largest ethnic minority in Britain, and Leicester has, as a population proportion, one of the largest Indian communities in Britain (almost 30 percent of residents in 2011), since it became a home to many East African Indians who fled Uganda during the Idi Amin regime. In 2001 about half of Leicester's Indians resided in wards where their group was in the majority. Nevertheless, just seventy-two thousand Indians lived in Leicester, so only thirty-six thousand were found in Indian enclaves. In most British cities, Indians in areas of ethnic concentration are greatly outnumbered by those in areas where whites form the majority. The picture for London needs qualification because of its large minority population: in 2011 more than a third of London's minorities resided in majority-white areas, and another quarter in areas where whites typically made up the plurality. The pattern of living in neighborhoods dominated by whites is particularly pronounced among the Chinese.[51]

Residing outside of areas of group concentration is also common for the Pakistanis, one of the two most segregated groups in Britain (see figure 4.1). About half of Pakistanis in Bradford, once a flourishing textile manufacturing center, lived in Pakistani-majority areas in 2001, although most of these neighborhoods had bare majorities of Pakistanis and hence were significantly mixed. In London, with the largest Pakistani population, the majority of Pakistanis as of 2011 resided in neighborhoods where whites were the plurality or the majority. A significant concentration of Bangladeshis in London is located in the council housing of the Tower Hamlets borough, where many Bangladeshis landed upon arrival in Britain; as of 2001, 42 percent of London's immigrant Bangladeshis lived in this borough.[52] Since the immigration of the group crested during the 1980s and has been ongoing, it is scarcely surprising to find such initial concentration persisting into the beginning of the new century.

Black groups also live mostly in areas where they are outnumbered by whites. For instance, London in 2011 was home to nearly 350,000 black Caribbeans and 400,000 black Africans, populations large enough, one would think, to generate group enclaves. Yet neither group lived in wards that could be considered enclaves. Most black Caribbeans and Africans lived in areas where whites were the largest group, though their greatest concentrations were in areas where whites lived side by side with significant numbers of nonwhites.[53]

A new pattern on the British scene is the emergence of mixed neighbor-hoods where no single group predominates. At least, this is true in London, where between 1991 and 2001 nearly sixty wards (about a fifth of the wards that had a significant minority presence in 1991) went from majority white to a majority composed of a mixture of minorities, a trend that continued during the first decade of the new century.[54] The groups most likely to reside in such neighborhoods include Bangladeshis and Indians, with Pakistanis not far be-hind. In contrast to American neighborhoods where mixtures of Latin Ameri-cans are prevalent, these British areas contain groups that are linguistically and religiously distinct.[55] These neighborhoods bear monitoring as areas of poten-tial disadvantage for their residents and where contacts with the native major-ity may be limited.

If Canada and Great Britain could be said to exhibit a certain degree of simi-larity to the United States when it comes to the residential segregation of im-migrant groups, any similarity has been strongly contested for continental Eu-ropean countries. The strongest case on behalf of difference has been made for France. Loïc Wacquant has led the way in arguing that the areas of immigrant-group concentration, especially in the notorious suburbs (*banlieues*) around Paris, are essentially different from the American ghetto. While the black ghetto is not the right standard for evaluating immigrant-group concentrations in any event, Wacquant makes two critical points: first, the banlieues, like inner-city immigrant-group concentrations (for example, Belleville in Paris), are quite diverse and home to many poor and working-class native French; and, second, they are by no means as impoverished in institutional terms as some inner-city American neighborhoods.[56]

In fact, the data about residential segregation in France indicate that the concentrations of immigrant-origin groups are not as great at those in the United States. The Paris region, home to 40 percent of France's immigrants, is a prime example.[57] French studies are of immigrant segregation, and they reveal modest segregation levels for the major groups, although the magnitudes may be somewhat deflated by the large spatial units involved.[58] For example, in 1999 the indices of dissimilarity for the African immigrant groups—Algerians, Mo-roccans, Tunisians, and sub-Saharan Africans—were all just above 30. The sole exception has been the Turks, who are a small group in the Paris region. As of 1999 their index of dissimilarity (in relation to the native French of the Paris region) was just under 50.[59] Since this is in all probability an underestimate in comparison with the indices measured in U.S. metropolitan regions, it suggests that Turks in France are about as segregated on this measure as are Hispanics in their U.S. regions of high segregation (for example, Los Angeles).

The modest degree of segregation in the Paris region is also underscored by the limited number of areas in which immigrants and the children living with them make up a majority of the population. Among more than one thousand areal units in the Paris area, only fourteen have non-European immigrant-group majorities, and they show up in the well-known immigrant suburbs, such as Clichy-sous-Bois (where the episode that sparked the 2005 riots took place) and Seine-Saint-Denis. Just 5 percent of the non-European immigrant population resides in these areas. In other words, the great majority is found in more ethnoracially mixed areas of the Paris region—a pattern that applies to France in general and appears to be holding steady as of the early twenty-first century.[60]

In the Netherlands, too, the segregation of immigrant-origin minorities is quite moderate. Because Dutch immigrant groups are concentrated in just four cities, studies of segregation tend to be city-specific, with Amsterdam serving as a critical case. The focus is usually on the four main immigrant groups in the Netherlands, two postcolonial groups, the Antilleans and Surinamese, and two former guestworker groups, the Moroccans and Turks.

For Amsterdam in 2004, the Surinamese and Antilleans exhibit index-of-dissimilarity values just above 30 in relation to the native Dutch (that is, Dutch-born individuals with Dutch-born parents). The Moroccans and Turks show values around 40, not unlike Asians in the United States. The patterns are similar in Rotterdam, the second largest Dutch city.[61] The levels of group concentration in Amsterdam's immigrant areas are modest by the standards set in the United States by Hispanics. The presence of coethnics in the neighborhoods of the average group member is relatively low: the highest value of the isolation index (in 2000) is around 19 for the Surinamese and the next highest is for Moroccans at 16 (see figure 4.2). The largest group present in the neighborhoods of all four groups tends to be the native Dutch. In short, these groups are generally not locating in neighborhoods that concentrate members of diverse immigrant groups and isolate them from the native majority. The Amsterdam neighborhoods that stand out for their immigrant presence are also quite distinct for the four main immigrant-origin groups.[62]

The role of social housing is more significant in the Netherlands than in any other country we are considering. About 40 percent of all housing there is classified as social housing, and the fraction is even higher in large cities like Amsterdam.[63] That social housing is not limited to the poor and ethnoracial minorities may help to account for the moderate degree of segregation in Amsterdam. However, immigrants are still disadvantaged in obtaining social housing, for which there are long waiting lists. When they are recently arrived and have a pressing need to find a place to live, immigrants often end up taking the first available apartment. Native Dutch, by contrast, are already in some form of housing and, when considering social housing options, can wait for

social housing: problem or solution?

something desirable. Moreover, immigrants, once settled, frequently stay in place; their concentrations can often be traced to the initial neighborhoods they occupied. A notable 2000 concentration of Surinamese is found in the southeast of Amsterdam, in the social housing complex of Bijlmermeer, which was developed in the 1970s, shortly before the Surinamese arrived in large numbers.[64]

In Germany, too, the segregation of immigrant groups is modest. Working against high concentration is the dispersal of the immigrant-origin population across numerous cities and smaller places. In 2004 the twelve largest German cities housed only 27 percent of the foreign population. Among the former guestworker groups, this dispersion is a function of the links tying immigrants to employers at the moment of arrival. Hence, dispersal characterizes Turkish settlement, even though the Turks are the immigrant group provoking the greatest concern in Germany about group concentration and supposed proclivity to form a "parallel society." The city with the largest number of Turkish residents is Berlin, but just 7 percent of all Germany's Turks reside there.[65]

Segregation index values suggest a level of segregation in German cities well below that observed for Hispanics in the United States. For Berlin, where the absolute number of foreigners is the largest, the index of dissimilarity between Germans and non-Germans was 30 in the mid-1990s and had been declining. For Frankfurt, where the population share of foreigners is especially high, the index of dissimilarity between Germans and Turks was just 27 in 1994. For Cologne, the index of dissimilarity between Turks and non-Turks was 35 in 2000 (see figure 4.1).[66] The levels of immigrant-group concentration in specific neighborhoods also appear modest. German cities contain few if any ethnically homogeneous areas, and immigrants frequently reside in neighborhoods that mix together immigrants from different countries with the German majority. Examining 1,800 neighborhoods in thirty-three different cities, Karen Schön-wälder and Janina Söhn find only one in which the population share of a single immigrant group (the Turks) came close to 40 percent.[67] One weakness of their data is that nationality, that is, citizenship, is used to indicate immigrant origin; the data lose sight, in other words, of members of a group who have become German citizens. Even so, the most residentially concentrated of the major groups, Turks, has only a handful of neighborhoods where its population share exceeds 20 percent; since a minority of first- and second-generation Turks are German citizens, it is reasonable to conclude that there cannot be more than a few neighborhoods in major German cities where Turkish-origin individuals are a majority among residents. After the Turks, the next most concentrated group is immigrants from the former Soviet Union, most of whom came under the special provisions for the immigration of "ethnic Germans." Their degree of concentration is possibly a consequence of their recent arrival, since most came during the 1990s.

NEIGHBORHOOD DISADVANTAGE AND
IMMIGRANT-GROUP CONCENTRATION

Important as it is to document segregation patterns, they only get us so far. A crucial issue concerns the kinds of neighborhoods where immigrant groups concentrate. Are they worse than the neighborhoods where the native majority predominates? A priori, one would presume so, since many immigrant groups—and here we think especially of those coming in search of low-wage work—arrive with limited financial resources and are forced to find housing as quickly as possible in an unfamiliar environment. To be sure, the residential contexts described as ethnoburbs in North America demonstrate that not all immigrant-rich areas are inherently disadvantaged, although the Asian immigrants in ethnoburbs are typically high in human and financial capital.

The most in-depth picture of the conditions in immigrant neighborhoods comes from the United States, where investigations take place against the backdrop of African American ghettoes.[68] In general, the finding has been that the areas of concentration for low-income immigrant populations, such as those from Mexico, Central America, and the Caribbean (save for Cuba), suffer from a variety of disadvantages, which come close to the conditions encountered in African American neighborhoods. Douglas Massey has demonstrated that in the United States "segregation concentrates poverty," a process that impacts Latinos as well as African Americans. Employing an index of neighborhood disadvantage that combines such rates as unemployment, high school dropout, female-headed households, and poverty, one study found that neighborhoods where Latinos are the prevalent group—sometimes referred to as *barrios*—exhibit high levels of disadvantage, including high crime rates.[69]

It is possible that positive features of these immigrant areas in the form of social capital, such as social networks and communal institutions supporting mobility, have been overlooked in the literature on residential segregation, because the kinds of data deployed, typically from the census, are limited. But with some exceptions, such as the Cubans of Miami, such features have yet to be demonstrated as general characteristics of barrios. And some comparisons reveal these areas to be lacking in institutions found elsewhere—for example, the ethnic after-school programs that Asian children attend are absent for Mexican and Central American children in Los Angeles neighborhoods.[70]

The negative impact on the Latino second generation of growing up in segregated American neighborhoods is potentially severe. It is evident in educational life chances. The schools that youngsters in segregated neighborhoods attend are also generally segregated. In 2003, for example, three-quarters of Latino students in public schools attended schools where most students were members of ethnoracial minority groups, and nearly 40 percent were in "intensely segregated" schools, where at least 90 percent of students were minorities. Mostly minority schools are usually deficient in a number of ways, including less experienced and less qualified teachers and a more constricted range of course offerings, especially at the advanced end. Mostly Latino neighborhoods also house an unusually large number of idle teenagers, who are neither in school nor at work and thus at risk of joining gangs or engaging in other forms of deviance.[71]

Across the Atlantic a central question concerns immigrants who live in mixed neighborhoods that contain substantial numbers of the native majority, which are common in European cities. In the theory of spatial assimilation, entry into neighborhoods of the majority is a way that immigrant families improve their residential situation when their finances and level of acculturation allow this. Members of the majority population presumably occupy better neighborhoods. Living among them should give immigrant families access to better neighborhood-based resources and amenities. On this basis alone, one would expect the neighborhoods where immigrants live in Europe to be better residential environments than the more concentrated immigrant neighborhoods in the United States, where immigrants and their children predominate.

Differences in urban policy strengthen this expectation. In general, European national and local governments, especially on the continent, are more concerned about neighborhood-based disadvantages, including concentrations of disadvantaged individuals and families, and are more active in developing policies to counteract them. In France, for example, the government has systematically identified "vulnerable urban zones" (ZUS, in the acronym for the French expression). There are more than seven hundred such zones in the country, which housed about 4.5 million people in 1999, or about 8 percent of the population. The policy intervention is modest, however: the zones benefit from various tax exemptions intended to attract businesses or subsidize their expansion and hence to expand the employment base. France has also attempted to disperse poor populations across the full range of communities: the 2000 law on *Solidarité et Renouvellement Urbain* requires municipalities above a certain size to establish a minimum percentage of public housing. How successful the law has been is unclear. In the Netherlands, local governments have actively pursued policies to foster socially mixed neighborhoods. Unlike, say, public housing in the United States or France, Dutch social housing includes many middle-income households. In some Dutch cities, such as Amsterdam, city authorities in the name of urban renewal have built some middle-class housing in districts that were previously low-income in character. These efforts are supported by a national Big Cities policy that provides funding.[72]

It turns out, however, that, as far as one can tell, the European neighborhoods where immigrant families concentrate are also disadvantaged, even though they tend to have smaller concentrations of immigrants and a larger presence of the native majority than in the U.S. Consider France, where an activist state and a generally lower degree of ethnoracial segregation might be expected to ameliorate any degree of neighborhood disadvantage. Yet the evidence suggests strongly that most neighborhoods in which many low-income immigrants live and raise their children concentrate households at or near the bottom of the social class ladder. Thus, even though ethnoracially diverse, the neighborhoods seem to be fairly homogeneous in terms of social disadvantage rooted in low social-class position.

Despite the French government's attempts to assist vulnerable urban ZUS neighborhoods, the percentage of households headed by foreigners is twice as high in these neighborhoods as it is elsewhere in the same metropolitan areas; and the percentage of individuals residing in low-income housing (called HLM in France) is three times as high. The housing estates, or *cités*, in the suburbs—for example, the notorious "*quatre milles*" ("four thousand," now partly demolished), in the Parisian suburb La Courneuve—represent the most socially distressed residential spaces in France and contain numerous immigrant families. The disadvantages associated with ZUS residence seem to afflict youth, especially when they are of immigrant origin, since they have, statistics indicate, a high risk of leaving school without a diploma and ending up unemployed. Wacquant's argument that these areas have not been abandoned by the state is undoubtedly true, but it is not clear how large a difference state involvement makes for the opportunities of residents.[73]

The Netherlands is another critical test case because of its activist urban policies and the much lower degree of immigrant concentration in neighborhoods. Yet, in Amsterdam, there are potentially some disadvantages associated with living in an area of immigrant-group concentration. The ethnic neighborhoods of the postcolonial groups, the Antilleans and Surinamese, have high numbers of welfare recipients and those of the guestworker groups, the Moroccans and Turks, have many low-income households. "White flight" by native Dutch away from the neighborhoods where immigrants congregate has been documented. This exodus has an impact on schools, which tend to be segregated as a consequence. The stigma attached to schools with many second-generation youngsters is borne out by their designation in common parlance as "black schools." To what extent students are disadvantaged by attending largely minority schools is unclear, especially given the government policy of giving schools additional funds for the disadvantaged children they educate.[74]

In general, whatever the country, low-status immigrant families settle in less desirable neighborhoods, which impose disadvantages of various sorts on them and their children. This appears to be true even in countries where the state is more active in trying to ameliorate place-linked inequalities than it is in the U.S. What is hard to judge from the research record is whether there are differences among our countries in the social and economic distance between immigrant neighborhoods and those of the native majority middle class. We suspect that the place-based disadvantages for low-status immigrants are great-est in the United States, which not only has the most extensive and concen-trated immigrant neighborhoods, but also has suffered over decades from an extreme growth in the degree of segregation by income. This growth entails an increasing concentration of individuals and families in poor neighborhoods, where the average income is substantially below that of native majority middle-class neighborhoods. One study has found that the percentage living in poor tracts in the United States doubled between 1970 and 2009 to include one of every six residents of large metropolitan regions.[75] We have no doubt that these poor tracts—and others just a little more prosperous—encompass large shares of low-status immigrant families today.

MOVEMENT AWAY FROM IMMIGRANT ENCLAVES

It is one thing to observe that the areas of concentration of low-status immi-grants tend to possess deficits such as relatively inferior schools. The obvious next question is whether immigrant families are confined to these neighbor-hoods for long periods by discriminatory barriers or whether they are able to move to better neighborhoods once they have adjusted to the new society and achieved a modicum of economic mobility. Particularly important are the life chances of the second generation: if the immigrant generation often stays within enclaves, we have to ask whether the next generation is able to leave them.

These questions have much less relevance for the ethnic communities estab-lished by high human-capital immigrants, such as most Asian groups in Can-ada and the United States. These immigrants are able to enter more privileged neighborhoods and, in the United States in particular, often reside with large numbers of affluent whites. The thorn of residential disadvantage, which can spur the exodus of immigrant families from enclaves, does not hurt most mem-bers of these groups. In truth, we know very little about their movements. However, in the United States, residence in mixed neighborhoods with many whites reduces the social distance between the white majority and Asians, at least to judge from the high intermarriage rates of second-generation Asians.[76]

The thesis of spatial assimilation provides a sort of yardstick for evaluating the mobility of immigrant families and the second generation. Its core concep-tualization is that the immigrant enclave is a "way station" or "decompression chamber," necessary to immigrants during the initial phases of settlement. Eco-nomic improvements, which many immigrants achieve with longer residence, are presumed to enable families to leave the enclave and move to better, and frequently more mixed, neighborhoods. Likewise, some degree of accultura-tion, especially in terms of language, allows them to maneuver more adroitly within the housing market. To be sure, discrimination can prevent immigrant families from succeeding in the effort to improve their residential context. In addition, "white flight" by natives away from immigrants moving into their vicinity can cause mixed neighborhoods to take on increasingly the character of an immigrant enclave, also thwarting the mobility attempts of immigrant families.

Once again, we know the most about mobility by immigrant-minority families in the United States, where a large body of research has been conducted on the ability of Latino families to enter better neighborhoods. This research indicates that mobility out of disadvantaged neighborhoods occurs at a robust pace. For example, a five-year study found that 15 and 12 percent of Mexican and Cuban families, respectively, left their original neighborhood (census tract) during this period. A substantial portion of these movers left a poor neighborhood for a non-poor one. Many were also moving to mixed neighborhoods with higher percentages of non-Hispanic white residents. As the spatial-assimilation model would predict, better-educated, English-speaking, and higher-income Latinos moved into such neighborhoods, though dark skin was a hindrance for some Cubans. Another study, of residents of Chicago neighborhoods, found that some mobility by Latinos, just as among non-Hispanic whites, is motivated by the desire to escape neighborhoods with a growing nonwhite presence.[77] There appears, then, to be "Latino flight," though it is hardly of the magnitude that white flight has been.

The research on residential location, which includes Latinos who have remained in the same place over a long period of time as well as those who have moved, shows again that, for Latinos, socioeconomic advance, language acculturation, and departure from an immigrant enclave are associated with greater numbers of neighbors who are native whites and neighborhoods that contain more affluence and presumably more amenities and resources.[78] An obvious question is whether Latinos ever achieve residential parity with non-Hispanic whites. There is not a definitive answer. According to one analysis, high-income Latino families outside of immigrant neighborhoods start to close the residential gap with socioeconomically similar white families. On the whole, though, whites hold important advantages in terms of residential location and all that it entails for living conditions, social capital, and opportunities of various kinds, even though Latinos tend to improve their residential situations over time. One study of Mexicans in Los Angeles found that only in the fourth and later generations did they achieve spatial assimilation.[79]

Of the remaining countries, the most information about mobility exists for the Netherlands, which makes a good comparison to the United States because immigrant families tend to live in mixed neighborhoods there, which are not as deprived as are some barrios in the United States. But, in Dutch cities, too, there is substantial mobility out of immigrant concentrations. One study of Moroccan and Turkish clusters in Amsterdam between 1994 and 2004 found that nearly a quarter of the original Turkish residents had left their group's areas in a decade's time, though the rate of out-migration by Moroccans was much less, just 7 percent. In line with the spatial assimilation model, Moroccan and Turkish families whose heads are better educated or employed are more likely to live in mainstream neighborhoods. In the case of the postcolonial groups, Antilleans and Surinamese, generation comes into play, as the second generation is more likely than its parents to live in such neighborhoods.[80]

In sum, for many immigrant families in Europe and North America the ethnic enclave is probably a way station, as they move on when their economic circumstances and proficiency in the mainstream language permit. However, mobility does not necessarily bring immigrant families into neighborhoods that are equal to those in which the native majority is found; this conclusion is justified for Latinos in the United States and probably applies to some other low-status immigrant groups there and elsewhere as well. Moreover, geographic mobility is not inevitably a sign of or spur to increased assimilation. Some mobility is between ethnic neighborhoods or even into neighborhoods with a greater coethnic concentration than the original one.[81]

For some immigrant families, the enclave is undoubtedly more than a temporary harbor. Questions that cannot be answered on the basis of existing research are how many families remain in enclaves and to what extent they and their children are disadvantaged as a consequence. It has been noted in Germany that some Turkish immigrant women do not learn German and therefore prefer to live in neighborhoods that allow them to shop and otherwise function in their native tongue.[82] And there are other barriers. Immigrant families may be prevented from spatial mobility by a failure to improve their incomes sufficiently or by encounters with prejudice and discrimination outside of the enclave.

Geographic mobility is also impeded by a lack of legal status, which is especially consequential for some Latino groups in the United States. Immigrants who lack the legal right to live and work in the receiving society are anxious about any exposure of their status to others, and this anxiety imposes numerous constraints on their lives.[83] Many undoubtedly prefer to live in immigrant neighborhoods because of the protection these afford from the scrutiny of unsympathetic outsiders. This limitation on residence probably contributes to the sizable disadvantages found among children growing up in undocumented families, even for those with citizenship in the receiving society.[84]

SUPER-DIVERSE NEIGHBORHOODS

One of the new phenomena linked to immigration is the emergence of what could be called "super-diverse" or "global" neighborhoods, where members of the native majority and multiple immigrant groups congregate.[85] Such neigh-

Table 4.1. Super-diverse and Other Neighborhoods in 24 Highly Diverse U.S. Metropolitan Areas, 2000

	Type	Percent distribution of neighborhoods (census tracts)	Average ethnoracial neighborhood composition			
			%W	%A	%B	%H
Heavily minority neighborhoods	A	0.0%	6.3	86.2	1.2	2.5
	H	2.2	6.1	0.7	0.8	92.4
	HA	2.3	6.7	20.3	1.4	71.6
	B	4.2	1.8	0.4	94.8	2.6
	BA	0.5	3.5	10.5	81.6	3.9
	BH	7.1	3.6	0.8	48.4	47.0
	BHA	5.4	6.4	12.5	30.7	49.9
All-white Neighborhoods	W	4.4	93.7	1.1	0.9	3.8
Neighborhoods where whites and minorities mix	WB	1.2	64.4	0.9	30.0	4.3
	WA	10.8	83.7	10.5	1.3	4.2
	WH	5.9	62.7	1.1	1.3	34.2
Super-diverse neighborhoods	*WBA*	3.4	72.0	10.0	12.7	4.9
	WBH	5.9	44.0	1.1	20.1	34.3
	WHA	17.7	61.6	11.7	1.7	24.6
	WBHA	28.9	47.9	11.9	13.1	26.7
		100.0%				

Note: Letters indicate significant presence of groups, A for Asians, B for Blacks, H for Hispanics, W for non-Hispanic whites.
Source: Logan and Zhang (2010).

borhoods appear in many European cities, such as Amsterdam, where two or more immigrant groups are concentrated in neighborhoods that are also home to many native Dutch families; there are many examples in the United States, some of the best known located in New York City's borough of Queens, such as Jackson Heights and Astoria. In the United States, immigrations in the past gave rise to neighborhoods with a welter of groups from different countries. The historical record reveals that many ethnically identified neighborhoods in the early twentieth century were in fact quite diverse.[86] But, so far as we know, these neighborhoods did not contain much of a presence of the then white-Protestant majority. Today's settlement patterns are different.

The highly diverse neighborhoods in the United States may prove an augury of things to come in other countries. In many parts of the United States, whites have to resort to extraordinary measures to avoid having diverse neighbors.

One study of twenty-four highly diverse metropolitan areas found that, in the year 2000, three-quarters of the neighborhoods mixed a significant presence of whites with that of one or more minority groups (Asians, Hispanics, or blacks).[87] In nearly half of all the neighborhoods, whites lived with substantial numbers of both Asians and Hispanics, showing the broad impact of immigration (see table 4.1).

Moreover, the white presence in super-diverse neighborhoods tends to be considerable: in the highly diverse metropolitan areas of 2000, it averaged 48 percent in the quarter (29 percent) of all neighborhoods that brought all four major groups together. The average was 62 percent in white-Asian-Hispanic neighborhoods. Looked at another way, the great majority of members of immigrant-origin groups in these areas live as neighbors of whites: two-thirds of the Hispanics and 85 percent of the Asians in 2000.

To be sure, there is white flight from some of these diverse neighborhoods, especially as the percentage of minority residents climbs. However, for white families wanting to stay in these metropolitan areas, few bastions of whiteness remain, as a tiny percent of neighborhoods (less than 5 percent in 2000) lack a significant presence of at least one minority group. White families can find a mixed neighborhood with a higher percentage of white residents, but it is very difficult to avoid diversity altogether.

Just because members of different groups live in proximity to one another and encounter each other on the street and in public places does not mean that their relationships have become friendly. They could pass each other by with little mutual recognition, or even hunker down into mutually antagonistic sub-communities.[88] In her ethnographic study of a London borough, Susanne Wessendorf observed what she calls commonplace diversity in public space. The residents of Hackney, one of Britain's most ethnically diverse boroughs, are about a third white British, with the rest having origins in more than fifty countries, including significant numbers of West Africans, West Indians, and South Asians as well as Turks, Chinese, and Poles. Ethnic, religious, and linguistic diversity has come to be seen as a normal part of social life, and an "ethos of mixing" has developed in which it has come to be expected that people should mix and interact with residents of other backgrounds in public space and associations. At the same time, private relations were more parochial, with people's closest ties tending to be with those most like themselves in terms of ethnicity, race, and social class.[89]

We do not know yet what the long-term significance of highly diverse neighborhoods will be for interethnic relationships.[90] But we do think that such neighborhoods will become more common as populations become more ethnoracially diverse, an inevitable result of contemporary demographic forces, and as diversity spreads outside of its current areas of concentration. That likelihood makes it all the more urgent to learn more about these super-diverse neighborhoods.

CONCLUSION

The idea that immigrant-origin groups are establishing "parallel societies" that evolve separately beside, and apart from, the mainstream seems wildly overstated when confronted with the empirical evidence. Yet immigrant residential concentrations are apparent in all immigration societies, even though the degree of concentration and the quality of the neighborhoods vary among groups and from one national context to another. The extent to which these neighborhoods function as transit stations on a journey to integration, as opposed to traps holding families back, is hard to adjudicate with precision. There is a kernel of truth in both conceptions.

In continental Europe, where states generally have taken a larger role in developing policies to promote the mixing of different groups and socioeconomic strata in neighborhoods, the areas of immigrant concentration are not as homogeneous as in North America and, in many cases, include a substantial fraction of the native majority. In contrast to the situation in the United Sates, moreover, when these neighborhoods mix different immigrant groups, they typically bring together groups that speak different languages—for example Turks and Moroccans share some Amsterdam neighborhoods—or practice different religions, such as Hinduism and Islam in some London neighborhoods.[91] In the United States, neighborhoods of Latino concentration are frequently ones in which a Latino majority, often composed of a mix of Spanish-speaking groups, dominates.

On both sides of the Atlantic, neighborhoods of immigrant concentration, at least for the low-status groups that are our major concern, are usually inferior to those in which the native majority typically lives. This inferiority tends to be reflected in more dilapidated and overcrowded housing, more segregated and lower-quality schools, more unemployed adults (who therefore lack the connections to the labor market to help young adults find jobs), and a greater risk of criminal victimization, though the precise configuration of these conditions varies from one context to another. These problems are reflected in, and intensified by, the out-migration of natives, "white flight," from these areas, a pattern that has been documented in the Netherlands as well as in the United States.

Arguably, the disadvantages associated with residence in immigrant neighborhoods are most severe in the United States. We cannot verify this hypothesis directly because the research on neighborhood quality outside the United States is too sparse to make a well-calibrated comparison. But what make it plausible are the degree of income and wealth inequality in the United States, which is much higher than in most other wealthy societies, and the translation of this inequality among individuals and households into inequality among neighborhoods.[92] Housing and spatial location are allocated in the United

States largely based on market forces—in general, one can live only where one can afford to live—and many government policies, in the form of zoning regulations, for example, tend to enhance socioeconomic distinctions among different areas. In the hierarchy of communities and neighborhoods, those at the bottom, where poor individuals and families are concentrated, tend to be very deprived by comparison with the average area. As we noted earlier, research has shown that neighborhoods of Latino concentration typically are quite disadvantaged.[93]

In principle, immigrants and their adult children can move out of heavily immigrant areas. Indeed, the negative features of these neighborhoods create an incentive to do so, as families move up economically and gain proficiency in the mainstream language. While this subject has not been investigated in-depth in all of our countries, we find evidence that this dynamic is at work in contexts as different as the Netherlands and the United States. Needless to say, the possibility of mobility into better neighborhoods may not be available to everyone. In the United States, it is clearly not. Race is a barrier for Afro-Caribbean immigrant families and no doubt for some Latino ones. Lack of legal status impedes the mobility of many immigrant families. The degree to which equivalent barriers to mobility operate in other societies remains unknown.

Geographical mobility generally results in residential improvement, but the extent of that improvement—and of segregation from the mainstream society—remains uncertain. Not enough research has been done on the residential contexts of immigrant and second-generation families living outside of immigrant concentrations. The research in the United States, by far the most extensive, indicates that Latinos make a large advance in their living situations by leaving immigrant neighborhoods, but at the same time they are channeled into neighborhoods with more minorities and less affluence than those housing socioeconomically comparable whites.[94] This picture affirms the privileged position of the native majority in the United States with respect to residence; despite the reduction in segregation associated with departure from immigrant enclaves, members of immigrant minorities do not usually attain full parity with whites.

There is also the question of whether residential integration leads to integration in other respects, such as friendships across ethnoracial lines. Merely living in a mixed area need not in and of itself imply more than visual exposure to members of other groups; more-than-incidental social relationships across ethnoracial lines are not guaranteed. By the same token, residence in immigrant neighborhoods need not be a bar to developing amicable relations with those in different groups in other contexts or to other sorts of integration, especially economic.[95] Research in the Netherlands comes down on both sides of the question of contacts with the native majority: one study underscores that mixed neighborhoods do not necessarily promote much in the way of social interaction among different groups, while another found the reverse—that immigrants' contacts with the native Dutch are inversely related to the degree of immigrant concentration in the neighborhoods where they live.[96]

In reflecting on the relationship between residential integration and other forms of integration, it is important to keep in mind the distinction between the immigrant and the second generation. Immigrants who arrive in a new society as adults tend to be limited in the degree of change they can undergo, and it is unrealistic to expect the average labor-seeking immigrant, who is significantly less educated than the average native, to become socially integrated with the native majority population to any great extent. However, the situation of their children is potentially quite different, and, moreover, as they are growing up, they are more vulnerable to the influences of the social environment in which they are located than adults are. Here is where the most critical impacts of neighborhoods are probably registered and where the explanations for the mobility of many immigrant families out of immigrant concentrations are likely found. As Özüekren and Ergoz-Karahan point out for Turkish families in Berlin, some choose to reside in German-dominated neighborhoods to ensure that their children master the mainstream language, for their futures in Germany depend on their doing so.[97]

Overall, then, we conclude that, for immigrant minorities, residence in mixed areas, where members of the native majority also live generally implies a greater connection to the mainstream society. In this respect, one of the keynotes for the future appears to us to be heterogeneity in the residential situations of immigrant minorities. This seems obvious as one looks *across* groups: the residential situations of many Asians in the United States, who live in affluent areas of ethnic concentration that also contain numerous whites, are very different from those of many Latinos and Afro-Caribbeans. But it will also prove to be true *within* groups: the quality of the residential environment for the many Latinos who live outside of immigrant neighborhoods is much superior to that of those who live within such concentrations.[98] This sort of intragroup heterogeneity may prove to be a hallmark of the contemporary era of immigrant incorporation on both sides of the Atlantic.

CHAPTER 5

THE PROBLEMS AND PARADOXES OF RACE

The problem of the twentieth century, W.E.B. DuBois wrote in 1903, is the color line—a problem that unfortunately remains with us at the beginning of the twenty-first century. DuBois was writing primarily about the black-white divide in the United States, and he was not concerned with immigrants. Yet the color line—and, more generally, color-coded race—is of critical importance to the dynamics of integration in the United States for immigrants and their children. Race-as-color is relevant in Western Europe and Canada as well, particularly in countries where immigrants who trace their origins, in the recent or more distant past, to sub-Saharan Africa are a substantial presence. These immigrants (and their children) of course are not the only ones who are racialized in terms of color. This is true of many Mexicans in the United States, for example, and large numbers of North Africans and South Asians in Western Europe. But we focus frequently in this chapter on immigrants whose roots are in black Africa and the Afro-Caribbean, because they are racialized everywhere and confront especially high hurdles as a result. In addition, they are present in sizable numbers on both sides of the Atlantic and thus represent a particularly intriguing case for comparison.

If the realities of and inequalities related to color-coded race are not unique to the United States, there are ways that the United States is exceptional when it comes to the dynamics of racialization. This exceptionalism is closely tied to the legacy of the past. Europeans oversaw slavery regimes in their colonies, but this was far from home; Canada had slavery on its territory until the early nineteenth century, but large-scale plantation slavery never existed and the number of African slaves was tiny, never more than several thousand.[1] By contrast, not only was African slavery on America's soil since its formation, but also "the peculiar institution" was the basis for the economy of the American South, involving, by the middle of the nineteenth century, several million slaves and followed by a harsh regime of legal segregation that lasted until the mid-twentieth century. The United States, in short, has long had a large, subordinated black population inside its territorial boundaries.

The consequences of the historical legacy of slavery, segregation, and ghettoization for immigrants have been complex and contradictory. On the one hand, people of African ancestry, native and foreign born alike, experience barriers in the United States that are more severe than those facing their counterparts in Europe. On the other hand, the special position of the large American black population has been an essential element in how ethnic or racial groups of immigrant origin have defined themselves and their position in American society, providing them with certain advantages that immigrant minorities lack in Europe and Canada. In particular, the civil rights movement and legislation of the 1950s and 1960s, which sought to redress and overcome the institutionalized disadvantages following several hundred years of slavery and legal segregation, created policies, practices, and institutional mechanisms that have had no parallel in Europe or Canada—and despite rollbacks in recent years—have had positive effects for the integration of contemporary immigrants and their children.

SLAVERY, COLONIAL HISTORY, AND COLOR-CODED RACE

Race acquires its "searing reality," as the historian Gary Okihiro has put it, through the deep impact "of history, through [a] . . . nation's laws and institutions, through popular culture and everyday practices."[2] By "race," we refer to the belief that visible physical differences or putative ancestry define groups or categories of people in ways that are seen to be innate and unchangeable.[3] Race, in our view, is closely connected to racism—a widely believed ideology asserting the enduring and essential inferiority of a subordinate population; and also a system of privilege and dominance of one group over another that is buttressed by the incorporation of racial distinctions into core societal institutions (for example, segregation of residence and schools).[4] In principle, race can refer to a social distinction that is only weakly reflected in outward physical characteristics—examples are the racism directed against Jews in Nazi Germany and against the Irish by their English overlords in the nineteenth century. Though racist literatures in both cases employed caricature to portray the subordinate groups as visually distinctive, membership in these groups was not directly discernible by sight. However, the racism with the greatest significance for contemporary immigration is in fact linked to physical markers of membership, particularly (but not exclusively) skin color, because the vulnerable groups, the ones we describe as "low status," come from outside Europe. Racism of this sort—"color-coded" racism—can be especially systematic because group membership is readily apparent (or thought to be).

The power of color-coded racial differences in Europe and North America is linked to historical realities of conquest, colonialism, and enslavement. All of the countries we are studying were involved in one or more of these forms of domination. The European countries had colonial empires that subjugated people of non-European ancestry in Africa, Asia, and the Americas. In Canada and the United States, European settlers established their dominion over peoples indigenous to their territories, a process that was especially harsh in the United States, where military conquest bordered on outright genocide, and survivors were forced onto reservations to make way for white farmers and ranchers. The United States also defeated Mexico and usurped its northern portion, incorporating at one stroke tens of thousands of Mexican citizens. On the other side of the Atlantic and at about the same time, France forcibly extended its territory into North Africa, making Algeria into three *départements*. In general, these subjugations were justified on racial grounds. To put it another way, an essential rationale for white dominance was the belief in the superiority of "civilized" whites over "barbarous" or "savage" peoples.[5] This belief was apparent in the ferocious prejudice and discrimination that greeted Asian immigrants to the United States in the late nineteenth and early twentieth centuries.

The most enduring racism stems from the experience of slavery and affects persons of African descent. France, the Netherlands, Britain, and the United States were involved in the enslavement of millions of Africans on plantations in the Caribbean and American South. "The long association of black people with a form of servitude never imposed on whites," the historian George Fredrickson has written, encouraged "the belief . . . that blacks were servile in nature and therefore incapable of being . . . self-governing citizens."[6] The quest to provide justifications for enslavement that were morally satisfactory to many whites gave rise to racist ideologies that were especially pernicious and difficult to extirpate.

The social and cultural significance of slavery as an institution was much greater in the United States than in Europe or Canada because it involved massive numbers on the country's home territory and left a deep imprint on societal institutions. It has only been since the immigrant influxes after World War II that European countries and Canada have had black populations of substantial size. For France, Britain, and the Netherlands, the confinement of slavery and most blacks to distant colonies did not corrupt home-society institutions through the incorporation of racist practices and distinctions. The black-white color line, by contrast, has been a central feature of the U.S. national experience from its very founding. Slavery was a domestic, not far-off, institution. The United States was founded as a nation based on African slavery, and it took a bloody civil war to lead to its official abolition in 1865 with the passage of the Thirteenth Amendment. In 1860, slaves made up a remarkable 13 percent of the U.S. population—nearly four million people. Abolition was followed by a harsh regime of institutionalized racial oppression, entailing a century of legal segregation in the South and a new era of white supremacy that defined African Americans in Southern states as second-class citizens, confining them to separate schools, public places, and public transportation and depriving most of the right to vote.

Europeans' sense of identity was far less dependent on whiteness than was that of most Euro-Americans.[7] In the United States, white entitlement was encoded in foundations of the nation through citizenship law. The right of naturalization was only extended to blacks after the Civil War (through the passage of the Fourteenth Amendment) and to Asians only in the middle of the twentieth century. Ian Haney López's book *White by Law* chronicles the legal attempts by Asian immigrants in the late nineteenth and early twentieth centuries to prove they were white to overcome the barriers preventing them from becoming citizens.[8] Despite enormous changes in U.S. law and social institutions, the close connection between privilege and pigmentation remains. In everyday discourse in the contemporary United States, race is a color-coded concept, the main divisions now between black, brown (Hispanic), yellow (Asian), red (Native American or American Indian), and white. Frequently, Asians, blacks, Hispanics, and Native Americans are lumped together as "nonwhite" or "people of color" in contrast to whites.

Race-as-color may be less central and prominent as an organizing principle in Europe, but Europeans are far from color-blind. This is particularly so in countries where postwar immigration has involved very significant numbers of people of black African ancestry—in our study, the Netherlands, France, and Britain.

In France, about 13 percent of the immigrant population in 2008 was from Africa south of the Maghreb, with another 232,000 born in the Caribbean overseas departments of Guadelupe and Martinique (who as French citizens are not considered immigrants). Despite the taboo on the term "race" in France, and a definition of "otherness" primarily in terms of culture and religion, it has been said that skin color has made "black French nationals . . . in the reality of daily life, into foreigners"; those with origins in the French Caribbean and sub-Saharan Africa often perceive discrimination against them as based in large part on color.[9] In the Netherlands, according to one account, the "strong emphasis, in common sense and political discourses, on national, cultural and European belonging, seems to leave little if any explicit space for ideologies and identities of whiteness to get a stronghold."[10] Still, color is relevant as a symbolic marker of difference for the large number of Antilleans and Surinamese from the Caribbean, who in 2012 made up a quarter of the non-Western first and second generations ("allochthones") in the Netherlands. To further complicate matters, the term "black" is not always reserved for those of sub-Saharan African descent. In a practice that would seem strange to most Americans, "black" schools in the Netherlands refer to those where the majority of pupils have a foreign background, especially Moroccan or Turkish although also Surinamese or Antillean. Moreover, the metaphor of whiteness is sometimes used to differentiate minorities of non-Western origin from the "white" long-established native Dutch.[11]

Color-coded race is more prominent in Britain and Canada than mainland Europe. Discrimination on the basis of color has been a central concern in Britain since the early days of the postwar immigration, when politicians and policymakers emphasized skin color as a critical factor in understanding race.[12] One argument is that color identities became a major focus in Britain partly because of the presence of the huge Afro-Caribbean population and its activism against color-based racism—nearly half of all net immigration between 1955 and 1967 was from the Caribbean. Another line of thought stresses that British policy leaders self-consciously modeled their ideas about race and race policy on the U.S. experience. Whatever the reason, race-as-color has been a pivotal element in policy and public discourse in Britain and focused on non-white immigrants from the Caribbean, Africa, and South Asia. Although the term "black" was widely used in the 1970s and 1980s to include South Asians, it now commonly refers only to people of African ancestry and, indeed, most South Asians do not think of themselves as black.[13] Blackness, however, remains an important identity and issue for Afro-Caribbeans and Africans in Britain; those defining themselves as black in the 2011 census represented 3.4 percent of the population of England and Wales, or about 1.9 million people. At the same time, anti-Muslim sentiment has become a highly significant element in Britain in recent years, more so than in the United States. Britain's 2.7 million Muslims, most of them with origins in Pakistan and Bangladesh, have mobilized around religious and related identities rather than identities based on color. Indeed, the strong focus on a race relations framework in discourse, laws, and policies has been critiqued as giving insufficient weight to religious inequalities and discrimination.[14]

Color-coded race is also central in Canadian society, where, according to one analysis, whiteness is an "enduring meta-narrative."[15] Immigrants from Asia and the Caribbean and their descendants are officially referred to as "visible minorities," a term defined by the Canadian government as "persons, other than Aboriginal peoples, who are non-Caucasian in race or non-white in colour" and thus differentiated from people of European origin who, prior to the 1970s, made up the overwhelming majority of the Canadian population, as high as 97 percent in 1961. By 2011 visible minorities represented 19.1 percent of the Canadian population, with blacks the third largest group, 2.9 percent of the national total. Still, historically, the French-English language divide has been the pivotal conflict in Canada and at the root of the official policy of multiculturalism emphasizing ethnic and cultural diversity; the U.S. version of multiculturalism centers on racial categories and has been shaped by the long history of the black-white color line, what Irene Bloemraad calls race-based multiculturalism.[16]

Quite apart from the role of skin color in racial divisions, the very use of the term "race" in public discourse differs in Europe and North America. In the United States, race is a commonly used word in public, political, and academic discourse. Newspaper stories and television coverage refer to race all the time; so do politicians and activists, as well as scholars. Race is used to officially categorize people—the census being a case in point, with people now allowed to report themselves as belonging to more than one race, and the questionnaire in 2010 listing fifteen categories (including White, Black, American Indian or Alaska Native, Asian Indian, Chinese, Japanese, Filipino, Korean, Vietnamese, and Other Asian). While some American scholars have sought to substitute other terms for race—communities of descent or ethnoracial or racialized groups—the Census Bureau and much of the American public, as David Hollinger observes, remain "in the thrall of the concept of race."[17]

This is not the case in Canada, where, although race is commonly used in public discourse, especially in English-speaking provinces, official statistics refer to "visible minority" rather than race. In Britain, the census classifies people by ethnic groups. The terms "race relations" and "racism" remain important in the language for publicly discussing social issues, and the use of "race" is common in the media and popular discussion, although, according to one sociologist, "the word 'race' and certainly the word 'races' are less part of the public discourse in the UK as compared with the USA."[18]

On much of the European continent, the association of the term "race" with the Holocaust and the Nazi past has delegitimized its use as a category for public discourse and led to discomfort with the word and the concept it stands for. There is a concern that using the term gives legitimacy to discriminatory tendencies and inequalities by reifying races as biologically distinguishable groups. In the Netherlands, race is a "sensitive, if not a taboo word" and "references to race are shunned"; in Germany, even the term "racism" is rarely used in public discussion. In France, the term "racism" is acceptable, but race as a category generally is not. In French public life, "racism" is commonly used to criticize beliefs (and practices based on these beliefs) that people are innately inferior owing to their pigmentation, religion, or culture, but there is widespread disapproval of using race or ethnicity as categories for the collection of statistics or the basis for government programs, the argument being that these distinctions are inherently socially divisive and harmful.[19]

SOCIAL SEPARATION OF BLACKS: THE UNITED STATES STANDS OUT

Whatever the discourse about race or symbolic meanings attached to skin color, on-the-ground social realities reflect, reinforce, and help to shape views about race. Distinctions based on color certainly have an impact in Europe and

Canada, yet the United States is in a class of its own. Available data on residential segregation and mixed unions indicate that in the United States skin color is a greater divide and barrier to integration for people of African ancestry, including those of immigrant origin, than it is for their counterparts in Western Europe and Canada.

As the chapter on residential segregation has shown, individuals of African ancestry remain highly segregated from whites in the United States, a situation that has no parallel in the other countries in our study. This is not just the case for African Americans but for West Indians as well, the major black immigrant population. The remarkably high residential segregation rates reduce day-to-day interactions and informal contacts with whites. Familiarity, of course, can breed contempt. Proximity to whites may increase opportunities for racial tensions and conflicts to develop. However, it also increases opportunities for interracial friendships in informal settings and for blacks and whites to become comfortable with each other in a way that does not happen when they live apart. Confinement to predominantly, or virtually all, black or racial minority neighborhoods in the United States also has a variety of pernicious effects: it limits access to mainstream institutions, including decent schools, and increases exposure to crime.

Patterns of marriage are another indication of the distinctive social distance separating whites and blacks in the United States. Mixed unions are of great significance because of their potential for reducing the salience and rigidity of racial boundaries. That mixed unions occur in the first place reflects the ease with which racial boundaries can be moderated or crossed. Rates of black-white intermarriage are much lower in the United States than in the other countries in our study. This is not surprising given the large pool of African American potential partners, the higher levels of black-white residential segregation, and, of course, America's legacy of racial discrimination. In fact, for much of the nation's history, black-white intermarriage was illegal in most states; many states repealed anti-miscegenation laws after World War II, but the laws remained on the books in most Southern states until a 1967 Supreme Court decision declared them unconstitutional.

Given the weight of the past, one can view recent changes as quite remarkable. "In 1961, the year Barack Obama's parents were married," a Pew Center report notes, "less than one in 1,000 new marriages in the United States was, like theirs, the pairing of a black person and a white person. By 1980, that share had risen to about one in 150 new marriages. By 2008, it had risen to one-in-sixty." Still, intermarriage for blacks remains much less frequent than for Hispanics and Asians. Among the newlyweds of 2008, about 22 percent of black men and 9 percent of black women were intermarried, compared to almost half of U.S.-born Asians and nearly 40 percent of U.S.-born Hispanics; the majority of all intermarriages were to whites.[20]

In the Netherlands, black-white mixed unions have become so common that two Dutch sociologists argue that the black-white boundary is relatively weak and skin color less a barrier than religion and language. By the second decade of the twenty-first century, about seven in ten of the Antillean and nearly half of the Surinamese second generation were in unions with Dutch natives (see chapter 9). The Surinamese of African origin have much higher rates of partnership with Dutch natives than do those of Asian Indian descent or do Turks or Moroccans. Interracial couples are also common in France, where a major recent survey found that over two-fifths of the second generation of black African origin has taken partners from the mainstream French population.[21]

Mixed unions in Britain between black Caribbeans and British whites are also widespread, reflecting the relative ease and frequency of relations between the groups, especially in working-class communities where so many black Caribbeans live. While mixed-race couples still find themselves "stared at even in the most cosmopolitan metropolitan areas" of the United States, in Britain, they "draw virtually no notice in the metropolitan areas where they tend to reside."[22] According to an analysis of 2004–8 data, a remarkable 63 percent of 1.5 and second-generation black Caribbean men in couples and 45 percent of their female counterparts had a partner from a different ethnic group, no doubt most of them whites. Already by 2001, more children in England and Wales under the age of fifteen had one black Caribbean and one white parent than two black Caribbean parents. The contrast with the United States is striking. An analysis of census data for 1990–91 found that native-born West Indian men in Britain (40 percent) were nearly four times as likely as those in the United States (12 percent) to have a white partner.[23] North of the border, in Canada, too, white-Afro-Caribbean unions seem to be more common than in the United States: one in four blacks in couples in Canada in 2006, and nearly two-thirds of those born there, were in mixed marriages or common-law unions with a person of another ethnic group, presumably most with white partners.[24]

Another kind of social separation is devastating for communities of African descent in the United States: extraordinary rates of incarceration, which have removed an unprecedented number of young black men from civil society. The United States is the world leader in imprisonment, with 2.3 million prisoners in 2008; it locks up its residents at rates five to eight times greater than Canada and Western Europe. Black men are more than six times as likely to be incarcerated as white men. Although England has a high rate of black imprisonment, the sheer numbers in the United States stand out. Non-Hispanic blacks, about 13 percent of the U.S. population, were a staggering 43 percent of prison inmates, with more than 900,000 black men and women behind bars in 2009; in England and Wales (2013), blacks made up 2.8 percent of the general population fifteen and older but 13.2 percent of the prison population, or slightly over 11,000 people.[25] Around the turn of the twenty-first century, almost one out of every seven black men in the United States in their twenties was in prison or jail. Among black men in their early thirties, nearly twice as many had prison records as bachelor's degrees. The rates of incarceration are much lower for foreign- than native-born blacks, although, according to a New York study, the arrest rates for second-generation West Indian young adult men are not far behind those of African American young men.[26]

High rates of incarceration wreak havoc on U.S. black communities. Black men with prison records are at a huge disadvantage in the labor force, and they are poor candidates for husbands.[27] Their incarceration contributes in multiple ways to the high rates of poverty in many African American communities— not only do black men with criminal records earn low incomes when they are able to find work, but incarceration also makes for many one-adult families, consisting of a woman raising children by herself, frequently in poverty.

Although London, Amsterdam, Paris, and Toronto may be more at ease with black-white mixing than American cities are, it is well to remember that European countries are not yet "postracial." Racial prejudice and racial in- equalities, unfortunately, persist there, and young people of Caribbean and black African origin continue to encounter racism in numerous contexts. France may be color-blind in theory, but as one political scientist argues, it is race-coded in practice.[28] Many black young people in France believe they are discriminated against in housing and the workplace on the basis of color. In a recent survey, about half of immigrant and second-generation sub-Saharan Af- ricans and Caribbeans reported experiencing racist insults. Research shows that they also experience severe ethnic penalties in employment. In the Nether- lands, field experiments reveal that the Surinamese confront discrimination in securing work, and studies report Afro-Caribbeans in Britain experiencing ra- cial prejudice in educational institutions and from the police.[29] Nor is Canada free of racial discrimination, despite a common belief that it is not a significant problem there. A high proportion of Canadian blacks report experiences of discrimination, and statistical studies show them suffering earnings disadvan- tages as compared to Canadians of European origin.[30]

COLOR-CODED RACE AND U.S. IMMIGRANT MINORITIES

Once the pattern of color-coded racism has been established, it can be general- ized to new groups. Color-coded racism is especially entrenched in the United States, which we now focus on, not only because of its history with a highly developed system of slavery but also because of the more than two centuries of conquest of what became its home territory. Racism historically has affected not only African Americans and black immigrants but also American Indians,

Mexicans, and Puerto Ricans.[31] Its durable power raises the question of how it affects contemporary immigrant populations, who have come mainly from outside of Europe and Canada.

The most obvious implications concern immigrant groups whose members have a greater or lesser degree of visible African ancestry. These include not only Afro-Caribbeans from Haiti and the English-speaking West Indies, but also Spanish speakers from the Caribbean, most notably many Dominicans, the fifth largest Hispanic group in the United States (and many Puerto Ricans, although as U.S. citizens by birth they are not, strictly speaking, immigrants). African ancestry is also present in some other Latin American groups as a result of slavery during the Spanish and Portuguese colonial periods—for example, among Brazilians, even Colombians and Mexicans.

Indigenous ancestry in Latin American and Caribbean groups can also pose racial challenges in the U.S. context. It is not just associated with skin color but also physical features such as facial appearance and height. As David Lopez and Ricardo Stanton-Salazar put it, speaking of Mexicans, "[T]hose who fit the mestizo/Indian phenotype, who 'look Mexican,' cannot escape racial stereotyping any more than African Americans, though the stigma is usually not so severe."[32]

How Mexicans are seen is of particular consequence given that they are by far the largest group of contemporary U.S. immigrants. That Mexicans are often stigmatized as inferior, illegal, and foreign and seen as nonwhite has led some scholars to label them a racialized ethnic group. Another view stresses that Mexican Americans are targets of prejudice and discrimination because of nativism, or intense opposition based on their foreign connections, rather than because of beliefs about their racial inferiority. According to one argument, Mexican Americans experience a racialized form of nativism in which their presumed foreignness is central and their right to be in the country is questioned; third- and later-generation Mexican Americans may thus encounter discrimination because they are associated with and often mistaken for new Mexican immigrants. Pigmentation may also be involved. Skin color among Mexicans and other Latinos has been shown to matter for socioeconomic standing and residential integration, the lighter, not surprisingly, the better. A historical analysis of racial boundaries among Mexicans in the past argues that those whom "Anglo individuals and institutions judged sufficiently light-skinned, educated, or well-to-do could gain acceptance as whites, at least in some contexts, in some places, and at some times"—a dynamic that may remain true today. A recent ethnographic study shows that Mexican Americans and Mexican immigrants, including those attaining middle-class status, often experience discrimination in their daily lives because of their skin color and surnames. [33]

This is not to say that any skin-color difference creates unalterable barriers. The Asian American experience contradicts such notions. There can be no disputing the vitriol of the racism directed against Asian groups from the late nineteenth century until the middle of the twentieth. Racial prejudice against Asians was enshrined in restrictive immigration and naturalization laws, including the Chinese Exclusion Act of 1882, which singled out the Chinese as the first group to be excluded from the United States on the basis of race, ethnicity, or nationality. For much of the nation's history, Asian immigrants were denied the right to become citizens, and on the West Coast, numerous states adopted laws in the late nineteenth and early twentieth centuries prohibiting intermarriage between Asians and whites. Most devastating of all, during World War II, more than one hundred thousand Japanese Americans living on the Pacific Coast were forcibly confined in internment camps. Racism against Asians has faded considerably since the opening of immigration to them in 1965. Granted, the Asian immigration has been, to a large extent, a high human-capital one. Yet the degrees to which Asian families have prospered in the United States, enjoying on average incomes higher than those of white Americans, and to which young Asian Americans have gained entry into colleges and universities, including the most elite, and intermarried with whites speak against any notion of unbridgeable racial divides. This conclusion, it should be noted, does not mean that anti-Asian prejudice and discrimination can be consigned to the dustbin of history; but they are clearly on the wane.

For the Latin American groups, it is becoming apparent that, especially among the U.S. born, their position is increasingly inconsistent with a simple narrative of racial exclusion (or, by the same token, with one of universal assimilation). Already by the end of the twentieth century, according to one analysis, about 40 percent of U.S.-born Mexicans showed evidence of approaching the mainstream in one or more ways—through high educational attainment, geographic mobility away from regions of Mexican American concentration, intermarriage, and/or being children of mixed unions. This figure has undoubtedly increased since then if only because of continuing substantial rates of intermarriage (which are still less than those of Asians) and the expansion of the group with mixed ancestry, especially with Mexican combined with one or more European origins.[34]

Yet, at the other end of the spectrum, on the exclusion side, the disadvantages for many Mexican Americans and other Hispanics can be as severe as those faced by poor African Americans. One telltale sign is the rate of Hispanic incarceration, which if not as grave as it is for young African American men is quite high. Another source of disadvantage is widespread lack of legal status, which creates barriers not just for the immigrant adults but also for the children growing up in their families, including those who are U.S citizens by virtue of jus soli. In 2010 one in four Hispanics lived in a household with one or more undocumented adults.[35]

What remains uncertain is the extent to which variations in racial appearance within Latin American groups are responsible for the position of individuals along this spectrum. Put somewhat differently: is it the case that more successful Hispanic Americans are much more likely to be European American in appearance, while those at or near the bottom of the socioeconomic hierarchy are much more likely to be perceived as nonwhite? Research so far has come out on both sides of this question, but an answer is central to any diagnosis of the present-day role of skin-color as a factor in racism against immigrant minorities in the United States.[36]

BENEFITING FROM THE AFRICAN AMERICAN PRESENCE

To end the story here is to paint an incomplete—and overly bleak—picture of the impact of America's racial history and hierarchy on nonwhite immigrants and their children. There are some surprising ways that the legacy of the past and the attempts to redress the injuries incurred by centuries of legalized oppression have ended up benefiting immigrants in ways that have not been available or possible in Europe or Canada.

Of central importance is the effect of African Americans' struggles for civil rights. The civil rights movement of the 1950s and 1960s, which gripped the nation and challenged the southern Jim Crow system, gave rise to landmark legislation that ushered in a new era of race relations. The Civil Rights Act of 1964 outlawed discrimination in education, employment, and public accommodation and created the Equal Opportunity Employment Commission; the Voting Rights Act of 1965 ensured blacks the right to political participation; and the Fair Housing Act of 1968 prohibited racial discrimination in renting or selling housing.

These sweeping legal changes were partly responsible for recent large-scale immigration in the first place. What was key was the passage of the 1965 Immigration Act, which ended discriminatory national origins quotas and severe bars on Asian immigration. As many studies have shown, a dynamic interplay of factors led to the 1965 law, including international pressures and national political alliances, but concerns about the racial and ethnic biases of existing immigration law in the context of the civil rights era's drive to achieve formal racial equality were undeniably at work.[37]

Once in the United States, immigrants and their children who are seen as racial minorities or people of color have profited from the institutions, political strategies, notions of rights, and public discourses on diversity that developed in the aftermath of the civil rights movement. This is particularly so for blacks and Latinos. Of great significance have been affirmative action programs. These programs were originally justified as a response to the caste-like status of African Americans, and later were extended to other groups, especially Latinos; they were designed to promote greater representation of African Americans by requiring employers and educators to take race into account, giving advantages to membership in a specific racial group.[38] Over time, the diversity rationale for affirmative action—to ensure minority representation in educational institutions and the workplace—has become more common than that of redress for past injustice. Federal contractors and subcontractors have been required to take affirmative action to recruit and advance qualified minorities (as well as women, persons with disabilities, and veterans) through training programs, outreach efforts, and other positive steps; and those with over fifty employees have had to develop a written affirmative action program. In education, the nation's public (and private) universities adopted policies to consider race in admissions procedures to achieve diversity in their student bodies.

Though America's native black population continues to suffer severe inequalities and disadvantages, affirmative action has made a major difference. As Ira Katznelson has written, it "has done more to advance fair treatment across racial lines than any other recent public policy." It has sustained and expanded a growing African American middle class "that is better connected to the central institutions of American life than ever before. . . . If affirmative action did not exist, the United States would be a vastly more segregated country. Without such efforts, most white Americans would have far less contact with their fellow black citizens. . . . It is no longer conceivable to imagine American society without [the] gains to racial integration in our universities, firms, professions, and public bureaucracies promoted with the backing of judicial opinion and governmental regulation."[39]

Without question, affirmative action and other diversity programs have provided mobility opportunities for immigrant minorities and their children in the past few decades, even if this was not their original intent. Research conducted in the late twentieth century makes this clear. An extensive study of second-generation young adults in the New York metropolitan area, which included comparison groups of native blacks and Puerto Ricans, even contends that affirmative action and other diversity programs have ended up working *better* for immigrants and their children than for the native minorities for whom they were designed. Affirmative action, the study argues, has worked exceptionally well as a second-generation integration policy. The American-born children of immigrants may not be aware of how much African Americans' struggles against racism have affected their lives, but they are well positioned to take advantage of the results of those struggles. The argument is that the children of nonwhite immigrants are "perhaps best suited to a program designed to locate and help qualified but disadvantaged youth": on one hand, they suffer from racial discrimination, substandard schools, and lack of knowledge of America's educational system, but on the other, they are optimistic and come from families who invest a great deal in their success.[40]

A study of freshmen at more than two dozen selective U.S. colleges and universities found that immigrants and their children were substantially overrepresented among black students. In much the same way, programs originally designed for Mexican Americans and Puerto Ricans have been used by the children of an "ever-broadening category of recent 'Latino' immigrants." Educational institutions have gone along with this, it has been maintained, because it is less difficult to admit the children of dark-skinned but middle-class, often college-educated, immigrants than to truly confront the heritage of America's racial past.[41]

Since these studies were done, affirmative action has come under sustained attack in the courts and at the ballot box. As of 2014, eight states prohibited the use of racial preferences in admissions to the states' public universities, and the Supreme Court has recently upheld such bans. To what extent, and in what form, affirmative action will survive is unclear, but it seems safe to say that some of its benefits for immigrant minorities will be a thing of the past. It is also likely, however, that some policies and procedures will pass the strictest legal scrutiny, such as actions taken to encourage university applications from minority-group members.[42] Indeed racial and ethnic diversity has become a publicly stated goal of major universities in the post–civil rights era, replete with administrative staff to promote it.

An additional positive side effect of the civil rights movement for immigrants and their children—which will no doubt continue—has been the growth of school programs, clubs, and curricula (for example, ethnic studies courses) to meet the needs of African Americans as well as Latinos and Asians. These have promoted a sense of ethnic and racial pride and provided environments that, in some cases, have been a help in the quest for mobility.

Legal changes of the civil rights era also created opportunities in the workplace for some immigrants and their children by leading to new institutional arrangements and monitoring and enforcement mechanisms that have increased the cost of discrimination. Title VII of the Civil Rights Act of 1964 established the Equal Employment Opportunity Commission to eliminate unlawful employment discrimination, and subsequent Congressional legislation gave it the authority to bring lawsuits. Admittedly, enforcement of Title VII has been inconsistent under different federal administrations, and enforcement agencies have had only limited powers. But the law led to an expanded cadre of personnel managers who installed a range of equal opportunity programs in corporations, from diversity training to grievance procedures. Various corporate diversity measures, and the many human resource professionals who implement them, are unlikely to disappear anytime soon. How effective the programs have been in equalizing opportunities for racial minorities is another—and open—question, although a recent analysis suggests that targeted recruitment efforts, mentoring programs, and diversity officers and taskforces have made the most inroads.[43]

Obviously, racial barriers and discrimination have not disappeared in places of employment, but the desire to demonstrate diversity has no doubt helped many children of immigrants move up the occupational ladder. In general, it has become widely accepted in the United States that blacks, Latinos, and Asians should be represented (and improve their representation) in universities, corporate and government offices, and political bodies. That ethnic and racial diversity in the post–civil rights era is now often celebrated in public discourse contributes to a sense of national belonging among immigrants and, even more, their U.S.-born children (see chapter 9). In the political sphere, the Voting Rights Act of 1965, a hallmark civil rights–era law, helped immigrant minorities achieve political representation in a number of places, including northern cities like New York, by allowing the creation of voting districts where they had a better opportunity to elect their own representatives. (However, the law was severely weakened in 2013 when a conservative-dominated Supreme Court struck down key provisions.) Not only has the civil rights movement of the 1960s achieved "canonical status as a model for combining vigorous protest with political mobilization and electoral success," but also on occasion immigrants have been able to ally with black leaders to promote their own civil rights.[44]

The United States, of course, is not alone in creating policies to combat racial discrimination and seeking to expand opportunities for racial minorities. In Europe and Canada, these policies have been a response to the influx of non-European immigrants—not, as in the United States, to ameliorate the enduring damages of slavery and segregation—and, in large part, they have been much less extensive. They have lacked, as one scholar suggests for Britain, the backing of a social movement on the scale of the American civil rights movement.[45] Of the non-U.S. countries in our study, Britain and Canada have been the most proactive in laws and programs to reduce and prevent racial discrimination, although by now the European Union and its Western European member countries have adopted laws prohibiting discrimination on the basis of race and ethnicity (and in some countries, nationality and religion as well) and provide victims with means of legal redress. According to the Migrant Integration Policy Index, Canada (89), the United States (89), and the United Kingdom (86) had "favorable" scores in terms of antidiscrimination policy, and France (77) and the Netherlands (68) "slightly favorable" ones; Germany was "halfway favorable" with a score of 48.[46]

At the same time, whatever the name—affirmative action, positive discrimination, or some other term—official programs involving preference for or giving special advantages to racial minorities in employment and education have been stronger and more far-reaching in the United States than in the other countries in our study. France and Germany have stood back from affirmative action policies for ethnoracial minorities, France being famously averse to race-conscious approaches (though one of the elite *grande écoles*, Sciences Po in Paris, created in 2001 a selective admissions track for students from disadvantaged neighborhoods, many of whom come from immigrant backgrounds). Positive-action policies and programs for recruiting racial minorities in Britain have been localized and implemented by some local authorities; and in the Netherlands, they have tended to be piecemeal, with, for example, efforts to hire ethnic minorities in some jobs (like the police force) and, until 2006, with explicit use of immigrant status as a basis for additional funds for schools with substantial numbers of first- and second-generation children whose parents had low-levels of education or low-skilled jobs.[47]

Canada has come closest to the United States in its official commitment to affirmative action, enacting employment equity legislation in 1986 requiring employers in federally regulated industries to advance the representation and promotion of visible minorities (as well as women, people with disabilities, and aboriginal people). However, the legislation did not extend to education, and Ontario, home to more than half of Canada's visible minorities, repealed its provincial Employment Equity Act in 1995 on the grounds that it gave undue preference to racial minorities.[48]

In their comparative analysis of immigrant political incorporation in the United States and Europe, John Mollenkopf and Jennifer Hochschild put it well when they write that European countries "have little experience with robust affirmative action laws, voting rights laws, minority advocacy groups, litigation against discrimination, minority business set asides, and all the other policies and organizational strategies intended to help mitigate the consequences of centuries of racial hierarchy." Even if these programs have not always worked in the United States (and, in some important ways, have been diluted by recent Supreme Court decisions), they have provided "a scaffolding upon which migrants and their supporters have been able to hang some policy innovations. Migrants to European countries have lacked such scaffolding and find it difficult to construct one from scratch."[49]

Quite apart from being able to piggy-back on gains won by native blacks through civil rights–era programs and policies, immigrants and their children in the United States have benefited in another way from America's racial history: the very presence of a large black native minority population, which obviously does not exist in Europe or Canada. Coming to a society with a large native black population has had particularly far-reaching implications for black immigrants in the United States. Admittedly, the U.S. foreign-born black population is fairly small, around 9 percent of the immigrant total in 2008–9, and constitutes a similar share of the entire U.S. black population.[50] But in several cities, most notably New York and Miami, the proportion is much larger. In New York, about half of the city's approximately two million non-Hispanic blacks belong to the first or second generation of Caribbean or African background. Immigrant-origin blacks there have, at times, united with African Americans in a "black bloc" to elect black officials who speak to issues of concern to immigrant and native blacks alike. In the absence of a large African American population, black immigrants in Canada and Europe lack, racially speaking, a critical mass of this kind.[51]

For blacks and Hispanics of immigrant origin in many American cities, the long-established populations of African Americans and Hispanics may be a more welcoming presence than the white working- and middle-class communities that have greeted immigrants in Western European and Canadian cities. While the U.S.-born children of black (and Hispanic) immigrants often feel excluded from white America—and embrace aspects of their ethnic heritage—they generally come to feel a part of the large black (and Hispanic) minority communities.[52] Probably the best-known example is Barack Obama, the son of a Kenyan father, who, as an adult, defined himself as a black American.

Nationwide, there is now a sizable African American middle class; incorporation into the African American middle-class "minority culture of mobility" provides resources for upward mobility for the black immigrant and second generation, including black professional and fraternal associations and organizations of black students in racially integrated high schools and universities. The presence of African American "strivers" in their high schools has been shown to benefit the children of Latino immigrants on an upward mobility path, who in some cases develop close ties with and model themselves after successful African American students.[53] Outside the educational arena, black immigrants and their children have profited from their ability to enter and gain contacts in other institutions dominated and controlled by black Americans, such as some labor unions and political groups.

Immigrants' identity in the United States is also bound up with how they see themselves—and are seen by others—in relation to black Americans. The novelist Ralph Ellison once wrote that "one of the first epithets that many European immigrants learned when they got off the boat was the term 'nigger'—it made them feel instantly American."[54] Ellison was referring to European immigrants in the past, and the "N word" is now strictly taboo in mainstream American society, but his comment captures an important racial dynamic that still operates in the United States. Whites in America may now reject racial segregation and discrimination in principle, but negative sentiments, beliefs, and stereotypes about African Americans persist. African Americans are widely seen to be at the bottom of the racial hierarchy, thereby enabling immigrants to avoid this position. In Europe and in Canada, non-European immigrants and their children are often seen as *the* disfavored and stigmatized groups. Indeed, there the term "black," to the extent that it is used, frequently refers to them; in the United States, it generally means African Americans.

Part of the process of adapting to life in the United States is learning America's culture of race and that identification with African Americans is something to avoid, at least much of the time. This distancing from African Americans is especially pronounced among immigrants who share a common African ancestry with black Americans or are close to them in phenotype. Distancing and identification are not mutually exclusive. Black immigrants may identify with African Americans around a sense of a "linked racial fate," and, along with other immigrants, align and cooperate with African Americans on some occasions, but they also often seek to set themselves apart to avoid the stigma associated with American blacks and to claim superior status. Frequently such claims are regarded as legitimate. Much has been written about this dynamic among Afro-Caribbean immigrants, whose ethnic pride develops and is bolstered by their sense of distinctiveness from and superiority to African Americans, especially poor African Americans.[55] Distancing from African Americans has also been reported for Dominicans and other dark-skinned Latinos, who find it unsettling to be mistaken for African American. Although South Asians, many of dark skin color, realize they are not white, there is also a strong sense among most that they are not black. As Vijay Prashad puts it in *The Karma of Brown Folk*: "In a racist society, it hard to expect people to opt for the most despised category."[56]

To be sure, immigrants in Europe and Canada often claim superiority to those in other immigrant-origin groups on the grounds, for example, of cultural assets or length of time in the receiving society. But in Europe and Canada, there is no large, racialized native minority group with whom nonwhite immigrants might be confused, and thus not the kind of distancing strategies so common among nonwhite immigrants in the United States.

For the children of black immigrants, identity struggles also assume different forms on the two sides of the Atlantic. In the United States, many second-generation West Indians strive to have their West Indian identity recognized, but find that without an accent or other cues to immediately signal their ethnicity to others, they are seen as African Americans and their black race is what matters in encounters with whites. Becoming American for the Afro-Caribbean second generation often means becoming African American and thus subject to the same kind of racial prejudice and exclusion as black Americans experience. In Europe, the Afro-Caribbean second generation's central identity struggle is to have their claims to "Frenchness," "Dutchness," or "Britishness" recognized and not simply to be identified on the basis of their national origins or skin color. Foreignness, in short, can be an advantage for blacks of immigrant origin in the U.S. context, while it is generally experienced as a disadvantage across the Atlantic.[57]

CONCLUSION

The problem of race is the age-old "American Dilemma" that has plagued the United States since its founding. Slavery is long gone but its impact lingers on. Post-1965 immigrants enter a society that has been deeply affected by the division—and durable inequalities—between blacks and whites. Despite changes in recent years, blacks remain the quintessentially racialized Americans, and their history and presence have had profound consequences for how post-

1965 immigrants and their children experience and take their place in American society.

The United States, as we have seen, stands out in the remarkably high degree of separation of blacks and whites and the weight of color-coded race in political and popular discourse. Yet, at the same time, attempts since the 1960s to ameliorate the enduring damages of slavery and legal segregation have had unexpected benefits for immigrants of color and their children. These include opportunities provided by civil-rights legislation and related policies and programs, although the recent weakening of two pillars of the civil rights era, affirmative action and voting rights, are bound to reduce the benefits for the cohorts of the first and second generations now coming of age. In addition, the very existence of a large native black population has given immigrants in the United States advantages that their counterparts across the Atlantic and north of the border lack.

This chapter has focused mainly on minorities with roots, in the near or distant past, in sub-Saharan Africa, yet it is important to emphasize that color-coded race is not just a matter of black and white. In Britain, for example, the huge South Asian population is seen in racial terms as nonwhite, in Canada as visible minorities. In the United States, one of the consequences of the massive Hispanic, Asian, and Caribbean immigration of the past half century has been to complicate racial issues. Nonwhites include the growing number of Asians, 5 percent of the U.S. population in 2010. Hispanics have now overtaken African Americans to become the nation's largest minority group; Hispanics are often seen through the prism of race as a brown-skinned minority in between blacks and whites. Although "Hispanic" is not classified as a race on the census, in popular discourse the category tends to be treated this way, with "black" and "white" implying non-Latino.[58]

Still, the groups for whom skin color is the most salient racial marker are those of sub-Saharan African ancestry. Their presence in significant numbers in Canada and Europe is something new. In the European countries in our study, immigration has made people of color a significant part of the population for the first time.[59] There and in Canada, racial dilemmas of a color-based kind are a recent development; and they are focused, to a large extent, on those of immigrant origin from the Caribbean and black Africa. Without a long-oppressed, large native-black minority group and a history of momentous black civil rights struggles, Western European countries and Canada lack the extensive civil rights measures that the United States has instituted. Yet in part because they do not have the same sordid racial history on their soil when it comes to blacks, it has been possible for people of immigrant origin with African ancestry to become more integrated into European and Canadian societies than in the United States, at least if measures of mixed unions and neighborhood integration are anything to go by. Indeed, in much of Europe, it is the reaction to the huge numbers of Muslim immigrants that has taken center stage in recent years—with aspects of culture associated with Muslims, not skin color, a principal source of stigma and concern. In Britain, France, Germany, and the Netherlands, religion has emerged as a critical dividing line between immigrants and the dominant native-born population; in the United States, race-as-color remains primary.

CHAPTER 6

IMMIGRANT RELIGION

Religion is at the heart of concerns about immigrant integration in Western Europe, and the central issues have to do with Islam.[1] From the wearing of headscarves and burqas to the building of mosques and the public funding of Islamic schools, there are widespread popular fears that Islam not only will prevent the successful adaptation of immigrants and their children to European society but also damage, even undermine, Western democratic institutions, values, and practices.

Western Europe is not alone in experiencing a rise in anti-Islam sentiment targeting immigrants. There have been controversies about the veil in Canada, sharia law in Canada and the United States, and mosque construction in a number of American towns and cities. In the post–9/11 era, many Muslim immigrant men in the United States have been subject to police surveillance and FBI interrogations. Anti-Muslim discourse is acceptable in American public life in a way that no longer is true for anti-black rhetoric.

Yet these broad similarities, important as they are, obscure real and significant transatlantic differences in religion's role in the integration of immigrants and their children, with the United States and continental European countries in our study providing the most striking contrast. In Western Europe, religion has become a bright boundary that separates a significant proportion of immigrant minorities from the mainstream or the cultural, institutional core of their societies.[2] Or to put it somewhat differently, religion is a key site for the demarcation of boundaries between the native majority and individuals of immigrant origin, many of whom are perceived as "other" because of their religion.

Immigrant religions in the United States are a less serious basis for contention. Religion is not a central dividing line between immigrants and long-established residents in the United States, and, in general, immigrant religions are not seen as a major threat to American institutions and identities. By and large, religion is an accepted avenue for immigrants' and their children's inclusion in American society. To the extent that there is hostility to Islam, it tends to be more focused on security issues. In Western Europe, by comparison, threats to civilizational and core values loom larger. Canada stands somewhere in between Europe and the United States, with immigrant religion seeming to pose fewer problems for integration than in continental Europe but engendering controversies in the public sphere, particularly in French-speaking Quebec. [3]

Why has immigrant religion generally become a more significant marker of a fundamental social divide, a greater challenge to integration, and a more common source of conflict with mainstream institutions and practices in Western Europe than in the United States? There are three main reasons. Of paramount importance are basic demographic facts. The religious backgrounds of immigrants in Western Europe and the United States are different, mostly Christian in the United States as compared to Western Europe, where a large proportion is Muslim. Muslims of immigrant origin in Western Europe also have a lower socioeconomic profile than those in the United States. But this is not the whole story. Western European native majorities have more trouble recognizing claims based on religion because they are more secular than religiously involved Americans. Furthermore, historically rooted relations and arrangements between the state and religious groups in Europe have led to greater difficulties in incorporating and accepting new religions than is true for the United States and, to some degree, for Canada as well.

In developing this argument, our emphasis is on common features of Western European societies, yet all exhibit nation-specific institutional, historical, and ideological differences in recognizing and managing religious diversity in general and Muslim religious demands in particular, differences that we consider as well. There is also the question of possible changes in the future that have the potential to make Islam less of a barrier for immigrant-origin populations in Western Europe, as well as in the United States, and to blur the distinctions among the countries in our study.

WESTERN EUROPE

In much of Western Europe, religion has come to be viewed as a problem for immigrant minorities and for the societies in which they now live. The concerns and tensions are almost exclusively about Islam, which numerically overwhelms other non-Western religions. Nearly 40 percent of migrants from outside the European Union are Muslim. Discussions about Muslims' alleged failure to integrate have dominated public debates in Western Europe since the 1990s, and a prevalent view is that the culture of Islam and that of the West are irreconcilable.[4]

Anti-Muslim sentiment in Europe is sometimes conceptualized as "cultural racism." This kind of racism occurs when culture and religion are essentialized to the point that they become the functional equivalent of biological racism, and groups are seen as inherently inferior on the basis of their culture or religion. Scholars have written that "Muslimophobia is at the heart of contemporary British and European cultural racism"; used terms like "European Muslimania" and "Islamophobia"; and referred to racialized perceptions of Islam and the racial dimensions of Islam. Anti-Muslim discourse prevalent in Europe, José Casanova notes, is a fusion of anti-immigrant xenophobic nativism, secularist antireligious prejudices, liberal-feminist critiques of Muslim patriarchal fundamentalism, and fear of Islamist terrorist networks.[5]

Whether labeled cultural racism, religious prejudice, or xenophobia—or all three rolled into one—polling data show considerable antipathy toward Muslims, especially in continental Western Europe. The 1999–2000 wave of the European Values Study indicates that prejudice against Muslims there was more widespread than prejudice against other immigrants. According to a 2005 Pew Research Center report, substantial numbers of Dutch (51 percent), Germans (47 percent), and French (34 percent), although fewer British (14 percent), viewed Muslims unfavorably.[6]

There is considerable evidence of socioeconomic disadvantage and even of discrimination experienced by Muslims, including those in the second generation who have grown up in European societies. For the most part, Muslim immigrants arrived with low levels of education, sometimes no formal schooling, and took jobs at the bottom of the labor market. Their subsequent employment levels have been much lower than the national average (chapter 3).[7] Studies of the second generation reveal patterns of inequality in European educational systems that steer the children of these low-status immigrants toward less-valued outcomes (chapter 8). And there appears to be discrimination against them in the labor market: in France, young adults with parents from North Africa, sub-Saharan Africa, and Turkey, the groups in which Muslims are prevalent, are far more likely than native French to believe they have been the victims of discrimination by employers; frequently they perceive this discrimination to be commonplace rather than exceptional.[8]

Most visible are the conflicts that have developed with long-established European residents and institutions as Muslims struggle to practice their religion and build up their institutions. The conflicts, usually over fitting Muslims' practices into legal frameworks and public arenas, have been repeated across Western Europe, although with variation in themes, emphasis, and severity in different countries.

Among the issues leading to controversy have been ritual animal slaughter, burial in municipal cemeteries according to Islamic practices, exemption from co-ed physical education classes, provision of prayer rooms at work and in educational institutions, and the construction of mosques. Islamic teachings that proscribe the stunning of animals before killing have given rise to debates about ritual slaughter and challenges to the legality of Islamic practices by animal rights activists. There have been tensions over the establishment of state-funded Muslim schools and teaching Islam in the curricula of state schools as well as what has been called "the delicate question" of state-sponsored schools to train imams. Another source of conflict has centered around the building of mosques, and the prospect of minarets as high as church steeples. Requests for permits to construct new mosques have often come up against various arguments to justify refusal, including problems of traffic and of noise nuisance (often over the Muslim electronically amplified call for prayer), incompatibility with existing zoning rules and urban planning, and nonconformity with security norms.[9]

A major concern is that Islam is threatening the liberal values of European states, such as free speech and equal rights for women and homosexuals. This concern is especially common in France, Germany, and the Netherlands. In the Netherlands, Geert Wilders, the controversial leader of the Party for Freedom, one of the major Dutch political parties, has called Islam a "backward" religion and advocated banning the Koran. "If we do not stop Islamification now," Wilders has said, "Eurabia and Netherabia will just be a matter of time. . . . We are heading for the end of European . . . civilization as we know it."[10] While Wilders' apocalyptic and shrill stance is extreme—and critiqued by many Dutch opinion leaders and politicians—the anxieties he expresses about Islam are commonly heard there and elsewhere in Europe. In Germany, a 2010 best-selling book by Thilo Sarrazin, *Deutschland schafft sich ab* (Germany Does Away with Itself), blamed Muslims for lowering the country's intelligence level, and argued that Germany will eventually turn into a Muslim-majority country. Polls showed a majority in Germany agreeing with the thrust of the book's arguments, although Sarrazin was harshly criticized in the media.[11]

The view that European culture should be defended against Islam is not confined to cultural conservatives. That Muslims pose a threat to Western values is a common element in anti-Islamic sentiment among Europeans on the left. As Olivier Roy has put it, "For the left the issue is more generally secularism, women's rights and fundamentalism." Or as the Dutch writer Ian Buruma notes, Islam "with its antiquated ideas on homosexuality or the role of women threatens to overthrow the very gains that progressives fought for in the last century." For the Dutch, Muslims' "strict sexual morals remind [them] . . . too much of what they have so recently left behind" and, especially among Dutch on the left, the painful wresting free from the strictures of their own religions.[12]

Free speech issues have inflamed European publics in recent years. The 2015 murders in Paris of staff at the satirical magazine *Charlie Hebdo* by Islamist members of the second generation shook mainstream France to its core. Previously, the Danish cartoon affair—when in 2005, the *Jyllands-Posten* published twelve Mohammed caricatures—had invoked mocking images of the Prophet. The *Charlie Hebdo* murders produced huge marches in Paris and elsewhere to support a free press, just as a decade earlier leading German, French, and Dutch papers made a point of republishing the Danish cartoons.[13] In the Netherlands, criticism of Islam as a danger to freedom of speech surged in the reaction to the 2004 murder of filmmaker Theo van Gogh by a young Dutch Moroccan, who targeted Van Gogh for his anti-Islamic statements and making a movie, *Submission*, which depicted abused women with passages from the Koran written on their skin. The secular European notion that "everything must be said no matter how offensive" has justified deliberately provocative anti-Islam statements in respectable public forums by certain well-known figures—intolerance in the name of tolerance, one might say.[14]

Much of the public criticism in Europe of Muslim practices focuses on the subordination of women associated with Muslim immigrants (even though many of the practices involved are not required by Islam). In Germany and Britain, for example, "honor killings" carried out by Turkish, South Asian, and Middle Eastern men against daughters and sisters who have taken partners not approved by their families have received attention and come under attack in the media, as have "forced marriages" in some groups, such as Pakistanis in Britain and Turks in Germany, in which arranged marriages are common. The state, it has been argued, should uphold universal rights for children and women in the face of many oppressive practices found in Muslim communities.[15]

In France, the controversy over the headscarf has assumed enormous symbolic and political importance in the context of the French principle of secularization, or *laïcité*. A 2004 law banned conspicuous religious symbols and dress in public schools. including large crosses and Jewish skullcaps, yet "everyone knew the issue was France's four to five million Muslims." In Germany, half of the sixteen states (*Länder*) passed laws between 2004 and 2009 prohibiting the Islamic headscarf for public school teachers at work, although at the same time, some allowed the teachers to wear Christian symbols and clothing.[16]

Throughout Europe, the *jilbab*-plus-*niqab*, black head-to-toe veiling that leaves only two slits for the eyes, has been the subject of public debate. Proposals have been put forward to ban it either altogether or in certain institutions and occupations, even though the number of women wearing such clothing is small, fewer than two thousand in France, according to one estimate. Still, in 2010, the French parliament voted to prohibit veils fully covering the face in public places. Even Britain's "fabled tolerance," according to one account, "has shown signs of wear," with the High Court affirming in 2007 the right of schools to exclude certain extreme Islamic dress if they choose to do so. A 2010 survey found widespread support in Western Europe for banning the full veil covering the whole face except the eyes, with 82 percent in France, 71 percent in Germany, and 62 percent in Britain endorsing the measure (but only 28 percent in the United States).[17]

Finally, Islam has become an oppositional identity for some Muslims in European societies, or a way of marking their rejection of the European mainstream, which they perceive as condemning them to positions of inferiority. A strong Muslim identity has provided a way to claim dignity in the face of exclusion, particularly for some members of the European-born generation, who adopt what might be called a reactive religiosity. As an in-between group—often not accepted as fully French, Dutch, or German—some second-generation individuals have come to see themselves as Muslims, identify with "things Muslim," and look for a "pure Islam" free from the defects of the parental culture in a search for a sense of belonging and self-esteem. Just how extensive this development has become is unclear, and many in the second generation are becoming less involved with Islam, not more.[18]

This development has fed widespread concerns in Europe that the involvement of some of the second generation in fundamentalist Islam may lead to acts of violence and terrorist attacks like the 2005 London underground bombings and 2015 Paris killings—anxieties also stoked by the growing participation of European-raised Muslims in Islamist military groups fighting in the Middle East. Large majorities of Germans (85 percent), Dutch (87 percent), French (89 percent), and British (56 percent) in a 2005 survey said that a growing sense of Islamic identity among Muslims in their respective countries was a bad thing, with many worried that it would prevent integration and lead to violence.[19]

Hostilities and concerns about Islam in Western Europe are so prominent in public discourse that there is a risk of overlooking more encouraging developments. Islam can serve positive functions for Muslims as they adapt to living in European societies. For the second generation, a religious allegiance may offer a refuge and sense of collective self-worth in the context of discrimination, and help keep young people away from crime and delinquency.[20] For the first generation, engagement in Islam and mosque culture can provide psychological ballast in the face of the strains of adjustment in a new country as well as social networks of support with coethnics.

Everyday interactions are often more positive, or at least less conflict-ridden, than public discourse and policies tend to suggest. As long-time Europeans have more day-to-day interactions with Muslims, especially those born and raised in Europe, in schools, neighborhoods, and other social settings, they have frequently become more comfortable with and less prejudiced toward people of Muslim background. Practices of Muslims that once seemed strange often become familiar in the context of increased intermingling in everyday contexts. When the Dutch government was considering banning headscarves in public spaces, the biggest supermarket chain in the Netherlands introduced them—in the company color!—for the many Turkish and Moroccan women working as cashiers, and evoked little public reaction.[21]

On a policy level, European governments have been realizing they must find ways to fund and support the development of an independent Islam and offer some accommodations for Muslim religious practices, although they have differed in their acknowledgment of and adaptation to Muslims' socio-religious needs. Britain is particularly liberal on this score. On the whole, the accommodation of many tenets and practices of religious minorities, including Islam, has been considerable and progressive there. As early as the 1980s, Muslims' claims for the toleration of religious symbols and autonomous organizational spheres were granted in Britain, including building and registering mosques, establishing Muslim sections of cemeteries, permitting ritual slaughter, and exempting children from school worship and religious instruction.[22] Whereas mosque-building has been the subject of bitter controversy elsewhere in Europe, for the most part in Britain, getting permission to build a mosque or Islamic center has not been "more difficult than securing permission for any other similar building." British traditions have recognized the right of Muslims to settle personal affairs among themselves (including in sharia councils) as long as the outcomes do not conflict with prevailing laws.[23]

The Netherlands has also accommodated many Muslim religious demands despite a shift since the 1990s to tougher integration policies for Muslim minorities and, especially since the slaying of Van Gogh, fierce criticisms of Islam in public discourse.[24] To what extent the old pillarization system—in which religious differences were institutionalized in separate, state-subsidized organizational structures or "pillars" in all spheres of public life, including parallel labor unions, newspapers, political parties, and even hospitals, schools, and universities for Protestants and Catholics—has influenced the accommodation of Muslim demands is the subject of debate.[25] Muslims arrived as the system of pillarization was on the decline, so there was no question of a Muslim institutional pillar, comparable to the Protestant and Catholic ones of the past. Yet the legacy of the pillarized system has shaped responses to Muslims and contributed to the accommodation of certain Muslim group claims, even if this did not always occur without a struggle. On the whole, it has been observed, local governments in the Netherlands were supportive of the establishment of mosques in the 1980s and 1990s. A comparative analysis of Muslim claims-making ranked the Netherlands in 2002 with a perfect score of 1 in allowances for "Islamic religious practices outside of public institutions."[26]

France fared poorly on the same scale—with a score of 0, on the bottom along with Germany—and Muslims have faced roadblocks in many French localities in the quest to build mosques. Perhaps the most important step forward has been the establishment in 2003 of a French Council of the Muslim Religion (Conseil Français du Culte Musulman) as a liaison between the government and Muslim communities. This council, which exists on both national and regional levels, finally puts Islam on the same plane as other religions in relationship to the French state, for each of the major religions is represented by a similar body; the Jewish Consistoire Central, for instance, dates to the emancipation of Jews in the Napoleonic era. The French Council of the Muslim Religion has a mandate to negotiate with the French state over issues affecting Islamic religious practice, such as the training of imams and the regulation of ritual slaughter; and as Jonathan Laurence and Justin Vaisse note, it represents an attempt by the state to establish an Islam *of* France rather than simply tolerate Islam *in* France. In 2006 the German government, too, established an Islam Council, the Deutsche Islam Konferenz, drawing on a core of elites to engage in exchanges with administrators to try to resolve the practical challenges of religious observance facing Muslims—with initial discussions on, among other topics, the future of mosque construction and Islamic burials in Germany.[27] Although judged less accommodating than the Netherlands and Britain by many scholars, Germany has granted increasing rights to Muslims in the cultural sphere and gradually accommodated some Muslim religious practices.[28]

Encouraging as these developments are, the fact is that the tensions surrounding Islam have hardly disappeared. One journalist writes about the tortured debate in Britain about how to reconcile Islam with Britishness—and the same could be said for France, Germany, or the Netherlands.[29] Immigrant issues in Western Europe are frequently viewed as issues about Muslims. Seeing a man of Turkish origin walk down a Berlin street several paces ahead of his headscarved spouse, an ordinary German observer, according to one scholarly account, will attribute this picture "to 'Islam' rather than to the man's rural . . . peasant background."[30] Anti-immigrant sentiment tends to be closely linked with anti-Muslim sentiment, something that right-wing populists and even centrist parties have exploited, and at the same time strengthened, in the quest to rally support. All over Western Europe, "populist parties have heightened fear of Islamization, claiming that multicultural societies are making themselves vulnerable to an activist, fundamental Islam in which religious beliefs lead young Muslims to cultivate loyalty only to their own ethnic group, not to the nation."[31]

THE UNITED STATES

If religion has become a major cleavage in Western Europe between long-time residents and a large segment of the immigrant population, this has not happened in the United States, where, by and large, immigrants' religious beliefs and practices are viewed in a more positive light.

Not that the contemporary United States is a paradise of religious tolerance—far from it. In a national survey conducted between 2002 and 2003, a

substantial minority (about a third) of respondents said they would not welcome a stronger presence of Muslims, Hindus, and Buddhists in American society. About four in ten said they would not be happy about a mosque being
built in their neighborhood (about a third also would be bothered by the idea
of a Hindu temple being nearby), and almost a quarter favored making it illegal
for Muslim groups to meet (a fifth in the case of Hindus or Buddhists). In a
2009 Gallup Poll, more than four in ten Americans admitted to feeling at least
a little prejudice toward Muslims, more than twice the number who said the
same about Christians, Jews, and Buddhists.[32]

Since the terrorist attacks of September 11, cases of discrimination, hate
crimes, and bias incidents against Muslims in the United States have increased.
So has state surveillance of Muslims, even in a relatively immigrant-friendly
city like New York, where a 2013 lawsuit against the New York Police Department for violating the constitutional rights of Muslims highlighted the opera-
tion of a widespread surveillance program of Muslim neighborhoods, mosques,
social events, and campus organizations. Controversies over the building of
mosques have arisen in some towns and cities. Most notable was the high-
profile dispute in 2010 over construction of a Muslim community center and
prayer space in Lower Manhattan a few blocks from the World Trade Center
site. The anti-Muslim rhetoric of national conservative figures such as Newt
Gingrich, demanding the relocation of the proposed Muslim community center near Ground Zero and conflating Islam with terrorism, reinforced antago-
nism toward Muslims among segments of the American public. In response to
politically stoked anxieties about Muslim demands for sharia law, several
states have enacted statutes banning judges from considering foreign or religious law.[33]

Yet it would be a mistake to conclude from this litany that religion is the
kind of deep divide between immigrants and natives in the United States that
it is in Europe. It is not. Immigrants' religion has not aroused the same bitter
reaction as it has in Europe nor is it as frequent a subject of public debate
about integration or assimilation. Immigration debates in the United States, as
one scholar puts it, have not been Islamicized—or systematically connected
with anti-Islamic rhetoric—as they have been in Western Europe. Muslims in
the United States are largely framed as an external threat, as an enemy from
outside the country committing acts of terrorism and threatening national
security, not as an enemy from within undermining national cultural values,
as in Western Europe.[34] In general, immigrant religion has functioned as an
element in the Americanization process, and religious institutions generally
serve as places where immigrants can formulate claims to inclusion in American society.[35]

While there may be suspicion toward Muslims by the state, some conservative politicians and commentators, and parts of the general population, it is
more than offset by the widely viewed positive role of religion. The argument

that immigrant religion operates this way in the United States dates back to what are now regarded as classic historical studies of immigrant religious life, primary among them Will Herberg's 1955 *Protestant, Catholic, Jew*. Herberg asserted that it was "largely in and through . . . religion that he [the immigrant], or rather his children and grandchildren, found an identifiable place in American life." Herberg was writing about the assimilation into the American mainstream of Jews and Catholics from eastern and southern Europe in the years after World War II; this was a period when Catholicism and Judaism were becoming core American religions and, at the same time, America was becoming a "Judeo-Christian" nation. Today, in the midst of a massive immigration, which is bringing new diversity to America's religious landscape, Herberg's themes are still seen as having relevance, as a substantial share of today's immigrants "become American" through participating in religious and community activities of churches, mosques, and temples.[36]

To be sure, Americanization sometimes happens by conversion to Christianity, given its charter status in American society. For instance, the proportion of Christians among Asian immigrants to the United States is generally much higher than in their countries of origin. To some extent, this may be the result of selective immigration by those who were already Christian in the homeland. But there is little doubt that for many immigrants the move to America involves conversion to Christianity, a common pattern among the Taiwanese. Whereas in Taiwan some 4 percent of the population is Christian, this is true for about a fifth to a quarter of the Taiwanese in the United States. Among the Taiwanese in California, evangelical Christianity has mediated their acculturation to American society by repackaging some Taiwanese values in Christian trappings; at the same time, it has facilitated and reinforced assimilation to middle-class American family practices, such as recognizing children's autonomy and building more "democratic" parent-child relationships.[37]

Nevertheless, it is obvious that many immigrants retain non-Christian religious attachments, and consequently the religious diversity of the United States is growing rapidly as a result of immigration. Yet as far as anyone can tell, some immigrant religions that are relatively new to the United States, such as Buddhism and Sikhism, have many of the same integrative effects as the Christian denominations do. Asserting a religious identity remains an acceptable way to be different and American at the same time. The main title of a much-cited article "Becoming American by Becoming Hindu," captures this "Americanizing" impact of immigrants' engagement in religion. Prema Kurien argues that emphasizing Hinduism, albeit a recast and reformulated Hinduism, has helped Indian immigrants fit into American society and claim "a position for themselves at the American multicultural table."[38]

Whether asserting a Muslim identity operates in the same way is open to question in the political climate since 2001. Yet among Muslim Americans, protests and responses to discrimination reflect an Americanization dynamic.

In the wake of the backlash after 9/11, Muslim American advocacy organizations, it has been argued, "responded in typical American fashion," through political activism and legal challenges and urging constituents to claim their rights as Americans. Several Muslim American organizations shepherded a campaign to make Islam one of the core religions of American society, as a way to become integrated into the American mainstream.[39]

The religious institutions and practices that immigrants have brought from the old country tend to become "Americanized" in a variety of ways. There is a trend toward developing congregational forms, that is, local religious communities comprising people who come together voluntarily along the lines of a reformed Protestant congregation and in which, among other things, governance is in the hands of the local lay body and religious leaders are selected by this group. In the American environment, the congregational structure not only gives religious groups legitimacy but also, and importantly, tax-exempt nonprofit status.[40] In line with a change to congregationalism, a Buddhist monk, to give one example, may assume a more specialized and professional role closer to that of a minister. Moreover, immigrant religious groups often adopt American forms and practices—for instance, using the English language, holding weekly services, or having a sermon as the focal point of the service.[41] Partly this may happen because of the sheer exigencies and constraints of everyday life, including immigrants' work schedules and the availability of buildings for meetings. But immigrants (or their religious leaders) are also often consciously emulating American religious institutions and attempting to become more "American." In adopting congregational forms that are a dominant model in the United States, churches, synagogues, temples, and masjids are "more than houses of worship or prayer and become authentic community centers with different kinds of educational and social services, fellowship and recreational activities, and task-specific associational networks."[42]

In New York City, with its large and influential Jewish population, there is a different twist as immigrant religious groups sometimes take Jewish institutions as models. Interestingly, the developer involved in planning the controversial Muslim community center near Ground Zero, Sharif El-Gamal, consciously modeled it after Jewish community centers in New York that provide educational, cultural, and recreational programs for the broader New York community. Indeed, his daughters learned to swim at Manhattan's Jewish Community Center, where he was a member.[43]

Whether the integrative role of religion for contemporary immigrant groups represents a long-standing American pattern or is the fruit of the resolution of religious conflicts during preceding eras of immigration is a legitimate question. Certainly, American mainstream society had a decidedly Christian, even Protestant, character for much of the country's history. Anti-Catholicism and anti-Semitism are threaded through the fabric of that history, and Catholics felt forced to establish their own school system in the middle of the nineteenth century in order to protect their children from the overtly Protestant character of the state-supported school system. The full acceptance of Catholicism and Judaism as American religions was not accomplished until the middle of the twentieth century, around the time that Herberg wrote his famous synthesis. Yet, what was not in doubt was the ability of these previously minority religions to form their own institutions, without much interference from the outside society. That Catholics could erect a separate school system, and eventually a panoply of organizations to channel their social and professional lives within a religiously circumscribed subsociety, was not in question. Nor was Catholicism in this respect at a disadvantage compared to Protestant churches, for, aside from temporary holdovers from the established churches of the thirteen colonies, no denomination enjoyed state support. In this sense, there is a distinctively U.S. pattern implicated in the contemporary bridging role of immigrant religion. At the same time, the newer immigrant religions benefit from an acceptance that is the result of the difficult integration of Catholicism and Judaism into the mainstream.

There is a long tradition of recognizing, and accepting, ethnically based religious congregations as part of the American immigrant experience—and of taking for granted that immigrants' religious institutions will not only reproduce and reassert aspects of home-country cultures but also nurture and strengthen a sense of ethnic identity. In the context of contemporary American pluralism, it is normal and acceptable that immigrant churches and temples are places where newcomers can enjoy the rituals, music, foods, and festivals of their native lands, speak their native language, and pass on the cultural heritage to the next generation.

Immigrant churches, temples, and mosques, as a growing literature notes, serve a broad range of integrative functions. Religious membership offers a refuge for those separated from their homeland, creating a sense of belonging as well as a community of support and shelter from the stresses and difficulties of life in a new land. Religious groups may serve as an alternative source of respectability for newcomers, typically providing opportunities for leadership and service that bring prestige, something that is particularly important for those who feel denied social recognition in the United States or have suffered downward occupational mobility as a result of migration. They also usually provide many "this-worldly" resources and services to newcomers that help them to adjust and ultimately integrate into American society. These range from information about jobs, housing, and business opportunities to classes in English and seminars on various practical topics. Korean Christian churches are important social service agencies in the New York Korean community, offering job referrals, business information, Korean-language and after-school school programs for children, educational counseling, and even marriage counseling.[44]

Religious groups have been shown to provide a training ground for entry into the wider American society and for civic skills as immigrants serve on boards of directors and organize elections in church and temple associations and Islamic societies. A study of congregations in Washington, D.C., tellingly subtitled, 'How Faith Communities Form Our Newest Citizens," describes how immigrants develop and hone skills in public speaking, planning events, and conducting meetings in their congregations. The religious groups often sponsor citizenship classes and voter registration programs and efforts to lobby elected officials. Many mosques and churches encourage volunteer services to the larger community beyond their own religious group, from volunteering at senior citizen centers to serving food in soup kitchens.[45]

Interestingly, in the post–9/11 period, Muslim organizations in Chicago responded to public attacks and government targeting of Muslim and Middle Eastern Americans by joining with mainstream human-rights organizations investigating abuses of prisoners, private philanthropies supporting community defense work, and immigrant coalitions protesting against government excesses. In this way, the protests and political engagement, according to one account, pulled in some Muslim religious groups "from the margins of social exclusion and forged a new level of individual and organizational integration in American society."[46]

Involvement in ethnic congregations can keep the second generation on the right (upward mobility) track. According to a study of Vietnamese immigrants in New Orleans, church attendance and participation in church-sponsored activities protected young people from neighborhood gangs and "immoral" influences of American culture by strengthening attachment to the ethnic community and reinforcing parental aspirations for educational achievement. Some religious groups give assistance of a more direct kind, providing formal educational training, such as English-language or SAT classes, for the children of members. Classes that inculcate homeland traditions and language skills, it has been argued, can also have positive effects for mobility. They encourage and reinforce habits of study. By doing so in a setting controlled within the ethnic community, rather than provided by benevolent outsiders, they reinforce a sense of identity and cultural pride and perhaps also add to their effectiveness.[47]

EXPLAINING THE U.S.-EUROPE DIFFERENCES

And so we come to a critical question: why has religion been more problematic and created more barriers for immigrant integration in Western Europe than in the United States?

A major reason is that in the United States, in contrast to Western Europe, the vast majority of immigrants, like most of the native-born, are Christians, and those who are Muslim are relatively successful in socioeconomic terms. In addition, Americans are considerably more religious than Western Europeans, and their state institutions and constitutional principles provide a foundation for the easier acceptance and integration of non-Christian religions. To put it another way: in Europe, Muslim immigrants confront, on the one hand, majority populations that are mainly secular and therefore suspicious of claims based on religion and its requirements and, on the other, societal institutions and national identities that remain anchored to an important extent in Christianity and do not make equal room for Islam.

DEMOGRAPHIC FEATURES

It is not surprising that immigrant religion is seen in a more positive light in the United States, where most immigrants, nearly 75 percent, share the religious orientation, Christianity, of the majority of long-established Americans. In Western Europe, by contrast, Muslims have become the largest religious minority as a result of postwar inflows; an estimated sixteen to eighteen million people in 2010, nearly all of immigrant background, they constitute a growing share of the population. The highest proportion is found in France, where Muslims represent about 8 percent of the total population, compared to around 6 percent in the Netherlands, 5 percent in Germany, and 5 percent in Britain. In France, more than half of the nearly five million Muslims are of Algerian or Moroccan origin, with sizable numbers also of Tunisians, Turks, and sub-Saharan Africans; about two-thirds of Germany's 4.1 million Muslims have origins in Turkey; close to three-quarters of the Netherlands' nearly one million Muslims are of Turkish and Moroccan origin; and about three-quarters of Britain's 2.7 million Muslims are of South Asian background.[48]

Equally significant is that in Western Europe Islam is associated with large immigrant groups whose prospects for successful incorporation are a cause of public anxiety and concern. Western Europe's major Muslim groups include the most visibly disadvantaged immigrant minorities in terms of poverty, unemployment, and education rates—in France, these are Maghrebins from Algeria and Morocco; in Germany, Turks; in the Netherlands, Moroccans and Turks; and in Britain, Bangladeshis and Pakistanis.

Overall, only a tiny proportion of the foreign-born in the United States, about 5 percent, are Muslim. The largest immigrant group by far, more than a quarter of the foreign born, and the most problematic in terms of legal and socioeconomic status, is Mexicans, who are overwhelmingly Christian, mainly Catholic. There are hardly any Muslim Latinos (under 1 percent), and only 4 percent of adult Asian Americans are Muslim (mostly South Asian). According to a recent estimate, around one out of eight of the 2.75 million Muslims in the United States in 2011 were African American. The Muslim foreign born are diverse in national origin—more so than in the four European countries in our study—with about four in ten from the Middle East or North Africa, more than one in ten from sub-Saharan Africa, and about a quarter from South Asia, including Pakistan, India, and Bangladesh.[49]

Moreover, unlike Western Europe, where Muslims are often stuck in neighborhoods with poor housing conditions and low-paying jobs and stand out on account of their relatively high levels of unemployment, Muslim immigrants in the United States have done fairly well. Indeed, one factor reducing or counteracting negative attitudes to them is that so many are well educated and in the middle class. Even at a time when the recession had taken a toll, Muslim immigrants were holding their own compared to the wider U.S. population. According to a 2011 Pew Research Center study, 35 percent of foreign-born Muslims had annual household incomes of at least $50,000, with 18 percent over $100,000, about the same as the general public. In education, the Muslim foreign born were doing better than the general public: nearly a third had graduated from college and a quarter were currently enrolled in college or university classes.[50]

RELIGIOUS COMMITMENT AND SECULARIZATION

Whatever immigrants' particular religion, the fact is that religion generally is more accepted in the United States than Western Europe. The United States is characterized by unusually high levels of religious belief and behavior. To be religious is to be in sync with mainstream norms, which put great emphasis on the value of religious faith.[51] This is not the case in most of Western Europe, where the religious are members of a decided minority. A secular mindset dominates in most Western European countries. Claims based on religion have much less acceptance and legitimacy there—and when the religion is Islam, these claims often lead to public unease, sometimes disdain and even anger, and, not surprisingly, tensions and conflicts.

Figures from numerous surveys bring out the U.S.-Europe contrasts in religious commitment. In a 2004 Gallup poll 44 percent of Americans said they attended a place of worship once a week, while the average figure in Europe, according to a European Values Study, was only 15 percent—and the proportion was actually below 15 percent in France, Germany, Britain, and the Netherlands. The differences are striking with regard to reported beliefs. Half of the Americans in a Pew Research Center survey said that religion was very important in their lives; for the Germans, British, and French it was a fifth or less. According to the International Social Survey Programme (ISSP), 61 percent of Americans, compared to about a fifth to a quarter of French, Dutch, German, and British, said they know that God really exists and have no doubts about it.[52]

Admittedly, Americans, as many observers note, tend to exaggerate their rates of church attendance and the seriousness of their religious beliefs, and there is a growing retreat from identification with organized religions, reflected in the increasing proportion of American adults expressing no religious preference (still only 20 percent, however).[53] Yet religion's place in the national collective consciousness remains strong—and much stronger than in Europe. The very tendency of Americans to exaggerate their religiousness, in contrast to the opposite tendency of Europeans, is itself part of the different and consequential definitions of the situation in both places: "Americans think they are supposed to be religious, while Europeans think they are supposed to be irreligious."[54] Indeed, atheists arouse more criticism in the United States than do Muslims. In a recent national survey, fewer Americans held a favorable view of atheists than of American Muslims, and in another, more said they would disapprove if a child wanted to marry an atheist (48 percent) than a Muslim (34 percent). And whereas Muslims in Europe are much more likely than non-Muslims to be opposed to abortion and homosexuality, the gap is far narrower in the United States. Indeed, American Protestants and American Muslims disapprove of homosexuality in equal measure.[55]

The higher degree of secularization in Western Europe means that forms of social and cultural activity based on religious principles are frequently seen as illegitimate. This is particularly the case when it comes to Islam. The public nature of Islam and its demands on how followers conduct their lives make Islam seem in flagrant contradiction with modern European norms. Casanova writes of the "intolerant tyranny of the secular, liberal majority" in Europe: "While conservative religious people are expected to tolerate behavior they may consider morally abhorrent, such as homosexuality, liberal, secular Europeans are openly stating that European societies ought not to tolerate religious behavior or cultural customs that are morally abhorrent, insofar as they are contrary to modern, liberal secular European norms."[56]

In the United States, demands made on the basis of religion are a common feature of American life, put forward by a broad range of religious groups, including most vocally by fundamentalist and evangelical (mostly native white) Christians, who represent a significant proportion of Americans.[57] (In 2007, more than a quarter of U.S. adults were evangelical Protestants.) Thus, as the scholarly literature on immigrant religion emphasizes, becoming more religious is a way of becoming American, whereas it is often seen as a problem in Europe.

INSTITUTIONALIZED IDENTITIES AND ARRANGEMENTS

The way religion has been institutionalized is markedly different in the United States and Western Europe; and it has implications for whether immigrants' religious beliefs and practices are seen to contribute or create barriers to integration and inclusion. The hand of constitutional and legal history is heavy in this respect.

In the United States, key constitutional principles were fashioned because of the religious diversity among the original colonies and the resulting impossibility of institutionalizing a single state church in the new republic. The resulting principles of religious freedom and separation of church and state, enshrined in the Constitution's First Amendment, have provided the framework for a multireligious nation and religious pluralism, which has characterized American society from the very beginning.[58] The Constitution prohibits the government from establishing a state religion, guarantees the right to the free exercise of religion, and, through the equal protection clause of the Fourteenth Amendment, bans government-supported religious discrimination.

This does not mean, of course, that non-Protestant immigrant religions were welcomed with open arms. Hardly. In the late nineteenth and early twentieth centuries, Protestant denominations were more or less "established" in that they dominated the public square, crowding out Catholicism and Judaism, both associated with disparaged immigrants and seen by nativist observers as incompatible with mainstream institutions and culture.[59] (In this respect, one hears an echo of the contemporary European debate about Islam's place.) Non-Protestant religions either separated themselves from the dominant society by creating their own institutions—Catholic parochial schools and universities are a major example—or, as was true for much of American Judaism, confined their religious beliefs and practices to the private realm and "thus acceded to Protestant domination in the public realm." From the middle of the nineteenth century, the Irish, who constituted the first mass immigration of Catholics to the United States, were the target of deep-seated and virulent anti-Catholic nativism. Many native Protestants viewed the assimilation of the Irish as blocked by what was seen as a fanatical and unholy devotion to the Catholic Church and a foreign, antirepublican pope. The fear that a Catholic president would be under the influence of the Pope helped defeat Democratic Irish Catholic nominee Al Smith in 1928 and remerged in 1960 to confront John F. Kennedy.[60]

Yet by 1960 there were definite cracks in the Protestant hegemony. What is important is that Catholics and Jews were eventually incorporated into the system of American pluralism; or, to put it another way, the boundary dividing Catholics and Jews from the Protestant majority moved to include their alternative models of religious belief and practice. The separation of church and state was critical in enabling the religions imported by past immigration streams to achieve parity with Protestant versions of Christianity. Because the state did not officially support or sponsor Protestantism, the newer religions were able over time to become part of the American mainstream as the descendants of the immigrants did. By the mid-twentieth century, Americans had come to think in terms of a tripartite perspective—Protestant, Catholic, and Jew—with Judaism treated as a kind of branch or denomination within the larger Judeo-Christian framework, a religion of believers attending synagogues rather than churches. And in the late twentieth and early twenty-first century, opponents of multiculturalism were referring to "our Judeo-Christian heritage" in upholding the value of Western civilization.[61]

In recent years, public figures have made appeals to constitutional principles of religious freedom to support Muslim immigrants' claims to equal treatment. A case in point is the controversy over the Muslim community center near Ground Zero in lower Manhattan. New York City's then Mayor Michael Bloomberg made an impassioned speech, with the Statue of Liberty as a backdrop, supporting the planned center, saying, "This nation was founded on the principle that the government must never choose between religions, or favor one over another. . . . We would betray our values if we were to treat Muslims differently than anyone else." Jocelyne Cesari argues that the protection of religious minorities by law in the United States and the philosophy that religious freedom is a "cornerstone of individual dignity" has worked in Muslims' favor: "They are able to use America's long history of judgments supporting the free expression of religion to their advantage, even when Islamic beliefs themselves are ridiculed or disparaged."[62]

The very transformation of America into a "Judeo-Christian" nation has meant that post-1965 immigrants enter a more religiously open society than their predecessors did a hundred or a hundred-and-fifty years ago. Today, the encounter of immigrant religions with American society benefits from the earlier incorporation of Jewish and Catholic immigrant groups. Casanova points to an "ambiguous and tortuous process of public symbolic recognition of Islam as an American religion that resembles the processes of incorporation of Catholicism and Judaism," with an imam, for example, now often present, along with a Protestant minister, Catholic priest, and Jewish rabbi on the podium at public ceremonies in Washington, D.C., state capitals, and large cities. At the White House, President Obama has hosted an annual Ramadan Iftar dinner, a tradition, he noted, "that goes back several years just as we host Christmas parties, seders, and Diwali celebrations."[63] This does not necessarily mean that the new religions will eventually attain the charter status now occupied by Catholicism and Judaism. It is important to stress this point. The outcomes of the current encounter between non-Western religions and the American mainstream are not predictable.

If the past struggles by Catholics and Jews for religious parity have led to a more welcoming environment for newer immigrant religions, so too, the legacy of the civil rights movement has aided Muslim Americans in their struggle to integrate on equal terms into American society and helps explain the quickness of their advocacy and grassroots organizations in responding to targeted attacks in the wake of 9/11. Muslims, one sociologist argues, often see their experiences as "another chapter in the American story of the fight for social inclusion that all racial, ethnic, and religious minorities have to wage."[64]

In Western Europe, the ways in which Christian religions have been institutionalized have made it difficult for Islam to achieve equal treatment and are implicated in many of the problems and conflicts that have arisen. As secular as Europeans are, their societies have deeply institutionalized religious identities, which are the result of historic settlements to resolve profound and bloody conflicts between Protestants and Catholics. These settlements date back to the Peace of Westphalia in the seventeenth century, whose core principle was that "whoever rules the territory determines the religion." It ensured, at the very birth of the modern European state, a direct linkage with religion and a history of officially established Christian churches.[65] The resulting entanglements of sacred institutions and secular power have proven difficult to fully unwind.

While secular natives in Western Europe today may see religion as a minor feature of their societies, Muslims cannot help but be aware of the secondary status of their religion and the special privileges accorded to majority denominations, whose religious signs tend to be seen as elements of public culture. In France, *laïcité*, the exclusion of religion from the affairs of state, is the official ideology, yet a single religion, Catholicism, has for centuries been paramount and privileged. The state owns and maintains most Christian churches and allows them to be used for regular religious services. The same 1905 law that established state possession of religious edifices built before that year also prevents the state from contributing to the construction of new ones, thus keeping the country's nearly five million Muslims from enjoying the same privileges as Christians. Despite the recent construction of some large mosques in France— and the circumvention of the ban on state support for religion in some cases by using public funds for cultural centers associated with the mosques—most French mosques are makeshift structures in converted rooms in housing projects, garages, or even basements. (According to Laurence and Vaisse, two-thirds of Muslim prayer spaces are of this kind, and fewer than a hundred mosques in France can hold as many as five hundred worshipers.[66]) There is an inevitable contrast with the mainstream given the centrality of numerous impressive Catholic churches in the national narrative, perhaps most notably Notre Dame, built on the location of Lutèce, the original settlement by Celts that laid the foundation for the city of Paris, and the site of important events ever since. Adding to the religious divide is that half of the country's ten or so state-designated national holidays are Catholic in origin; no Muslim holiday has equivalent recognition.[67]

Likewise, in the Netherlands, the 1983 constitutional amendment instituting separation of church and state and the breakdown of the old system of "pillarization," with parallel, state-subsidized institutions for Catholics and Protestants, have had the effect of privileging mainstream religions while leaving stumbling blocks in the way of Islam. Between 1962 and 1975, the Dutch government offered significant subsidies for the construction of churches, but only one mosque was built with government money. The government subsequently provided some funds for the creation of prayer houses for Muslim guestworkers, but by the late 1980s secular political parties opposed the renewal of these subsidies as a violation of church-state separation, and the principle of "no financing of religion" became increasingly important in Dutch public policy toward Muslim associations. The shift to state neutrality was, notes Jan Rath, "like drawing up the bridge in front of the newcomers."[68]

Government support for religious schools has created other inequalities in Western Europe between long-established religions and Islam. In Britain and France the state provides financial support for religious schools as long as they teach the national secular curriculum. Inevitably, these arrangements, while seemingly fair to all religions, favor the most established ones. In Britain (where senior Anglican bishops sit in the House of Lords by right as part of the established state church), the government funds more than 6,500 Church of England and Catholic faith schools but, as of 2010, only eleven Islamic faith schools in a nation of nearly three million Muslims. In the Netherlands, the majority of children go to state-supported denominational schools, nearly all Protestant and Catholic, while the country's nearly one million Muslims in 2008 had only about forty-four of their own publicly funded schools educating about ten thousand pupils. In France, about 20 percent of French students go to religious schools (mostly Catholic) that receive the bulk of their budgets from the government, but the first publicly subsidized Muslim school, the Lycée Averroès, was not founded until 2003; as of 2009, there were only two Muslim schools funded by the French state.[69]

In Germany, the state, according to the 1949 constitution, must be neutral in matters of religion, but this does not preclude linkages between church and state. The long-established Catholics and Protestants as well as Jews—but not Islam, the third largest faith—are recognized as public corporations and entitled to federally collected church taxes and the right to run state-subsidized religious social services and hospitals. Because Islam is not organized the same way as the established religions, it is outside the state-supported mainstream. Further, the established religions are taught in public schools by regular teachers (i.e., civil servants) during hours set aside for religious instruction. Islam, however, has so far failed to be accorded the same status in most German states, and instruction in it is not universally available; when it has been, it has usually occurred in some nonregular form, such as on an experimental basis in Baden-Wurttemberg, Bavaria, and Lower Saxony.[70] (The state of Hesse in 2014 became the first to break this ad hoc pattern.)

The different ways that religion has been institutionalized in the United States and Western Europe have implications for the claims of immigrant religious groups and conflicts that may result. In the United States, immigrants with allegiance to minority religions have generally sought inclusion in the mainstream through public acceptance and recognition of their group. Although an important historical exception was the unsuccessful struggle by Catholics for public funds for parochial schools, some other minority religious groups—perhaps, most notably, many Jewish organizations—have fought for a strict adherence to separation of church and state as a way to prevent discrimination and obtain parity with dominant religions. In Europe, equal treatment for minority religions would require a radical structural change by removing institutionalized arrangements with long-established religions or, as Muslims have sought, achieving greater support from the state of the sort that the established religions already have, including subsidies for their own religious schools. At least so far, the kind of interlacing of the state and Christianity that we have described in Western Europe has no parallel in the United States.

WHAT ABOUT CANADA?

In many ways, the picture in Canada looks much like the one we have sketched for the United States: immigrant religion is neither a central dividing line between long-term natives and newcomers nor a major challenge to integration. Religious involvement is an acceptable way for immigrants in Canada to strengthen and preserve ethnic identity, which has facilitated immigrant adaptation and, particularly given Canada's official multicultural policy, access to government resources and programs. Muslims, in socioeconomic terms, are not a problematic group in Canada: they have high levels of education, and, as compared to Muslims in Britain, much lower rates of unemployment. Canada's Muslims are substantial in number—about 940,000 in 2010—but their share of the population is smaller (2.8 percent) than in each of the four European countries in our study.[71]

At the same time, however, Canada's highly publicized debates over the integration of religious minorities have a European ring and are connected to similar social and historical realities. In the past half century, Canada, like Western European countries, has witnessed a growing erosion of religiosity, which has reduced the legitimacy of demands made on the basis of religion, the most prominent in recent years coming from Muslims. While Canadians are less secular than much of Europe according to various measures, such as attendance at religious services and prayer and belief in God, they are far less religious than Americans. In a 2003 survey, 60 percent of Americans and 28 percent of Canadians said that religion is very important to them.[72]

In Quebec, the swinging of the pendulum in the direction of secularization after long years of Catholic hegemony partly explains why public controversies over "reasonable accommodation" of religious minorities have been more heated there than elsewhere in Canada. Before the 1960s the Catholic Church had virtual control over healthcare, education, and social services for French Quebecois. The so-called Quiet Revolution in Quebec in the 1960s radically reduced the sweeping power of the Catholic Church, one result being that the provincial government took over the fields of health care and education. Church attendance plummeted: in a survey in Quebec conducted in 2000, only

20 percent of respondents attended church on a weekly basis compared to 88 percent in the 1950s.[73]

The historically strong French connection also underlies some of the controversies concerning Muslims in Quebec. As a Francophone island in an Anglophone sea, Quebec has fought to maintain its language, culture, and history, requiring the children of immigrants to enroll in French schools. Identity issues are a central political matter and many in the province's Francophone majority fear that the arrival of outsiders will tip the balance away from their concerns and dilute or erode Quebecois cultural identity. In the context of rapid secularization over the past decades, private religious belief and practice are tolerated, according to Margarita Mooney, but public religious expressions and faith-based organizations are suspected of conflicting with Quebecois secular nationalism. Recent high-profile incidents involving Muslims focus on the veil, echoing those that have been prominent in France, and on more than one occasion, Muslim girls have been expelled from athletic tournaments for wearing the *hijab*.[74]

Throughout Canada, historically rooted relations between church and state have been implicated in controversies involving Canada's Muslims. On the one hand, church-state relations have changed radically since the 1960s, and especially since 1982 when the Charter of Rights and Freedoms guaranteed "freedom of conscience and religion" and equality under the law regardless of religion. Canadian churches, as one scholarly observer puts it, "lost much of their assumed and formal social control . . . [and] the Canadian state itself has also increasingly distanced itself from a simple endorsement of Christian values and beliefs. . . . [A] tacit agreement seems to have been reached within a variety of levels of society to confine religion (not just Christianity) to the private sphere."[75] Whereas in Ontario in the 1960s, religious education was obligatory and prayers were said each day in the classroom, these practices were struck down by the courts in the years after 1982 there and in other provinces.[76]

Yet, on the other hand, the legacy of earlier church-state links lingers on in ways that are reminiscent of the situation in Europe. If a wall of separation can be said to exist for Canadians, notes a church historian, they have been prepared to allow chinks in it that most Americans south of the border would regard as unthinkable.[77] The religious privileges of certain Christian groups remain guaranteed by the Constitution, something that stands out in the field of education. Alongside the secularization of the public schools throughout Canada, many provinces provide at least partial funding to faith-based, overwhelmingly Catholic, schools. In Ontario, the only province to fully fund Catholic education while not providing any funding to other faith-based schools, this inequality has been an issue. In 2007, when about a third of students at Ontario's publicly funded schools attended Catholic institutions, voters in the province strongly rejected a proposal to extend funding beyond Catholic schools, and so far the courts have upheld the existing system.[78]

It is worth noting that another controversy in Ontario involving Muslims and the courts ended with a more equitable result. When Muslims sought to include sharia in Ontario family tribunals in line with the province's recognition of Catholic and Jewish faith-based tribunals to settle family law matters, their demands were not successful. Concerned about the threat that Islamic family courts would pose to Muslim women, the provincial government decided in 2005 to reject the inclusion of sharia law. In a one-law-for-all approach, the government revoked parallel privileges previously available to Jews and Catholics, banning all legally recognized religious arbitration in the province.[79]

CONCLUSION

Our argument has been that a combination of factors—religious similarity between natives and immigrants, Muslim immigrants' socioeconomic status, the religiosity of the native majority, and historically rooted institutional structures—explain why religion is less of a barrier to inclusion of immigrant minorities in the United States than in Western Europe. The Canadian case also points to the role of state institutions and identities in creating difficulties for the incorporation of religious minorities.

What about the future? Are there signs of change on either side of the Atlantic? Are there lessons from the past that suggest what may lie ahead? The similarities between today's discourse on Islam as an antimodernist religion incompatible with democracy and yesterday's views on Catholicism provide some optimism about Islam's place in American society in the years to come. It may have taken more than a century, but the United States was able to overcome its fear of "the Catholic menace," offering hope that it can do so with regard to Islam as well. Perhaps in 2050, one historian writes, we will be talking about America as an Abrahamic civilization, a phrase joining Muslims with Jews and Christians: "America, at present, is a long way from that formulation of American national identity, but no further than America once was from the Judeo-Christian one."[80]

Less happily, there is the undercurrent of hostility to Muslims in the United States that has bubbled to the surface in various localities and on the national stage on a number of occasions in recent years. How widespread and sustained political attacks on Muslims Americans will be in the future remains to be seen. Nor do we know their consequences. By 2011 the Ground Zero controversy had died down in the public arena, in part because plans to build a large new Muslim community center had stalled, but of course other issues and events may bring sentiment against Muslims Americans back, front and center, into the national media and political focus. Still, Muslim Americans have the Constitution—and civil liberties advocates and liberal politicians—on their side if their rights to religious freedom are threatened, and the small size of the U.S. Muslim population makes the group seem less threatening. Its size can cut another way, however. The lack of personal exposure to Muslims, it has been argued, may actually fuel negative sentiments toward them. Even so, the future looks brighter since the more that Muslims mingle with others—and as a growing number of Americans count a Muslim among their friends, workmates, and family—the greater the likelihood of positive feelings toward them.[81]

Across the Atlantic, a number of developments provide grounds for cautious optimism about the integration of Islam in the future.[82] Familiarity can breed contempt, but, as just noted, it can also foster positive attitudes and relations. More and more, long-established Europeans have routine contact and interactions in a range of social settings with Muslims, including those born and bred in Europe, which often increases comfort with people of Muslim background and can reduce prejudice and lead to friendships. With a decline in the proportion of the foreign born, and a rise in the proportion of the second and third generations, the participation of Muslims in mainstream political and economic life is bound to become more common and increasingly be seen as "natural."

Over time, native European majorities are also likely to grow more used to Islamic religious observance, especially as Islam becomes more Europeanized—or, given internal divisions within Islam, "European Islams" take root.[83] According to writings on the Netherlands, for example, some Muslim leaders have sought to marginalize interpretations of Islam that conflict with liberal democratic values, and a development among many in the wider Muslim community is to blame ethnic cultures, not "pure" Islam, for customs and practices criticized by the native Dutch.[84] Some scholars predict that as members of the second generation in Europe take over in religious associations and institutions, they will generally strive for a more liberal version of Islam than their parents practiced, one that is focused on integration into Western European society and viewed more positively by the wider population.[85]

The jury is still out on the future of religiosity among the children of Muslim immigrants. Some studies indicate a fair amount of stability, and sometimes an increase, in religiosity among native-, as compared to foreign-, born Muslims, although we know little about the meaning and impact of religious beliefs and practices in their daily lives. Other studies suggest that, on average, members of the second generation are becoming less religious, and hold many views in sync with mainstream ideas.[86] In a large-scale survey of young adult second-generation Turkish Muslims in several major European cities, the majority did not actively practice their religion, agreed that religion should be a private matter, favored a strict separation of state and religion, and espoused gender equality in education and the labor market.[87]

In terms of policy, we have pointed to some ways in which European governments have begun to make accommodations for Muslim religious practices, but there is still a long way to go before Islam achieves parity with the mainstream religions. In Germany, where the institutional inequality between established churches and Islam is glaring, the major question is whether, or at what point in the future, Islam will be able to gain recognition as a corporate body, thereby entitling it to taxes collected by the state from its members and to have religion taught, at public expense, as part of the school curriculum. A major stumbling block has been Islam's lack of a central organization with which the state can consult; and the federal government has so far been unwilling to recognize one Islamic organization or federation as representative of the majority of German Muslims. Ultimately, it has been argued, ways will be found to give Islam parity with the Protestant, Catholic, and Jewish faiths, if only to preserve the corporate structure that benefits historically established religions, but how this will develop remains to be seen.[88]

There are other clouds on the horizon. Although most second-generation Muslims in Western Europe do not support a politicized Islam, a minority do. The aggrieved sense of exclusion felt by many Muslims who have grown up in Europe has created a pool of potential recruits for fundamentalist doctrines and radical Islamist groups, a development that could reinforce and indeed increase tensions with long-established Europeans. Terrorist incidents among "homegrown" Muslims and their recruitment to fight in Middle Eastern armed conflicts present a "serious challenge to integration," and could heighten antiMuslim hostility among the majority population and fuel anti-Muslim rhetoric. The prospects for relatively high rates of unemployment and stalled social mobility among many second-generation Muslims will provide fodder for "skeptics who will continue to argue that Muslims will never fit in or successfully adjust to European society."[89]

Exactly how the future will unfold is unclear. Changes may be afoot, but it is safe to say that immigrant religion will be a more contentious issue and pose more serious challenges for integration in Western Europe than in North America for some time to come. In light of the controversy over building a Muslim community center near the World Trade Center site, *Time* magazine asked in its August 2010 cover story on Islamophobia whether the United States has a Muslim problem and, to be sure, to some extent it does. Yet at least in the near future, religion is likely to continue to offer an acceptable way for the overwhelming majority of newcomers and their children to fit into American society just as in Europe it is likely to be more problematic for—and engender sharper tensions and conflicts with—important minorities seeking inclusion.

CHAPTER 7

ENTERING THE PRECINCTS OF POWER

Immigrant political incorporation, it has been said, is about "bringing outsiders in."[1] The political integration of groups originating in immigration could even be considered the paramount indicator of their overall inclusion. At stake is a fair share of societal power, a resource that tends to be monopolized by the native majority for as long as it can hold on. Despite the importance of political integration and the considerable amount of research it has attracted, much about the processes involved remains unknown.

Given the historical recency of many immigrant flows to the rich societies of the West, scholars have often looked at forms of political participation that do not require citizenship en masse and thus do not directly involve electoral influence and success. This focus is supported by, just as it supports, the view that noncitizen immigrants can obtain significant rights in the receiving society. Because excluded minorities often gain a measure of political inclusion through social movements, a great deal of attention has been given to immigrant and ethnic organizations that influence political actors or that become such actors themselves. Equally significant from this perspective are the claims made in political arenas by such organizations on behalf of immigrants.[2]

In this chapter, we take a different approach, putting the spotlight on an aspect of political life that has to do with electoral processes and outcomes: the ability of immigrant-origin politicians to be voted into office. This topic has been relatively neglected in studies of immigrant-group political incorporation,[3] although it is indisputably critical for the integration of immigrants and their children and indeed for their ability to influence the laws and policies that shape their lives in important ways. A half century or more after the onset (or renewal, as the case may be) of large-scale immigration to North America and Western Europe, it is appropriate to inquire into this form of inclusion. We argue that electoral success by immigrant minorities should be regarded as the gold standard for political inclusion. Success gives individuals from immigrant backgrounds—men and women who usually have an intimate understanding of the worldviews and interests of their coethnics—entry into the inner precincts of power and even seats at the table when important decisions are made.

From an analytic perspective, electoral outcomes provide a sensitive test of the idea that national institutional structures and identities, and the histories that lie behind them, exert a powerful influence on immigrant-group incorporation. The six countries we are considering exhibit a substantial range of variation in integration models and relevant legal and institutional structures: the integration models or philosophies range from multiculturalism in Canada to a fairly strict assimilationism in France; the citizenship regimes from absolute *jus soli*, or birthplace citizenship, for the second generation in the cases of Canada and the United States to, until 2000, a *jus sanguinis* citizenship regime in Germany, which has meant that even in the early twenty-first century the majority of second-generation adults there are not citizens; and the political systems from a first-past-the-post competition between the candidates of two parties in the United States to multiparty systems with proportional representation in the Netherlands. All of these features can be argued to potentially affect the success of immigrant-origin politicians.[4]

A counterpoint to the presumption of a role for distinctive national institutions and integration models is the notion of gradual institutional convergence. It posits that parallel political, demographic, economic, social, and cultural forces have been leading liberal democratic states in a common direction, toward similar state policies and laws relating to immigrants, in particular those involving citizenship, cultural practices, and welfare benefits.[5] A focus on convergence tends to stress national laws and policies, with less attention to other institutional structures shaping the concrete opportunities for immigrant minorities in different countries or to the potential impact of distinctive national models or ideologies of integration.

Our analysis gives something to both of these positions. Cross-national differences are apparent in the extent to which politicians from new immigrant backgrounds have been able to gain elected office. Immigrant groups have been least successful in Germany and France, the most successful in the Netherlands, with Britain, Canada, and the United States in between. At the same time, trends toward convergence are also evident. Just during a single decade, the opening years of the twenty-first century, there have been signs of progress in all the countries in our study as immigrant-origin groups have improved their representation in elected office.[6] Two opposing tendencies, in short, appear to be at work; and while immigrant origin-groups can hardly be said to be fully included in terms of political representation in any of the societies in our study, there are encouraging signs everywhere of their political advances.

CITIZENSHIP AND INTEGRATION MODELS

Since citizenship is usually (but not always!) a prerequisite for the most direct forms of political participation, such as voting and running for office, the rules under which immigrants and their children can become citizens would appear to be critical for an understanding of national differences. Yet citizenship has been a prime domain of convergence, where laws and policies have become more alike in Western Europe and North America in recent years (see table 7.1). Before World War II in much of continental Europe, *jus sanguinis*—the principle that citizenship is inherited from parents—was prevalent, so that many children of immigrants remained foreign even if they were born and had spent all their lives in the country. In contrast, in Canada and the United States, *jus soli*, or birthplace citizenship, has been the dominant principle in an automatic and unqualified form, with citizenship conferred at birth on all children born in the country. The dominance of *jus sanguinis* over *jus soli*, it has been argued, was a logical development in many continental European nations when they were countries of emigration seeking to maintain links with their citizens abroad, just as in settler societies like the United States *jus soli* was useful in integrating immigrants of diverse origins into a new nation. Not surprisingly, France, a country of large-scale immigration since the late-1800s, differed from its neighbors in developing a more expansive political citizenship in the late nineteenth century based on *jus soli*: automatic citizenship at birth for the third generation (*double jus soli*) along with easy access to citizenship for the second generation at the age of eighteen.[7]

The massive postwar immigration in Europe and North America has brought the two sides of the Atlantic closer together in citizenship law, with continental European countries generally moving in the direction of making it easier for immigrants and their children to acquire citizenship. (We speak of continental Europe here because Britain has a different, *jus soli*, tradition, and the large post–World War II immigration led to a move away from pure *jus soli* to a slightly more restricted form.) By now, the majority of Western European countries provide some form of *jus soli* citizenship to the second generation, although it occurs "not only automatically at birth [as in the United States], but also under conditions of residency or through voluntary acquisition, both of which are presumed to entail socialization."[8]

Germany is the most notable example of the shift away from descent-based to birthplace citizenship. Since a new citizenship law went into effect in 2000, birthright citizenship is granted to members of the second generation if at least one parent has lived legally in Germany for eight years; those with parents from non-EU countries were then supposed to decide by adulthood whether to keep German citizenship or the nationality of their parents, but since 2014 they are

Table 7.1. Citizenship Requirements in Six Countries

	Immigrants	Second generation*	Dual citizenship	Recent changes
Canada	Three years residence; knowledge of an official language; knowledge of Canadian history and governance	Unconditional *jus soli* at birth	Permitted	
France	Five years residence; knowledge of French; evidence of assimilation to French values	Conditional *jus soli*: passive acquisition at age 18 unless opts out; unconditional *jus soli* for the third generation	Permitted	During the 1993–98 period, second generation required to request citizenship
Germany	Eight years residence; knowledge of German; knowledge of civics; proof of livelihood	Conditional *jus soli*: dual citizenship at birth since 2000 (if parents resident for eight years)	Discouraged, but allowed for post 1999 2nd gen.	In 2000 shift from *jus sanguinis* to *jus soli*; in 2014, forced citizenship choice dropped
Great Britain	Five years residence; knowledge of English (or another U.K. language); knowledge about U.K. life	Conditional *jus soli* at birth (if one parent is a citizen or permanent resident)	Permitted	Prior to 1983, *jus soli* was unconditional; civic integration requirements strengthened in 2002
Netherlands	Five years residence; oral and written language test; knowledge about Dutch life	Conditional *jus soli*: can opt for Dutch citizenship from age 18 if resident since birth; unconditional *jus soli* for the third generation	Tolerated	Law covering second generation changed in 1985; language and integration requirements made more stringent in 2003
US	Five years residence; knowledge of English; knowledge of U.S. history and governance	Unconditional *jus soli* at birth	Tolerated	

* Defined here as children born in the country of reception to immigrant parents who are not citizens of that country, since the children of citizen immigrants are usually also citizens.

Sources: Ersanilli and Koopmans (2010); Vink and De Groot (2010); national government websites.

no longer forced to make this choice. In several European nations, including the Netherlands, a person born in the country to foreign parents can acquire citizenship at the age of majority after fulfilling certain residency requirements. In France, citizenship for a member of the second generation is acquired passively—automatically granted at age eighteen unless an individual rejects it.[9]

Why has there been this general trend from descent-based to civic-territorial principles of citizenship? Explanations have stressed the inherent principles or internal logic of liberal democracies in the context of mass immigration; the need to cope with similar sets of problems, including the integration of immigrants and their children; and mutual borrowing and emulation as states sometimes model policies on those of others. French political scientist Patrick Weil argues that a commitment to democratic values has forced states with restrictive acquisition rules to modify them; the old rules have been recognized as incompatible with modern democratic norms and as impediments to the integration of the second and third generations. Most *jus sanguinis* countries, as Stephen Castles and Alisdair Davidson note, have realized that "exclusion from citizenship is problematic, leading to social marginalization, political exclusion, conflict and racism."[10]

To what extent the emergence, within Europe, of transnational legal rules has been a factor is open to question. The increasingly important role of the European Union has meant that EU-instituted laws and policies, including some concerning immigrants and immigration, now pertain to all member states. One example relating to citizenship is the Maastricht Agreement of 1992, which has required EU members to award local voting rights to residents who are citizens of other EU countries. Still, policy about legal citizenship rules in Europe has basically remained a domestic, national, concern.[11]

There are thus limits to convergence, which are evident in policies regarding dual citizenship. To be sure, the general trend in recent decades has been toward greater toleration, allowing immigrants to hold onto the citizenship of the country where they were born and raised even as they acquire the citizenship of the country where they now live. Yet national differences remain. Of the countries in our study, Germany has been the least accepting of dual citizenship and usually requires individuals from outside the EU who acquire German citizenship through naturalization to renounce their prior one (though they sometimes reacquire it after becoming German citizens). This has had a depressive effect on naturalization by Turks, who often wish to retain their Turkish citizenship. None of the other countries is as restrictive as Germany in this respect. Canada, France, and Great Britain legally permit dual citizenship. The United States has a naturalization oath that requires renunciation of other citizenships, but U.S. law has "evolved in the direction of increased ambiguity or outright tolerance in favor of dual nationality"—in practice pursuing a "don't ask, don't tell" policy. Although officially immigrants in the Netherlands cannot keep prior citizenships if they naturalize, there are numerous exceptions to the policy, resulting in a de facto common practice of allowing naturalized citizens to maintain their prior citizenship.[12]

Some scholars claim that another kind of convergence has been occurring: in terms of the models or philosophies of civic integration. In the early years of the twenty-first century, there has been a retreat in some countries, at least in political rhetoric at the national level, from multicultural ideals, combined with a renewed emphasis on civic integration, one might even say "assimilation." That is, the rationale for some major new policies has been to narrow the cultural distance between immigrants and the receiving society and to ensure that immigrants understand societal norms, principles, and institutions of the mainstream society.[13] The Netherlands offers an example of a turn away from what some have labeled multicultural elements in policies—and others conceptualize as a shift from a tolerant to intolerant monoculturalism—partly based on the growing perception of the failure to produce the integration of important immigrant minorities, especially Muslim groups. Starting in the late 1990s, newcomers to the Netherlands have been required to take integration courses; in 2003 candidates for naturalization had to pass a more stringent examination in the Dutch language and take a new test on their knowledge of Dutch society; and since 2007, immigrants from outside the EU must pass tests on the Dutch language and their preparation for life in the Netherlands as a requirement for permanent residence. Several other European countries, including Germany, France, Britain, Austria, and Denmark, have adopted variants of the Dutch approach. The new formal and standardized naturalization tests in Britain, for example, impose more difficult language standards as well as require familiarity with British mores and day-to-day-life such as knowing the flower traditionally worn on Remembrance Day. Germany, while never multicultural in a policy sense, has instituted integration courses focusing on the acquisition of German.[14] With respect to citizenship, the general drift has been described as moving from a conception of naturalization "as a means of integration" to one of naturalization as the "crowning of a completed integration process."[15]

Yet here, too, there are limits to convergence. Canada has not abandoned its official multicultural stance. The United States, while hardly multicultural in any official sense, could be described as pursuing laissez-faire multiculturalism in the sense that it makes legal and political accommodations for ethnoracial diversity. And despite the backlash in Western European political discourse against multiculturalism, programs and measures once deemed "multicultural," such as recognition of ethnic minority organizations and public consultative bodies, generally remain (although as before European countries continue to diverge in the particular public institutional initiatives adopted).[16] France, it should be noted, offers the strongest contrast to de facto multiculturalism and emphasizes its own model or philosophy of integration, Republicanism, which denigrates any intrusion of ethnic origins and/or communities into public spheres. Nevertheless, as noted in the previous chapter, the French government provided the impetus for the creation of a French Council of the Muslim Religion (Conseil Français du Culte Musulman), established in 2003 to serve as a liaison to Muslim communities.

ELECTORAL POLITICS AND POLITICAL INTEGRATION

There are a number of reasons for focusing on the ability of minority candidates to be elected to office.

To begin with, election to political office is a direct measure of minority integration into the mainstream in the same sense that entry by minority individuals into high-status occupations is. It is an indication of a reduction, however modest, in the differentials in life chances between majority and minority.[17] Where immigrant minorities are not represented in elected office or are only minimally so, they experience very unequal life chances in attaining such highly esteemed and powerful positions as mayor, city councilor, and parliamentarian.

Moreover, the legitimacy of a political system, especially a democratic one, ultimately depends on its ability to give representation to different groups in the population. This would seem all the more true when the boundaries between groups are prominent and correlate with structures of inequality so that they effectively mark a societal cleavage. If immigrant minorities are unable to achieve significant electoral representation, then their attachment to the dominant institutions and norms of a society may ultimately come into question; and they are liable to define themselves, and be defined by others, as not just distinct from, but in opposition to, the native majority.[18] While lack of electoral representation is likely to reinforce a sense of outsider status, the sight of people like oneself being elected to office can nurture and strengthen a sense of identification with, and allegiance to, the society and its institutions, including the rules, procedures, and values of the political system, and can also be a source of pride.

These reasons concern what has been called the "descriptive," or "mirror image," political representation of a group, that is, the degree to which its representation in political positions reflects its population share. Descriptive representation is not the same as "substantive" representation, the reflection of a group's interests and concerns in political decision-making. As Irene Bloemraad points out, we should beware of assuming that politicians from a particular background represent the interests of their group of origin; indeed, their electoral success may depend on their distancing themselves from their origins.[19]

But substantive representation is nevertheless at stake in the electoral success of immigrant-origin politicians. They typically bring experiences and perspectives into the precincts of power that are not otherwise represented there. They can give mainstream politicians insights into a minority's concerns. Thus, the ability of members of an immigrant minority to occupy elected political office gives the group a voice in decisions that can directly affect it.[20] This is the case whether the office is part of the national government or a local one. As Nathan Glazer and Daniel Patrick Moynihan observed in *Beyond the Melting Pot*, many government decisions have differential ramifications for population groups, particularly the native majority versus ethnoracial minorities.[21] A minority group that is unable to achieve some degree of electoral representation has little or no ability to influence such decisions in its favor or to ward off those with potentially negative impacts. Indeed, majority-group politicians may believe that they can impose unfavorable decisions with impunity.

There are other quite tangible benefits of electoral success. Elected politicians usually have an influence on many of the routine decisions of government, which are often formally made by civil servants, such as the awarding of contracts. They also often exert influence on the hiring of individuals to occupy public offices that are exempt from civil-service regulations; indeed, such offices may be regarded as part of the "patronage" that is the spoils of electoral victory and can be doled out to supporters. Thus, when a group fails to achieve electoral success, it generally loses out when such offices are distributed. By contrast, groups that achieve electoral success can use it as leverage to raise the socioeconomic position of many group members and, perhaps eventually, of the group itself. The Irish offer a compelling historical example in the United States, as they used their leadership of Democratic political machines that dominated many U.S. cities a century ago to bring about massive municipal employment of their coethnics.[22]

The analysis we present here is focused on the ability of candidates from immigrant-minority groups to be elected to local, regional, and national offices. A group's political representation is measured as the ratio of its share of elected offices to its population share.[23] As one would expect, the degree of representation tends to be greater at lower levels of the political system, since immigrant concentrations in particular neighborhoods, cities, and regions guarantee some degree of representation. Moreover, there is usually a lag between subnational and national electoral success, since politicians typically begin their careers at the local level, and it takes longer to build up the kind of support, resources, and influence necessary to attain national, as opposed to local and regional, offices. Nevertheless, the degree of political voice achieved by immigrant populations at the national level is also important because of the generally greater concentration of power there.

MINORITIES IN THE ELECTORATE

In looking at the entry of immigrant-origin groups into the precincts of power, we have had to rely on existing studies of electoral representation, and this fact helps to determine the groups we can consider. As in other chapters, we focus as much as possible on low-status immigrant-origin groups, whose successful incorporation is seen as problematic by many in the native majority—the population that considers itself to constitute the core of the national community and occupies the lion's share of the seats of power.[24] The immigrant groups coming from Africa, Asia, the Caribbean, and Latin America best meet the notion of problematic incorporation in the political realm. This is especially true when it comes to electoral success because as candidates they generally stand out owing to their skin color, names, and religions. In continental Europe, these groups are frequently defined in political and citizenship studies as "non-Western," whereas in Great Britain and North America, they are seen as nonwhite minorities. Our definition of the populations includes not only the immigrant generation but also the second and sometimes later generations; citizenship is usually much more common among the second and third generations, whose members are therefore more likely to be voters. Table 7.2 provides basic data about these minority populations, including their percentages in the electorate, which we equate with citizens of voting age.

Given our concern throughout with the role of institutions, a relevant question is whether convergence in some aspects of citizenship law has led to cross-national equivalence in the degree to which members of immigrant populations possess citizenship and the political rights that typically go along with it, including voting and the ability to run for office. It has not. Although in all countries under study, as table 7.2 reveals, there are gaps between immigrant-origin groups' shares of the population and of the electorate, the size of these gaps varies by country.

The contrast between France and Germany in the table illustrates the electoral impact of different citizenship regimes. In France, our focus on non-Western groups, many of whom originated in former colonies, excludes insofar as possible European colonials who migrated to France when the colonies where they were living achieved independence.[25] It hardly needs to be said that the political incorporation of the two populations has been very different. The best available data (from the 2008 survey *Trajectoires et Origines*) possibly overstates somewhat the minority percentages in the population and electorate (because the data, restricted to individuals between the ages of eighteen and sixty, do not include the elderly, who are less likely to have an immigrant background).[26] Still, owing to the relatively easy access to French citizenship, especially for the second generation, the population and electorate percentages of

Table 7.2. Electorate and Population Data for Immigrant-Origin Groups[1]

	Population percentage	Electorate percentage[2]
Canada (visible minorities), 2011 *Source:* Census	19.1%	No data
France (non-western immigrants and their children), 2010 *Source:* our calculations from Beauchemin et al. (2010), ages 18–60	~10.8%	~8.2%
Germany (non-western immigrants and their children),[3] 2009 *Source:* Statistisches Bundesamt (2010)	5.8%	~1.6%
Great Britain (England and Wales here) (nonwhites, including mixed), 2011 *Source:* Office for National Statistics; Heath (2013)	14.0%	~12%
Netherlands (non-Western origins), 2006 *Source:* Statline (2014); Dekker (2006)	10.5%	8.9%
US (Hispanics), 2010–12 *Source:* 2010 Census, Pew Hispanic Center (2012)	16.3%	11.7%

Notes: ~ indicates an approximate estimate.

[1] "Immigrant origin" includes first and subsequent generations wherever possible.

[2] Percent of minority citizens in the voting age population.

[3] Persons originating in the Asian parts of the former Soviet Union are not included here because they mostly have come as part of the "ethnic" German migrations and received special treatment (for example, immediate citizenship).

the non-Western groups are not very different (approximately 10.8 percent versus 8.2). This strongly contrasts with the picture in Germany. Non-Western groups (including the Turks) form about 6 percent of the German population, but their weight in the electorate is much smaller because of Germany's history of restrictive citizenship.[27]

In the Netherlands, the population and electorate percentages of the non-Western groups, among whom Turks, Moroccans, Surinamese, and Antilleans stand out, are more closely aligned than in neighboring Germany. The main immigrant populations are of long residence, and many have therefore naturalized (or, as ex-colonials, brought Dutch citizenship with them). The Netherlands is the one country where these groups can form different portions of the electorate in local as compared to national elections. Since 1985 immigrants with five years of residence have the right to vote in local elections; the right to vote in national ones remains reserved for Dutch citizens.

In Great Britain, electoral studies have typically focused on nonwhites, a population overwhelmingly derived from colonial and postcolonial immigration, especially from the Caribbean (namely West Indians) and the South Asian subcontinent (namely Bangladeshis, Indians, and Pakistanis). According to the 2011 Census, these groups form about 14 percent of the population (this figure includes individuals describing themselves as "mixed," on the presumption that most racially mixed individuals would be socially perceived as nonwhite). Since most members of nonwhite groups have had the right to vote on arrival as immigrants from Commonwealth countries, they form a percentage of the electorate almost as large as their percentage of the total population. In Canada, the relevant groups are also defined racially, as "visible minorities," and make up an even larger percentage of the population, almost one-fifth. Oddly, however, data on their percentage of the Canadian electorate are not easily available. Since Canada has the shortest residence requirement before immigrants can naturalize and also, supported by its multicultural logic, employs proactive policies to encourage them to do so, we suspect that minority voting and population shares are closely aligned there, too.[28]

In the United States, our choice is constrained by the complexity of the origins of the nonwhite population, with its large African American component, mainly not of immigrant origins, and by the available studies. The best record of electoral outcomes exists for Hispanic groups, who form a large part, almost half, of the U.S. foreign born. However, the situation is complicated by the fact that some Hispanic families have lived in the United States for a century or more, and one of the important groups, Puerto Ricans, is not an immigrant group in the strict sense of the term. (Island-born Puerto Ricans are U.S. citizens at birth.) Nevertheless, the great majority of contemporary Hispanics are immigrants or descended from immigrants who have entered the United States since 1950. The group therefore seems a suitable choice for examining electoral outcomes.

The sizable gap between population and electoral shares in the case of Hispanics is partly attributable to the large undocumented immigrant population, which is ineligible to apply for naturalization and concentrated among Latin Americans. In addition, the naturalization rate of documented Hispanic immigrants is relatively low, compared to other immigrant groups such as those from Asia, possibly because of the proximity of their homelands and the ease of return.[29]

ELECTORAL SUCCESS AT THE LOCAL AND REGIONAL LEVEL

Electoral success may be the gold standard, but immigrant-origin groups generally have had a hard time achieving it in mainstream elective bodies. Nowhere does their electoral representation at the local and regional levels approach the proportion of immigrant minorities in the population, especially when the second generation is taken into account, although it varies across the six national settings we consider. However, the variations are not as great as they were the first time we examined this topic at the very start of the twenty-first century. That is, immigrant minorities are generally making significant progress in achieving representation on elected bodies. For instance, in France, the percentage of politicians with non-European origins elected to municipal councils more than doubled between 2001 and 2008, going from 3.2 percent of all councilors to 6.7 percent. In Germany, an almost equivalent rise happened in the same period, as the total number of councilors with any sort of immigrant background rose from 114 to 190.[30]

Our data (see table 7.3), we admit, are less than ideal for comparative purposes because of our dependence on existing studies, which are sometimes for city councils, sometimes for regional bodies (state legislatures in the United States, *Landtage* in Germany), and in some cases for both. Moreover, most of the studies are limited to cities of a certain size or cities or regions of high immigrant concentration, such as the eleven-city study in Canada. In such cases, the data on the national electorate (in table 7.2) understate the percentage of immigrant minorities in the local population that elects these representatives. We have also chosen to present the data for selected major cities, such as Amsterdam, where immigrant minorities make up a large part of the population, in order to give a sense of their representation in places where they are most concentrated.

In the past, Germany, one country for which we have both city and regional data,[31] has presented arguably the worst record of immigrant-group electoral success among our cases at the subnational level. It still appears to hold down the bottom, but not by nearly as much as only a few years before.[32] In 2011 just 2.8 percent of the members of various *Landtage* had any sort of immigration background (European included), compared to a population percentage about 7 times as high (19.1 percent of Germany's population belongs to the first and second generations; see tables 2.1 and 2.2).[33] The figure was 2.4 percent for non-Western minorities on the city councils of large cities (excluding Berlin, Hamburg, and Hannover, all of which are also federal states), where immigrant groups are more concentrated. The non-Western representation on the city councils is on the order of a quarter of the non-Western population share. (This fraction depends on our rough estimate of 9 to 10 percent as the percentage of these cities' populations with non-Western origins.) Viewed against the backdrop of Germany's history of restrictive citizenship laws and their impact on the electorate, the underrepresentation may not seem so extreme.

The number of immigrant-origin politicians tends to be small even in German cities with very high immigrant concentrations. The largest contingent of city councilors of foreign origin (Western backgrounds also included) is in Frankfurt, making up 16 percent of the council. Few other cities have

Table 7.3. Immigrant-Group Representation on Regional and Local Legislatures, 2000–10

Canada (visible minorities)		
Elected public officials, 11 major cities, 2001–14	8.7%	
Source: Andrew et al. (2008)	(N=552 officials)	
Elected public officials, 3 gateway cities, 2001–14	12.3%	
Source: Andrew et al. (2008)	(N=unknown)	
France (non-Western groups)[1]		
Municipal councils, after 2008 elections, cities and towns with more than 9000 inhabitants	6.7% (N=33649)	
Source: Amadieu (n.d.)		
Municipal councils, Ile-de-France (including Paris), 2008	10.8%	
Source: Amadieu (n.d.)	(N=9519)	
Regional councils, 2010	5.3%	
Source: Keslassy (2010)	(N=1722)	
Germany		
Landtage (state parliaments), 2011 (all immigrant backgrounds)	2.8%	
Source: Schönwälder (2013)	(N=1860)	
City councils, 2011 (non-Western backgrounds), 77 large cities (population > 100,000)[2]	2.4% (N=4670)	
Source: Schönwälder et al. (2011)		
Great Britain (England) (nonwhites)		
Local councils, 2008	3.4%	
Source: Local Government Association (2008)	(N=18809)	
London boroughs, 2008	15.9%	
Source: Local Government Association (2008)	(N=790)	
Netherlands (non-Western immigrant backgrounds)		
Councils of all cities, 2006	3.2%	
Source: IPP (2006)	(N= 9558)	
Councils of four largest cities, 2006	20.6%	
Source: IPP (2006)	(N=261)	
Amsterdam, 2010 (all councilors with foreign origins)	16.0%	
Source: Vermeulen, Michon, and Tillie (2014)	(N=45)	
US (Hispanics)		
State senates (upper houses), 2010	3.4%	
Source: NALEO (2012)	(N=1972)	
State assemblies (lower houses), 2010	3.5%	
Source: NALEO (2012)	(N=5411)	
State senates, nine states with high Hispanic concentrations, 2010	14.0%	
Source: NALEO (2012)	(N=378)	
State assemblies, nine states with high Hispanic concentrations, 2010	14.7%	
Source: NALEO (2012)	(N=893)	

[1] Data at regional level for "visible minorities," including some French from outside metropolitan France.

[2] Berlin, Hamburg, and Hannover are not included because they are also German states (*Länder*).

substantial-sized groups of non-German councilors. There are also a number of cities with large immigrant-origin populations that have no councilors of immigrant origin at all. This is true of Mannheim, for example, a moderate-sized industrial city (with approximately three hundred thousand inhabitants) in Baden-Württemberg, even though nearly 40 percent of its population has immigrant origins.[34] One account, based on interviews with immigrant-origin parliamentarians in Germany, found that these politicians are so rare in German legislative bodies that they have tended to be treated as outsiders by their colleagues and be seen as representing the interests of foreigners rather than Germans.[35]

France has also been identified as a country where immigrant minorities, especially groups from former colonies like the Maghrebins from North Africa, have had difficulty in attaining electoral success at the local level. The lack of immigrant political representation has been cited as a factor behind the 2005 riots of second-generation youth in the *banlieues*. However, in the aggregate, the French situation appears more favorable to minority politicians than many accounts suggest. A survey of cities and towns with more than nine thousand inhabitants undertaken on behalf of the Haut Conseil à l'Intégration (High Council for Integration) found that non-European representation on municipal councils was nearly 7 percent, almost two-thirds of the population share for non-European groups in France as a whole (see tables 7.2 and 7.3). This is the highest fraction of representation in our results, and the electoral presence of these groups has more than doubled in less than a decade. In regional councils, the non-Western immigrant groups achieved a somewhat lower level of representation, 5 percent.[36]

Where French immigrant minorities appear to face the greatest barriers is in the large cities. Certainly, studies of Marseille and Paris, the two largest cities in France, point in this direction. One study of Marseille that focused on Muslim politicians in the 1990s found very limited representation. This is striking in a city that is home to very large immigrant populations and has developed a political culture that, in deviation from French Republican norms, has been "*communitairiste*" (giving explicit political and policy recognition to immigrant and ethnic communities).[37] Probably because of this politics, Marseille was widely noted as the one place in France that remained peaceful during the 2005 riots. Yet immigrant-origin representation in Marseille is no different from what it is on average in French cities. The same holds for Paris, where in 2008 only 5 percent of councilors had a non-European origin.[38] Representation appears stronger when the region around Paris is included, since it includes many suburbs with extremely high immigrant concentrations: in Île-de-France as a whole, more than 10 percent of municipal councilors came from non-Western backgrounds. Since, however, the Paris region is home to about 40 percent of the immigrant population of France, this figure still indicates a substantial underrepresentation.

The data presented in table 7.3 for Canada appear similar to that for France. When we look at the broadest geography for which data are available—an eleven-city study[39]—the representation of visible minorities among city elected officials is relatively high at nearly 9 percent, more than half of the proportion of minorities in the national population. However, in the three cities—Montreal, Toronto, and Vancouver—where immigrants have their highest concentrations, the picture is less favorable. Visible minorities are only 12 percent of the municipal officials and are underrepresented on the order of more than three-to-one. This degree of underrepresentation is surprising in light of Canada's proactive citizenship stance, and it is not uniform across the three cities. The underrepresentation is starkest in Montreal, about six- or seven-to-one and least in Vancouver, about two-to-one. Still, in all three cities the political influence of visible minorities is not commensurate with their weight in the cities' population: in 2008 in Toronto, for instance, they were just 11 percent of elected officials, though they formed more than 40 percent of Toronto's population.

Relative to the sizes of immigrant groups in their populations, Great Britain and the Netherlands appear to have even lower aggregate rates of immigrant-group representation on city councils than Canada or France do. For instance, the 3.2 percent of Dutch city councilors who in 2006 belonged to visible immigrant minorities (see table 7.3) is quite low compared to the minority percentage of the Dutch population, especially given the access to local voting by noncitizen immigrants. However, the aggregate national figures fail to capture the extent to which immigrant minorities in Britain and the Netherlands have been able to win office in cities with large immigrant concentrations, in contrast to the situation in Canada or France. Since immigrant-origin populations are concentrated geographically in all these countries, this may be the more relevant test. In London, 16 percent of the local councilors in 2008 were non-white minorities at a time when about four in ten Londoners were nonwhite. In the Netherlands as of 2006, councilors from immigrant backgrounds were 20 percent of Amsterdam's council, below the 35 percent of ethnic minorities in the city's population, but still a sizable proportion. Immigrant minorities have achieved high levels of representation on the councils of several other large cities, such as Rotterdam, the second largest Dutch city. Mayors in Dutch cities are appointed, not elected, yet it is noteworthy that Moroccan-born Ahmed Aboutaleb became mayor of Rotterdam in 2008—the first mayor in the Netherlands born outside the country (he holds dual citizenship) and the first Muslim mayor. Despite these favorable indicators of incorporation, however, the local political representation of immigrant minorities was heading downward as of 2010 in Amsterdam.[40]

The U.S. data refer to regional legislatures, that is, those of the fifty states; to our knowledge, no systematic data are available for the city level, where we would expect electoral representation to be greater than at the regional level.[41]

Relative to the minority share of the population, the electoral representation of Hispanics is superior to that of minorities in Germany but inferior to that of minorities in France. At 3 to 4 percent of the aggregate membership of state legislatures, it is about one-fifth of what one would expect if population proportion were the sole determinant. An important factor contributing to this discrepancy is undoubtedly the citizenship gap for Latin American immigrants. Nevertheless, the Latino electorate is growing rapidly because of the maturation of the youthful second generation and is expected to account for 40 percent of the total growth of the U.S. electorate between 2012 and 2030.[42]

Hispanics, though spreading to new destination areas, are not distributed uniformly through the fifty U.S. states. The nine states with the largest Hispanic populations, have a much more sizable presence of Hispanic politicians in state legislatures: in 2010, an average of 14 to 15 percent of their lower and upper houses. Since Hispanics then constituted 30 percent of these states' populations, the ratio of their electoral representation to their population share had risen to almost one half.

The situation in the major gateway cities of the United States is less clear-cut because of the lack of systematic data. Nevertheless, Hispanics have begun to gain political office in many of them. In 2005 three of the mayors in the nation's top ten gateway central cities were Hispanic; in another three cities, the main challenger in the prior mayoral election was Hispanic. For example, in the "mega-gateway" of Los Angeles, the mayor at the time, Antonio Villaraigosa, was Mexican American, and his successor, Eric Garcetti, is of partial Mexican descent. In another major U.S. city, Miami, one immigrant group, Cubans, has attained a degree of political clout that is unmatched, to our knowledge, among all the major cities in the six countries under study—by the end of the twentieth century, six of the thirteen Miami-Dade commissioners were Cuban Americans as was the mayor. One sees the impact in the Miami-Dade school system, for example, where all students, including native English speakers, are encouraged to become bilingual.[43] However, in New York City in 2009, when the foreign born and their adult children made up almost half of voting-age citizens, only nine of the fifty-one-member City Council (18 percent) belonged to the immigrant or second generation (they included three West Indians, four Dominicans, and two Chinese).[44]

In all six countries in our study, then, immigrant-origin minorities are underrepresented in city councils and regional legislatures, although there are signs of improvement for countries like France and Germany, where political representation was slight before. (In the Netherlands, by contrast, where the record of political representation has been a strong one, some signs point downward as of the end of the first decade of the twenty-first century.) At the same time, differences in immigrant minority electoral success still stand out when we narrow our focus to cities and regions where immigrant groups have concentrated. National electoral data dilute the political impact of these groups because such data include many areas where the immigrant presence is virtually nil. But we might hope to see minorities achieve substantial political influence in those areas where their presence is large. Again, nowhere do they achieve a representation proportionate to their numbers, but the discrepancy between the two varies and seems greatest in Germany with the gap also substantial in Canada and France.

NATIONAL LEGISLATURES

If immigrant minorities have had difficulties entering the precincts of power at the local and regional levels, these difficulties are compounded at the national level. Constituencies for election to national legislatures are usually much larger than those at the local level and therefore coethnic voters' support for an immigrant-origin politician carries less electoral weight—though in systems where legislators are elected through party lists, such as the Dutch one, this disadvantage may be offset by the ability of parties to include politicians with immigrant backgrounds on the lists in order to attract these voters. In addition, there is the issue of substantive representation: will mainstream voters see a minority politician as capable of representing them? Many times, the answer seems to be no.

The representation of immigrant minorities in lower houses of national legislatures, whose members are directly elected (not always the case for upper houses), is well below their population proportions (see table 7.4), with one notable exception: in the Netherlands, the non-Western immigrant minorities have achieved a presence in the Second Chamber of Parliament (Tweede Kamer) very close to their population share. Elsewhere, however, the representation gap—between the proportion of immigrant-origin groups in the national population and in national legislative bodies—tends to be large, varying from the roughly eight-to-one disproportion in the French National Assembly to the two-to-one disparity in the Canadian Parliament. In Germany, Great Britain, and the United States, the representation gap is on the order of three-to-one. (In the German case, the figure 5.6 percent appearing in table 7.4 counts Bundestag members with any immigration background and must therefore be compared with its equivalent for the population, 19.1 percent.)

France stands out for presenting immigrant-origin politicians with especially marked difficulties in gaining access to higher levels of the political system, the tiers at which power is concentrated. Even though the presence of these politicians in the National Assembly is quite low, it represents an improvement over the very recent past, since in 2007 this legislative body contained not a single member of Maghrebin background. The National Assembly is elected from single-member constituencies, a system like that in Great Britain and the United States, where many immigrant-origin politicians have been

Table 7.4. Immigrant-Group Representation on National Legislatures, ca. 2010

Canada (visible minorities)		
House of Commons, 2011	9.4%	
Source: Crawford (2011)	(N=308)	
France (non-Western immigrant backgrounds)		
National Assembly, 2012	1.3%	
Source: Tiberj and Michon (2013)	(N=555)	
Germany (all immigrant backgrounds)		
Bundestag, 2013	5.6%	
Source: Migazin (2013)	(N=622)	
Great Britain (nonwhites)		
House of Commons, 2010	4.2%	
Source: House of Commons FAQs, Sobolewska (2013)	(N=650)	
Netherlands (non-Western immigrant backgrounds)		
Second Chamber, Dutch Parliament, 2006–10	10.0%	
Source: Michon (2012)	(N= 150)	
US (Hispanics)		
House of Representatives, 2010	5.5%	
Source: NALEO (2013)	(N=435)	

successful. However, in France, the political parties, which have control over candidacies, operate in a more top-down manner, and this appears to restrict the opportunities for minority candidates to effectively compete. Moreover, the Republican model of incorporation, strongly supported by the French political elite, challenges any notion that minorities have special interests that are best represented by politicians from the same backgrounds.[45]

The figure for Germany represents a very recent surge in electoral success for politicians with immigrant origins. Although, at the national level, the representation gap appears to be in line with that in some other countries such as the United States, the Bundestag contingent of immigrant-origin politicians was much smaller in the beginning years of the twenty-first century. The Turks, Germany's largest ethnic minority at 3.1 percent of the population, are the group for which the change has been most rapid. The Bundestag elected in 2013 had eleven parliamentarians of Turkish origin, a large increase from the previous Bundestag, in which there were just five. That small group was itself a substantial advance from the preceding Bundestag of 2005–9, in which there were just two. Germany can boast, in addition, that Cem Özdemir, a German politician of second-generation Turkish background, became co-chair of a major national party (the Greens) in 2008. Despite this rapid political advance, the Turks account for a mere 1.7 percent of Bundestag members, hardly a basis for much influence on that body. A representation gap remains, testifying to how rare the electoral successes of Turkish-origin candidates have been in the very recent past. However, the growing share of the Turkish group with German citizenship, an inevitable consequence of the switch to a *jus soli* system, will likely shrink the gap further. The representation gap for other immigrant-origin groups remains more sizable at this point.[46]

For the three English-speaking countries, the range of underrepresentation for immigrant-origin groups is relatively narrow, but nevertheless substantial, with Canada achieving much greater representation of immigrant-minority politicians than either Great Britain or the United States. (It is curious, and we have no explanation for the finding, that the representation of visible minorities in the national Canadian Parliament, in relation to the minority percentage of the population, seems superior to that among elected officials in the three major gateway cities.) Citizenship and voting rights are a big part of the story. Canada, as Bloemraad has shown, has been more proactive, and more successful, in encouraging citizenship among immigrants than the United States has.[47] In the United States, an enormous barrier has been the high percentage of Latin Americans who are undocumented and therefore not eligible to begin the process ending in naturalization. In Britain, the voting strength of immigrant-origin minorities does not depend so much on naturalization but on the fact that a large portion of the immigrant-origin population has come from Commonwealth countries and so has been eligible to vote upon arrival.

The generally low levels of immigrant-minority representation in national legislatures revealed in the data thus indicate, not surprisingly, that it is more difficult for outsiders to gain access to positions at the top of the political hierarchy—where power is more concentrated—than at the bottom. But the lack of uniformity in the degree of underrepresentation points to the significance of nationally specific factors in translating demographic presence into political representation.

HOW CAN THE DIFFERENCES BE EXPLAINED?

What accounts for the differences in representation among the six countries at both the national and local levels? There is no simple explanation. Certainly, social and political institutions in each society, often conceptualized as political opportunity structures, play a large role, as we have already suggested. These include citizenship and voting laws as well as the nature of the electoral system and the part that political parties play in it. At the same time, the opportunities for immigrant minorities to attain electoral office are affected by particular national integration models or discourses. These integration models can make the native majority more-or-less amenable to minority-group mobilization efforts and thus have an effect on immigrant minorities' abilities to forge successful careers in politics.

There is also a place for group-specific factors, such as a group's social cohesion, broadly construed. Groups that are more cohesive in the sense that they possess well-developed organizational infrastructures, as well as identities and group consciousness that are salient for their members, are more likely to do well in the electoral realm. The Turks in the Netherlands, in comparison with Moroccans, are an example. Moreover, residential segregation, which is usually associated with disadvantaged living situations, can be an advantage when it comes to electoral success. In addition to social capital, some degree of human capital—a significant part of the group holding professional credentials—contributes to political success by supplying a pool from which viable candidates can be recruited.[48]

To tick off the principal factors on the institutional side, there is the basic ability to vote: immigrant-origin politicians typically depend heavily on support from coethnics in order to gain office and thus their chances are far better when immigrant minorities can take part in elections in large numbers. Because members of the majority are reluctant to surrender power—especially to groups that are seen as outside the mainstream—minority politicians rarely gain widespread support in the majority population. (This point highlights the extraordinary accomplishment of the Obama campaign of 2008, since he initially vaulted to the front of the pack of politicians competing for the Democratic nomination for president based on his success in a heavily white state, Iowa, and won the election with substantial support from white Americans.)

Voting rights are largely, but not entirely, a matter of citizenship law. EU citizens have been guaranteed local voting rights when they migrate to another EU country; and, as we have already noted, the Netherlands has extended these rights to all foreigners with at least five years of residence, which explains why non-European immigrant minorities there have attained a considerable degree of local representation in the major cities. Citizenship law, it should be noted, often does not treat all immigrants equally, but bestows citizenship more readily on those with favored origins. "Favored" could mean a presumption of ethnic similarity to the mainstream society, as is evidenced, for example, in the immediate awarding of German citizenship to ethnic German immigrants. Or it could reflect old ties of empire, which are involved in the liberal British award of immediate and full voting rights to immigrants from colonies or former colonies in the Commonwealth. The considerable electoral success of ethnic minorities in Britain in cities of high immigrant concentration, especially in London, has much to do with this fundamental fact.

The nature of the electoral system also plays a prominent role in the electoral results we have analyzed. Systems involving party lists, as are found in France (at the local level), Germany (at the subnational level and partly at the national one), and the Netherlands, hold a double-edged significance for immigrant-group electoral success. On the one hand, such systems offer advantages because political parties can include some immigrant minorities on their lists without alienating mainstream voters. On the other, these systems place the power to promote or constrain minority candidates in the hands of the parties, making political hopefuls' fate dependent on the decisions of party leaders and selection committees. A consistent finding, for example, is that elected minority candidates come largely from the parties of the left (as in France); apparently, the more conservative parties see little incentive in promoting the success of minority candidates (though this reluctance is weakening in Great Britain and Germany). And, as in France and the Netherlands, placement on the party list can be an issue, since the lower a candidate's position on the list, the less the chance of being elected. A further complication in the Dutch case is the ability to cast preferential votes, which can help ethnic minority candidates. Even though the party decides on the order of candidates on its list, voters can select a listed candidate who can independently earn a seat by getting enough votes. Consequently, minority candidates who are placed in seemingly hopeless, or low, positions on electoral lists might still win if a critical mass of ethnic voters mobilizes for their election.[49]

First-past-the-post systems (with single-member districts, where voters can cast one vote each and the candidate with the most votes wins), such as are found in Britain, Canada, and the United States (along with France for election to the Assemblée Nationale and Germany for election to half of the Bundestag seats) likewise hold a double-edged significance for minority electoral success. Because members of the majority often will not vote for an immigrant-minority candidate, majority politicians have an advantage in demographically mixed districts and frequently can hold onto their seats even as the population in their districts shifts in the direction of a greater minority share. Yet first-past-the-post systems can facilitate change "from below" by allowing immigrant candidates to challenge native ones in electoral districts with heavy immigrant representation. There may even be a "contagion effect" in heavily ethnic minority areas; if one party selects an ethnic minority candidate in a constituency, other parties may feel pressure to name ethnic candidates as well. The downside is that immigrant electoral success depends on residential concentration of ethnic minority voters that coincides with constituency boundaries—in other words, on residential segregation. As has been observed for Britain, relatively few ethnic minorities are selected as candidates outside of areas with sizable minority communities.[50]

In the United States, two legal aspects of electoral districting may play a role in minority representation. Because electoral districts are based on resident population (as required by the U.S. Constitution), not numbers of voters, this may be an advantage for large immigrant minorities who heavily occupy a district despite low citizenship rates. Also the Voting Rights Act of 1965, though recently stripped of its teeth by a Supreme Court ruling, has helped stimulate the creation of some electoral districts where immigrant minorities are at least competitive, as in the carving out of city council districts for West Indians and

Dominicans in New York City. Another factor affecting Hispanic representation is the long-time presence of Mexicans and Puerto Ricans in the United States; Hispanics had achieved some political voice even before the latest waves of immigration greatly increased their numbers.[51]

The structure of the party system, particularly as it shapes candidate recruitment and the selection process, is also involved in the electoral success of immigrant minorities. In Britain, the ward-based system of local candidate selection in the Labour Party, Romain Garbaye contends, reinforces the advantages of the single-member district system in the context of high ethnic-minority concentration. It has allowed minorities to get a foot in the door by giving the ward-level party organization the ability to designate candidates. In addition, procedures exist to appeal to higher levels of the party in case of conflict over the choice of candidates. By contrast, the party system in major French cities—Garbaye presents Lille as representative of a large number of medium-range and large French cities—tends to be "top down," partly because prominent politicians are allowed to accumulate elected positions (the so-called *cumul des mandats*), serving simultaneously in national and local offices. Consequently, they have a great deal of influence over local party decisions. In Lille, selection of candidates by the dominant Socialist Party usually has been made consensually in favor of local notables or incumbents, thereby reinforcing a feeling of powerlessness and inaccessibility for outsiders. A revealing story concerns a successful Maghrebin politician in Marseille—during the late 1990s the only Maghrebin on the city council—who in 2001 was forced off the party list of candidates at the direction of national Socialist headquarters, although after vigorous local protest, she was placed back on in a lower position.[52]

Then there is the role of national political ideologies or integration models, which have their roots in particular national traditions. Admittedly, such models are often more a matter of political rhetoric than actual on-the-ground practices, but this is not the whole story. Integration models or philosophies can influence political opportunities in a number of ways. The countries that seem to have provided the most scope for immigrant-origin politicians in mainstream offices (when local, regional, and national positions are considered)—Britain, Canada, Netherlands, and the United States—have been the most willing to acknowledge immigrants as ethnic minorities with distinct needs and cultural rights, even if this recognition is now often contested in the Netherlands. Perhaps most notably in the United States, this recognition has played a role in the acceptance of ethnicity as a basis for political claims and campaigns. In general, migrants and minorities may "have greater access to the political system where . . . their organizations [are] facilitated, and where their claims can refer to existing legal frameworks for equal opportunity, anti-discrimination, and cultural rights."[53]

In the Netherlands, for example, the granting of local voting rights to foreign residents in the mid-1980s was an extension of minority policies promoting equality before the law and deriving from the notion that individuals should not be disadvantaged by foreign citizenship. Just how multicultural the Netherlands was, and for how long, are topics of contention. In the early 1980s, building on the legacy of pillarization, policies emphasized group empowerment and "integration with the maintenance of cultural identity," but this emphasis, according to one line of thought, soon faded. The backlash against multicultural ideals during the 1990s, Floris Vermeulen and his colleagues argue, helps explain the decline in the number of immigrant-origin city councilors in Amsterdam between 2006 and 2010. Whereas candidate selection committees had previously given priority to including more immigrants on party lists, with the shift away from multicultural elements of policies of the 1980s and greater suspicion of group-based politics, this was no longer the case.[54]

In Britain, Canada, and the United States, state models of multiculturalism or ethnic pluralism have reinforced the effects of the electoral, political, and party systems in providing scope for ethnic minority candidates. Whether Britain's multicultural policies in the late twentieth century (along with extensive and progressive race relations legislation) were a product, as Christian Joppke suggests, of Britain's historical model of pluralism in dealing with empire and various ethnicities within Britain or, as Adrian Favell contends, of the long-held British conception that the individual should be protected from the state, the fact is that these policies helped foster political mobilization along ethnoracial lines and legitimated ethnic minority claims to political office. In the United States, urban ethnic politics has a longstanding legitimacy, dating back to the nineteenth century when the Irish were able to infiltrate and take over the helm of big-city Democratic politics by mobilizing the "ethnic" vote. The efforts of today's Latino or Asian politicians to gain local office by wooing coethnic voters are viewed as a fully acceptable, even normal, path to political influence. Successful attempts by African Americans to win office in the wake of the civil rights movement have also provided a model for immigrant-origin politicians to follow. In post–civil rights America, it has become widely accepted that ethnoracial minorities, especially blacks and Latinos, who together make up more than a quarter of the nation's population, should be represented in important political bodies.[55]

In contrast, the ways in which France and Germany have defined immigrants, and their integration into the state, have hindered ethnic minorities' ability to gain elected office. Germany held onto the guestworker model for much of the postwar period and insisted it was not a country of immigration— what one journalist refers to as the "you're a guestworker, so you'll be going home" model. Consequently, German politicians have tended to view their immigrant-origin colleagues in terms of their original nationalities and to question their ability to represent German constituencies.[56] France, with its strong assimilationist principles, does not officially recognize ethnic groups and has been loath to accept group-specific approaches, which may be an added barrier that immigrant-origin groups face in gaining access to the mainstream through political office. Indeed, Republican principles have provided a basis for objecting to the very notion that immigrant-origin politicians are needed in order to include the views and interests of these constituencies, although the increasing prevalence of a new symbolic language of diversity in France, in which political parties are obliged to declare that they promote diversity as a moral and political imperative, may be shifting the ideological terrain.[57]

When it comes to the interaction of specific immigrant groups and their characteristics with the political system, the story is also not straightforward. Bloemraad has argued in fact that "we might need distinct models of political integration and representation for different sorts of immigrant-origin groups."[58] A key distinction, in terms of ideal types, is between groups whose members seek individual "assimilation into politics" and others that envision "group-based political incorporation." Groups whose experiences better fit a "minority" model—in that they have suffered significant discrimination, social exclusion, and socioeconomic disadvantage—may ironically be better poised for electoral success. To be sure, this is a matter of degree. Even among groups that are alike in terms of minority experiences, some may be more predisposed to collective strategies of advancement, as has been argued for the Turks,[59] and this may be helpful for their electoral success. In similar fashion, groups with a rich organizational life are better able to nurture aspiring politicians, who can gain vital early experience in the institutions of the ethnic community. Yet much still depends on the political system, for the Turks were rather quick to gain elected positions in the Netherlands, in contrast to their slow and still limited ascent in Germany.

CONCLUSION

When they move to a new land immigrants settle into neighborhoods, send their children to school, and join the workforce, but there is no such inevitability about members of their group obtaining elected office. Indeed, this development is generally resisted by a significant portion of the majority, which is reluctant to give up power to groups that are defined by many as standing outside the mainstream, as not belonging to "us" who are the "nation." For immigrant minorities, gaining political office is about acquiring influence and power as well as prestige and recognition. It is a major—even arguably the ultimate—indicator of integration.

Our comparative look at the success of immigrant-origin politicians in winning elective office, though limited of necessity by available studies, provides no simple or monolithic convergence or divergence story. Reality is complicated, as the positions of France and Germany at the low end of immigrant-group political success reveal. For some time, these two countries have stood for opposing models of incorporation, one civic, the other ethno-cultural,[60] which continue to matter and, paradoxically, help to explain their similar results. More generally, the review of the data on electoral representation for our six countries shows that substantial differences remain among them despite some trends toward convergence. One question is whether the differences are likely to erode further in the near future.

One certainly can support convergence with our results insofar as we have found immigrant minorities to be making progress in achieving greater political representation, and this seems especially true in France (at the subnational level) and Germany (at the national one). Partly it is a matter of sheer numbers of potential voters, especially as a growing second generation comes of age, in Germany under changed citizenship rules. Along with political parties' desire to attract the ethnic minority vote, there are also growing pressures from below as immigrant-origin activists push for more and better positions in a variety of ways, including informal lobbying, grass-roots mobilization, and formal organization within political parties.[61] It could also be argued that increasing convergence with regard to citizenship will soon undercut key national differences that emerged in our study. The case of Germany stands out in large part because of the barriers posed by its citizenship laws through the mid-1990s. Since 2000 *jus soli* citizenship has been granted to second-generation children, but will Germany's electoral pattern increasingly converge with those in the other democracies? We think it might, but a conclusion is not justified as yet. The 2013 national elections showed positive signs of change, with the number of Turkish German lawmakers in the Bundestag doubling, and the first two blacks elected, one a Senegalese immigrant and the other born in Munich to a Senegalese mother and German father.[62] At the other end of the spectrum, the Netherlands has promoted an unusual degree of immigrant electoral success by granting the right to vote in local elections to resident immigrants since 1985. It is not apparent to us that other countries will emulate it in the near future.

The case of France, which has a *jus soli* citizenship regime for the second generation, demonstrates that other factors besides citizenship law, an area of convergence, are also in play when it comes to immigrant electoral success. The political weight of immigrant-origin minorities in cities and regions where their concentration is dense remains quite modest; and it is almost nonexistent in the national legislature. In France, both the model of integration preferred by the political elite—Republicanism—and the standard practices of the party system seem to have worked against immigrant representation in elected bodies. The Republican model has made it difficult for political actors to deliberately sponsor the careers of immigrant-origin politicians as a way of diversifying the political elite, as is shown by the uproar that greeted Jacques Chirac's appointment of Algerian-born Aïssa Dermouche as the only Muslim prefect (out of more than one hundred) in 2004.[63] Change is taking place, however: since Nicholas Sarkozy appointed an immigrant-origin Muslim to a cabinet position in 2007, the appearance of immigrant-origin politicians in French cabinets has become de rigueur. All French political parties now regularly nominate candidates in national and local elections who are labeled "candidates of diversity," and it seems likely that in the future the parties will field even more ethnic minority candidates in districts with large ethnic minority populations.[64]

In short, national differences still matter, and they are likely to continue to matter, when it comes to immigrant minorities' ability to enter the precincts of power in Western Europe and North America. Yet we do think that, over the course of the next several decades, the political significance of immigrant-origin minorities is bound to increase as a result of demographic shifts in all of the Western countries. Perhaps the United States, which has the most ethnoracially diverse population in North America and Western Europe, is the beacon showing the way to the future. Not only is it the first country to elect a non-white leader, but Barack Obama's reelection in 2012 suggests that, for the first time in the nation's history, whites by themselves are no longer in control of the national political destiny. Minority votes, including importantly the votes of Asians and Hispanics, immigrant-origin groups, determined the 2012 outcome; and the rapid growth of the Hispanic second generation promises that the electoral weight of Hispanics will continue to increase in the nation as a whole and in the states where they are concentrated. In the aftermath of Obama's second victory, the Republican Party is debating its future electoral strategies and whether it must find ways to reach out to Hispanic and other minority voters or can continue to rely almost exclusively on white support. The choice may appear meaningful in the short term, but in the long term it is not. Immigrant-driven demographic change will render a "whites-only" strategy untenable.

CHAPTER 8

EDUCATING THE SECOND GENERATION

If wealthy societies are to benefit fully from the talents brought by recent waves of immigrants, then their schools must face up to the challenges of integrating the second generation. These challenges are especially acute for the children growing up in low-status immigrant families, in which parents often have limited educations, acquired moreover in another society, and work at low-skill jobs. The families are typically unable to provide much guidance or assistance to their children in school. To be sure, not all children from immigrant homes face high educational hurdles: the children from professional or entrepreneurial immigrant families often excel in school, sometimes outperforming the best students from native families.[1] However, as we have seen, the labor forces in North America and Western Europe will depend on the futures of children from low-status immigrant backgrounds, too.

Integrating these children through schooling is complicated by a tension fundamental to the educational mission. On the one hand, educational systems are in the business of sorting among students and providing them with an education appropriate to their adult lives, one that equips them for positions they are likely to occupy in unequal societies. Hence, educational systems play a major role in generating, indeed perpetuating, inequalities in a new generation. All studies show that educational outcomes reflect social origins to a greater or lesser extent. Not surprisingly, schools tend to reproduce inequalities, at least in the aggregate, between native and immigrant-origin students.

On the other hand, educational systems are charged with providing opportunities for advancement, especially for children from disadvantaged backgrounds. This aspect of their mission is obviously relevant to children from low-status immigrant families. In the most rudimentary sense, all the school systems in wealthy societies of the West provide such opportunities: it is common for members of the second generation to make an educational leap beyond their parents, if only because they are growing up in societies where the legally mandated period of school attendance is far longer than it is in many societies of origin. But how far do these opportunities allow the children of immigrants to go? While no modern society can afford to exclude completely the talented members of a disadvantaged group from access to the higher levels of educational and professional accomplishment, strong pressures operate on, and within, educational systems to maintain, or at least not overturn, established inequalities.[2]

An added element is that schools are sites where advantaged groups work to preserve their superior position. This is true of middle- and upper-middle-class parents everywhere, who seek to ensure that their children obtain a favorable educational outcome and starting position for adult life. The systems we consider are by and large set up to facilitate the preservation of these advantages. For instance, all of the educational systems in the six countries in our study employ tracking in some form, that is, providing students with instruction that varies according to their supposed abilities to learn. Tracking is consistent with the desires of parents who themselves have relatively high levels of education, because their children, simply by virtue of exposure to education–relevant advantages at home, tend to be placed in better tracks. Tracking tends to have negative consequences for children from low-status immigrant homes, where mainstream cultural and social capital is in scarce supply.

The tension in the educational mission may be universal, but there are critical institutional differences among the educational systems of the main receiving societies of North America and Western Europe that can affect the balance between the provision of opportunities and the production and reproduction of inequalities, with important implications for the life chances of the children of immigrants. Systems differ, for example, in the degree and fatefulness of tracking, with the northern European systems, especially the German one, featuring formal tracking at an early age that separates students into distinct streams directed toward different outcomes, ranging from university degrees to labor-market entry once mandatory schooling is finished. The systems differ also in their funding schemes in ways that have tangible consequences for the schools the children of immigrants attend. At one end is the United States, which relies heavily on local and regional funding, leading to marked inequalities among schools that correlate to an important degree with the social origins of the students they serve. The result is that the children of immigrants frequently go to schools that are poorer in resources and in teachers' qualifications than those that middle-class white students attend. At the other end are France and the Netherlands, which provide additional funding to schools to support the education of immigrant-origin students.[3]

Ultimately, the fundamental question is this: what are the consequences of these institutional differences for the second generation or, to phrase it somewhat differently, how much do they matter for the second generation's educational achievements? We cannot simply assume a priori that certain structural characteristics in different educational systems will have positive, or negative, effects for the children of low-status immigrants; it is necessary to show, empirically, that they do. Nor should we assume that educational systems, taken as a whole, lead these children to have school outcomes that are below those of native majority students. These systems each feature an array of distinctive characteristics, some that may be impediments, others that may be helpful. In the end, the cross-country comparison offers hints for an understanding of what works, suggesting particular features of school systems that may improve the second generation's chances for successful integration. The proof, however, of these beneficial effects requires more detailed studies than have been conducted to date; the same goes for research on how educational training affects the second generation's trajectories when they leave school to go into the labor market, a topic we turn to at the end of the chapter.

DIMENSIONS OF SYSTEM DIFFERENCE

In principle, numerous features of schools potentially matter for the opportunities and challenges that immigrant-origin students confront. One useful scheme for mapping the differences among school systems in the six countries focuses on the dimensions of standardization and stratification (see figure 8.1).[4]

By standardization we mean "the degree to which the quality of education meets the same standards nationwide."[5] It is indicated by several features of educational systems, including the following: the extent to which they tolerate disparities among schools on a regional or local basis or along the public/private divide; and the extent to which the content of education is rendered uniform by a national curriculum. Alongside a national curriculum, there may be a uniform, comprehensive examination at the end of the period of mandatory education, such as the GCSE (General Certificate of Secondary Education) examination in England and Wales.

The degree of standardization can have significant repercussions for the children of low-status immigrant parents. Insofar as education is not standardized, immigrant-origin students may attend schools of less-than-average quality and receive an education inferior to what is available to middle-class members of the native majority. However, one aspect of a standardized education could disadvantage students from immigrant backgrounds: namely, comprehensive examinations of students in academic tracks, such as the German *Abitur*, which may intimidate some of these students, pushing them toward vocational training. Moreover, in systems like the American and Canadian ones, which do not have national qualifying examinations for entry to the university sector, the evidence suggests that, other things being equal, immigrant-minority students are more likely to continue into post-secondary education.[6]

Of the countries in our study, France is the most standardized because of the centralization of education: school funding is to a large extent under the con-

| | | Stratification | | |
| | | Nature of tracking | | |
	Standardization	Informal	Late	Early
Funding: primarily local and state/provincial; Curriculum: state/provincial; Culminating comprehensive examinations: limited (some states/provinces)	Low ↑	U.S. Canada		
Funding: primarily national; Curriculum: national; Culminating comprehensive examinations	↓ High		England/ Wales France	Germany Netherlands

Figure 8.1. Standardization and stratification of educational systems. *Notes:* Canada's school funding has historically mixed local and provincial sources but is shifting toward less local and more provincial funding; Germany's school curriculum and funding are primarily determined at the regional (*Land*) level; U.S. high-stakes testing, introduced by No Child Left Behind law, is focused on basic skills, occurs mainly during grades 1–8, and is determined at the state level. *Sources:* Almendinger (1989); Lessard-Phillips et al. (2014); OECD (2013e); Shavit and Müller (1998: 12).

trol of the national Ministry of Education, and education is governed by a curriculum determined at the national level. Passing a nationally uniform examination at the end of high school is required to earn a *baccalauréat,* the credential for entry to university. The Dutch system is also centralized, depending heavily on funding from the national government and employing a national examination at the end of primary school to help determine subsequent track placement. The British system features standardized culminating examinations, the GCSE and subject-specific A-level examinations (the latter required for university entry). In Germany, education is a state (*Land*)-level matter according to the constitution, but there is national coordination among the states, making the system more standardized than is the case in Canada and the United States. The two North American countries are the least standardized (see figure 8.1). In both, educational funding and governance are mostly situated below the national level, at state, provincial, and communal levels. Neither system imposes a uniform examination at the end of secondary schooling to measure students' performance according to standardized norms.[7] (The standardized testing in the United States, mandated by the No Child Left Behind Act of 2002, is more for the purpose of evaluating school progress than for grading individual students. The focus is on basic reading, writing, and mathematics skills rather than competence in subjects such as biology and history.)

The United States is the paragon of a decentralized system, tolerating large disparities among schools, rooted in traditions of local control.[8] For funding, the American system relies much more heavily than the other five countries on local sources, with regional (state-level) sources in second place and the federal government accounting for a small share of the total K-12 budget. Because the bulk of local funding comes from the property tax, it is dependent on community wealth. This situation contributes greatly to the stark inequalities among U.S. primary and secondary schools. According to economic journalist Eduardo Porter, in 2010–11 the wealthiest 10 percent of school districts in New York state spent an average of $25,505 per pupil, while the poorest 10 percent spent just $12,861—in other words, a two-to-one disparity. In the state of Tennessee, average spending per pupil was even lower, $8,200.[9] The resulting system is a complex patchwork in its inequalities, but on the whole students from disadvantaged backgrounds tend to attend schools with weaker funding.

The dimension of stratification refers to the extent and nature of tracking—broadly speaking, the differential education of students based on presumptions about their varying abilities and prospects. Tracking is a critical mechanism channeling students toward different educational destinations, which, in turn, have distinct, often fateful, consequences for their prospects in adult life. Stratification disadvantages the children of low-status immigrant parents in many of the ways that standardization does. Immigrant-origin children from disadvantaged, typically minority-language, homes often have trouble in quickly demonstrating their academic abilities in mainstream classrooms and therefore may be consigned to lower tracks, putting impediments in their way. A common estimate is that children from minority-language homes may need five to seven years to acquire academic competence in the mainstream language.[10] Furthermore, the judgments of teachers and school administrators about these students' abilities often play a role in track assignments—and are likely to be influenced by ethnoracial stereotypes. Since immigrant parents generally do not have the kind of cultural and social capital possessed by the middle class of the mainstream society, they are not likely to be effective advocates for their children as these judgments are formulated.[11]

Germany represents the extreme case of stratification. Like other stratified systems, it offers a variety of secondary-school credentials, each associated with distinct educational and labor-market life chances. In most *Länder* (states in the federal system), students are divided among three unequal tracks at the end of fourth grade, with different educational and occupational destinations: the *Hauptschule*, the bottom track, provides a general education followed in many cases by an apprenticeship for students destined for less-skilled blue-collar occupations; the *Realschule*, the intermediate track, prepares students for more-skilled occupations, including some white-collar ones, and can culminate in an apprenticeship or a vocational post-secondary track; and the *Gym-*

nasium, prepares students for the university, which they enter after passing the *Abitur* examination.[12] The students on different tracks typically attend different schools (that is, located in different buildings), adding to the difficulty of improving track placement in this system, though students may move from a higher to a lower track.

The German case highlights three features of stratification that matter for students' educational chances. Tracking varies according to its *formality*, the degree of separation among different streams of students, and *rigidity*, the degree to which students are unable to change tracks. In addition, the *age* at which tracking begins is consequential: the earlier the onset of differentiation, the greater the role that social origins are likely to play in determining where students are placed.[13]

The Dutch system bears some similarities to the German one but differs significantly in these three key features. In the Netherlands, students may enroll in one of several streams, including vocational and academically oriented tracks, but only the lowest track, the purely vocational one, involves separate schools; the others are housed within comprehensive schools.[14] Moreover, tracking comes later, after the sixth grade, when students are twelve years old; and except for those on the most vocational track, students spend two more years together in a comprehensive curriculum, giving them additional time to improve their track position.

At the other end of the stratification dimension are the Canadian and U.S. systems. Tracking is less systematic and typically takes place in the same building; secondary-school students attend comprehensive schools but are distributed over different classrooms, where they receive different levels of instruction according to estimates of their academic abilities. (In many cases, the same subject is taught at different levels of depth.) In contrast to European systems, the final credential, the high-school diploma, is largely undifferentiated. But transcripts reveal inequalities in educational experiences, such as the number of honors or advanced-placement courses taken. Such systems are often seen as "forgiving" in that weak performance at earlier levels of education does not preclude students from attaining high academic outcomes at the next level.[15]

The other two systems, in Britain and France, involve late tracking. Students attend comprehensive schools for much longer than is the case in Germany, entering tracks late in secondary school. Generally speaking, students also have more choice about their tracks than in early tracking systems (though, in France at least, guidance counselors play a significant role). In France, the delay in separation into distinct streams, which takes place at the high school (*lycée*) level, is a historically recent innovation, part of an effort to democratize the system by giving more students from working-class and immigrant backgrounds the opportunity to earn the *baccalauréat* and thereby the passport to a university. Also part of the reform is the development of new professional and technical forms of *baccalauréat*, whose overt link to the labor market was designed to appeal to students from these backgrounds, and which offer pathways into post-secondary education.[16]

There are, of course, other dimensions of educational systems, not included in the standardization/stratification scheme, that matter. Perhaps the most important concerns the division of educational labor among schools, families, and communities. In no system is all education conducted in schools—from the very first day, students come into the classroom with already developed differences in school-relevant skills, whether they involve the ability to sit still or read some words. These initial skill differences are brought from homes and communities, outside agents that continue to play a crucial role throughout children's school careers. Since schools can compensate to some extent for the inequalities associated with family and community backgrounds, those systems that place less responsibility on schools enhance the disadvantages of immigrant-origin students.[17] Immigrant-origin youngsters who speak a mother tongue at home may be handicapped at the outset by lack of proficiency in the mainstream language of school. Moreover, their parents generally are unfamiliar with the school system of the receiving society and consequently not able to strategize and assist their children's school careers. The parents often are neither capable of successfully intervening on their children's behalf, nor of compensating at home for what children may be missing in school. They typically cannot help their children with homework (though older siblings, if successful in school, may be able to do so) nor interact easily with teachers and school administrators. They may even be unable to read the notices the school sends home with their children.[18]

One aspect of the school-family-community division of educational labor relates to the age at which children enter school or school-like settings and the amount of time they spend there on a daily and annual basis. The systems we are considering differ significantly in these respects. At one end is France, which introduces children at very young ages to school-like settings through its *maternelle* system, which begins at the age of two-and-a-half and includes virtually all three-year-olds. The *maternelle* system has especially positive consequences for children from immigrant homes because it brings them into French-speaking environments well before they will need to use French for academic performance.[19]

At the other end are Germany and the United States. German schools have an unusually short day; during the primary years, children go home at lunchtime and are expected to complete substantial amounts of homework with the help of a parent or older sibling. The United States has an unusually short school year and lengthy summer vacation. According to *The Economist*, American children "have one of the shortest school years anywhere, a mere 180 days compared with an average of 195 for OECD countries. . . . Over 12 years, a 15-day deficit means American children lose out on 180 days of school, equivalent to an entire year."[20] The long summer layoff in the United States has been shown repeatedly to be associated with a regression in learning, especially for poor and minority children.[21]

Some of the systems we are considering have been attempting large-scale interventions to support the educations of disadvantaged children, including children from immigrant homes. We have already mentioned the democratization effort underway in France since the 1980s. To further it, France has provided supplemental funding for schools that educate children living in areas associated with social problems by designating Zones of Educational Priority (ZEP), whose schools benefit from the extra financial support. The Netherlands has also crafted a policy to give more funding to schools that educate immigrant-origin and other disadvantaged students. It has also attempted to strengthen communal institutions that can help immigrant-origin students with homework and educational guidance, thus compensating for some of the weaknesses of immigrant homes. The United States is unusual for its experiments with bilingual education, which range from intensive efforts to help minority-language children in regular classrooms make the transition to English to providing some education in the children's home language. The positive effects of these interventions are debatable: in France, the literature on the investment in ZEPs is generally skeptical of its impact, and in the United States, bilingual education, under the best circumstances, does not seem to have had more than modest educational benefits.[22]

Finally, one should not overlook the way that educational systems are entangled with other institutional domains. In other words, the implications of school systems for immigrant-origin students cannot be understood solely from the institutional features of the education sector: they interact in important ways with other institutional domains, especially residence and the labor market. In the United States, we will argue, the significance of inequalities among schools due to the nature of the funding system, particularly its reliance on local sources, is enhanced because of the high level of residential segregation by ethnicity/race, immigrant status, and economic standing. In some other countries where the second generation expects to encounter labor-market discrimination and other difficulties—France and Great Britain are cases in point—some students from low-status immigrant backgrounds may stay in school longer in the hope that more advanced credentials will help them to overcome employment hurdles.

STUDYING EDUCATIONAL SYSTEMS AND OPPORTUNITIES FOR IMMIGRANT-ORIGIN STUDENTS

In assessing how school systems affect immigrant-origin students' opportunities we have adopted certain strategies with regard to which of these students to focus on, which students from native families to compare them to, and which educational outcomes to examine.

As in other chapters, we focus the analysis, insofar as we can, on immigrant-origin students from disadvantaged backgrounds, from groups where immigrants with low levels of human capital predominate; sometimes, because of data limitations, we use as a substitute those whose immigrant parents lack a secondary-school diploma, the basic educational credential needed in the labor forces of economically advanced societies. It makes little sense to include students with highly educated, professional parents, or groups where such parents are the majority such as Asian Indians in the United States, because they are unlikely to challenge the ability of educational systems to recognize the intellectual talents of youngsters from disadvantaged immigrant backgrounds or to assist them in catching up to mainstream educational norms.

For native comparison groups, we mainly look at *all* students from native families. It may seem strange not to compare students from disadvantaged immigrant backgrounds with their counterparts in the native population, for example, those whose parents also failed to complete secondary school. The logic of multivariate analysis strongly suggests that this is the appropriate comparison; otherwise, it presumes, we may be confounding what we view as a native/immigrant difference with a social-class effect. However, this logic, otherwise so convincing, become problematic in the immigration context. The difficulty is that immigrant parents often have been educated in countries where the average level of schooling is very low. Even if they achieve higher-than-average education for their home-country communities—which is frequently the case owing to the selectivity of most immigration streams[23]—their levels of education place them at the lower rungs of the host-society educational distribution. Hence, "controlling for" parental status is, in effect, to calibrate second-generation schooling by the educational outcomes of native children from the most deprived social strata, where parents have uncommonly low levels of schooling and families are beset by a variety of problems, including low levels of optimism about the future. Immigrant parents often have high levels of aspiration for their children—immigrant "optimism," which often carries over into the second generation.[24] And since immigrant parents often have talents and abilities not measured by formal schooling and lack the personal and social problems (for example, alcoholism, drug use, and criminal records) afflicting many native parents on the bottom rungs of the economic ladder, controlling for socioeconomic background is likely to produce unrealistically optimistic results: that is, the children of immigrants will appear to be doing very well by comparison with their socioeconomically "similar" counterparts in the native population.

A recent analysis of immigrant selectivity bolsters our concern.[25] It compared immigrants' educational levels to those of residents of their home countries. The analysis shows that the selectivity of immigrant populations varies—for example, it is uniformly high in Canada for non-European immigrant groups thanks to the admission system, and also very high in different destination countries for immigrants from East Asia. What is key here is that the study also demonstrates that, when family socioeconomic position is controlled in analyzing second-generation educational attainment, important group differences remain that correlate with the selectivity of immigrant streams—in short, the children from more selective streams perform better in school (better also than native students). This finding supports our supposition that the positive selectivity of immigrants in general can distort the apparent disadvantages of children from low-status immigrant homes when they are compared to native children of similar socioeconomic background.

With regard to what aspects of educational outcomes we should investigate, two kinds of data, we argue, are essential to understand how immigrant-origin students are faring: one is the educational credentials earned by students from different ethnic and nativity backgrounds; another is the skills students have acquired by the time they are in the later stages of compulsory education. For the latter, we draw on PISA (Programme for International Student Assessment) data, the most consistent, widely available data on educational performance in different countries, collected triannually.[26] While skills measures give insights into the competencies young people are acquiring, they risk underestimating second-generation academic performance because children from minority-language homes take a substantial period to catch up to their peers from native families. In fact, immigrant-origin students often go further in school than their test scores would predict,[27] and the final credentials young people earn, for which we rely on data from a number of recent studies, are critical for their futures and their position in the labor market.

INEQUALITY OF OUTCOMES

DIFFERENCES IN SCHOOL-TAUGHT SKILLS

What, then, do the data reveal? The PISA data show major academic-skills differences between native-origin students and the children of low-status immigrants at the age of fifteen, when the data are collected and when students are at the upper secondary level, corresponding, for example, to the second year of U.S. high school.

As table 8.1 shows, the second-generation children lag substantially behind native students in all the countries we are studying except perhaps Canada. (We describe the differences as "substantial" because most are on the order of what the PISA researchers regard as a proficiency level in reading and math skills—for example, the difference between students with basic reading

Table 8.1. Average Scores on Skills Tests in Reading and Mathematics for Working-Class Second-Generation and Native-Origin Students by Country, PISA Studies, 2000–2009

	Canada	France	Germany	Great Britain	Netherlands	US
Reading						
2nd-gen. w/ parents < final secondary credential	504	450	414	468	473	441
Native origin	533	511	518	515	528	509
Difference	29	61	104	47	55	68
Mathematics						
2nd-gen. w/ parents < final secondary credential	501	456	425	463	492	428
Native origin	535	520	526	515	554	494
Difference	34	64	101	52	62	66

skills and those who can manage reading tasks of greater complexity.[28]) As one might expect, the differences between immigrant-origin and native students are larger in table 8.1 than they would be if the comparison were to working-class native students, though there would still generally be differences in that case. Interestingly, the gaps separating second-generation from native students are as large for mathematics as for reading, even though students from immigrant homes where minority languages are spoken could be expected to have greater trouble on language-skills tests. These results suggest a more general disadvantage than one would predict from an immigration background alone.

Nevertheless, immigrant-origin students fare worse in some countries than in others, whether in terms of the average gap in basic skills separating them from native students or absolute scores on the reading and mathematics tests. The most stratified system, Germany, comes out worst in the comparisons, with the lowest average reading and mathematics scores for working-class second-generation students. Indeed, the gap between them and native students is more than one hundred points on each scale. No other country comes close to a gap of this size. The rigid tracking system in Germany appears to hurt the skills acquisition of students from immigrant homes, who are much more likely to be placed in the lower tracks. Strengthening this inference is the extraordinary level of variation in student performance among schools in Germany, which is regularly among the highest of all the countries participating in the PISA study.[29] The type of school in which students are placed in Germany makes a difference in their learning—and in their test results.

The other highly stratified system, the Netherlands, does much better. Second-generation students trail their native counterparts by gaps that are about average, but they score relatively well on the skills tests compared to their peers in other countries. The students from native backgrounds score even better, attaining some of the highest scores among all the countries in our study. The Dutch case suggests that delaying the moment of tracking, when students are shunted along separate academic pathways, can have beneficial consequences for students from low-status immigrant homes. In addition, the Dutch have been more proactive in crafting policies to address the disadvantages faced by these students. While we cannot regard the better results in the Netherlands as proof of the efficacy of these policies, they are indications that the policies deserve careful scrutiny.

The situation of immigrant-origin students in the United States makes clear that disparate treatment of these students can come about without a formally stratified school system like Germany's. In the United States, this disparate treatment seems to be a function of highly unequal schools combined with substantial class and racial segregation. Indeed, the United States exhibits large differences between second-generation students and those of native backgrounds. Moreover, the average reading and mathematics scores for working-class second-generation students in the United States are generally worse than those of their peers in Canada, France, Great Britain, and the Netherlands. Ironically, the gap separating immigrant- from native-origin students is restrained by the relatively weak performance of the natives. Nevertheless, the gap is still usually larger than in the other countries in our study, with the exception of Germany. The educational life chances of immigrant-origin students in the United States are affected by the relatively weak performance of the American educational system in general in the context of international comparisons, combined with the strong disparities among schools in a system that depends heavily on decentralized funding.

In yet another demonstration of how immigrant/native educational inequalities can appear similar in systems structured in quite different ways, France is close to the United States in terms of the magnitude of the differences in table 8.1, even though it is the polar opposite of the United States in terms of standardization. One way France differs from the United States, however, is in the higher mathematics skills of second-generation (and native) students; this may be an instance where a system does a better job of preparing students in a specific skill domain since the reading scores in the two countries are quite similar. In Great Britain, skills inequalities are somewhat less pronounced than in France and the United States; and the average skills of students from immigrant backgrounds tend to be higher, implying that its schools are doing a better overall job of preparing them. There is no obvious explanation for this, but the British case bears more attention because recent data reveal an unusual development—that the children from Bangladeshi and Pakistani families, who enter school with test scores well behind their white British peers, appear to catch up to them by age sixteen.[30]

The Canadian system is in a class by itself. The differences between immigrant- and native-origin youth are much smaller there than everywhere else, and the skills levels of youngsters from immigrant backgrounds are quite high, sometimes approaching or exceeding the levels of native students in other countries. Is the absence of native/immigrant inequality a function of the school system or a consequence of immigration policies? Both probably are involved, but we strongly suspect that immigration policies play the major role; the Canadian system for admissions, as we have emphasized throughout the book, is highly selective and gives substantial weight to educational and professional qualifications. The large weight of Asian source countries in the immigration flows to Canada and the well-demonstrated academic performance of Asian-origin students suggest that not too much credit should be given specifically to the Canadian school system. (Supporting this inference are low native-/immigrant-origin inequalities on the PISA tests in Australia, which, like Canada, has a skills-driven immigration system bringing in large numbers from Asian countries.) In class-diverse Asian communities, educational advantages flow downward from more to less advantaged families through such mechanisms as after-school programs and networks and media that spread information about the school system.[31]

DIFFERENCES IN EDUCATIONAL CREDENTIALS

The data on educational credentials, summarized in table 8.2, compiled from a series of post-2000 studies, also tell a story of second-generation disadvantage, yet a more mixed one than provided by the PISA data on skills and with more significant variation among the six countries. At the lower end of the educational system, France, Germany, the Netherlands, and the United States produce severe handicaps for substantial fractions of the second generation. In Canada and Britain, those of native origin have little or no advantage in completed education.

Two measures are telling. The proportions of groups advancing to, and earning credentials in, the higher-educational system (or "tertiary" education) provide clues about immigrant-origin students' chances of obtaining middle-class and upper-middle-class jobs. The proportions failing to attain the final secondary-school credential indicate the probability that these students will wind up, like most of their parents, at the lower end of the host society's labor market since, without any meaningful educational credentials, they are likely to be condemned to the ranks of low-skilled labor.[32] As we have throughout, we concentrate on second-generation youth of selected disadvantaged ethnic backgrounds, such as the Turks in the Netherlands or Germany, in comparison with their counterparts from native families (and from the native majority population in the cases of Canada and the United States).

Table 8.2. Educational Attainment of Selected Second Generations Compared to Native Majorities

		No secondary credential	Basic secondary Credential	Some post-secondary	University Degree
Canada (ages 18–59, Public Use Microdata Sample of 2001 Census)					
Males	3rd-gen. British	23.0	25.0	33.4	18.6
	Caribbeans	19.5	39.5	28.1	12.8
Females	3rd-gen. British	19.3	27.3	33.6	19.8
	Caribbeans	14.9	35.5	34.1	15.5
England and Wales (various ages, Youth Cohort Study and Longitudinal Survey [see notes])					
	White British	39.5	—	—	28.8
	Afro-Caribbean	54.4	—	—	41.7
	Pakistani/Bangladeshi	48.4	—	—	32.0
France (ages 26–35, 2008 *Trajectoires et Origines* survey)					
Males	Native French	12.5	36.4	27.6	23.5
	North Africans	27.4	30.1	26.4	16.1
Females	Native French	12.2	31.9	30.1	25.7
	North Africans	20.5	32.0	30.9	16.5
Germany (ages 18–35, Berlin & Frankfurt, 2007–8 TIES data [see notes])					
	Native Germans	13.2	67.1	19.7	
	Turks	31.2	62.1	6.7	
Netherlands (ages 18–35, Amsterdam & Rotterdam, 2007–8 TIES data [see notes])					
	Native Dutch	9.5	26.9	62.6	
	Moroccans	25.0	45.3	29.7	
	Turks	29.1	42.2	28.7	
US (ages 26–35, 2005–9 American Community Survey)					
Males	Non-Hispanic white natives	8.0	28.2	31.4	32.5
	U.S.-born Dominicans	14.0	34.0	35.5	16.5
	U.S.-born Mexicans	20.8	34.3	31.8	13.0
Females	Non-Hispanic white natives	5.8	21.1	33.3	39.8
	U.S.-born Dominicans	9.5	18.3	39.5	32.8
	U.S.-born Mexicans	16.3	29.1	36.8	17.9

Notes: The TIES data (Germany and the Netherlands) include young people who are still in school, and therefore the distinction between university completion and attendance-only is not available. The data for Great Britain are put together from two different, not fully consistent datasets; only the extreme categories are consequently reported.

Sources:
Canada: Yu and Heath (2007)
France: calculation for us by Yaël Brinbaum
Germany: Crul et al (2012)
Great Britain: Waters et al. (2013)
Netherlands: Crul et al. (2012)
U.S.: calculation for us by Ruby Wang

Germany and the Netherlands

Large differences between immigrant- and native-origin young people appear once again for the formally stratified systems, Germany and the Netherlands—and also again, they are especially remarkable in Germany. The differences are particularly sizable at the upper end of the educational distribution, where Germany stands out among economically advanced nations for its overall low level of post-secondary attainment. As of 2007–8 about 20 percent of native German men and women were attending an institution of higher education, but just 7 percent of the Turkish second generation were doing so (the data do not allow us to estimate the percentages obtaining degrees). Put another way, the chance of a German native obtaining some level of post-secondary education was about three times that of a youth from a Turkish immigrant family.

There are also major differences at the lower end of the educational distribution in Germany. For those in the lowest track in the German system, the *Hauptschule*, what matters is whether they obtain an apprenticeship and what its market value is. Those who complete a good apprenticeship are well positioned in the labor market, typically entering highly skilled blue-collar occupations with considerable earning power. There is substantial evidence that some second-generation groups, the Turks especially, are much more concentrated in the *Hauptschulen* than are native Germans, and that they are significantly disadvantaged in obtaining an apprenticeship in the first place and gaining a desirable one in the second.[33] For those who fail to pursue an apprenticeship, the lower end of the labor market, where jobs involve modest skills, is typically all that is open. The high percentage of second-generation Turks who leave the school system without a credential in table 8.2, nearly a third, reveals a group with such limited economic prospects.[34] (Those who have completed or are pursuing an apprenticeship are recorded in the "secondary credential" category.) Native Germans are only 40 percent as likely to find themselves in this situation.

A similar, if less troubling, picture is found in the Netherlands, where higher percentages of key second-generation groups, Moroccans and Turks, are able to enter post-secondary education. Still, the native-/immigrant-origin differences at the upper end of the educational system are large, on the order of two-to-one. It is possible that they are somewhat exaggerated in the data, which are confined to the two largest cities in the country, a sample no doubt more representative for immigrant groups than for the native population (which is less concentrated in large cities, where overall education levels are higher). Yet at the lower end of the educational system, the differences are also large. The disparity in relation to the native Dutch majority is on the order of three-to-one, as great as in the German case, with a quarter or more of the Turks leaving school without any useful credential.

In the Dutch case, the relative success of the Antilleans and Surinamese is notable, and has been shown in other research. The rate of university of education for Antilleans is not far behind that of the native Dutch, and the children of the Surinamese occupy an in-between position, doing better than the children of low-wage immigrants of Moroccan and Turkish origins, but not as well as Antilleans.[35] Although Antilleans are often counted among postcolonial migrants, they are Dutch citizens who can move freely between their Caribbean home islands and the European metropole; in this respect, their status is unlike that of an immigrant group. Perhaps the parents' special status, plus their greater knowledge of the Dutch language and educational system, gives their children a more favorable position than those of other immigrant groups; the second-generation Surinamese, a postcolonial group, may also have been helped by their parents' premigration knowledge of Dutch and Dutch institutions.

France and the United States

Clearly, a highly stratified system with early tracking—the German system par excellence—puts children from low-status immigrant homes at a great disadvantage, with little opportunity to demonstrate their academic abilities before their academic fate is decided.[36] Does later or less systematic tracking make a big difference then? Not necessarily. In France and the United States, where tracking has a much less rigid character, the credentials data show large native-/immigrant-origin disparities. Nor does it seem to matter much that France is the paragon of a standardized system and the United States a decentralized one.

Admittedly, in both France and the United States, some of the large immigrant groups—primarily of southern European origin in France and Asian origin in the United States—are doing well, with educational attainment generally at least as high on average as that of the ethnoracial majority. However, the children of large, low-wage immigrant groups are not faring so well. The differences between disadvantaged groups and the native majority are pronounced at the lower end of the educational distribution, as shown in table 8.2. In France, a quarter of North African young men leave school without a culminating secondary-school credential; recently in the United States, about a fifth of Mexican young men were in the same boat. The percentages of dropouts generally have been lower in the United States, but Mexicans have stood out for their striking difference from the native majority. In the data in table 8.2, which reflect cohorts of youth who were in their late teens during the last decade of the twentieth century, the rate of dropout verged on being three times higher for Mexican youth than for their non-Hispanic white counterparts—higher than the disparity between North Africans and the native majority in France. Since 2000, the high-school graduation rate of Hispanics in general has surged, although it has not yet caught up to that of whites. For Mexican Americans, the largest Hispanic group, the disparity has surely narrowed, but to a degree that is yet uncertain.[37]

When it comes to university credentials, such as the bachelor's degree in the United States, there are also large differences—more than two-to-one between U.S.-born Mexicans and native whites. The differences from national native-white norms are not as large for another generally disadvantaged group, Dominicans, perhaps owing to their proximity to higher educational opportunity in New York City, where a large proportion of Dominicans live and the campuses of the City University make a low-cost college education readily accessible. (A study of the second generation in New York City finds that Dominicans are especially dependent on the less-prestigious campuses of this system.[38]) Inequalities among U.S. groups soften somewhat when we consider overall rates of post-secondary education, for substantial percentages of immigrant origin groups have spent some time in a community or four-year college. For Hispanics, these percentages are climbing, according to post-2000 data for college-age groups. High rates of entry to the post-secondary system reveal one "benefit" of open systems like the Canadian and U.S. ones, where entry to the university is not foreclosed by tracking in secondary school.[39] Such systems afford working-class and minority students more "second chances." However, their rates of earning post-secondary credentials may be low. This is especially the case in the United States because of the sharply rising costs of post-secondary education. Inequalities in terms of credentials remain substantial.

Two additional factors complicate the U.S. picture. On the one hand, unlike in continental Europe, the American post-secondary system is highly differentiated internally, with large quality, and social, differences even within the same nominal tier. For example, four-year undergraduate institutions range from renowned, elite private campuses to weakly funded public institutions that accept virtually all who apply. Second-generation students from low-status immigrant origins appear to be concentrated in schools at the lower end of this hierarchy.[40] On the other hand, U.S. colleges and universities have used affirmative-action policies to improve access for minority students (see chapter 5). While these policies have been disputed, and in some states negated at public institutions by court action or voter-approved referenda, they have had substantial effects on the upper levels of the higher education system. Their benefits have gone, to a large extent, to young people from immigrant backgrounds, as opposed to those from long-standing racial minorities. Among black students at elite institutions, for instance, those of immigrant origin are disproportionately represented.[41] Nevertheless, as important as affirmative action is in providing opportunity for minority students, it has not greatly counteracted the overall, and overwhelming, concentration of young people from disadvantaged immigrant backgrounds in the lower-quality parts of the system.

In France, inequalities in university credentials are moderately lower. Second-generation North Africans acquire university credentials at rates below those of the native French, but not by the large gaps evident for Mexicans in the United States. (The rates for the native French exceed those of the North Africans by about 50 percent.) Moreover, acquisition of a vocationally oriented postsecondary diploma is more common in France than in the United States, and there is a smaller gap in these diplomas with the native majority.[42]

What stands out in France is the remarkable underrepresentation of second-generation North African and other immigrant-origin youth in the most prestigious tier of the post-secondary system, the *grandes écoles*, schools that are as selective as the American Ivy League and prepare students for elite careers in government, business, and the sciences. For working-class immigrant-origin students, even to attempt entry into the *grandes écoles* may involve an unacceptable level of risk because it requires two years of specialized education beyond the *baccalauréat* at the end of high school and then passing a competitive entrance examination. Unlike elite schools in the United States, the *grandes écoles* have mostly been unable to create diversity among entrants through affirmative-action, or positive-discrimination, policies because these are condemned by the widely accepted ideology of Republicanism. One school, though, Science Po in Paris, has experimented with a special admissions program for students from disadvantaged neighborhoods.[43]

Canada and Britain

Once more, Canada is a special case, and, once again, the selectivity of immigration owing to policy doubtless plays a key role. The second generations of various immigrant groups (such as the Chinese, not shown in table 8.2) have records of university education that, on average, are equal or superior to those of native Canadians.[44] Sociologist Jeffrey Reitz and his colleagues argue that, even though immigrants have frequently failed to find jobs that match their educational and professional qualifications, their children's school success demonstrates the value of the points system for selecting immigrants.[45] However, second-generation Afro-Caribbeans present a mixed picture. In the national data (table 8.2), they have lower rates of university education than the native white comparison group, defined as third- and later-generation British Canadians. But at the lower end of the educational distribution, they are less likely to drop out of secondary school than the British-descent Canadians.

In Britain, too, those of native origin do not have the highest levels of educational attainment; that honor goes to the Chinese, a group that includes many immigrants with high human capital (and is not shown in table 8.2). But even groups commonly thought of as disadvantaged—Afro-Caribbeans, Bangladeshis, and Pakistanis—are not far behind the native white British. Indeed, the combined category of Bangladeshis and Pakistanis has essentially the same rate of earning university credentials as the native British group, and Afro-Caribbeans have pulled ahead.

At the very top of the British educational system, the native British group, or at least that slice of it from the right class backgrounds, has a definite edge. The British post-secondary system, like the American one, is internally stratified, with a group of highly prestigious, long-established universities at the apex and a group of new universities, recently upgraded from vocationally oriented polytechnics, at the bottom. Whites who attend university are more likely to go to the most prestigious institutions than the members of many second-generation groups; this is particularly true in relation to Afro-Caribbeans, Bangladeshis, and Pakistanis. Second-generation black Britons are extremely underrepresented at the top of the system, as was revealed by a 2011 controversy over black admissions to the University of Oxford.[46]

The rates for leaving school without a diploma look astoundingly high in Britain for the white group (40 percent)—although the rates for Pakistani, Bangladeshi, and Afro-Caribbean youth (around 50 percent) are even worse (table 8.2). These figures, however, are misleading in the context of an international comparison. The British system has an escape hatch for students who do not like school or who want to enter the labor market at the earliest possible age. At sixteen, students take the GCSE (General Certificate of Secondary Examination), and many leave school after passing it. Although these students do not have a secondary-school *diploma*, they do have a school *credential* that is useful in the labor market.[47] Without knowing more about the circumstances under which young people leave school and their labor-market prospects, it is difficult to evaluate whether passing the GCSE is equivalent to secondary school graduation in other systems. It is nonetheless fair to conclude that this educational outcome is on average more favorable for the white British than for members of minority groups because of the difficulties the latter encounter in the labor market.[48]

This aspect of the British case raises a general issue, which applies also to the continental European systems, regarding the relative value of a vocational as opposed to university degree. In France, Germany, and the Netherlands, students can earn a variety of vocational credentials that connect them to job opportunities, sometimes with good salaries and security. A question that is extremely difficult to answer is whether many working-class immigrant-background students would be better off pursuing a vocational credential that is valuable (admittedly, not all are) rather than a university education, especially when their educational disadvantages make it unlikely that they will graduate.[49] The situation in France sharpens this question. In France second-generation Portuguese students often have aimed for vocational credentials, while second-generation North Africans have been more likely to head for the university system (but not necessarily to complete a degree). Portuguese students, coming from a community with substantial economic resources, including ownership of construction firms, possess the social capital, that is, the family connections, to get good jobs, whereas the North African students do not. A limited amount of university education often does not serve the North Africans youth well, for they still experience high levels of un- and underemployment.[50] Indeed, the suspicion is that some of them continue into the university system for this reason, where they often fail to complete their degrees. This example underscores that the simple equation of more education with better adult economic outcomes is problematic, especially in the differentiated educational systems of continental Europe, with their complex panoply of diplomas and credentials. Given the current state of knowledge, however, we have little alternative but to make comparisons in which university education represents the most favorable educational outcome.

GENDER AND EDUCATIONAL ACHIEVEMENT

A few words about the female educational advantage that comes out in many second-generation studies, and is especially pronounced in some groups like Dominicans in the United States (table 8.2). Even among immigrant groups from countries where cultural traditions favor limits on young women's education, second-generation females, according to a recent investigation of nine Western societies, on average go further in school than their male counterparts, just as is the case in the native majority populations.[51] What are the reasons for this gender pattern, which in many immigrant groups reverses home-country inequalities favoring boys' education?

Paradoxically, gender inequalities that tie second-generation girls to the home and reward female compliance may end up helping them succeed academically. Being responsible for domestic chores and helping to look after younger siblings take time away from studies, yet these activities also keep girls away from the temptations of the street. Boys have fewer family responsibilities and are encouraged to be independent, which is often counterproductive for school work. In schools, teachers may reward what are seen as traditional female traits such as cooperativeness and obedience, and see girls as less menacing than boys; and second-generation girls may experience less direct and virulent racial or ethnic hostility from school authorities than do boys.[52] At the same time, the frequent reversal of home-country gendered patterns points to changes taking place in immigrant families as a result of moving to societies that typically have greater formal equality between the sexes as well as wider educational opportunities for women; these changes include a greater willingness of parents in many immigrant groups to encourage daughters to achieve more advanced education than would have been supported or possible in the home societies.[53]

THE SECOND GENERATION IN THE LABOR MARKET

Given the overall conclusions so far—that the second generation usually makes substantial educational advances but fails to achieve parity with the native majority—there is a final question: to what extent do these advances translate into gains in the world of work? Unfortunately, we know next to nothing about the cumulative work careers of the second generation. Because the members of this generation are still generally quite young, most research on them has focused on their school trajectories rather than their experiences in the labor market. What research we have is truncated, that is, concentrated on young adults, generally tracking them no further than the first few years after the end of schooling.[54]

What we can say is this: members of the second generation are, by and large, entering the mainstream economy rather than an ethnic subeconomy; and they are improving their economic position by comparison with their immigrant parents. In the United States, a New York study suggests that the second generation is doing better than native minorities.[55] Even so, for a number of key groups in the countries in our study, this does not mean pulling even with the native majority.

Britain is a particularly relevant case since the most disadvantaged minorities, such as Afro-Caribbeans, Bangladeshis, and Pakistanis, have done well in educational terms, achieving at least parity with the white British in obtaining university degrees. Research shows, however, that while the second generation makes occupational progress compared to the first, economic disadvantages persist, especially for Muslims.[56] The employment and occupational penalties suffered by Bangladeshi and Pakistani immigrants, the two overwhelmingly Muslim groups, are still evident in the second generation, as Sin Yi Cheung has demonstrated with 2010 data. The Bangladeshi and Pakistani second generations show relatively high rates of unemployment as well as high rates of employment by ethnic minority employers (a trait shared by Indians). That large numbers end up working for ethnic minority employers strongly suggests a pronounced disadvantage in the mainstream labor market, which drives some of the second generation into the ethnic economy. At the same time, second-generation Bangladeshis and Pakistanis are less likely to work in the ethnic economy than the immigrants are, another sign of some intergenerational progress.

In the United States, where we know most about the Mexican and other Hispanic native born, the Great Recession has taken a toll. Before then, in the 1995–2005 period, the Mexican American second generation was not lagging behind in labor-market entry: rates of labor-force participation and employment were similar for second-generation Mexican and native white men, although this was not the case for the quality of jobs. Even if members of the second generation generally moved beyond the "immigrant jobs" of their parents, research by Renee Reichl Luthra and Roger Waldinger found that second-generation Mexican men's jobs were on average lower in "quality" than those held by third- and later-generation white men. The jobs typically paid less and were less likely to provide such benefits as retirement plans and health insurance. These disadvantages were explained only partially by educational differences between the groups.[57]

In the wake of the economic downturn, the economic position of second- and third-generation Latinos has showed signs of deterioration. Five years after the onset of the recession, the employment rate of U.S.-born Hispanics remained relatively low and the unemployment rate relatively high. In the last quarter of 2007, when the recession began, the unemployment rates of native-born Hispanics and all workers were fairly close, 6.8 versus 4.6 percent. By late 2009 the rate for native-born Hispanics soared to 13.8 percent, and remained high in 2012 at 10.3 percent, while falling for all workers to 6.7 percent.[58] Since the U.S.-born Hispanic group includes many young workers, it may suffer disproportionately from the "scarring" that many economists predict for young people beginning their work lives during the labor-market turmoil unleashed by the Great Recession. The heightened risks of unemployment are undoubtedly one of the reasons for the surge in Latino college enrollment in the early twenty-first century. Since much of this surge was likely absorbed by two-year colleges and degree-completion rates still lag for Latinos, it remains to be seen whether this educational advance will significantly improve the second generation's employment situation.[59]

The labor-market disadvantages of some second-generation groups show up even more starkly in France and Germany, despite advances beyond the position of their immigrant parents. In France, various studies reveal the problems confronted by the North and sub-Saharan African, as well as Turkish, second generations in the mainstream labor market. Compared to second-generation Mexicans in the United States, for example, members of these French second generations are less likely to have employed relatives who can help them get a foothold in the labor market through a first job. Moreover, they frequently complain of discrimination at the hands of French employers. They also have much higher rates of unemployment—and correspondingly lower rates of employment—than those in the native majority population. For instance, in 2008, when the rate of unemployment of native majority men was about 7 percent, the rate for the North African, sub-Saharan African, and Turkish second-generation men hovered in the 17 to 21 percent range. When employed, the young men and women in these second-generation groups relatively often hold jobs below their level of qualification.[60]

In Germany, too, the second generation makes progress but lags behind the native majority in economic outcomes. This is especially so for the Turkish group, but the children of some other guestworker migrants are also disadvantaged. In the 1990s, the unemployment rates of second-generation Turkish men and women were almost as high as those of their immigrant parents, and more than twice as large as for their native German counterparts. More recent data indicate that the Turkish second generation is overrepresented in the working class, that is, less likely to hold salaried positions, compared to the native German population. Educational inequalities cannot adequately explain this gap in occupational status, which also appears to be associated with inadequacies in German-language proficiency and embeddedness in Turkish social networks. These additional explanatory factors can be read in different ways, but we believe that they underscore the barriers the children of Turkish immigrants face in acceptance by, and assimilation into, the German social and cultural context.[61]

In sum, the limited research on the employment and economic prospects of the contemporary second generation is of a piece with what we know about its educational outcomes. The second generation makes substantial advances beyond the immigrant generation. But, for most of the low-status groups, these advances still leave the second generation on average well behind the native majority group. This is true in education, as we have demonstrated, and when we take the educational disparities into account, it is independently true, it appears, for the world of work and its economic benefits.

CONCLUSION

Overall, this chapter has shown that the second generations emerging from low-status immigrations—the offspring of low-wage immigrants such as Mexicans in the United States, Algerians in France, and Turks in Germany—begin their adult lives with substantial disadvantages compared to young adults who grew up in native majority homes. Not surprisingly, these disadvantages are manifest in the worlds of both education and work. They are of particular concern in light of the demographic transition that will occur during the next quarter century in Europe and North America, which, as we have emphasized throughout, will involve the massive exit of the baby boomers from the workforce. This transition will create a need for the social mobility of many children of immigrants if the departing baby boomers are to be replaced; at the same time, of course, it will generate potential opportunities to move up for the second generation, including individuals from families in humble circumstances. The integration of these youth is vital for their own futures and has enormous implications for the futures of the societies of North America and Western Europe.

Granted, the immigrant-origin young adults on whom we have focused do not represent the entire second generation. Some in the second generation are the children of high human-capital immigrants, who hold university degrees and pursue highly skilled technical and professional jobs. These children have significant advantages and often surpass members of the native majority group in educational attainment. It is, however, the children of low-status immigrant parents who face limitations and handicaps owing to their backgrounds and who challenge the openness of the educational systems of the societies where their parents have moved and they have grown up.

The disadvantages of students from low-status immigrant families result from a combination of factors. Their parents generally have very low levels of education by the standards of the receiving society—sometimes no formal schooling at all, like many Moroccan immigrant mothers in the Netherlands[62]—a disparity that, in turn, has a number of consequences, including an inability to provide guidance to their children in important educational decisions and assistance with homework. The children frequently grow up in homes where the immigrant, rather than mainstream, language, is used on a daily basis, and so often enter school behind other children in their proficiency in the language used there. And they stand out, and sometimes apart, in schools because they are ethnically and sometimes racially and/or religiously different from the society's majority population. This last may mean isolation from fellow students who belong to the ethnoracial majority when immigrant-origin and mainstream students attend the same school; it almost certainly implies some degree of distance from teachers.

These accumulated disadvantages mean that most immigrant-origin students need extra attention in the classroom if they are to have a chance to catch up to native majority peers. The evidence is that they do not usually receive such help—if anything, they typically receive less enriched classroom instruction. This happens in different ways in different systems. In the United States, the financing system produces rather gross inequalities among schools that correspond in a rough manner with the social origins of the students they serve. Then, in secondary schools, the differences in school-taught skills channel students into different "tracks," though these are defined more informally than in many European systems. By contrast, in countries like Germany and the Netherlands, formal tracking separates students into different instruction streams at an early age—at the end of the fourth year of primary education in most German states—and thereafter they attend different schools that prepare them for different academic and labor-market destinations.

There are some important exceptions to the general pattern of native-/immigrant-origin educational inequalities. They are muted or absent in Canada and Britain. Canada, as we emphasized, should be bracketed as a special case because of the selective nature of its immigration system, which contributes to unusually high second-generation educational achievement. Britain is the more pertinent example for other immigration societies of the West because the children of disadvantaged groups in the immigrant generation, such as Afro-Caribbeans and Pakistanis, appear to have caught up to the native white British in terms of university credentials (even if they are less likely to earn them from the top institutions). This is an important development, and one for which there is as yet no persuasive explanation. Tariq Modood has suggested that the resources and cohesion of the communities of the Muslim groups help to explain their educational success in the second generation, and this accords with observations about the role of Asian-community institutions in promoting educational achievement in the United States.[63] (This argument does not address the Afro-Caribbean case.) However, it is also possible that the British exception is entangled with the class rigidities that operate among whites, many of whom leave school at age sixteen, after the GSCE examinations, to enter the labor market; these departures lower the white rate of university entrance and completion. In addition, some members of the second generation from disadvantaged groups such as the Pakistanis may persist in education in the hope that an additional credential will overcome the difficulties that they anticipate in the labor market.

The inequalities in the other four countries in our study—France, Germany, the Netherlands, and the United States—show that no one type of system can ensure second-generation educational parity. Neither standardization nor lack of stratification *per se* seems to greatly reduce second-generation educational disadvantage. This said, another point needs to be underlined: extreme lack of standardization or a high level of stratification does reinforce disadvantage. Highly stratified systems with early choice points, like that in Germany, create substantial drawbacks for immigrant-origin students.[64] Because of the short period that such systems give students to adjust to schooling and demonstrate their academic abilities, the systems give a great deal of weight to social origins; and their tracking, owing to such factors as the distinctiveness of the curricula on different tracks, is fateful. In addition, a very decentralized system, coupled with high levels of class and ethnoracial residential segregation—the U.S. system, in other words—has a built-in social inertia that can be difficult to overcome because of the correlation between the quality of the education students receive and their social origins.

What about the implications for change? It is not realistic to expect a wholesale reorganization of educational systems in order to facilitate the success of immigrant-origin children. But this does not mean we should feel hopeless about policy measures to ameliorate inequalities. To some extent, each system can learn from others; almost every system has some features that are worthy of emulation. Consider a few examples. The universal preschooling found in France can compensate to some degree for the inequalities among homes and communities in knowledge, skills, and other cultural capital relevant to school performance; it can play a powerful role in helping children from immigrant homes adjust to contexts where the mainstream language is dominant. Interestingly, bilingual education has not been raised as an issue in France, where proficiency in French is virtually universal in the second generation despite the widespread use of other languages in immigrant homes.[65] The Dutch program of subsidizing community organizations employing coethnic mentors to help immigrant-origin students with homework and educational guidance is another idea that may be worth promoting in some other systems.[66] This program suggests a way to provide a counterweight to the weakness of mainstream cultural capital in immigrant homes. The use of coethnic mentors who have good grades in school is, in a sense, a policy substitute for a pattern often found in academically successful families, in which older siblings serve as mentors for their brothers and sisters.

An in-depth analysis of all the noteworthy, and potentially beneficial, features of these different systems is beyond the scope of this chapter, which has been devoted largely to documenting inequalities that hinder the successful integration of children from low-status immigrant backgrounds. Writing prescriptions for contemporary school systems requires intricate analyses that pay close attention to system features and institutional history. As an example, we close with an intriguing puzzle about the United States that international comparisons can help to illuminate. The puzzle concerns the successful integration in the past of groups that lagged educationally well behind mainstream norms. If this happened in the past—and in a very brief period, the quarter century following World War II—why does it not appear to be happening in the present?

The exemplar of this educational catchup is the Italian group. Their case bears a strong resemblance to the situation of some low-status immigrant groups today. The immigrants came from the economically backward regions of the *Mezzogiorno*, the Italian south, and brought with them few skills, apart from construction trades, of value in an industrial economy. The school system of the *Mezzogiorno* was very limited in 1900, and many of the immigrants were illiterate. The expectations of Italian immigrant parents set up a series of clashes with American schools. Italian children had high rates of truancy and frequently left school as early as the law allowed. Even as late as 1930, only 11 percent of Italian Americans who entered New York City high schools earned diplomas, at a time when over 40 percent of all the city's high school students stayed through to graduation. The obvious consequence was low educational attainment for second-generation Italians and channeling toward jobs where educational credentials were not important. This is where Nathan Glazer and Daniel Patrick Moynihan found them at midcentury in *Beyond the Melting Pot*.[67]

Yet, during the quarter century following the end of World War II, the Italians' educational attainment accelerated, and they caught up to native white Americans in such key respects as college attendance and graduation. The critical shifts occurred across cohorts and reflect the historical evolution of the group's life chances. For the Italian children born on American soil during the period of mass immigration, the gap separating them from the educational levels of mainstream white Americans, typified by those of British ancestry, was very large. A substantial narrowing of the gap occurred for the cohort born during the late 1930s, a group whose education took place mainly after the war. For those born after 1950, the differences vanished, not to return.[68]

Undoubtedly, there are any number of differences between the big-city schools of the postwar period, where the children of Italian immigrants were educated, and the urban and suburban schools attended by the children of today's immigrants. To be sure, there are also differences in the societal context—most notably, that the United States of the postwar decades was enjoying not just a period of rapidly advancing prosperity, but also one of unusually low economic inequality; neither is true today. But, from the perspective of educational systems, two differences seem especially relevant: one has to do with "quality," that is, the academic skills and proficiencies, of teachers; the other with public investment in educational opportunity.

Public investment was critical and was particularly potent at the postsecondary level. It began with the GI Bill of 1944, which led to a higher level of attendance at colleges and universities just after the war. This momentum was accelerated by the enormous expansion of higher education, almost entirely due to growth in the publicly funded portion. As a result, the size of the postsecondary sector, as measured by the number of students attending colleges and universities, quintupled between the end of the war and 1970. In 1940 less than 10 percent of eighteen- to twenty-four-year-olds were college students; by 1970, more than a third were.[69] Many students from homes with limited educational horizons were able to enter higher education.

The dimension of teacher quality is one that appears to have experienced decline in the United States since the post–World War period, when the predominant aspiration of the select group of female college students at that time was to enter the teaching profession. There are still many excellent teachers in American schools, but teacher quality is more uneven than in the past. Owing to expanding occupational opportunities for women and the declining prestige and working conditions of teaching, there has been a downward trend in the measured academic skills of the men and women recruited into teaching during the past half-century. In a system with great variation in teacher pay and working conditions, the better teachers are recruited by schools that can offer superior opportunities; these are typically schools that also serve advantaged students.[70] Since there is compelling evidence that the quality of teachers matters—that students learn more when their teachers have better credentials, more teaching experience, and higher levels of verbal skill according to standardized test scores—the sorting of teachers among schools creates another handicap for students from low-status immigrant backgrounds.[71]

International comparisons show that U.S. teachers are not paid very highly on average, substantiating the notion that recruitment to the profession is a problem. OECD data indicate that American elementary-school teachers with ten years of experience earned $43,700 on average in 2011. This was well above the average salary in France ($31,000) and just below the averages in England ($44,300) and the Netherlands ($45,000), but further behind those in Germany ($47,500 at the start) and Canada ($53,600).[72] However, since overall average salaries in the U.S. workforce are higher than in the other countries, teacher salaries look low in the United States in relation to other possible jobs. In other words, when young people consider career options in the United States, they see teaching as requiring extended education but yielding salaries inferior to those of other occupations within their reach. The case of Finland provides an illustration of a successful path for change. The turnaround of educational achievement there in recent decades depended heavily on the upgrading of teachers' status and earnings and consequently on a highly selective recruitment into the profession.[73]

This example illustrates one way that international comparisons can provide lessons for developing policies to improve the integration prospects of low-status immigrant populations. There are, of course, particular constraints in each national setting owing to deeply embedded and interconnected institutional features in the educational system. But specific elements or aspects of the system—rather than the entire system, writ large—may be amenable to change. In more narrowly defined ways, such as early preschool education for children from immigrant families, systems can be compared to evaluate the benefits, often quite specific, that could follow from policy change. In this manner, different immigration contexts—at the national as well as local levels—can learn much from one another. To come back to the tension in the educational mission with which we began, educational systems can seek to shift the balance in the direction of producing opportunities for students of immigrant background and away from reproducing inequalities that hold them back.

CHAPTER 9

___

WHO ARE THE "WE"?
IDENTITY AND MIXED UNIONS

Being recognized as, and coming to feel like, an "insider" is a central element in the process of integration. Issues of national identity loom particularly large for the second generation. Understandably, immigrants who grew up in and spent much of their lives in another country may continue to have strong allegiance to it and, owing to their language and other cultural attachments, are often seen as foreigners. Their North American– and European-born children, however, are living in their home country. To what degree do they feel at home there and see themselves included in the broader national identity? Is the second generation considered American, for example, or German, or Dutch? Are the societies in which the children of immigrants live open to and accepting of hyphenated identities in which the second generation combines a sense of belonging to the nation and their ethnic group?

Then there are the actual social relations that descendants of immigrants develop with members of the native majority. Indeed, the frequency and nature of these relationships are an indication of how accepted individuals with immigrant backgrounds are in the mainstream society. Especially revealing is when individuals of different origins form families—which simultaneously involve intense intimacy between two people and have ramifications for relations within two extended-family networks. Our focus on mixed partnerships not only reflects their importance as a social indicator, but also the existing data. The most widely available, and internationally comparable, measure of intergroup social relations is based on intermarriage and, increasingly, mixed cohabiting couples. Hence we can ask, How extensive is mixed partnering in the second generation, especially with members of the majority group? How do intermarriage rates vary among national-origin groups? How much does the national context matter? And what are the consequences of mixed unions for integration into the mainstream?

On both counts—identities and mixed families—the available evidence suggests a role for historically evolved ideologies about the place of immigrants in the society. The identities of immigrants and the second generation, along with the extent to which these groups are seen as part of the national "we," appear to reflect a warmer welcome that Canada and the United States have, in some important ways, extended to them. The most obvious reason is the North American experience as settler societies founded on immigration, which engenders more acceptance of immigrants. However, this is too simple. Our analysis makes clear that other factors are also involved in explaining the transatlantic differences, such as the historical experiences of civil rights and diversity gains in the North American societies.

The phenomenon of mixed families is even more complex, influenced, for example, by the relative sizes of groups. Yet we find traces of national models or ideologies in partnership choice, with the distinction in this case lying between Canada, France, and the United States, on the one hand, where most major second-generation groups have relatively high rates of mixed unions, and Britain, Germany, and the Netherlands, on the other, where rates for some of the most important groups are much lower. Entangled with this contrast, however, are also the powerful roles exerted by religion, specifically the exceptional position of Islam in Europe, and the cultural patterns associated with most Muslim groups. In addition, race, that is, visible African ancestry, has a big impact on marriage patterns in the United States. Given that some of the largest immigrant populations in Europe are dominated by Muslims, the religious divide reflected in family formation in some European countries potentially will have a sizable influence on the societal cleavages that could arise from immigration.

Of course, the differences in identities and intermarriage we document are not fixed or immutable. Ultimately at issue is whether mixed unions will become more common across the divides of religion and race and whether our analysis points to ways that countries may support more inclusive identities in the future.

EXTENDING NATIONAL IDENTITY TO THE SECOND GENERATION

IDENTITIES AND BELONGING

Studying national identity is a tricky business. Much of the evidence comes from surveys that suffer from inherent limitations. Identity can be fluid and situational, often shifting from one context to another in ways that questionnaires and surveys have trouble adequately capturing. One American study of the second generation (based on a large-scale survey as well as in-depth interviews) argues that it is actually impossible to use survey research to "make the subtle contextual distinctions necessary for understanding the subjective meanings of identity."[1]

Also, the research conducted to study identity among immigrants and the second generation reflects different orientations and practices on the two sides of the Atlantic. A recent examination of major surveys of second-generation young adults in U.S. and European cities notes that the U.S. surveys did not even think to ask about feelings of national belonging (with the exception of a question about feeling at home in Los Angeles), instead posing many questions about racial and ethnic identity. European researchers, by contrast, placed a great deal of stress on the supposed problem of nonidentification with the host society, reflecting "the mainstream's lack of imagination [in Europe] about how people can hold multiple forms of belonging."[2]

This said, the Los Angeles survey found that a whopping 95 percent of the Mexican and 99 percent of the Chinese-Taiwanese second generation said that the United States felt more like home than their parents' country of origin. By contrast, in the Frankfurt, Amsterdam, Rotterdam, Paris, and Strasbourg surveys, a substantial minority of the Turkish second generation—about a fifth to a quarter—indicated weak or no feeling of belonging to the country where they were born and live. Generally, the second generation in Europe identified much more strongly with their city of residence and felt more accepted there than in the nation as a whole, and this was especially pronounced in Rotterdam and Amsterdam, which in recent years have promoted a more inclusive discourse with regard to cultural diversity than many other parts of the Netherlands.[3] A strong city identity is not unique to Europe, of course. Second-generation New Yorkers also have a strong city attachment, and identify as New Yorkers because they see this as an "inclusive identity that encompassed both natives and immigrants and differentiated them from a generic American identity that might be conceived as white and Midwestern and thus exclusionary."[4]

Identities hinge on social-category schemes that are specific to different societies, and even to local contexts within them. A key feature of any scheme structuring national identities is whether they are easily hyphenated, that is, combined with other ethnic labels in socially acceptable ways. If not, as is generally the case in France and Germany, for example, then the boundaries between national and ethnic identities can be regarded as "bright," forcing members of the second generation into an uncomfortable choice between national identity and parental heritage. Where identities can be hyphenated, as in North America, then the boundaries are "blurred," allowing the children of immigrants to identify with the national mainstream without having to give up their ethnic identities.[5]

To put it somewhat differently, those in the U.S. second generation, unlike their European counterparts, generally feel that their hyphenated identities are socially viable. Two recent national surveys of adult second-generation Americans by the Pew Research Center indicate that ethnic and American identities frequently go hand in hand.[6] While most adult Asian and Latino children of immigrants identified in ethnic (for example, Mexican) or panethnic (for example, Hispanic) terms, about six in ten said they also considered themselves to be a "typical American." The fact is, too, that adopting a panethnic or racial identity as Hispanic or black (or African American) as one of their identities gives the second generation a sense of belonging to an American native minority group—a kind of societal membership that as yet has no counterpart in Europe.

The notion of American identity, it has been said, is like an umbrella that can encompass different ethnic and cultural backgrounds. Holding onto earlier identities and cultures is acceptable for immigrants in the United States, as well as in Canada, as long as these are additions to a fundamentally American or Canadian core. As Roger Waldinger has put it, new Americans can retain what they wish of the old country but they need to "master the native code."[7] To be sure, the phrase "new Americans" nearly always refers to those legally resident in the country. Large sectors of the U.S. population view the undocumented, even those living in the United States for many years, as outside the pale of American-ness, and substantial numbers have opposed offering the undocumented a path to legality and citizenship. Nor should we forget that racial prejudice excludes many black and Latino immigrants and their children from being seen as part of the American mainstream, and Asians often complain that no matter their American birth, they may be perceived as "forever foreign."[8]

Still, when it comes to the second generation, Americans are comfortable with hyphenated identities. You can be American and "ethnic" at the same time. In the United States, moreover, it is not just the children of immigrants who often embrace hyphenated identities. So do many long-established natives, at least some of the time. Being a hyphenated American, one might say, is the American way and not something that makes the second generation stand out as a group apart. Just as there are Chinese Americans and Mexican Americans with immigrant parents, so, too, there are millions of Irish Americans and Italian Americans, well established in the mainstream, whose immigrant ancestors go further back. Being Canadian and ethnic is also normal and accepted, and of course a large proportion of the long-term native white population in Canada identifies as Francophone Canadian. As for immigrants, a high proportion express a strong or somewhat strong attachment to Canada—87 percent in one poll of immigrants in Canada's three largest cities; at the same time, two-thirds had a strong sense of belonging to their country of origin and ethnic group. Evidence from a large-scale national survey, however, indicates that being a visible minority (and second-generation racial minority) dampens a sense of belonging and feeling Canadian.[9]

The second generation in the United States displays a strong sense of patriotism. In one survey, native-born Hispanics exhibited more patriotism than whites, with a hyphenated identity compatible with a "strong love of country"; another survey found Mexican Americans, no matter the extent of their Latino identity, had more pride in being American than Anglos.[10] In a third survey, more than three-quarters of the second generation chose American as their primary identity; whether they identified as American or in ethnic or panethnic terms did not affect patriotism: "A person of Mexican ancestry who identifies primarily as Latino or as Mexican is just as patriotic as a person of Mexican ancestry who identifies primarily as American."[11] Accompanying this patriotism are high rates of military service, particularly among Latinos. Latinos—including a great many immigrants and children of immigrants—make up a growing proportion of enlisted personnel, 11 percent in 2006. In a 1999 national survey, Mexican Americans, Cuban Americans, and Central and South Americans were more likely than whites to support enlistment.[12] A complex mix of factors explains why Latinos sign up for the military, including the possibility of gaining skills that will stand them in good stead when they return to civilian life, but a sense of belonging to America and feelings of patriotism are generally involved. And no matter what the reasons for enlisting, being in the armed forces tends to strengthen attachment to the United States.

Across the Atlantic, the second generation feels more pressured to express an exclusive national identity. At the same time, they confront barriers to acceptance on the same footing as long-established natives. Germany, as a study of second-generation belonging notes, does not support the idea of hyphenated identities but promotes exclusive ethnonational labels, with notions like *Deutschturken* (German Turks) only recently gaining some presence in public discourse: "anyone with non-German . . . family roots faces an ambiguous task in defining themselves as German. . . . The wider society and much of the political discourse insinuate that it is not possible to be German and also Turkish."[13]

In France, the dominant assimilationist model emphasizes that immigrants and their descendants must become—and feel—French, and is "actively unfavorable" to the expression of multiple or hyphenated identities.[14] At a minimum, ethnic characteristics are supposed to be muted in the public sphere; individuals are expected to become part of the French nation as individuals, not as groups defined by a common ethnicity or religion. Dual identities, however, are common among the descendants of immigrants, torn between the draw of the mainstream society and their distinctive experiences as ethnics. According to a recent survey in metropolitan France, two-thirds of the children of immigrant parents have a dual sense of belonging, to France and their country or group of national origin. Another problem is that while most in the second generation, including more than half of the Algerians, Moroccans, Tunisians, and sub-Saharan Africans, said that they strongly felt French, this identity may not be recognized by others. Many descendants of non-European immigrants said that they are not viewed as French—or, as Patrick Simon puts it, they feel their Frenchness is denied on the basis of their origins.[15]

The Dutch may not be as strongly assimilationist as the French, but they have moved more and more in that direction. In the 1970s and 1980s, policies in the Netherlands were shaped by the view that ethnic and racial differences were a positive basis for participation in mainstream Dutch society, but since the 1990s, integration policies have become tougher. Immigrants and their children have felt pressure to identify with and show loyalty to the Dutch nation and its culturally progressive values, including those on gender and sexuality. Although surveys show that most second-generation Turks and Moroccans say they are or feel Dutch, many believe that others do not recognize them as fully Dutch.

The terms widely used in public discourse in recent years exacerbate the feeling of many second-generation Moroccans and Turks that they are not accepted as "really" Dutch. In the Netherlands, non-Western immigrants—and their children and sometimes even their grandchildren—are commonly called "allochthones" in contrast to "natives" or "autochthones." The term "autochthones" literally refers to those who originate from the soil; it is, as two Dutch sociologists observe, a nativist concept in which the "original" inhabitants are seen to own the nation because they were there first. Being a citizen born in the Netherlands is thus not enough to be truly Dutch. Indeed, a large-scale study of second-generation young adults in Amsterdam found that some felt excluded from a Dutch identity because they were continually labeled by others as "allochthones," Muslims, and foreigners. "No one sees me as Dutch because I wear a headscarf," said a young woman of Moroccan descent interviewed in another study. "I will be addressed as *allochtoon* for the rest of my life. I can't stand this, I have to admit. I do have the Dutch nationality, and don't I speak Dutch well? Am I not born here, raised, and what do you want in addition?" This "thick" notion of what it means to be Dutch, Jan Willem Duyvendak argues, is inherently exclusionary and makes it difficult for the second generation to be recognized as "one of us."[16] This includes the Afro-Caribbean second generation, as revealed in the 2013 cultural battle over whether "Black Petes," whites in black face accompanying Santa Claus in the annual December festivity, are offensive or acceptable. The Dutch-born Surinamese were largely excluded from the public debate—in which a pro–Black Pete Facebook page received two million "likes"—because, it has been argued, "many native white Dutch define 'Surinamese' citizens as non-Dutch" who do not have the right to decide on Dutch traditions.[17]

Of the Europeans, Britain is closest to Canada and the United States in terms of emphasizing civic integration while also recognizing the cultural or ethnic identity of migrants and their children. "We . . . want each community to feel proud of its heritage," a Home Office report said. "We need a type of multiculturalism in which everyone supports the values and laws of the nation, whilst keeping hold of their cultural identity." A high proportion of the second generation indicates a sense of belonging to Britain. In a 2010 national election survey, over three-quarters of second-generation South Asians said they felt equally or more British than Asian, and about three-fifths of second-generation black Caribbeans felt equally or more British than black. In 2008 Gallup polls of European Muslims (of any generation), a much higher proportion in Britain (77 percent) identified extremely or very strongly with the country of residence than in France (52 percent) or Germany (40 percent). Yet despite British Muslims' strong identification with their country and pride in being British, public discourse about Muslims' identity often takes a different tack. Fears about Muslims' loyalty to Britain are widespread, and leading journalists and politicians often portray Muslims as having difficulty feeling British. This public discourse, it has been argued, contributes to and reinforces a sense among many in Britain that Muslims, or at least a good many Muslims, are outsiders and do not belong.[18]

WHY ARE CANADA AND THE UNITED STATES DIFFERENT FROM WESTERN EUROPE?

What explains the trans-Atlantic differences in how the second generation identifies and is identified by others? As is already obvious, Canada and the United States have models or public philosophies of integration—involving widely held values and beliefs about how immigrants can and should become members of the national society—that differ from those predominating in European, particularly continental European, countries (which also differ from one another). A fundamental question, however, is why these values and beliefs have developed in a distinctive way in North America to more readily extend national identity to the second generation.

One explanation is that Canada and the United States are settler or classical immigration societies, with national narratives emphasizing histories of immigration that go back to their very founding. As such, the practice has generally been to encourage new immigrants to see themselves as linked to the new society as rapidly as possible. Inclusive national identities have been the result. By contrast, the European countries in the course of their development as nation states constructed identities founded on histories that go back centuries, even millennia. Such identities are more exclusive in the sense that they pose social and psychological barriers for those who cannot link their family origins to such historical roots. The argument, as one sociologist puts it, is that "the sense of common peoplehood spanning centuries is not as foundational to North American self-conceptions as in the 'older' European nations. . . . [And] Canada and the United States are . . . better able . . . to frame national identities to include immigrants and their children."[19]

There is a good deal of truth to this argument. Notions of an historical family attachment to a country and its soil, like that embodied in the Dutch notion of "allochthones," are not prominent in public discourse in North America, and there is no dominant sense, as in European countries, of a core majority population that has occupied the national territory since time immemorial.[20]

The different citizenship regimes in North America and Europe also are implicated in identity issues. That Canada and the United States give automatic and unqualified birthright citizenship (*jus soli*) to those born on their territory no doubt reinforces a feeling of belonging among the second generation. The strongest contrast is with Germany, which until 2000, did not accord birthright citizenship to the children of immigrants and until 2014 required that they ultimately choose between German citizenship and that of their parental homeland, when it was outside the EU. Even Britain, France, and the Netherlands, with stronger traditions of or longer experience with birthright citizenship, do not offer unconditional citizenship to the native-born children of migrants. These countries all attribute citizenship to those born on their soil but only if certain conditions are met (see table 7.1), and in the cases of France and the Netherlands citizenship is acquired at age eighteen or later.[21] (France and the Netherlands do give automatic citizenship at birth to the third generation through so-called double *jus soli*, whereby children born in the country receive citizenship provided one of their parents was also born there.)

However, the settler/nonsettler society distinction—and citizenship regime contrasts—only gets us so far. Neither Canada nor the United States was so accepting of ethnic or hybrid identities a hundred years ago, despite being settler societies and having birthright citizenship rules then. As late as 1947, the Canadian prime minister warned in the House of Commons that large-scale immigration would change the "fundamental character of the Canadian population," which was then overwhelmingly of British and French origin (80 percent in the early 1940s). Becoming a real Canadian in pre–World War II English-speaking Canada meant one had to become British.[22] The emphasis in early-twentieth-century United States, in the midst of a massive eastern and southern European influx, was on "100 percent Americanism." "There is no such thing as a hyphenated American who is a good American," former president Theodore Roosevelt thundered in a 1915 speech. "The only man who is a good American is the man who is an American and nothing else." To some at the time, hyphenated Americanism even "amounted to *un*-Americanism."[23]

The history behind the expansive national identities in North America is readily discernible. A critical element was the incorporation of earlier European immigrants and their descendants in the mid-twentieth century, which shaped the development of identities allowing for civic inclusion and persisting ethnic affiliations. To start with, the immigrant inflows were huge and dramatically transformed the ethnic character of the two nations. Indeed, the majority of Canadian and U.S. citizens today are descendants of European immigrants, most of whom arrived in the pre–World War II period. According to one estimate for the United States, over one hundred million Americans can trace their ancestry to a man, woman, or child who entered the country through Ellis Island, having arrived between the 1890s and 1920s. Their ethnic attachments, based on their ancestral origins, often remain very much alive, contributing to the acceptance and legitimacy of ethnic identities in the United States today.

In the United States, as we discussed in an earlier chapter, the integration of nineteenth- and twentieth-century immigrants and their children led to the acceptance of Judaism and Catholicism as American religions so that by the 1960s "the Judeo-Christian tradition as the American way had become ubiquitous."[24] The cessation of massive inflows after the 1920s meant that immigration aroused less anxiety; and the ethnic groups that had arisen from immigration were increasingly represented by the U.S.-born second and even third generations. Their economic and social mobility, which combined a rise up the economic ladder with social intermixing, especially in new suburbs, and acculturation to mainstream ways, contributed to greater acceptance of ethnic identities. The ethnics' patriotic embrace of America during World War II also played a role. As the children and grandchildren of immigrants fought together in the 1940s, the image of the multiethnic platoon, with Protestant, Irish, Polish, Italian, and Jewish soldiers fighting side by side, became part of popular and official culture and "presaged . . . a vision of America, which for the first time included white ethnics as potential members of the charmed circle of full-fledged Americans."[25]

It was in the postwar period that the national narrative was refashioned to elevate immigration, and the identities that grew out of it, to a central role in the U.S. myth of origin. This did not happen without a struggle, and historical accounts were one arena in which the battle took place. By the 1940s, the notion that America was a "melting pot" had entered the majority of American history textbooks. In the next two decades, as "Ellis Island identities" began to replace "Plymouth Rock" ones, socially and academically ascendant intellectuals with recent immigrant backgrounds insisted that the stories of people like themselves receive prominent attention in the national narrative. In 1963, for instance, two Harvard professors, Nathan Glazer and Daniel Patrick Moynihan, revised the American self-image with their seminal book, *Beyond the Melting Pot*. Around this time, the phrase "nation of immigrants" became widely and popularly used as a celebration of the United States.[26]

For nonwhites at the time, most not of immigrant background, the civil rights movement and the "minority rights revolution" it brought about were critical in the creation of a more inclusive national identity. The effect of the acknowledgment of racial and ethnic minority experiences in the dominant discourse of national civic life that followed the civil rights legislative successes of 1964 and 1965 was "electrifying."[27]

Policy and legislative changes that began in the civil rights era to combat discrimination and open up opportunities for blacks in schools, workplaces, and at the ballot box were extended to other racial minorities and thus to non-

European immigrants and their children. Legal changes thus added momentum to the decisive move of "the discourse of integration in the United States beyond a singular focus on Americanization."[28] Diversity is not just tolerated but also often celebrated as part of America's founding principles and, by the 1990s, had become central to a program of national belonging. The "Black Is Beautiful" movement, along with the growing prominence of immigration-derived ethnic groups who were simultaneously claiming the right to pride in their own cultures, challenged narrow, rigid conceptions of American-ness, "broadening and intensifying the effort to locate America's vitality in its ethnic and racial diversity."[29] Ethnic hyphenation became a "natural idiom of national belonging" and, as the history textbooks make clear, the United States, once conceived as male and Anglo Saxon became filled with blacks, white ethnics, women, Latinos, Native Americans, and Asians.[30]

The civil rights successes of the 1960s as well as the thoroughgoing incorporation of earlier European immigrants have also contributed to a sense of national belonging among the descendants of contemporary immigrants by making it acceptable to organize politically along ethnic lines. Appealing to voters on ethnic grounds has long had legitimacy in urban America, owing to the efforts of the Irish, and later southern and eastern Europeans, in the late nineteenth and early twentieth centuries to rally voters, build coalitions, and gain political influence (see chapter 7). The civil rights movement reinforced and strengthened this pathway to political influence for nonwhite groups. Candidates of all colors and ethnicities in presidential and local elections now eat tacos on the campaign trail and sprinkle their speeches with Spanish in the quest for the large and growing Hispanic vote. In the 2012 presidential campaign, both Barack Obama and Mitt Romney ran ads in which they spoke Spanish. It is hard to imagine Turkish or Arabic being used this way in Dutch, French, or German campaigns in the bid for high office.

In Canada, issues arising out of the historical French-British divide were significant in creating a more inclusive national identity, which has made room for people with a variety of ethnic backgrounds. Largely in response to the rising threat of Quebec separation and grievances by Francophone Canadians, in the 1960s a series of policy changes at the federal level ushered in a new era. In 1969 bilingualism became official policy, with French and English now the official languages of the Canadian government. When other groups protested that they were out of the loop, an official multicultural policy was adopted two years later based on the principle that all "citizens can keep their identities, can take pride in their ancestry and have a sense of belonging"—a policy that has had the effect of including immigrants and their children as part of the Canadian national community. Polls show that Canadians regard multiculturalism as a key feature of their national identity, equal in importance to the Royal Canadian Mounted Police and above hockey.[31]

If Francophone Canadians, the largest ethnic group in Canada, have been so important in national identity developments there, in the United States the very presence of long-established native minority groups has played a role in giving newcomers and their children a feeling of belonging. This is not just because African Americans' struggle for civil rights led to a new "diversity regime," but also because black and Latino immigrants share a racial or panethnic identity with native minorities. Whereas immigrants and their second-generation children in Europe are confronted with white working- and middle-class communities and structures, for the U.S. black and Latino second generation, long-established African Americans and Latinos provide resources for civic and political organizing as well as potential allies in some circumstances, for example, in election campaigns and on the job. This is not to deny the stigma and disadvantages associated with racial minority status in the United States or conflicts that may develop between native and foreign blacks and Latinos.[32] Still, second-generation blacks and Latinos in particular generally come to feel part of the African American and Hispanic communities—together more than a quarter of the nation's population. They may be racialized Americans, but Americans nonetheless. There is no structural equivalent in Europe.

MIXED UNIONS

SOME PRELIMINARY POINTS

As the saying goes, "it takes two to tango." The frequency of amicable social relations between people from different ethnoracial groups depends upon the willingness of both sides. A refusal or reluctance to interact at times lies more on the immigrant-group than the mainstream side, but often enough it is the other way around. In many situations, members of low-status immigrant groups are willing to take steps to engage with those in the dominant groups, unless they perceive that they are likely to be rebuffed by discrimination and subject to prejudice.[33]

The extent of intergroup social relations, it seems reasonable to say, is thus a reflection of the acceptability of immigrant-origin individuals to the native majority. Of course, this acceptability need not be—rarely if ever is—felt by all members of the majority population. Yet, even when only a relatively small proportion is accepting of large immigrant subgroups, this can lead to numerous relationships between individuals of native majority and immigrant backgrounds. This is particularly true when the more tolerant members of the majority are concentrated in the same cities as the immigrant groups are, which is often the case.

The outcome of at least some of these interactions is marriage, or, increasingly, long-term cohabitation. (The changing status of marriage as the bond uniting couples who live and raise children together is a complex subject that we do not want to let distract us from our main purpose here. Suffice to say that the percentage of births to unmarried mothers, rising in the rich societies to heights unimaginable a half-century ago—41 percent of all 2012 births in the United States, for instance—is an indicator of a decline in marriage's formerly privileged status.) Mixed couplehood may seem like a simple measure of intergroup social relations, but this is far from the case. As the large literature on intermarriage reveals, a variety of forces shapes the frequency of mixed couples. For one thing, the sizes of the groups matter; all things being equal, those in smaller groups tend to outmarry more because they have greater difficulty satisfying their full set of preferences (for example, for education level or attractiveness) within their own groups. For another, religion plays a role, a profound one, with respect to the possibility of marriage between the Muslim second generation and potential partners from the native majority population. Certainly, in the past, the Jewish-Christian divide was wide enough to deter frequent intermarriage—in the United States, for example, the rate of intermarriage by Jews, a very small group, was below 10 percent until fairly late in the twentieth century—though this is no longer true today. Race, too, can pose an immense barrier, though one that is variable. In the United States, African Americans for some time have been the ethnoracial minority with the lowest intermarriage rates. However, in Britain, unions of Afro-Caribbeans with whites are common, even unremarkable.[34]

Generational distinctions in immigrant-origin groups, especially between immigrants and their descendants, also come into play. Immigrants are much less likely to intermarry than the second and third generations, partly because many are already married when they arrive, and because those who are not lack the prerequisites for easy interaction with the native born, such as proficiency in the mainstream language.[35] The situation of their descendants, born and raised in the host society, is different, especially as many have at least some contacts with peers from different backgrounds, including the majority, from childhood on. As a general rule, the second and later generations enter into mixed partnerships at a much higher rate than the immigrant generation. To be sure, those in the immigrant generation who came as children and attended school in the receiving society, the 1.5 generation, no doubt resemble the second generation in this respect, but the distinction between the 1.5 and 1.0 generations is not usually available in intermarriage data. The intermarriage rate tends to increase further in generations after the second, but, again, this generational distinction is not always available.[36] In general, the most revealing mixed-partnership rates are for the second generation, although for the United States, because of the limitations of U.S. census data, the rates usually are calculated for all U.S.-born members of a group.

Table 9.1. Rates of Mixed Unions in the Second Generation

	Total	Men	Women		Total	Men	Women
Canada				**Great Britain** (*cont*)			
Arabs	41			Bangladeshis	12	5	
Blacks	63			Chinese	36	58	
South Asians	35			Black Caribbeans	63	45	
Chinese	54			Black Africans	39	36	
Filipinos	64			**Netherlands**			
Japanese	69			Antilleans	71	69	
Koreans	63			Moroccans	22	12	
France				Surinamese	48	45	
Algerians		44	42	Turks	14	8	
Moroccans/Tunisians		52	36	**US**			
Sahelian Africans		47	26	Afro-Caribbeans	12	9	
other sub-Saharan Africans		66	64	All Asians	31	38	
Southeast Asians		81	57	Chinese	26	43	
Turks		41	7	Filipinos	35	43	
Germany				Indians	27	21	
Turks		11	13	Japanese	38	43	
Great Britain				Koreans	34	45	
Indians		19	21	Vietnamese	21	24	
Pakistanis		10	10	All Hispanics	38	35	
				Mexicans	36	37	

Note: Except for the US, all data include cohabitations. The rates refer to partnerships with members of the native majority populations, except in Britain and Canada, where the rates include all non-coethnic partnerships.

Sources:

Canada: Milan et al. (2010)

France: Hamel et al. (2010)

Germany: Hamel et al. (2012)

Great Britain: Platt (2009)

Netherlands: Central Bureau for Statistics (2013)

US: Asian data: Min and Kim (2010); Afro-Caribbean data: Model and Fischer (2002); Hispanic totals: Qian and Lichter (2011); Mexican data: Duncan and Trejo (2007).

PATTERNS AND EXPLANATIONS

Despite the complicated set of factors affecting partnership choices, the rates of second-generation partnerships with members of the native majority population are sufficiently variable to allow us to draw some major conclusions. Table 9.1 presents figures for some key immigrant-origin groups in the six societies we focus on in this volume. For the most part, the rates have been calculated to include cohabiting as well as married pairs and to count only relationships involving native majority partners. (The inclusion of cohabiting pairs, we want to emphasize, does not extend to same-sex partnerships; all of the data presented are for heterosexual couples.) In the United States the data, which come from four different sources, are for married couples only. In Canada and Great Britain, the rates are for all mixed partnerships, not just for those with members of the native majority.[37] (The variation in the nature of the categories in the table, such as the appearance of the umbrella category "Asian" in the U.S. data, reflects different national conventions about reporting meaningful ethnoracial differences.)

There are some striking differences both within and across national contexts. The differences between groups in the same country can be quite large. In France, to take an extreme case, the rate of mixing in partnerships goes from roughly 80 percent for second-generation Southeast Asian men to under 10 percent for second-generation Turkish women. A variation of similar magnitude occurs in Britain.

Some countries feature higher mixed-partnership rates than others, with high rates especially evident in Canada, which, as we have seen, is also quick to extend national membership to immigrants and their descendants. Rates of mixed unions vary from a low of 35 percent among second-generation South Asians to 60 percent or more among some east Asian groups. (Because in the Canadian and British cases we are unable to limit the rates to those involving only native majority partners—marriages involving partners from different immigrant origins are also included—the rates may be modestly inflated compared to those elsewhere.)

South of the border, intermarriage is common, although it does not reach the levels prevalent in Canada; and race is a barrier to mixing for the children of black immigrants. The rates of marriage of U.S.-born Asians and Hispanics to native majority (that is, non-Hispanic white) partners are quite a bit higher than some intermarriage rates in northern Europe, but fall short of the 50 percent mark. For Hispanics in general and for the largest group, Mexicans, the rates are 35 to 40 percent. For Asians in general and most Asian national-origin groups (except Indians and Vietnamese), the rates vary roughly between 30 and 45 percent, depending on gender (with women more likely to intermarry). (These percentages are modestly depressed because mixed-race Asians, numerous in the youthful Asian-descent population in the United States, are not included and they have relatively high rates of marriage to whites.[38]) However, only about 10 percent of the Afro-Caribbean second generation have white partners. The mixed-union rate of blacks in Canada, most of them the descendants of Caribbean immigrants, is much higher.

In the European countries, the low rates of mixed unions among second-generation Muslim groups stand out—with the intriguing exception of France. Given that these are sizable and highly visible immigrant-origin groups, this is especially significant. For Turks in Germany and the Netherlands, the rates for men and women of unions with native majority partners are in the 8 to 15 percent range. For Moroccans in the Netherlands, they are in the same range for women, but higher for men, at 22 percent. These are, overall, low rates by any standard and indicate that the immigrant groups and the national majorities have relatively little contact with one another in family circles, even extended ones.

One reason why the lowest intermarriage rates in Europe involve Muslim groups is that a religious chasm sets them off from the secular/Christian mainstream, no doubt adding to the reluctance of potential partners on both sides. In addition, these groups have cultural traditions of marriages arranged by parents, which, needless to say, are endogamous. The mixed-union rates are not as low for other immigrant populations in Germany and the Netherlands, especially those from elsewhere in Europe. For Germany, data on the Yugoslavian second generation (not in table 9.1) show that they are much more likely than Turks to form partnerships with individuals from the majority population; about half do. Since the Yugoslavs are more likely to be Christian or secular, this disparity testifies in part to the salience of the Muslim–non-Muslim divide in northern Europe. In the Netherlands, the two major postcolonial groups, the Surinamese and Antilleans—many of them of African descent and Christian— are much more likely to have a partner in the Dutch majority than are Moroccans and Turks.[39] About half of the Surinamese do and for the Antilleans, the rates of mixed unions are startling: about 70 percent. However, the two largest immigrant-origin groups in the Netherlands are the Turks and Moroccans, and the Antilleans are by a good margin the smallest of the four groups.[40]

Great Britain also illustrates the salience of religion and culture over race. As we have already observed, the rates of mixed partnerships (especially with white Britons) are much higher for Afro-Caribbean men and women in Britain than in the United States. The rates of mixing for second-generation Chinese Britons, especially women, are also high, though in this case there is little difference with the United States (the U.S. rates in table 9.1 appear lower because they include only marriages to white partners). However, the mixed partnership rates of the second generations from two of the largest immigrant groups, Indians and Pakistanis, are much lower, with the Pakistani rates just above the low rates already noted in the Netherlands. Mixing is very infrequent for Bangladeshis also.

France is a key test of the influence of the national context because, like Germany and the Netherlands, some of its major immigrant groups are Muslim, but like Canada and the United States, its national ideology, Republicanism, envisions immigrants and their descendants as attaining membership in the national community, as entitled to call themselves, and be viewed as, "French." The existence of such an ideology does not mean, as we have seen, that immigrants and the second generation necessarily feel, or are accepted as, fully French. The ideology may, however, facilitate the social acceptability of those of immigrant origin in many day-to-day social situations. In fact, in

France, rates of partnership with members of the native majority are on a par with those in Canada. The critical cases are those of the heavily Muslim groups from North Africa, that is, Algerians, Moroccans, and Tunisians. Their rates of union with members of the native majority are at least as high as those for Asians and Hispanics in the United States, reaching to about 50 percent for young men with Moroccan or Tunisian parents. Obviously, then, not all of the Muslim groups and not all of the groups with traditions of arranged marriage are fated to have high rates of endogamy or of marriage to partners brought from the homeland.

There is an exception in the French context, however—the Turks, although the data on them are ambiguous. In one survey, Turkish second-generation men have a rate of choosing native majority partners close to those of the other Muslim groups; in another survey, their rate is much lower, under 20 percent.[41] Both surveys agree that second-generation Turkish women are unlikely to be in unions with members of the majority population: the rate is under 10 percent in each case. What is unclear is whether the Turkish exception, which unquestionably applies to second-generation women and may be true of second-generation men as well, is a consequence of the unusual ethnic solidarity of the Turkish group, a characteristic of Turkish communities throughout Europe, or of something else. In France, the something else could be the relative recency of the Turkish immigration, which dates mainly to the late 1970s and the 1980s.[42]

A key aspect of the low mixed-union rates for most major Muslim groups in Europe concerns transnational marriages, which involve importing partners from the homeland for the second generation. This practice might even be considered the diametric opposite of cohabitation with native majority partners. Second-generation transnational marriages take place in an environment where a partner with residential rights in a European country has value as a route to immigration; they are facilitated and encouraged by cultural traditions of arranged marriage, often with those from home villages and sometimes within the extended family network, as in first-cousin marriages among Pakistanis in Britain.[43] We know little about how transnational marriages affect ongoing social relations of the second-generation partner, but it is likely that in a good many cases they limit, and even reduce, interactions with those in the mainstream.

In some European countries, such as Great Britain, visas for prospective or actual spouses have been the most common pathway of entry for immigrants from outside the European Union. Some countries have imposed restrictions on transnational marriages—for instance, by raising the minimum age required to enter on a spousal visa, testing language knowledge before arrival, and insisting that sponsors meet minimum earnings requirements—since these marriages have become a political issue, partly owing to the presumption that the European-born partner may not have been free to choose (see chapter

2). This may or may not be true, although when it comes to the restrictions, they appear to have lowered the rates where they have been introduced. While some young people (especially second-generation daughters) resent and struggle against marriage to a home-country partner, others accept or may even welcome it. As Elizabeth Beck-Gernsheim points out, a transnational marriage market holds some advantages for second-generation young women: their European residence adds to their value as prospective partners because restrictive immigration laws make it extremely difficult to enter Europe other than through marriage; and the brides' established position in, and knowledge about, European society, along with proficiency in the mainstream language, may, at least initially, give them advantages in the marital relationship. Marrying a man from their parents' home country, it has been suggested, may free young women from direct influence of their in-laws, and second-generation young men may prefer a more "traditional" and less "Western" wife.[44]

Whatever the advantages, transnational marriages have not been common to all second-generation groups. They are most often found where there are traditions of arranged marriage, demonstrating the immigrant generation's involvement in facilitating the unions since young people born and raised in Western Europe lack familiarity with home-country family networks and places of origin to make choices on their own. (The immigrant generation's role in the transnational marriage market raises a question of how this market will function for the third generation, whose parents are born in Western Europe rather than the original homeland.) Even in these groups, which are usually but not exclusively Muslim (witness the frequency of transnational marriages among Hindu and Sikh Indians in the United States), transnational marriage rates vary by national context.

Table 9.2 shows the great variation across groups and national contexts in rates of second-generation unions with partners born in parents' home countries. Among Moroccans and Turks in the Netherlands and Pakistanis in Britain, at the extreme end, more than half of second- generation women have entered into this kind of union; the rates for the second-generation men are lower but still hover around 40 percent. At the other end are groups like Latin Americans in the United States, for whom the rates of marriage in the second generation to homeland-born partners are much lower, under 20 percent.

There is a danger, it should be said, in overstating the extent of transnational marriage from the existing data. Some foreign-born partners are members of the 1.5 generation, that is, they were brought as children to the receiving country and have grown up there. From a cultural and social point of view (if not always a legal one), marriages to 1.5-generation partners generally are not different from those to other members of the second generation. The usual limitations of the reporting of mixed-partnership data make this distinction difficult to discern. However, according to an analysis of the marriage patterns of U.S.-born Asians, more than 40 percent of homeland-born partners are members of

Table 9.2. Rates of Second-Generation Unions with Homeland-Born Partners

	Men	Women		Men	Women
Canada	Not available		Netherlands		
France			Antilleans	15	17
Algerians	22	26	Moroccans	31	58
Moroccans/Tunisians	19	38	Surinamese	21	28
Sahelian Africans	35	45	Turks	44	56
other sub-Saharan Africans	7	23	US		
Southeast Asians	2	8	All Asians	15	12
Turks	38	74	Chinese	11	8
Germany			Filipinos	15	8
Turks	12	14	Indians	26	33
Great Britain			Japanese	7	2
Bangladeshis	39	55	Koreans	18	7
Indians	24	24	Vietnamese	15	13
Pakistanis	43	57	All Hispanics	13	17
			Mexicans	14	17

Sources (and notes):
France: Beauchemin et al. (2010)
Germany: Hamel et al. (2012)
Great Britain: Dale (2008), counts only foreign-born partners who came to the UK at the age of eighteen or later
Netherlands: Central Bureau for Statistics (2013); counts the foreign born of any country
US: Asians : Min and Kim (2010), excludes 1.5 generation; Hispanic totals: Qian and Lichter (2011); Mexicans: Duncan and Trejo (2007)

the 1.5 generation.[45] (In table 9.2, where the data allow, we have not counted unions with 1.5-generation partners as homeland marriages.) The fraction is not likely to be as large in Europe because of the restrictions on immigration there, which means that there are fewer members of the 1.5 generation of marriageable age than in Canada and the United States. In the case of the Netherlands, nevertheless, homeland marriage, while quite prevalent in the recent past, has declined steeply since 2001, at least in part because of restrictions imposed by the government on the immigration of foreign partners.[46]

France and Germany are conspicuous for having substantially lower rates of marriage by the Muslim second generation to homeland-born partners. In Germany, second-generation Turks have a high rate of ethnic and religious endogamy, mainly because of marriages between two German-born partners, since a large number of potential partners are now available in the Turkish community; data indicate that transnational marriages were more common in the recent past.[47] In France, the rates of union with native majority partners are already high for some Muslim groups, thereby reducing the likelihood of choosing homeland partners. This is true for second-generation Algerians and also for young men of Moroccan and Tunisian backgrounds. The higher rate of homeland partners for second-generation Moroccan and Tunisian women suggests that a transnational marriage market has been operating to some extent for these groups, even though it is less in evidence than for, say, Pakistanis in Britain.

Gender differentials in marriage to homeland-born partners reflect gender roles, norms, and values as they operate in the context of transnational marriage markets. Immigrant parents generally have more influence over the marital choices of daughters than of sons. Moreover, daughters' social activities outside the home are typically more restricted by immigrant parents than are those of sons,[48] which can prevent the young women from establishing romantic liaisons with young men in the place where they live. In groups where transnational marriages have been common, second-generation women have higher rates of union with partners from the homeland. For instance, among Turks in France, the rate for women is 74 percent, almost double that of young men. In groups with low rates of transnational marriage, by contrast, the gender differentials are small or absent. Among U.S.-born Mexicans, 14 percent of men, compared to 17 percent of women, have Mexican-born partners.

SIGNIFICANCE OF MIXED UNIONS

If these are some basic facts about rates of mixed partnership, what about its consequences—or, to put it another way, its broader significance? It has been argued, for example, that intergroup unions need not mean that the minority partner is fully accepted by majority family members.[49] Nor is it clear that mixed-ancestry children who result from such a union will gain full acceptance in the mainstream society; they may be marginalized and forced to find their home in the minority community, as dictated by the so-called one-drop rule of race relations in the American past (in which anyone with any visible African ancestry was considered black).

This said, available research suggests that mixed unions not only reflect interaction between individuals from immigrant and majority groups—after all, they would not take place without interaction—but also in many cases further integrate immigrant-origin partners and their children into the mainstream society. The ramifications of this mixing, however, tend to vary by minority group, as research reveals in the United States, where the findings are by far the most extensive. For Asians and Hispanics, intermarriage is associated with substantially greater integration into U.S. mainstream society, but for those of African ancestry this outcome is more doubtful.

One indicator of the social situations of mixed couples is where they live, which tells a lot about the contexts in which the minority partner feels comfortable and about the social surroundings in which the children will be raised.

An analysis of residential segregation patterns of mixed-race individuals in the United States—using 2000 Census data, in which reporting of mixed race was concentrated among children—shows that mixed-race individuals are "in-between" the single race groups. Those who are a mixture of Asian and white are less segregated from whites than single-race Asians and less segregated from Asians than single-race whites. The same is true for individuals with both black and white heritage. Generally they live in neighborhoods with many more members of the white majority than single-race minorities do, although their neighborhoods are more mixed than those of single-race whites.[50]

Additional insight into the consequences of mixed unions comes from the experiences of the children themselves—the degree to which they feel accepted in mainstream settings and the choices they themselves make, for example, in terms of marriage partners. A 2010 study based on in-depth interviews with the children of unions between native whites and U.S.-born Asians and Hispanics reveals that they did not perceive any impediments to mixing in the mainstream society and felt they had the option to identify along ethnic lines or as whites, without having their decisions questioned by outsiders or institutions. (These data, we must note, are more suggestive than conclusive because of the small scale of the study.) Data on the partnership patterns of children of mixed unions are scant, but one study shows that individuals with one Mexican and one non-Mexican parent have much higher rates—five times higher—of marriage to a white partner than individuals whose parents were both Mexican. The conclusion that most mixed-Mexican individuals have been raised in much more mainstream contexts, and generally found acceptance there, seems unavoidable. The experiences of the children of black-white unions are different. Blacks who intermarry with whites find that they are often seen as black only, underscoring the continued stigma attached to African ancestry in the United States and that the "one drop rule" is not altogether a relic of the past.[51] To what extent this is also true in Britain, the Netherlands, and France, with their large African ancestry populations, or whether a mixed-race or biracial identity has become more widely accepted and recognized there, is an open question.

If in a race-conscious society such as the United States mixed unions for major nonwhite immigrant-origin populations, specifically Asians and Hispanics, are associated with greater integration into the mainstream society, we can feel reasonably confident that their significance is similar in Canada and Western Europe as well. Indeed, the United States case is instructive in other ways about the long-run consequences of mixed partnership on a sizable scale. The overall frequency of intermarriage has been rising steadily in the United States, with about one out of seven marriages contracted in 2010 crossing the major divisions of race and ethnicity. Moreover, cohabitations are about as likely to cross ethnoracial boundaries as marriages.[52] The incidence of intermarriage was more than double what it was three decades before, in 1980, when the equivalent figure was 6.7 percent. Most of the intermarriages, about 70 percent, involve a white partner married to a nonwhite or Hispanic.

Intermarriage on this scale is increasingly taken as "normal" in American society. More than a third of all Americans have a close relative through marriage who is of a different race; the figure is not quite as high for the white majority population, but nearly 30 percent of whites claim a nonwhite or Hispanic relative. About two-thirds of Americans declare that it is fine with them if relatives marry outside their ethnoracial group. Among young Americans, who are mostly the ones choosing partners, the acceptance of intermarriage reaches 75 to 90 percent.[53] Owing to differential population size, intermarriage's effects are more pronounced for minority populations than for the white majority, but intermarriage is gradually spreading among whites, too. In 2010 almost a tenth of whites married Hispanics or nonwhites, a figure that has more than doubled since 1980.[54] The demographic dynamics of the United States—the shrinking pool of whites in the age groups where most partnership choices are made—favor a steady rise in the white out-marriage rate and consequently growing diversity in the family circles of the white majority. There is something of a paradox here, for, all else being equal, the expanding pool of potential partners in the immigrant-origin groups may drive down their rates of mixed unions. Yet the approaching balance in the sizes of minority and white majority populations favors, overall, a growing incidence of intergroup partnerships, as has been the trend in recent decades.[55] This trend will be supported by two other developments: a shifting generational distribution among immigrant-origin populations, with a rising share in the third generation, and the expansion of the racially and ethnically mixed population, whose marriage patterns are distinct from those of unmixed descent.

This does not mean that intermarriage is a panacea for a society's ethnoracial problems. It is not. Certainly in the United States, the ramifications of intermarriage are not as favorable for blacks as for Asians and Hispanics. There are other caveats, as well. Obviously, not every descendant of new immigrant groups will partner with someone from the majority population, and the rates of endogamy for these groups are, and will remain, substantially higher than would be predicted by chance. Nor will every individual in a mixed union be oriented toward the mainstream society rather than an ethnoracial community. Despite these reservations, this sort of mixing is, and will be, generally associated with integration into the mainstream society. At the same time, it is a mechanism through which the mainstream society itself will evolve and change. In societies where mixed couples are common, they are a factor that will lead to the remaking of the mainstream—as it expands to take in the mixed descendants of new immigrants and possibly other minority groups and becomes considerably more heterogeneous as a result.[56]

CONCLUSION

As compared to the European countries in our study, Canada and the United States seem to be more comfortable with extending a national identity to immigrants and their children, thereby drawing them into the national fold. Indeed, it is easier for newcomers and their children to feel American or Canadian than German, French, or Dutch.[57] In general, there is not the same level of fear and anxiety about national identity in North America as in Western, especially continental, Europe, and public debates about immigrant minorities are less focused on national identity issues in North America.

Becoming American or Canadian is also seen as less problematic, and is expected as a matter of course. Americans, one historian has written, seem to find it normal and natural that immigrants choose their "'great' country and cannot imagine that they could have trouble identifying with America."[58] Moreover, it is possible—in fact typically considered quite normal—to be American or Canadian and ethnic at the same time. In Europe, ethnic identity is often seen as a threat to national cohesion, and ethnic and national identities tend to be cast in a competitive, or zero-sum, situation. The discourses on national identity contribute to maintaining, even hardening, boundaries between "us" and "them."

That Canada and the United States find it easier to extend a national identity to immigrants—albeit legal immigrants—and their children is, ultimately, embedded in history, both distant and close to the present. From the beginning, North American countries were settler or classical immigrant societies, which out of necessity encouraged new arrivals to see themselves as part of the new nation. But more recent developments are perhaps even more significant, especially when it comes to the acceptance of hyphenated or multiple identities. In the United States, the impact of the twentieth-century incorporation of earlier European immigrants as well as the legacy of the civil rights movement stand out. In Canada, the outcomes of the struggles over Francophone nationalism have been of great consequence.

Intuitively, mixed unions would seem to fit the same outlines as national identity; but mixture in family formation is also subject to a different set of social forces. On the whole, mixed unions are more common in Canada and the United States—but also France—than elsewhere in our study. In France, the Republican ideology could play a role similar to the settler-society experience of the North American societies. However, race and religion (and associated cultural patterns) are also powerful in the case of mixed unions in ways that are consistent with our previous discussion (in chapters 5 and 6). In the United States, the children of black immigrants are unlikely to form unions with white partners, reflecting a long-standing racial cleavage; in much of Europe, the children of Muslim immigrants are equally unlikely to marry outside their group. Both of these barriers are likely to prove consequential for future societal cleavages affecting descendants of immigrants.[59] The religious one is noteworthy in Europe because of the large sizes of Muslim-dominated immigrant groups.

Also, as we have seen, the immigrant groups in European societies with low rates of mixed unions in the second generation are generally those that have brought traditions of arranged marriage from their homelands. (In addition to Muslim groups, they include Indians in Britain and the United States.) Indeed, partly because of the value of marriageable children with permanent rights of residence in European countries and perhaps partly out of fear of inappropriate partner choices in the countries of reception, parents often encourage marriages to partners from the homeland. Strictly speaking, then, the low rates of mixed unions may not be determined by exclusion from the mainstream (though it certainly may play a role in keeping traditions of arranged marriage alive). Whatever the causes, the consequences of these low rates for integration in European societies are worthy of further observation.

The North American combination of inclusive national identities and frequent mixing between minorities and the majority in families could be potent for these societies' mainstreams. It suggests an incorporation of many individuals from the new immigrant populations that goes beyond what the term "integration" implies and should be understood as a form of assimilation. The distinction between assimilation and integration hinges on changes in social boundaries that divide or demarcate individuals and groups on the basis, for example, of ethnicity, race, or religion. Assimilation in the fullest sense involves more than the achievement of parity in the labor market and other public institutions; it encompasses parallel cultural and social changes, possibly on both sides of a minority-majority boundary, that bring immigrant-origin individuals closer to, or into, a society's mainstream. With assimilation, such boundaries become gradually less and less salient, and individuals from minority backgrounds are increasingly accepted as "just like us" when they are otherwise socially similar to, and intermingle with, members of the native majority. In this respect, North American mainstreams are expanding significantly, taking in portions (but hardly all, certainly not in the United States) of the descendants of the new immigrants from the global South. This is surely happening in Europe also, but we are less confident about its magnitude.

In this light, the struggles by minorities to open up North American societies in the several decades following World War II, we believe, were of great consequence and could carry lessons of value to European countries. These struggles resulted in mainstreams that were better able to recognize demographic diversity and allow for hyphenated identities that gave ethnic individuals the opportunity to preserve some parts of their family heritage while participating fully in their societies. The impacts in the longer term were not just on identities but also on social relations, as intermarriage rates soared. In the

United States, groups like the Italians and Japanese had intermarriage rates well beyond 50 percent by the last quarter of the twentieth century.[60] And Jews, a religious minority that had historically suffered various forms of social and economic exclusion and accordingly developed a panoply of institutions, from social clubs to summer camps, to promote endogamy, went from an intermarriage rate of less than 10 percent in the 1950s to one of about 50 percent three decades later.

Beliefs and discourse about national identities, the North American experience makes clear, can change over time in quite dramatic ways, serving as a powerful reminder that the patterns we have documented are not permanent and could shift in the future. If minority group struggles for rights and recognition in the United States—along with economic mobility and assimilation of the second and third generations—led in the past to more inclusive national identities there, so, too, these factors may operate in a similar way in the years ahead in Western Europe, where interethnic mixing and friendships, and partnerships with the native majority, are also bound to become more common.

Discourse about identity distinctions matters, too; and this is an arena where the native majority can help to bring about change. In reflecting on his experiences and identity in the Netherlands, a Turkish-born lawyer and novelist, who moved there when he was a young child, hints at some of the pressures for change. The Dutch government, he writes in a personal essay, should "scrap" the hurtful word "allochthone," which stigmatizes and excludes those, like himself, who belong to the new generation who have a Dutch passport or were born in the Netherlands.[61] Whether, when, or how this will happen are open questions, yet it is a good bet that collective efforts for more expansive identities by members of the second and third generation in the Netherlands and elsewhere will be part of the story.

CHAPTER 10

CONCLUSION: THE CHANGING FACE OF THE WEST

The wealthy societies of the West face immense challenges in dealing with the diversity created by huge immigration inflows since World War II. All have admitted large groups of immigrants who differ from native majority populations in pronounced ways—in ethnic, racial, and religious backgrounds, most prominently. And, except for Canada, whose admission system selects immigrants with relatively high educational and occupational qualifications, all have admitted major immigrant groups with human-capital characteristics well below norms in the wider society. Indeed, when postwar immigration policies were put in place, a primary aim was to bring in workers who could fill positions on the bottom rungs of the labor market. Now the full consequences of these policies are becoming evident.

If the challenges loom large, immigration, of course, has brought numerous benefits. For the European countries rebuilding their economies and infrastructures after wartime destruction, the immigrants were a godsend. Diversity itself has enriched, among other things, the cultural life of North American and European cities. The many immigrants arriving with advanced skills and education have boosted the economies on both sides of the Atlantic, as well as their own, and their children's, prospects. Less-skilled arrivals have provided an array of services that have supported the lifestyles of the middle and upper-middle classes, from caring for their children and frail elderly parents to tending their lawns and renovating their homes.[1] Whatever newcomers' skill levels, in Western Europe and North America, immigration has added an essential demographic dynamic, compensating for a fertility slowdown since the 1970s in the native majority groups that would have sent the populations of some of these countries into a sharply downward spiral. For those countries with ample welfare systems that take care of retirees, as well as others in need, the demographic bonus of immigration has given them at a minimum more time to adjust these systems to the growing demands on them.

Nevertheless, it is the challenges that have concerned us here. These are, above all, a matter of groups that have suffered from persisting economic and social disadvantages in their new societies and have been held apart from the mainstream through discrimination and other forms of social exclusion.

The challenges will be made acute during the next several decades by another major demographic feature of the wealthy societies of North America and Western Europe—what we have called the diversity transition, in which the adult population will come to include more of the first, second, and third generations derived from recent immigration and fewer from the native majority. The underlying dynamics trace back to the post–World War II baby booms, which extended in some cases, as in Germany, for as long as three decades. These large groups of natives, the first to enjoy mass higher education, have been disproportionately represented in the economic, political, and cultural leadership of Western societies and dominant on the higher rungs of labor markets. But their oldest members have entered retirement age, and over the next several decades the baby boomers will cease their economic activities and depart from positions of leadership. During this period, the youthful members of the native majority entering the active ages of adulthood will generally be fewer in number than the older members leaving them. Although we cannot predict the exact shape of the rich countries' economies in the future, it is safe to say that a wide range of higher-level positions will be vacated, and a question of cardinal importance is whether the children of low-status immigrants will be able to successfully compete for and fill them.

INTEGRATION AND ITS CHALLENGES

COMMON BARRIERS AND NEW OPPORTUNITIES

What have we learned so far about the challenges of integration for immigrant-origin groups in Western Europe and North America? To some extent, it is a story of common barriers and handicaps in the six countries under consideration. The majority in the groups we have identified as low in status—Turks in Germany, for example, North Africans in France, and Mexicans in the United States—start off in the immigrant generation with similar disadvantages. Not only do they arrive with relatively low levels of education and, in most cases, lack of proficiency in the host-country language, but they also must make their way in economies marked by growing inequality and a proliferation of precarious and low-wage jobs—precisely the kind of jobs in which they often end up. They tend to live in neighborhoods populated disproportionately, and sometimes exclusively, by poorer immigrant families; even when they move to other areas, the new neighborhoods often lag behind those of the native majority in

services and amenities. As for their children, everywhere the second generation confronts a series of hurdles in school systems that leave many by the way-
side; in most of the countries, they trail native-origin students in school-taught
skills and educational credentials. In the world of politics, immigrant-origin
minorities are underrepresented in city councils and regional and national legislatures. They are further separated from the majority population by racial,
ethnic, and religious distinctions that threaten to become the basis for permanent minority status.

Fortunately, this bleak view is not the whole picture. It is counterbalanced
by evidence of considerable progress in the integration of the first and second
generation in Western Europe and North America, and by signs that there will
be additional steps forward in the years ahead. One of the most striking is the
growing electoral success of immigrant minorities in winning local as well as
national offices, occurring in part because their numbers among eligible voters
are rising rapidly. Only two decades ago it would have been hard to imagine a
second-generation Turk serving as head of one of Germany's major political
parties, the mayor of Rotterdam being a Moroccan immigrant, or the son of an
African immigrant as the president of the United States.

There are also suggestions of other positive changes, including interethnic
mixing and friendships involving many children of immigrants in schools,
neighborhoods, and workplaces—a trend that is likely to continue, and may
well accelerate, in the future. Indeed, super-diverse neighborhoods, with residents from the native majority population as well as a range of immigrant-
origin groups, have emerged in many European and North American cities;
indications are that they contribute to a sense that ethnoracial diversity is a
normal order of things. Among some groups, rates of mixed unions are rising
substantially, with the result that more and more family circles bring together
members of the native majority with individuals from immigrant backgrounds. And despite the many disadvantages that children of low-status immigrants face in schools, everywhere at least some have been able to obtain
advanced academic credentials and move into better white-collar and professional jobs.

If religious and racial divisions seem like intractable obstacles to integration, over time the barriers may loosen and blur.[2] As Muslims and non-Muslims
in Western Europe have more interactions and become more comfortable with
each other in various settings; if segments of European Islam shift in a more
liberal direction; and if many in the second generation become more loosely
tied to cultural practices associated with Islam, the religious divide could become less sharp. Racial divisions seem less permeable and more resistant to
change, yet evidence indicates that they have already lost some of their potency
for segments of several immigrant-origin groups such as successful Asians and
Latinos in Canada and the United States; race also seems to be a less severe bar-

rier for the children of the large number of Afro-Caribbean and white unions in Britain, France, and the Netherlands than it was for their immigrant parents several decades ago.

One way of grasping this complexity involves considering the tension be- tween two fundamental—and opposing—principles simultaneously at work in all the societies. On the one hand are the social processes that promote integra- tion—the social mobility of individuals from immigrant backgrounds and the social mixing occurring in many domains from work to family. These processes are being enhanced by the demographic transition to diversity, which is associ- ated with the changing composition of many social contexts, such as neighbor- hoods and workplaces, and thus the greater exposure of majority and minority individuals to each other. Partly owing to openings created by retiring baby boomers, many in ethnoracial minority groups will be able to attain a socio- economic status like that of the middle-class native majority. On the other hand, there are the processes that tend to reproduce inequality, which sort in- dividuals according to their social origins and perpetuate social distinctions between members of native majority and immigrant minority groups. The in- creasing inequality in many Western societies will stretch the distance between those at the bottom, disproportionately minority, and those in the middle and impede mobility prospects. Furthermore, in most Western societies, new po- litical movements and parties—the Tea Party in the United States, for example, and the Party for Freedom in the Netherlands—have sought to block immigra- tion as well as implement changes that would impede minorities' chances for advancement, implicitly attempting to freeze the unequal ethnoracial order. The near future will be governed in important ways by the balance between these two sets of processes.

COUNTRY-BY-COUNTRY DIFFERENCES

This general assessment leads us to consider more specifically the differences among the countries in our study. One lesson of the analysis in the preceding chapters is that no country is successful, in every domain, in the integration process, or, alternatively, consistently lags way behind. Moreover, within the domains we have considered—from residence, the labor market, politics, and education to race and religion—no single type of institutional system ensures that immigrants and their descendants will achieve parity with those in the na- tive majority population.

Take the United States, which in some ways seems to create the highest bars to integration. The extent of residential segregation experienced by many im- migrant families stands out as extreme. This distinctiveness results from grow- ing overall economic inequality (and persistent racial inequality) in American society combined with the domination of market principles in a context where intervention of the state in housing policies is weak. Indeed, the disadvantages that immigrants and their children confront in terms of their economic status seem greatest in the United States, which has the most severe economic inequality.[3] Yet, at the same time, and as compared to the continental European countries in our study, the United States (like Canada) has been quick and comfortable in extending a national identity to immigrants and their children; moreover, rates of mixed unions between those of immigrant origin and the native majority are relatively high. The United States, despite the political exclusions created by massive lack of legal status, also has one of the better records in terms of electing immigrant-origin politicians, and, of course, it is the only country so far to vote in the child of a non-Western immigrant to the highest national office.

This discussion points to one of our major conclusions: integration's trajectory—the ways in which it plays out along different dimensions of social life—cannot be understood without a close examination of institutional histories and structures. For instance, one reason why religious divisions impede integration in Western European societies is because of the church-state relationships left behind by the histories of established religions. In every country, the historically rooted system of education plays a critical role in shaping opportunities for immigrant minorities. So does the structure of state economic regulations and welfare benefits as well as citizenship regimes. And to give one final example, in Canada, the selectivity of the immigration system has important effects for the positive outcomes we have documented there in a number of domains, perhaps most strikingly in education. The Canadian case also underscores the relevance of the composition of immigrant flows for immigrant integration. A significant transatlantic difference in this respect is the much larger proportion of Muslims in the immigrant streams to Western Europe as compared, in particular, to the United States.

And so we turn to the particular integration challenges that the different countries will face in the context of the diversity transition that lies ahead.

In two of the continental Northern European countries, Germany and the Netherlands, the demographic transition will be especially momentous because the sustained low fertility of the majority population has led to relatively small groups of native youth—substantially smaller than the postwar babyboom groups who will be leaving the workforce and many arenas of civic life during the next several decades. The two countries will thus be unusually dependent on immigrant-origin youth to replace many of their baby-boom adults, a process that may take up to three decades. In the Netherlands, a high percentage of these youth come from the global South, and in two of the main groups, Moroccans and Turks, a significant proportion of the second generation is experiencing difficulties. In Germany, the children of migrants from the global South make up a smaller group among immigrant-origin youth. However, as we have observed, the rigidly stratified German educational system generally has proven difficult for the children from immigrant homes to navigate and produces the highest native-/immigrant-origin differentials on the PISA studies among the countries we have examined.[4]

Looking at the prospects for the integration of immigrants and the second generation, each of the two countries presents a distinctive configuration of plusses and minuses. In Germany, a high percentage of immigrants have come from within the EU or from Russia, which implies that they bring higher levels of human capital than does the typical foreign-born resident of the Netherlands and that they present fewer ethnic and religious challenges to integration. Both countries present substantial barriers to Muslim incorporation, which affect a significant proportion of the immigrant-origin population, but in the Netherlands high rates of second-generation marriages to homeland spouses have reinforced home-country cultural patterns and proven to be a source of hostility from many native Dutch. Moreover, many of the guestworker immigrants ended up permanently out of the Dutch labor force from an early age and thus with little social capital to assist the second generation.

This said, the Netherlands has been more welcoming than Germany in terms of citizenship and voting rights, and as a consequence immigrant groups have gained stronger representation in political bodies, especially at the local level. And the school system of the Netherlands, though stratified at the secondary level like the German system, does not force students onto separate tracks at such early ages and allows for more fluidity across levels. The so-called long route to a Dutch university education has created mobility channels for the children of immigrants.

In France and Britain, the fate of their immigrant-origin populations will not hinge as critically on the demographic transitions resulting from the baby boomers' exit, for the fertility of the majority population did not decline as much as it did elsewhere in Europe. The decline of the majority youth population has not been as extreme in France and Great Britain, and the children of immigrants, though forming sizable groups, are proportionately smaller than in the other countries of our study. The upshot is that the purely economic pressures for integration may not be as intense in these two countries as in the other four.

Both France and Britain have immigrations with a pronounced postcolonial flavor. The Commonwealth countries have dominated the non-EU immigration to Britain, while African countries, both northern and sub-Saharan, loom large in France, which also receives migrants from former Caribbean colonies. The postcolonial immigrants are a more diverse group in Britain and include a large share of migrants with high levels of human capital, even professional qualifications (particularly among the Indians). Moreover, postcolonial immigrants appear to have fared somewhat better in the British than in the French labor market, and their overall economic position is considerably less marginal, as shown by their very different risks of poverty (table 3.4). And, then, there is the British exception: in a finding for which there is not yet an adequate explanation, the largest low-status second-generation groups, such as the Pakistanis, have caught up to the white British norm for university credentials. Perhaps this parity is somewhat overstated since the white British population contains a substantial group of working-class background, whose members frequently leave the educational system at the age of sixteen, as do many children from immigrant homes. Yet the rates of earning university credentials are high in an absolute sense in the British second generation. The educational success of low-status groups does not seem to be an illusion.

Still, the disadvantages of the low-status immigrant groups are undeniable in both countries. In Britain, the South Asian second generation experiences employment barriers in the labor market; equality with the white British in terms of university credentials does not translate into economic parity, in other words.[5] In France, the labor-market disadvantages of the African-origin and Turkish second generation are pronounced.[6] In both countries, many immigrants and their children confront barriers to full inclusion on the basis of race or religion, even though France sees itself as a "color-blind" society and Britain has been especially active in developing antiracism and antireligious discrimination measures.

At the national level and in cities with large immigrant concentrations, Britain has provided more opportunities than France for those of immigrant origin to win elected office, with South Asians being particularly successful. Britain has also been more tolerant of cultural practices associated with Islam. Unlike in France, for example, where full facial veils are banned in public and visible religious symbols may not be worn in public schools, Britain has no ban on wearing the veil in public and schools are allowed to make their own decisions on what students wear.[7] Yet, at the same time, the British government has sought to clamp down on "marriage migration" in light of the high proportion of second-generation transnational marriages among Muslim South Asians.

The two North American societies make up the final pairing, and on the surface they look alike in some ways. Both are exceptional for the numbers of permanent immigrants they welcome every year. The United States leads the world in this respect, although relative to its population size, Canada accepts a larger immigrant flow. The youthful populations of both countries are becoming rapidly more diverse, with growing shares of ethnoracial minorities, mainly the children and grandchildren of immigrants, though the process is significantly more advanced in the United States, where there are now as many babies born to minority mothers as to white ones. Among young minorities, those from Latin America are especially prominent in the United States and those from Asia conspicuous in Canada.

But there are also critical contrasts that give rise to differences in the challenges the two countries confront as highly diverse societies. Of great significance are the policies that regulate immigration and their consequences. The points system in Canada has made its immigration flow very selective by comparison with flows to the other countries we are considering, and it is dominated by migrants from Asian countries, with immigrants from Europe in second place.[8] Family reunification provides the major portal in the U.S. immigration regime, and many migrants come outside of legal channels. Some of the undocumented of the past few decades have subsequently achieved legal status; others, especially newer arrivals, have not. Migrants from the Americas have so far predominated in the overall immigrant flow and especially in its unauthorized portion.

Although many highly skilled immigrants in Canada have not obtained jobs commensurate with their credentials, their children do well in school, equaling or exceeding the performance of students from native majority families. Canada's immigrant population has achieved an unusual degree of political influence at the national level, as indicated by the high number of parliamentary members from visible-minority immigrant backgrounds, even though the representation of individuals from these backgrounds lags at the local level. And social integration is frequently advanced by mixed unions. In the United States, socioeconomic integration is bifurcated. Overall, the groups from Asia are doing well (with the exception of some refugee groups from Southeast Asia) and their children have been exceptionally successful in the educational system, but those in many of the major groups from the Americas confront serious difficulties.

The integration challenges faced by the United States reveal some distinctive aspects. First is the large size of the unauthorized immigrant group, which includes millions of Mexican and Central American immigrants, who are highly vulnerable in the labor market, ineligible for most federally funded social welfare programs, and constantly fearful of exposure and deportation. The severe disadvantages under which many families headed by unauthorized immigrants must live, in part because of the need to avoid detection of their status, are having a negative impact on the second generation, who are U.S. citizens by birth and account for about 80 percent of the children of undocumented immigrants.[9] Second, there is the intersection of deepening inequality in American society at large with the situations of low-status immigrants. The U.S. low-wage sector is the largest among our countries and disproportionately staffed by immigrants. The residential segregation of immigrant groups is far more extensive in the United States than anywhere else, and the economic and social distance between poor and middle-class communities has been growing. Needless to say, the educational differences in the aggregate between the native majority and the children of low-status immigrants are large. Third, race operates in a distinctive way in the United States. Although nonwhite immigrants have benefited from civil rights legislation and programs instituted to help African Americans, race continues to be a significant barrier to integration, especially for those defined as black, who experience a level of social separation from whites (in terms of residence and mixed unions) that is more extreme than that found in Canada or the European countries in our study.

Yet there are some optimistic signs for the future in the United States. The second generation, which receives unconditional citizenship by virtue of birth on American soil, reciprocates by overwhelmingly identifying as American (or hyphenated American) and widely embracing an allegiance to the country. And, if we take the upper tiers of the workforce as a window into the mainstream, it is apparent that the mainstream is diversifying as a consequence of the turnover engendered by the departure of the baby boomers and the arrival of youthful workers from Asian and Latino immigrant backgrounds. The labor force accomplishments of Asians are not surprising given the high human capital levels of many Asian immigrant families, but the expanding representation of second- and third-generation Latinos in top tiers is a significant development. Substantial rates of mixed unions, mainly involving partnerships of U.S.-born Asians and Latinos with whites, are giving rise to a growing group of mixed-ancestry individuals who mostly appear to feel themselves to be part of the mainstream. Still, the barriers of race remain high, as blacks are not participating to the same degree in these developments.[11]

HOW WELL DO THE GRAND NARRATIVES FARE?

How do the grand narratives raised at the outset of the book fare in light of our investigation? One of the tropes of much of the writing on immigration seeks to account for the success of integration, or lack of it, in a small number of grand ideas, which attempt to provide comprehensive explanations for cross-national contrasts and parallels: macro-models of integration, such as the French Republican model or Canadian multiculturalism; the nature of the political economy, that is, social market versus liberal market economies; or national history as a settler society, like that of Canada or the United States. Some scholars, in addition, see an almost inevitable trend toward convergence in democratic societies of the West, while a counter notion sometimes put forward concerns U.S. exceptionalism. Our analysis of integration in multiple domains across six societies in the preceding chapters sheds some light on the adequacy of these ideas. In brief, none provides a sufficient explanation of the patterns we have observed, though some help to illuminate integration in particular domains.

MODELS OF INTEGRATION

One of the most persistent ideas in the literature about immigration concerns national philosophies, models, or ideologies of immigrant integration that are presumed to guide policy decisions across multiple domains and thereby give a particular national cast to processes of integration. The models range from the multicultural tenets of Canada to strongly assimilationist principles in France and the ethnocultural nation in Germany. The laissez-faire United States is in between these poles, sometimes described as multiculturalist, sometimes as assimilationist.

How much national philosophies, cultures, or models of integration matter for the actual integration of immigrants and minorities is debatable. To begin with, the models can be hard to grasp below a very abstract level. Ambiguities about the particulars have given rise to a lively debate about whether the Dutch, for example, really had a multicultural model in the late twentieth century; and whether multiculturalism continues to exist in Britain or, as one interpretation goes, has been implemented there in a "thin" version.[11] Further, the labels for the models themselves may obscure dramatic shifts over time, as in the United States over the course of the twentieth century, which went from placing an aggressive emphasis on Americanization to an embrace of cultural pluralism. Attempts to give precision to the models through empirical measurements have not been entirely convincing. Keith Banting and Will Kymlicka—the latter a famous political philosopher of multiculturalism—have developed an index to determine the degree of multiculturalism in different nation-states, including such measures as: "the inclusion of multiculturalism in school curricula"; "exemptions from dress codes"; and "funding of ethnic group organizations to support cultural activities."[12] Such state measures foster a society in which a certain degree of visible ethnic distinctiveness is accepted, but it is not clear exactly how—and how much—they advance the overall integration of immigrant-origin groups.[13]

Furthermore, the national models sometimes seem in contradiction with on-the-ground social realities and institutional practices. For example, in direct opposition to French Republicanism, the French government provided the impetus for the 2003 creation of the French Council of the Muslim Religion to serve as a liaison to Muslim communities.[14] And in the Netherlands, even during the period when many believed it to be at the high tide of multiculturalism, the official designation for immigrants and the second generation, "allochthones," literally, "originating from another country," seemed to place them outside the national community.

This is not to deny that the models may have important influences and ramifications. One domain in which these may be traceable is identity. Multiculturalism seems to be an element implicated in the more capacious, more easily hyphenated national identity found in Canada today; and, with a shift in terminology, to a cultural pluralist ideology, one could say the same for the United States. In France, by contrast, the Republican model of assimilation generates pressures to express exclusive national identities—in other words, unhyphenated French ones.[15]

The domain to which the models of integration probably best apply is citizenship and therefore political inclusion. Canada's official multiculturalism policy has been invoked, for example, to explain the high rate of immigrant naturalization there.[16] In Germany the *jus sanguinis* principle (inheritance of parental citizenship) that until 2000 determined the citizenship of the second and even third generations has seemed to exemplify the idea of the ethnocultural nation. And, even though 1999 legislation accorded German citizenship to immigrants' children born subsequently on German soil, the previous citizenship regime has left a major legacy, given that a large portion of the Turkish group still lacks citizenship and is ineligible to vote.

Since, moreover, national cultures or philosophies of integration are connected to each polity's willingness to acknowledge immigrants as ethnic minorities with distinct needs and cultural rights, they can affect the openness to ethnically based political appeals. In France, the Republican idea has impeded the political expression of ethnic interests and the formation of blocs of minority politicians, which are commonplace in the United States. The model seems relevant in this instance. However, in Germany, which is presumed to operate from a diametrically opposed model, the wariness that minority politicians might act on behalf of what are seen as ethnic rather than general interests is equally strong. In both countries, the electoral success of immigrant minorities has been slow to develop.

Perhaps the most damaging problem with the models of immigrant integration has to do with institutional history: they do not jibe with many features of fateful institutional domains, which often took shape well before the post–World War II immigrations began and the contemporary forms of integration models emerged. For example, in Germany the highly stratified structure of the educational system seems at the heart of the educational disadvantages that the children of Turkish immigrants experience, disproportionately concentrated as they are in the lowest track of a three-tiered system. In the United States, the educational system, though structured quite differently from the German one, is also implicated in second-generation disadvantage. In this case, the extreme decentralization of school funding and control, especially when coupled to extensive residential segregation according to socioeconomic status and ethnoracial origin, is a major reason why the children of low-status immigrants lag behind native whites in educational attainments. These features of educational systems are not recent inventions; they have long histories.[17]

We conclude that national philosophies, cultures, or models of integration cannot provide an all-encompassing explanation for the successes or failures of integration and inclusion. They are not irrelevant. But they are just one piece of the puzzle in explaining some of the patterns we have observed, alongside a range of structural and institutional factors that nearly always turn out to be more important.

SOCIAL MARKET VERSUS LIBERAL MARKET ECONOMIES

Another idea with broad appeal locates the determinants of integration trajectories in the nature of the political economy, whether it more resembles the ideal type of the social market or liberal market economy. Most social-science opinion favors the benefits of the social market economy for integration, particularly because immigrant families are protected from a fall into poverty, which would distance them from the mainstream. However, the opposite argument could also be made, on the grounds that, in the absence of generous social welfare provisions, the economic necessity of labor-force participation imposes a degree of integration on immigrants.

Our findings suggest the limited power of this idea. The countries in our study divide fairly evenly between liberal market economies (Canada, Great Britain, and the United States) and social market ones (France, Germany, and the Netherlands). The distinction correlates poorly with the ranking of these countries in most domains. Thus, Germany and the United States, a social market economy and a liberal market one, have the weakest showings when it comes to second-generation educational attainment. Germany and France, which is another social market economy, reveal the slowest progress by immigrant-origin minorities in electoral politics. Granted, one could argue that the high poverty rates of some immigrant groups in the United States, which could be viewed as an outcome of its extreme liberal market economy, have contributed to its distinctively high levels of ethnoracial segregation. But Canada and Great Britain, liberal market economies like the United States, are unlike it in terms of residential segregation.

Even when it comes to measures of economic well-being, the explanatory power of the distinction is questionable. To be sure, some of its implications are true: on the one hand, immigrants are more likely to participate in the labor force in the liberal market economies, and their unemployment rates are lower. On the other hand, unemployed immigrants and their families have been able to stay on for long periods in the social market economies because of the income supports they receive. In the Netherlands, for example, these supports enabled Moroccan and Turkish families to weather high rates of unemployment in the 1990s.[18] In the liberal market economies, the prospect of long-term unemployment often forces immigrants to return home because, without income from the labor market, they cannot afford to stay. To the extent that social welfare benefits such as national health insurance and government-subsidized housing contribute to economic well-being, and indeed quality of life, then here, too, the immigrant-origin residents of social market economies also are, on average, better off—and their counterparts living in the United States, above all, lag behind.

However, when it comes to the income of immigrant families and their risk of falling into poverty, the liberal market/social market economy distinction bears little correspondence to the evidence. As we showed in chapter 3, in terms of the median income gap between native families and low-status immigrant families, two liberal market economies bracket the range, with the gap largest in the United States but smallest in Britain (and also the Netherlands). In addition, the vulnerability of immigrant families to falling into poverty appears to be almost as high in France, a social market economy, as in the United States.

A conclusion that the liberal market/social market economy distinction is inadequate to grasp integration differences across a range of institutional domains seems justified.

SETTLER SOCIETIES

Another commonplace idea is that integration proceeds more easily in the settler, or historical immigration, societies, which, in our study, are Canada and the United States. Unlike these two societies, Western European nations were not founded and peopled by continuous inflows of immigrants, and emigration was the main migration experience in the eighteenth and nineteenth centuries. The settler societies, it is suggested, feature immigration as a prominent aspect of their national identities and histories, and therefore are more welcoming of immigrants and more confident about their ultimate integration. By contrast, the former emigration societies have more exclusive national identities and narratives, which center on the experiences of the peoples who have occupied the national territory for centuries, often, in fact, since before there was a nation. They therefore have greater difficulty in including the newcomers in the national "we." North Americans, looking at Western European tensions over immigration, and especially the cleavages between the European secular/Christian mainstream and Muslim immigrants and their children, often see confirmation of this idea.

Our analysis complicates this idea, negating it in some major ways while supporting it in at least one respect. To begin with, lumping Canada and the United States together as settler societies ignores crucial differences between them that have consequences for integration. Canada needs to be treated as a distinct case, as we have stressed, because of the selectivity of its immigration policies since the late 1960s. They have meant that during the past half-century Canada has avoided the mass immigration of poorly educated workers from the global South that elsewhere has given rise on a large scale to the groups we have described as "low status." Canada has only small Latin American inflows, which in the United States constitute the bulk of the low-status immigrant population; immigrants from Asia predominate, with Europeans in second place.

Consequently, the issues of immigrant and second-generation integration take on a different flavor in Canada than they do in the other countries we have examined.

Then there is the fact that when we compare the United States and Western Europe, it is not the case that immigrants and their children are more successful in integrating in the United States despite its status as a settler society. For instance, in the United States a larger share of immigrant families live in neighborhoods of disadvantage, containing high proportions of minority households and extreme levels of poverty than is the case in Europe. These residential inequalities, which are directly linked to the life chances of the second generation, are intertwined with the problems of legal status, which loom much larger for the U.S. immigrant population than for immigrants in any other country in our study.

It is not surprising then that the United States has a mixed record with respect to the second generation. The high employment rates among immigrants do give the U.S. second generation a boost in getting jobs, at least first ones, through family and community networks—something that is less common for second-generation North Africans in France, for example, or Turks in Germany. However, as we have noted, the United States appears positioned near the low end of the spectrum in terms of the educational attainments of children from low-status immigrant homes. Despite affirmative action at many colleges and universities (especially private ones), the overall gap in university credentials between the children of, say, Latin American immigrants and white Americans is as large as, or larger than, that found elsewhere. In short, when it comes to socioeconomic life chances for the second generation, the integration advantages of the settler societies are not apparent in the U.S. case.

There is an additional problem with putting too much emphasis on the settler/nonsettler society distinction. Despite being founded as immigration societies, Canada and the United States have not always been open to ethnic diversity. As we argued in the previous chapter, the present-day transatlantic difference in the acceptance of hyphenated identities is the result of multiple factors. These include the development of more inclusive national identity discourses in the United States in the wake of the mid-twentieth-century incorporation of earlier European immigrants and the impact of the civil rights movement and legislation, and the struggles over Quebec nationalism in Canada. In both countries, as Irene Bloemraad has put it, the "civil rights and diversity gains [that] were institutionalized through law, bureaucracy, policy, and educational systems, [had] . . . real effects on national culture."[19]

This is not to dismiss the settler/nonsettler society dichotomy. It does have some purchase in helping to explain why North Americans are quick to extend the umbrella of American-ness or Canadian-ness to new immigrants and their children and why, at least from the limited evidence we have, these newcomers tend to embrace the new identities (including hyphenated options) and feel themselves to be a part of the societies where they reside. In general, Western Europeans are less quick to fold the newcomers into the national whole, as they tend to imagine their societies as derived from a core majority population that has occupied the national territory for centuries.

There may also be a social dimension to the easier acceptance of new immigrant populations in North America, which can be glimpsed in the rising rates of mixed unions. Mixed partnerships are very common in Canada, and interracial marriages now represent about one-in-seven marriages taking place in the United States. The U.S. case is indicative because intermarriage has been studied more thoroughly there. Intermarriage is frequent among second- and third-generation Asians and Hispanics, and its acceptance by the white majority has grown apace. Its intergenerational consequences are striking: The children of white-Asian and white-Hispanic marriages generally do not appear to perceive themselves as held back by racial barriers. Because of racism, intermarriage is neither as common nor as positive for the descendants of black migrants in the United States, however.

There is not a comparable overall level of mixed unions in the second generation in Western Europe. This does not mean that they are uncommon or inconsequential there. Mixed partnerships are as frequent for the second generation in France as in the United States. In Great Britain, unions between West Indians and whites are notable, though it is not evident that the children of such couples feel themselves to be part of the British mainstream. For other sizable groups, however, such as South Asians in Great Britain or Turks and Moroccans in the Netherlands, rates of mixed union are low; and homeland marriages, a significant concern to some European governments, have been a frequent occurrence. Religious difference from the mainstream and marriage customs are major factors in these cases and seem to be better explanations of North American/Western European differences than the settler-society idea.

The combination of more inclusive national identities and relatively high rates of mixed unions has the potential, we suggest, to lead to more expansive mainstreams in Canada and the United States. This combination makes it easier for members of the native majority to accept the immigrant-origin individuals who appear in their close social circles as "just like us." This expansiveness, we hasten to add, can occur even as many others in the immigrant and second generations remain outside of the mainstream. Given the picture of integration we have drawn in the United States, this is certainly the case there, even though its mainstream is visibly changing—for example, by the entry of Asians, blacks, and Latinos into the business and political elite.[20]

EXCEPTIONALISM AND CONVERGENCE

Finally, there are two countervailing grand ideas or perspectives that seek to account for integration. One, U.S. exceptionalism, stresses the uniquely positive or negative features of the United States. Along these lines, we have pointed to the historical legacy of slavery, segregation, and ghettoization as an exceptional feature shaping the U.S. racial landscape, in contrast to that of Western Europe, which did not have African slavery on its soil, or Canada, in which the number of African slaves was miniscule. Not surprisingly, racial barriers to integration are more severe for immigrants of black African ancestry in the United States than in Western Europe and Canada according to such measures as residential segregation and mixed unions. At the same time, immigrants of color and their children in the United States have benefited from the outcomes of the civil rights struggles of the mid-twentieth century and the very existence of a huge native black population in ways that have not been available to their counterparts across the Atlantic or north of the border.

Yet the facts do not support the kind of "good exceptionalism" for the United States that those who use the concept typically have in mind. For example, with a lower naturalization rate, the United States seems to be outperformed by Canada in giving membership rights to legal immigrants.[21] Nor, with its large low-wage sectors, does it provide greater opportunities for upward occupational mobility for immigrant-origin populations than do many other countries in our study.

If anything comes out of our study, it is that each country has many distinctive or exceptional features, and a perspective celebrating or demonizing the United States is not only too simple, but also misleading. So is a view that emphasizes only a society's singular aspects. There may be "many exceptionalisms," to use Aristide Zolberg's phrase, but the fact is that no country is unique in all ways. A focus on exceptionalism disregards the many similarities in patterns and processes of integration of immigrants and their children in the United States and other societies, and greatly overstates the degree to which the United States stands alone.

And this brings us to the notion of convergence, in which the master trend is alleged to be a growing similarity in government policies related to immigrants. Among the factors identified as pushing countries on both sides of the Atlantic toward more similar policies and practices is the need to cope with the problems of integrating immigrants and their children in liberal democratic societies. In fact, changing citizenship policies in many Western European countries since the end of World War II have brought them closer to those in North America in making it easier for immigrants and their children to acquire citizenship; in addition, antidiscrimination policies are now required by a European Union directive.[22] The sheer weight of demographic change and the growing number and proportion of immigrant minorities are behind their increasing representation in political office in all the countries in our study.

But if there is some evidence of convergent trends, there is also persistent divergence among the rich democracies in the domains we have studied. A tension exists, as Gary Freeman has observed, between "identifying unifying trends and [the] equally compelling need to pay attention to specificity."[23] Thus, while citizenship policies may be becoming more alike, no common citizenship policy has emerged in Europe and North America; and there are important national differences in the degree to which immigrant-origin politicians have been able to penetrate the precincts of power. In general, national differences in policies and practices as well as ideologies and institutions continue to shape both the successes and challenges of integration.

In sum, none of these grand ideas or perspectives offers a comprehensive explanation of the pathways of integration. They may shed some light on these patterns, but each is insufficient and each has serious failings. None brings out all of the elements that we argue are central, although these elements do not coalesce into one overarching "grand narrative." There are the characteristics or qualities immigrants bring with them when they move to Europe or North America, in terms of skills, education, skin color, and religion and culture, which shape the challenges that they and their families face and the successes they achieve. There are the demographic features of— and other social and economic trends in—the societies where they have settled and now live. And, perhaps above all, there are the broad range of historically rooted social, political, and economic institutions and structures in each receiving country that create barriers, as well as bridges, to integration and inclusion.

The failure of the grand ideas to systematically identify and explain successes or failures when it comes to integration has a salutary implication. No society is excluded from the possibility of improving integration because it falls on the wrong side of a grand idea; and no society is exempt from the need to take steps to improve integration because its institutional setup is the best. This need thus highlights one of the advantages of comparative analysis: its ability to suggest "borrowings," that is, features of one national context that can potentially be adopted to another to ease or facilitate integration.

POTENTIAL REMEDIES

Are there ways of improving the integration prospects of the low-status immigrant-origin groups in the wealthy West? We believe that there are. But just as there is no simple diagnosis for the problems of integration, which vary in their nature from society to society, there is no single remedy that will bring about a large-scale amelioration. Here, we first consider some common recommendations, before suggesting some of our own.

MORE SELECTIVE IMMIGRATION POLICIES

One idea, popular with politicians and many in the general public, is the adoption of more selective immigration policies, so that a larger fraction of immigrants arrive with educational and professional qualifications that enable them to fill jobs on the higher tiers of the labor market. As the case of Canada shows, selective immigration policies do not guarantee that immigrants can obtain such jobs. Nevertheless, their children frequently do well in the receiving society's educational system, positioning them to move up.

In the United States, economist George Borjas has championed the addition of a points system rewarding educational and skill-related qualifications to the immigration regime.[24] The immigration reforms that have been considered by the U.S. Congress in recent years have included some elements of this idea. In Germany, a so-called green card scheme was initiated in 2000, in order to attract highly qualified immigrants, but the results were meager. In France, in 2007, then President Sarkozy called for opening immigration to skilled immigrants, though nothing subsequently happened. Given the challenges of the diversity transition in wealthy Western societies, including the educational gaps generally separating a large part of the second generation from the upper tiers of the labor market, the notion of filling the need for highly trained workers with immigrants has obvious attractions.

But this is easier said than done. The German example shows that merely putting out a welcome mat does not mean that many of the desired immigrants will come through the door. Should many of the wealthy countries attempt at once to attract highly educated immigrants from elsewhere on the globe, it is not clear that there will be a large enough supply to fill all of their labor needs. In any case, such a large outflow of educated workers from countries such as China and India might, over the long term, threaten their own economic development. A new form of protectionism, involving human capital, could result.

Moreover, some of the wealthy societies will need low-skilled labor as well. Demographer Frank Bean and his colleagues have argued that one of the drivers for unauthorized immigration to the United States is the decline in the supply of native low-skilled workers willing to take many bottom-end jobs.[25] Reorienting immigration systems toward high-skilled flows might not satisfy needs at the lower end of the labor market. In the United States, such a reorientation, if it involved a significant reduction of family-based visas, would mean a pronounced shift in the geographic origins of immigrants toward Asia and away from Latin America. Given the well-established migration networks linking Latin America to el Norte, this shift would almost certainly bring about a rise in undocumented immigration. This would be counterproductive, in our view.

ETHNIC SOCIAL CAPITAL

One strategy for minority success in situations of hostility from majority groups depends on the development of ethnic social capital, embedded in networks of coethnics and in ethnic community institutions. Involvement in these networks and institutions can give minorities access to significant resources controlled by their own ethnic group, so that ethnic membership becomes a benefit rather than disadvantage. Ethnic social capital can take economic forms, for example, occupational niches and industrial sectors where high ethnic concentration, and sometimes ownership, allow a degree of control over recruitment to new jobs. It can also take the form of communal institutions, such as after-school educational programs, where children in the group receive an academic boost.[26] In the United States, where there is an extensive historical record detailing how earlier groups climbed the social ladder, we know that minority control over specific parts of the economy, such as what Jews achieved in the New York garment industry, was an effective mobility strategy for many immigrants and their children. There is every reason to think that ethnic social capital will prove consequential for new groups, as well.

The ethnic social capital strategy has appeared to some scholarly commentators as an attractive solution to integration problems. This is especially so when it is contrasted with assimilation to the mainstream, which is associated with various pitfalls, including the weakening of immigrant and ethnic cultures. Indeed, the highly influential segmented assimilation model puts the ethnic social capital strategy at the core of one of three main trajectories followed by contemporary immigrant groups. Since the other two—mainstream assimilation, which is assumed by segmented-assimilation theorists to be open only to those who are racially acceptable to whites, and downward assimilation, which entails incorporation into the ethnic-racial bottom of the receiving society and thus is associated with severe, permanent disadvantages—are deemed either hard to pursue or highly undesirable, the ethnic capital strategy gains in significance by comparison. Referring to the "resources made available through networks in the coethnic community," Alejandro Portes and Min Zhou write:

> Immigrants who join well-established and diversified ethnic groups have access from the start to a range of moral and material resources well beyond those available through official assistance programs. . . . In addition, the economic diversification of several immigrant communities creates niches of opportunity that members of the second generation can occupy, often without a need for an advanced education.[27]

This last condition implies that the ethnic path can lead to economic success for the children of immigrants who are unable to make full use of the mainstream school system.

The historical record strongly suggests that the most successful groups in the United States have used dual strategies, ethnic social capital *and* mainstream assimilation, often simultaneously; the ethnic social capital strategy has been most effective as a one- or two-generation effort by some families. Many immigrant parents prospered through the use of ethnic resources, thereby enabling their children to enter the mainstream economy, often at high occupational levels. However, our analysis of contemporary groups indicates that the ethnic social capital strategy does not provide a general solution to the dilemmas of integration in North America and Western Europe. The strategy is most effective in class-diverse immigrant groups. For resources to be available through ethnic networks, there have to be group members in positions to give others a leg up, for example, owning businesses that require numerous employees (not just ethnic groceries, in other words) or dominating occupational niches of some value (not just those needing low-wage workers). At the same time, there have to be group members with relatively few resources who can benefit from drawing on ethnic social capital to obtain, say, a better job than they otherwise would be able to get.

The groups seen as exemplars of the ethnic social capital strategy fit this profile. In the United States, the Cubans and the Chinese are the two most often cited. A "golden wave" of early Cuban exiles fleeing the Castro revolution brought to Miami many members of the former business, military, and political elites, who had the knowledge and experience to start businesses and organizations. A few arrived with financial capital; some benefited from massive U.S. government aid, including small-business loans, extended to the émigrés; and others obtained loans on favorable terms from coethnics. When later waves brought many members of the working and middle classes to South Florida, the ingredients were in place for the development of an extensive Cuban economic enclave.[28]

The Chinese case also involves class diversity, underscoring its potential value for the second generation's educational success. The class diversity within Chinese communities is associated with the circulation of information about the best schools and educational opportunities through the ethnic media as well as word of mouth; class diversity is linked, as well, to the proliferation of community after-school institutions, such as language schools and SAT prep classes, which enhance the academic skills of Chinese children. One study of the second generation in the New York metropolitan region revealed striking gaps in knowledge about elite public high schools in the city between Chinese and Dominicans; the latter had little information about how to get their children into the better schools partly because they are a relatively homogeneous poor group.[29]

For groups dominated in the first generation by low-wage workers, such as Mexicans in the United States and Turks in Western Europe, the ethnic social capital strategy is unlikely to be as effective. It may even lead to or accentuate social isolation, enhancing the consequences of the mainstream society's attempts at social exclusion. The major reason is the groups' inability to command enough economic and other resources to provide opportunities for the mobility of many group members. In the Mexican case, the rate of business ownership is low and what ownership there is tends to be found in the small-scale retail sector, such as food stores. The occupational niches controlled by Mexicans are mainly undesirable, featuring manual labor that does not require much training or skill. And group-specific educational institutions like the after-schools plentiful in Chinese communities are scarce.[30] For the Mexicans and groups like them, the best chance of economic mobility lies in pathways into the mainstream.

In the eyes of many observers, the Turks of Western Europe (or at least many of them) appear to be pursuing an ethnic social capital strategy. Their communities exhibit considerable closure with respect to the mainstream society and many Turks are owners of ethnic small businesses. They have high rates of endogamous marriage, often involving partners drawn from home villages, as well as high levels of maintaining the Turkish language in households that often encompass three generations (from immigrant grandparents to their grandchildren). Overall, the Turks in Western Europe lag in terms of a number of key socioeconomic indicators, such as educational attainment and employment. One analysis of the high rates of unemployment among the Turkish second generation in Germany traces its roots precisely to the embeddedness of many in exclusively Turkish social networks. In short, the ethnic social capital strategy does not seem to be paying off.[31]

THE SECOND GENERATION

For obvious reasons, the second generation is the key to the near-term future of diversity in wealthy Western societies. Our review of its position indicates that for the most part the children of low-status immigrant parents are disadvantaged, not as much as their parents, to be sure, but disadvantaged, nevertheless. A key institutional domain in which their disadvantages become manifest and then solidified is education: with some exceptions, such as the Bangladeshis and Pakistanis of Great Britain, these young people have higher rates of dropout and lower rates of post-secondary education than does the native majority. These facts raise disturbing doubts about the long-range ability of these second-generation young people to integrate into the mainstream labor market and also to replace the large number of native majority Americans, Canadians, and Europeans who will be leaving the economically active phase of their lives over the next quarter century.

The educational systems of North American and Western European countries are structured very differently from one another, but nevertheless produce broadly similar inequalities. That is to say, however structured, they function in ways that give a distinct edge to the children from majority-group, middle- and upper-middle-class families. For instance, in France and the United States (and undoubtedly in most or all of the other countries) the most experienced and qualified teachers are concentrated in schools attended by advantaged students and are few in number in those attended by poor, immigrant-origin, or other minority children. Ironically, all of these systems are subject to various forms of democratic control, which has ended up giving better-off parents an edge; thorough-going reforms on behalf of disadvantaged students are very difficult to introduce because the parents of advantaged students, who tend to have disproportionate influence, are unwilling to level the playing field.

But all is not hopeless. For one thing, as the number of majority youth declines, and therefore fewer appear at universities and other post-secondary schools, places will become available for minority students. Of course, the most elite and highly competitive universities and schools will still be able to pick and choose from a pool of qualified applicants from the long-established majority population. But as the decline in the number of students from "traditional" backgrounds occurs, other universities and post-secondary schools are likely to make efforts to recruit students from nontraditional groups in order to remain vital and viable. Moreover, all of these institutions, including the most elite, will face pressures to have student bodies that more accurately reflect the changed ethnoracial composition of the general population. (A telling example: in 2014, Hispanics for the first time outnumbered whites in admission to the University of California, the elite tier of public higher education in the state.[32]) Many minorities who gain admission will be the children of more economically successful and more educated immigrant parents, but some, who have been better prepared and done well in the earlier stages of the educational system, will come from poorer families in low-status groups.

In addition, reforms in educational systems need to be considered. In this respect, each country can potentially learn from others about what works to narrow the educational gap between native- and immigrant-origin youth. The United States, a country of great concern to us, stands apart from the others we have considered in the degree of inequality among schools—an inequality rooted in the educational financing system and exacerbated by private subsidies of public schools by affluent parents—and in the degree of ethnoracial segregation among schools, which is largely a consequence of residential segregation of ethnoracial and income groups. These are "sticky" features of a system, that is to say, hard to change by policy intervention, as is evident from the stubborn level of school segregation, which has been a concern at various levels of government since the 1954 *Brown v. Board of Education* decision of the U.S. Supreme Court. However, the inequality in school finances could be reduced if the federal government took a greater role, which could occur in a variety of ways—for example, by subsidies to states for universal pre-K schooling. Universal pre-K would also have the benefit of giving children from immigrant homes more preparation (in language, classroom readiness, and other ways) for the moment when their academic performance starts to matter.

As we argued in chapter 8, the United States also does not compare well when it comes to its teaching corps. It is well known that the "quality" of American teachers, as measured by formal qualifications and scores on standardized tests, has suffered a long-term decline, as the career options for women have expanded and the status of the teaching profession has failed to improve so as to attract educationally high-performing men and women. More and more, new teachers are in the profession for periods as short as two or three years, not long enough to become proficient in the classroom. Indeed, by comparison with the strongest national systems, such as in Finland, the status of teachers in the United States seems quite low.[33] This is something that could be ameliorated by investing in teacher training, improving teacher salaries and working conditions, and providing substantial salary differentials to teachers who move to schools in poorer districts. In order to recruit academically outstanding students to the teaching profession, it must not appear—as it apparently does today—decidedly inferior to other career options open to them.

When they leave school, members of the second generation confront new challenges on entry into the labor market, where their chances of getting jobs appropriate to their educational attainments are worse than those of their native majority age mates. One way to improve this situation is to strengthen the legal regime for countering discrimination. Discrimination persists in Britain, Canada, and the United States, even if they have strong institutional supports for its victims, according to the Migrant Integration Policy Index.[34] In Germany, cases against discrimination are harder to mount partly because the ability of private organizations—like the NAACP in the United States, which has been pivotal to anti-discrimination efforts—to assist victims in the courts is limited. So is the power of bodies of the German state to act on their behalf. In France, the collection of ethnic and especially racial statistics that might reveal patterns of discrimination has been an issue. Stronger legal mechanisms to counter discrimination will not eliminate the employment barriers facing many in the second generation, but they would be a positive step.

There is no question that affirmative action policies in the United States, giving special consideration to African Americans and other minorities in employment and education, have been a central force behind the significant expansion of the black and Hispanic middle classes and greater diversity in schools, professions, and public bureaucracies. Although affirmative action has been under legal attack in the courts and dismantled in publicly funded universities in some states, minority students have made good use of the opportunities it provides. The appointment to the U.S. Supreme Court of Sonia Sotomayor, the child of poor Puerto Rican migrants, who has written movingly—and gratefully—about how affirmative action at Princeton and Yale Law School was a door-opener that changed the course of her life, suggests the possibilities of affirmative action in higher education. Affirmative action, she wrote in her memoir, created the conditions to bring students, like herself, "from disadvantaged backgrounds . . . to the starting line of a race many were unaware was even being run."[35] Sotomayor's example also points to the need to reinvigorate affirmative action in the United States and, if possible, to concentrate its effects on those, like her, who have suffered disadvantages owing to class as well as race and ethnicity. Positive discrimination measures of this sort would be a benefit across the Atlantic, where robust and far-reaching programs of this kind have yet to be introduced.

OTHER POLICIES THAT CAN MAKE A DIFFERENCE

The residential contexts in which the second generation is growing up affect its prospects for integration. In many cities and suburbs where immigrants are concentrated, they experience some degree of segregation, which occurs partly by choice; and their neighborhoods are more disadvantaged than others, which is presumably not what they would choose. This problem is most severe by far in the United States, where large enclaves have developed in which immigrants and other poor minorities live. This sorting of immigrants and the native majority among residential locations interacts with increasing economic inequality to create neighborhoods in which large numbers of ethnic and racial minorities spend much of their daily lives, and have many of their most important interactions, in a world apart from the dominant majority.

Public policies of two sorts can address residential segregation and inequality. One sort can weaken segregation. European cities like Amsterdam have policies that encourage social mixing in neighborhoods, for example, by locating social housing in more affluent settings. Such policies are less systematic in the United States, where "public" housing, epitomized by clusters of multistory apartment buildings designed for poor families, has a troubled reputation and is associated with badly maintained buildings, crime, and violence. However, a recent study of a low- and middle-income housing development, imposed on the affluent New Jersey suburb of Mount Laurel by court decisions in the 1970s and 1980s, indicates that moving into the development had positive impacts for the newcomers—such as reducing their exposure to neighborhood disorder and violence—without having negative effects on the larger community.[36] An expansion of housing vouchers, which provide subsidies to low-income families to obtain housing that they otherwise could not afford, could also contribute to social mixing in American neighborhoods. In short, housing policies can counteract widening economic segregation and persistent ethnoracial segregation, which constrain the opportunities of immigrant families.

Another set of policies is needed to address the handicaps that come from living in neighborhoods with concentrated poverty, which include housing deficiencies, high crime, and inferior schools. In the United States, such neighborhoods tend to suffer from disinvestment, as banks, supermarkets, and other businesses withdraw and public services deteriorate. Renewed public investment can work against this downward spiral by locating sites of public employment in these neighborhoods and ensuring that the quality of public schools is improved. Social-welfare and public-employment policies, along with a rise in the minimum wage, can lift the economic resources of the residents and help to bring back critical services provided by the business sector.[37] We recognize that all of this is much easier said than done. But it is important, we believe, to reject the pessimistic view that residential inequality is a "natural" byproduct of market processes in an unequal society and to demonstrate that public policies that are within the realm of the possible (since they exist in some countries) can make a difference. Indirect evidence of this difference comes from a recent study showing that immigrant neighborhoods are less disadvantaged in U.S. cities where the political environment is more favorable to immigrants.[38]

Then there are policies that can seek to reduce the racial and religious barriers confronting immigrants and their descendants. In Europe especially, where Muslims are such a high proportion of the immigrant-origin population, policies to reduce the stigma and disadvantages associated with Islam should be high on the agenda, as they already are in some places. In Germany, recognition of Islam in the corporate structure of the German state would put Islam on an equal footing with other major religions. In France and elsewhere in Europe, providing more public space to Islamic institutions would give those of Muslim background greater representation in public life and assist with integration. Public discourse also makes a difference for racial and religious divisions. Free speech, of course, should be protected in a democratic society, but politicians, the media, and public intellectuals should avoid publicly expressing views that stigmatize Muslims. Some will say that this is simply political correctness, and that no matter what people say in public, they may display considerable prejudice in their private utterings. But encouraging a climate that makes it less acceptable for leading figures to utter blatant religious, as well as racial and ethnic, slurs in public would be a positive development.

Citizenship and legal status also require policy attention, particularly in Germany and the United States. In Germany, restrictive naturalization regimes have produced low citizenship levels, not only among non-Western immigrants but also the second generation born before the introduction of *jus soli*. In the United States, the great difficulties and disadvantages facing undocumented immigrants are a modern-day scandal. The effects ripple beyond the 11 to 12 million undocumented immigrants to their often mixed-status families, including children who are citizens by birth. As of this writing, the U.S. Congress has yet to pass legislation providing a path to legalization and ultimately citizenship for the undocumented. In 2012 and 2014, President Obama issued executive orders intended to ameliorate the legal vulnerability of a substantial fraction of them. We do not know yet how many will take advantage of these programs and with what consequences for their lives. But, at best, they constitute a modest and temporary fix, not the permanent change in status that will allow the undocumented to live as legal residents do. Clearly, then, legislation is necessary to provide undocumented immigrants, and their children, with access to rights and opportunities for which they are now ineligible.

THE CHANGING FACE OF THE WEST

This book has analyzed the experiences of immigrants and their children in Europe and North America in the contemporary period, and we have put a heavy emphasis on institutional factors shaping their successes as well as continued difficulties. Yet a consideration of potential remedies calls attention to the fact that the problems we have discussed are not inevitable or unchangeable. In the years ahead, a wide range of social, economic, and political changes are likely to have positive effects on integration pathways, including: the transformation of population structures; educational and occupational gains made by many children and grandchildren of immigrants who may also live near, work with, and sometimes form families with longer-established natives; and growing political representation of immigrant minorities. Government policies as well as strategies and political struggles by those of immigrant origin themselves also have the potential to ameliorate or reduce difficulties they currently face. We do not envision a problem-free future for the many in low-status immigrant groups who begin with, and are hampered by, innumerable disadvantages in the immigrant generation. As we have indicated, a great many challenges still lie ahead. Moreover, there are many imponderables in considering the future, including the extent of continued immigration and its consequences. Unforeseen economic and political developments may intervene as the second, third, and fourth generations grow up and take their place in societies that themselves have been altered by the large proportions of the population with immigrant backgrounds.

Yet, with all these caveats, it is safe to predict that the face of the West will continue to change. The image of the West has long been associated with phrases such as the "white man's burden" that link whiteness with hegemony and assume that the mainstream of Western societies is exclusively constituted by individuals of white and long-established European ancestry. This assumption will not hold much longer and, in some places—like the U.S. presidential office—it has already been defied. As the transition to diversity unfolds throughout the West during the next quarter century, it is inevitable that the most prominent individuals in mainstream society—the occupants of visible positions from the heads of large companies, to elite professionals, to newscasters and other personalities in the media—will become ever more varied in ancestral background, color, and religion, and that these societies will increasingly understand themselves as ethnically and racially diverse.[39] The degree to which this will happen is, of course, variable and contingent—it will be more apparent in some places than others depending on demography and the balance achieved between the principles we earlier labeled as "inequality" and "diversity"; and it will be contingent upon unforeseeable events and developments, as we have just observed. But, at some level, diverse mainstreams are inevitable—and, we believe, welcome.

NOTES

1: STRANGERS NO MORE

1. Chavez 2008: 41–43; Caldwell 2009: 20; Lewis quoted in *The Economist*, November 25, 2004; Huntington 2004; see Foner and Simon, forthcoming.
2. German Marshall Fund 2011.
3. Bendix 1964; Fredrickson 1997; see also Foner 2005.
4. For example, Alba 2005; Alba et al. 2013; Foner 1978, 2005; Foner et al. 2014.
5. Ji and Batalova 2012.
6. Portes and Zhou 1993; Portes and Rumbaut 2001; see also Gans 1992.
7. The potential impacts of immigrant groups on the mainstream are discussed theoretically by Alba and Nee 2003 and Orum 2005; Jiménez and Horowitz 2013 provide an empirical demonstration.
8. Marsden 1994; Hollinger 1996.
9. Alba and Nee 2003; Bean and Stevens 2003; Brubaker 2001; the classic statement, still relevant in important ways, is by Gordon 1964. On empirical measurement of assimilation, see Waters and Jiménez 2005.
10. Gans 1979; Alba 1990; Alba and Nee 2003; Waters 1990; for more on boundaries and ethnoracial distinctions, see Alba 2005; Lamont 2000; Lamont and Molnár 2002; Wimmer 2013.
11. Vermeulen and Penninx 2000: 2; Berry 1997; see also Penninx and Martiniello 2004; Alba, Reitz, and Simon 2012.
12. Gerstle 2001.
13. Brubaker 1992; Favell 1998; Kymlicka 2012; Schnapper 1991; see also Bauder 2014; Kivisto 2002; Van Reekum, Duyvendak, and Bertossi 2012.
14. Glazer 1997.
15. Bertossi and Duyvendak 2012: 239.
16. See, for example, Duyvendak and Scholten 2012; Cesari 2013; Uberoi and Modood 2013; Vertovec and Wessendorf 2010.
17. Bertossi and Duyvendak 2012; Bowen et al. 2014; Ireland 2004; Schain 2008: 15; Winter 2014.
18. See, for example, Esping-Andersen 1990.
19. OECD 2013b.
20. Cornelius and Tsuda 2004: 20, 25; Mollenkopf and Hochschild 2010: 20.
21. See, for example, Corak 2013.
22. Torpey 2009: 145.
23. Zolberg 2008: 177.
24. For example, Freeman 1995; Hollifield, Martin, and Orrenius 2014; Joppke 2010; Joppke and Morawska 2003; Kolb 2014; Soysal 1994; Weil 2001.
25. Vertovec 2004: 977.

26. Howard 2009: 199; Judt 2005.
27. Freeman 2004: 946.
28. Crul and Schneider 2010; Brettell 2003; Foner 2005.
29. For example, Foner 2000, 2005, 2007, 2013a, 2014; Foner and Waldinger 2013.
30. For the United States, see Alba 2009; Myers 2007.

2: WHO ARE THE IMMIGRANTS?

1. Rose et al. 1969: 78.
2. Bade 1994; Lucassen 2005: 150.
3. Cited by Gokturk, Gramling, and Kaes 2007: 36.
4. Castles and Miller 2009: 100.
5. Hollifield 2004: 189; Moch 2003: 181.
6. Moch 2003: 189; Muus 2004: 268.
7. Schain 2008: 68, 128.
8. Bade 1994.
9. Koikkalainen 2011.
10. Ibid.
11. Drew and Sriskandarajah 2007; *The Economist* 2013; Office for National Statistics 2013.
12. Massey, Durand, and Malone 2002; Fitzgerald 2009.
13. Alba and Nee 2003: 176.
14. Reimers 1992; Zolberg 1999: 79.
15. Zolberg 1999: 79; 2007: 31.
16. Alba and Nee 2003: 181–82; Batalova and Lee 2012; Bean and Stevens 2003.
17. Bakalian and Bozorgmehr 2009; Martin 2004b; Zolberg 2007: 41.
18. Tichenor 2008; see also Schuck 2007a, 2009; Zolberg 2007.
19. Zolberg 1999: 78; Massey, Durand, and Malone 2002.
20. Kelley and Trebilcock 1998: 331, 345; Reimers and Troper 1992: 25; Li 2003.
21. Reimers and Troper 1992: 52.
22. Li 2003: 24–25.
23. DeVoretz 2004: 135.
24. Li 2003: 32; Milan 2011; Reitz 2014.
25. Massey and Brown 2011; Milan 2011; Reitz 2014.
26. Grieco et al. 2012.
27. Bean et al. 2011; Massey, Durand, and Malone 2002; Passel and Cohn 2011, Yoshikawa 2011.
28. Alba and Silberman 2002; Lucassen 2005.
29. Layton-Henry 2004; Peach 1998; Rose et al. 1969.
30. Castles and Miller 2009: 103; Lucassen and Penninx 1997: 45; Muus 2004: 268; Loozen, De Valk, and Wobma 2012.
31. Beauchemin, Hamel, and Simon 2010; Lucassen 2005: 179.
32. Cornelius, Espenshade, and Salehyan 2001.
33. Li 2003: 26–31; Citizenship and Immigration Canada 2008.
34. Batalova and Lee 2012; Chagnon 2013; Challinor 2011; Galarneau and Morissette 2008; Reitz 2005, 2014.

35. Kolb 2014; Reitz 2005, 2014.

36. Batalova 2010.

37. Koikkalainen 2011; see also Favell 2008.

38. Vasileva 2012.

39. Parsons and Smeeding 2006: 15.

40. Kolb 2014; Murphy 2006; *Migration Information Source* 2009.

41. Castles and Miller 2009: 188; Russell 2002.

42. Zolberg 1999: 80; 2007: 32; see also Haines 2007.

43. Bean and Stevens 2003: 23; Li and Batalova 2011.

44. Bruquetas-Callejo et al. 2007; Kogan 2010a; UNHCR 2006, 2007, 2013.

45. Hansen 2007: 226; Eurostat 2012b.

46. Handl 1994; Martin 2004a: 233.

47. Joppke 1999; Martin 2004a; *Migration News* 2000.

48. Schain 2006: 362–63.

49. Beck-Gernsheim 2007: 278; see also Charsley et al. 2012.

50. Beck-Gernsheim 2007: 275–76; Kalter and Schroedter 2010; Statistics Netherlands 2011.

51. Beck-Gernsheim 2007: 284; Kelek 2005.

52. Castles and Miller 2009; Hansen 2007; Carol, Ersanilli, and Wagner 2014; Kulu-Glasgow and Leerkes 2013; Schain 2006: 363.

53. Passel, Cohn, and Gonzalez-Barrera 2013.

54. Bean and Lowell 2007; Chavez 2008; Gonzalez-Berrera and Lopez 2013; Massey and Sanchez R 2012; Passel, Cohn, and Gonzalez-Barrera 2013.

55. Zolberg 1999: 76.

56. Tichenor 2008.

57. Bean and Lowell 2007; Martin 2004b; Massey, Durand, and Malone 2002; Zolberg 2007: 36.

58. Bloemraad 2012; Reitz 2004: 127.

59. Martin 2004b: 80.

60. Morehouse and Blomfield 2011; Schain 2013; Clandestino Research Project 2009.

61. Office for National Statistics 2011b.

62. The projections are available at: http://www.census.gov/population/projections/data/national/2012.html.

63. Alba 2009; Coleman 2006; Myers 2007.

64. The population pyramid has been constructed from the data available on the Statistics Netherlands website: http://www.cbs.nl/en-GB/menu/home/default.htm.

65. Zolberg 1999: 83.

66. Engelen 2003.

3: ECONOMIC WELL-BEING

1. Louie 2012; Smith 2006. We use the term "immigrant bargain" in a somewhat different way than these authors, including immigrants' hopes for their own advances over time as well as for their children's success.

2. Corak 2013; Noah 2012; Pontusson 2005: chap. 3; OECD 2011.

3. Gautié and Schmitt 2010.

4. Kalleberg 2000, 2009; Gautié and Schmitt 2010.

5. For the United States, see Bernhardt et al. 2001.

6. Kalleberg 2000.

7. Gautié and Schmitt 2010 is the overview volume; the country-specific studies are: Caroli and Gautié 2008 for France; Bosch and Weinkopf 2008 for Germany; Salverda, Van Klaveren, and Van der Meer 2008 for the Netherlands; Lloyd, Mason, and Mayhew 2008 for the United Kingdom; and Appelbaum, Bernhardt, and Murnane 2003 for the United States.

8. Gautié and Schmitt 2010: 37.

9. Bureau of Labor Statistics 2014.

10. Bosch, Mayhew, and Gautié 2010: 134–38.

11. OECD 2013a.

12. Pontusson 2005.

13. The distinction we make here is related to Gøsta Esping-Andersen's (1990) famous classification among social-welfare regimes as liberal, corporatist-statist, or social democratic. It corresponds, however, more precisely to Pontusson's (2005) political-economy scheme, although he does not count France in the social market category because it does not exemplify what he sees as another characteristic of this category—namely, coordination among firms in an industry (see also Hall and Soskice 2001). However, we see this characteristic as not relevant for the purposes of our discussion, whose focus is the integration of immigrants in the labor market. The countries we examine would be classified by Esping-Andersen as liberal or corporatist.

14. Oorschot 2006.

15. Like the Netherlands, Germany in recent years has become less generous toward the poor and the unemployed. Still, even after the introduction of the controversial Hartz IV reforms in 2005, which cut back on social welfare benefits, German social expenditures (as a percent of GDP), according to OECD data, exceeded those in the Netherlands and the three liberal market economies, although by smaller margins.

16. Gornick and Myers 2003; Whitehead and Scanlon 2007.

17. OECD 2013a; Krugman 2014.

18. Kogan 2006; Reyneri and Fullin 2011.

19. Gautié and Schmitt 2010; Piore 1979; Sassen 1988; Waldinger and Lichter 2003.

20. Batalova and Terrazas 2010; Zeng and Xie 2004.

21. Borjas and Friedberg 2009; Park and Myers 2010; Portes and Rumbaut 2006.

22. OECD 2013d.

23. Demireva 2009; Silberman 2011; Waldinger 1996.

24. Castles and Miller 2009.

25. Wilpert and Laacher quoted by Castles and Miller 2009: 239.

26. Table 3.2 is constructed from varied sources: data compiled for European countries from a harmonized version of quarterly labor-force data; and census data from Canada and the United States. The time period covered by the data is 2006–8 (depending on the source), therefore before the Great Recession had produced large effects on labor-market participation and unemployment in the countries in our study.

27. Demireva and Kesler 2011; Kogan 2011; Reyneri and Fullin 2011.

28. Fleischmann and Dronkers 2007; Van Tubergen, Maas, and Flap 2004.

29. Velasco and Dockterman 2010.

30. OECD 2012; Fleischmann and Dronkers 2007; Kogan 2006.

31. Kalter and Granato 2007.

32. Cheung and Heath 2007; Demireva and Kesler 2011.

33. Tesser and Dronkers 2007: table 9.3A.

34. Silberman and Fournier 2007; Silberman, Alba, and Fournier 2007; Lhommeau et al. 2010.

35. Tesser and Dronkers 2007: 365.

36. Van Amersfoort and Van Niekerk 2006.

37. Hargreaves 1995: 49.

38. Model and Fisher 2007; Yu and Heath 2007.

39. Kochhar 2009; Reitz 2007: 42.

40. None of the restrictions on welfare applies to immigrants once they become citizens; consequently, their U.S.-born children, who are citizens at birth, are eligible for welfare programs. Empirical studies therefore find relatively high use of these programs by immigrant families, although the amount of benefit received is typically quite limited (Camarota 2011).

41. Massey, Durand, and Malone 2002; Passel and Cohn 2009.

42. Alba et al. 2013; Silberman 2011.

43. Tesser and Dronkers 2007; Kalter and Granato 2007; Silberman 2011.

44. Velasco and Dokterman 2010; also Model and Fisher 2007.

45. Hondagneu-Sotelo 2001.

46. Chiswick and Miller 2008; Pichler 2011; Reitz 2005, 2007.

47. King 2009; see also Buzdugan and Halli 2009; and Reitz 2005, 2007.

48. Quoted by Reitz 2005: 7; Reitz 2011.

49. Reitz 2007: 47–8.

50. Zeng and Xie 2004.

51. Alba 2009.

52. The European data come from published tabulations of Eurostat (2011). We are grateful to Janet Gornick and the Luxembourg Income Project for access to Current Population Survey data that allow parallel calculations for the United States, which were prepared by David Monaghan. Comparable Canadian data were not available, and Canada is therefore omitted from the table.

53. Buettner 2008; for a historical account of ethnic food businesses in the United States as they changed the tastes of native-born Americans, see Gabaccia 1998.

54. Kloosterman and Rath 2003: 11.

55. Rath and Kloosterman 2003: 134.

56. Guzy 2006; Ma Mung and LaCroix 2003; Wilpert 2003; Bundesagentur für Arbeit 2013; Wikipedia 2013.

57. Desiderio and Salt 2010; Rusinovic 2006:137, 152; Zhou 2004.

58. For useful overviews of the literature on immigrant small businesses, see the chapters in Kloosterman and Rath 2003 on the six countries in our study as well as Gold 2010; Light and Gold 2000; Waldinger, Aldrich, and Ward 1990; and Zhou 2004.

59. OECD 2010.

60. Fiscal Policy Institute 2012; Kalter and Granato 2007; Tesser and Dronkers 2007; Van Tubergen 2005.

61. Clark and Drinkwater 2007; Maxwell 2012.
62. Waldinger, Aldrich, and Ward 1990.
63. Min 1996, 2008; Kang 2010.
64. Kim 2004; Kalter and Granato 2007; Silberman and Fournier 2007; Tesser and Dronkers 2007.

4: LIVING SITUATIONS

1. Caldwell 2009; Kelek 2005.
2. Buruma 2006; Koopmans et al. 2005; Vertovec and Wessendorf 2010.
3. Massey and Denton 1993; Wacquant 2008; Wilson 1996; cf. Small 2008.
4. Quoted in Gillan 2005.
5. Logan et al. 2002.
6. Massey 1985.
7. Logan and Molotch 1987.
8. Breton 1964; Logan, Alba, and Zhang 2002.
9. Zhou 2009.
10. For example, Portes and Bach 1985; Portes and Stepick 1994.
11. Li 1998; Logan, Alba, and Zhang 2002.
12. Jiménez and Horowitz 2013.
13. Light and Johnston 2009; Marrow 2011; Massey 2008; Zuñiga and Hernández-León 2005.
14. Borrel n.d.; Pan Ké Shon 2011; Préteceille 2009.
15. Reitz and Zhang 2011; Statistics Canada 2013.
16. Peach 1996; Johnston, Poulsen, and Forrest 2013.
17. Schönwälder and Söhn 2009.
18. Peach 2006.
19. Préteceille 2009.
20. Massey and Denton 1988; Logan and Stults 2011.
21. The values are derived from the 2010 Census and taken from the data website of the US2010 Project at Brown University: see http://www.s4.brown.edu/us2010/Data/Data.htm. See also Sharkey 2014.
22. Massey and Denton 1993.
23. Ibid.; Telles and Ortiz 2008.
24. Logan and Stults 2011.
25. Alba et al. 2014.
26. Logan and Stults 2011.
27. Zhou 2009.
28. Logan and Stults 2011.
29. Marrow 2011; Massey 2008; Singer 2004; Zuñiga and Hernández-León 2005.
30. Logan and Stults 2011; Alba et al. 2014.
31. Iceland 2009; Iceland and Nelson 2008; Alba and Romalewski 2012; Emerson et al. n.d.; Villarrubia et al. n.d.
32. Logan and Stults 2011.
33. Li 1998; Matsumoto 2011.

34. Logan, Alba, and Zhang 2002.

35. Logan and Deane 2003.

36. Logan and Stults 2011.

37. Smith 1995.

38. Hou 2006; cf. Telles and Ortiz 2008.

39. Reitz and Zhang 2011.

40. Hou and Wu 2009.

41. Fong and Wilkes 2003; see also Hou 2006; Myles and Hou 2004; White, Fong, and Cai 2003.

42. Hou 2006.

43. Myles and Hou 2004.

44. Murdie and Ghosh 2010.

45. Hou and Wu 2009; Fong and Wilkes 2003.

46. Priemus and Dieleman 2002; Musterd and Andersson 2005; Verdugo 2011.

47. Poulsen and Johnston 2006; Peach 2009; Gillan 2005.

48. Peach 2009; Johnston, Forrest, and Poulsen 2002.

49. Peach 2009.

50. Poulsen and Johnston 2006; Peach 2009; Johnston, Poulsen, and Forrest 2013.

51. Johnston, Forrest, and Poulsen 2002; Johnston, Poulsen, and Forrest 2013; Poulsen and Johnston 2006; Peach 2009.

52. Johnston, Poulsen, and Forrest 2013; Peach 2006; Vertovec 2007.

53. Johnston, Poulsen, and Forrest 2013; Poulsen and Johnston 2006.

54. Ibid.

55. Peach 2006.

56. Wacquant 2008.

57. Pan Ké Shon 2011; Safi 2009.

58. Most studies of the Paris region are based on juridical units, *quartiers* within the city of Paris (a subdivision of the *arrondissement*) and place boundaries outside of it. Also, the only indicator of ethnoracial origin available in French census data is birthplace. Hence, the second generation is not taken into account.

59. Préteceille 2009.

60. Préteceille 2009; Pan Ké Shon and Verdugo 2014.

61. Musterd and Ostendorf 2009; see also Aalbers and Deurloo 2003; Logan 2006.

62. Logan 2006.

63. Boelhouwer 2002; Aalbers and Deurloo 2003.

64. Logan 2006.

65. Schönwälder and Söhn 2009; Kelek 2005.

66. Friedrichs 2008.

67. Schönwälder and Söhn 2009,

68. Massey and Denton 1993; Wilson 1996; Anderson 1999; Sampson 2012.

69. Massey and Fischer 2000; Krivo, Peterson, and Kuhl 2009; Alba et al. 2014; Rosenbaum and Friedman 2007.

70. Zhou 2009.

71. Orfield and Lee 2006; Alba et al. 2014.

72. Musterd and Andersson 2005; Boelhouwer 2002; CLIP Network 2007; Nieuwboer 2003.

73. Fitoussi, Laurent, and Maurice 2004; see Pan Ké Shon 2011; Silberman, Alba, and Fournier 2007; Verdugo 2011; Wacquant 2008.

74. Logan 2006; Bolt and Van Kempen 2010; Musterd and Ostendorf 2009

75. Reardon and Bischoff 2011.

76. Lee and Bean 2010.

77. South, Crowder, and Chavez 2005a, 2005b; Sampson and Sharkey 2008.

78. Alba, Logan, and Stults 2000; Alba et al. 2014; Iceland and Nelson 2008.

79. Alba et al. 2014; Brown 2007.

80. Musterd and DeVos 2005; Logan 2006; also Bolt and Van Kempen 2010; on France, see Rathelot and Safi 2014.

81. Rathelot and Safi 2014.

82. Özüekren and Ergoz-Karahan 2010.

83. Gonzales 2011; Menjivar 2006; Menjivar and Kanstroom 2014.

84. Bean et al. 2011.

85. Logan and Zhang 2010; Vertovec 2007, 2013; Johnston, Poulsen, and Forrest 2013.

86. Foner 2013a, 2013b; Philpott, 1978.

87. Logan and Zhang 2010.

88. Putnam 2007.

89. Wessendorf 2010, 2013.

90. But see Sanjek 1998; Jones-Correa 1998; Oliver 2010; Vertovec forthcoming.

91. Peach 2006.

92. Reardon and Bischoff 2011.

93. Krivo, Peterson, and Kuhl 2009.

94. For example, Alba et al. 2014; Pais, South, and Crowder 2011.

95. Bolt, Özüekren, and Phillips 2010; Britton 2014.

96. Blokland and Van Eijk 2010; Van der Laan Bouma-Doff 2007.

97. Özüekren and Ergoz-Karahan 2010.

98. Alba et al. 2014.

5: THE PROBLEMS AND PARADOXES OF RACE

1. Winks 1971.

2. Okihiro 2001: 54.

3. Foner and Fredrickson 2004; Fredrickson 2002.

4. Bonilla-Silva 1997; Feagin 2006; Omi and Winant 1994; Painter 2010; Winant 2002.

5. Fredrickson 2002: 108.

6. Fredrickson 2005: 89.

7. Ibid. 95.

8. Lopez 1996.

9. Giraud 2009: 46; Abdouni and Fabre 2012; Breuil-Genier, Borrel, and Lhommeau 2012; Beriss 2004: 37–38; Brinbaum et al. 2010; see also Byron and Condon 2008.

10. Essed and Trienekens 2008: 68; see also Duyvendak 2012.

11. For example, Delhaye, Saharso, and Van den Ven 2014; Ersanilli 2007.

12. Bleich 2003.

13. Modood 2007: 101; for figures on early Caribbean migration to Britain, see Rose et al 1969: 83; see also Bleich 2003: 36–37; Foner 2005: 114–15.

14. Modood 2005a: 464–66; Modood 2005b.

15. Peake and Ray 2001: 180.

16. Bloemraad 2006: 132–34; Li 2003: 126; Statistics Canada 2013.

17. Hollinger 2003: 1378.

18. Fenton 2010: 37; Song 2003: 147.

19. Koopmans et al. 2005: 144; Essed and Trienekens 2008: 52, 56; Hondius 2009; Klostermann 2008: 3; Beriss 2004: 6; Bleich 2003: 172.

20. Passel, Wang, and Taylor 2010.

21. Central Bureau of Statistics 2013; Kalmijn and Van Tubergen 2006; Hamel et al. 2010.

22. Patterson 2005: 98.

23. Platt 2009; Owen 2007; Model and Fisher 2002; see also Muttarak and Heath 2010.

24. Milan, Maheux, and Chui 2010; see also Rodriguez-Garcia 2007.

25. Maurer 2003; West 2009; Berman and Dar 2013.

26. Western and Wildeman 2009; Rumbaut and Ewing 2007; Kasinitz et al. 2008: 188.

27. Pager 2007.

28. Constant 2009: 246.

29. Beauchemin et al. 2010; Beauchemin, Hamel, and Simon 2010; Brinbaum et al. 2010; Silberman and Fournier 2006; Silberman, Alba, and Fournier 2007; Silberman 2011; Model 2008: 130; Back 1996; Solomos 2003; Cornell and Hartmann 2007.

30. Reitz and Banjerjee 2007; Attewell, Kasinitz, and Dunn 2010.

31. Blauner, 1972; Feagin 2006; Fox and Guglielmo 2012.

32. Lopez and Stanton-Salazar 2001: 75. On the racialization of Latinos, see also Massey and Sanchez R 2012.

33. Dowling 2014; Fox and Guglielmo 2012: 369; Roth 2012; Vasquez 2011; Massey and Sanchez R 2012; Alba 2005: 37–39; Waters 2014; Jiménez 2010.

34. Alba, Jiménez, and Marrow 2014; see also Telles 2010.

35. Rumbaut 2005; Perlmann 2011; Bean et al. 2011; Alba et al. 2014.

36. For data suggesting a role for skin-color inequalities among Mexicans, see Telles and Murgia 1990; however, Telles and Ortiz 2008 do not find such a role.

37. Alba and Nee 2003: 174; Skrentny 2002: 62; see also Reimers 1992; Tichenor 2002; Zolberg 1999, 2006.

38. Kasinitz et al. 2008: 303; Skrentny 1996.

39. Katznelson 2005: 148–49.

40. Kasinitz et al. 2008: 303, 331–33, 366.

41. Massey et al. 2007; Massey et al. 2002; Kasinitz et al. 2008: 332.

42. Alba 2009.

43. Dobbin 2009; Kim, Kalev, and Dobbin 2012; for an analysis of the impact of civil rights legislation on racial segregation in the workplace for black men and women based on EEOC records, see Stainback and Tomaskovic-Devey 2012.

44. Mollenkopf and Hochschild 2010: 28–29; Foner and Alba 2010.

45. Lieberman 2005: 512.
46. Migrant Integration Policy Index 2014; see Givens and Case 2012.
47. Sabbagh 2002; Lieberman 2005; Joppke 1999; Ladd and Fiske 2011.
48. Bakan and Kobayashi 2007; Reitz and Banerjee 2007.
49. Mollenkopf and Hochschild 2010: 28.
50. Capps, McCabe, and Fix 2011; see also Kent 2007.
51. Mollenkopf 2014; Foner 2001, 2005, Kasinitz 1992; Model 2008; Vickerman 1999; Waters 1999; Foner 2005: 119.
52. See, for example, Bashi and Clarke 2001; Foner 2011; Vickerman 2001.
53. Neckerman, Carter, and Lee 1999; Louie 2012; Smith 2014.
54. Quoted in West 1994: 3.
55. See, for example, Foner 2001, 2005; Waters 1999; Vickerman 1999.
56. Prashad 2000: 94.
57. Foner 2011; Imoagene 2012; Foner et al. 2014.
58. Roth 2012: 29; Fox and Guglielmo 2012.
59. Centre for Contemporary Cultural Studies 1982; Lucassen 2005.

6: IMMIGRANT RELIGION

1. As elsewhere in the book, our analysis focuses on four European countries. However, since the issues at stake have relevance for most other Western European countries, we often refer broadly to "Western Europe" throughout the chapter.
2. Alba 2005.
3. Lyon and Van Die 2000.
4. Pew Forum on Religion and Public Life 2012a; Lucassen 2005.
5. Casanova 2007: 65; Modood 2005b:37; Goldberg 2006: 262; Bleich 2011; Cesari 2004: 32, 34; Cole 2009; Fekete 2009.
6. Strabac and Listhaug 2008; Pew Global Attitudes Project 2005.
7. Pauly cited in Brub 2008; Heath and Martin 2013; Cheung 2014; Silberman 2011.
8. Silberman, Alba, and Fournier 2007; Alba et al. 2013; for analyses of Belgium and Spain that reach similar conclusions, see Kalter and Kogan 2006; on Germany, see Seibert and Solga 2005, but cf. Kalter 2006.
9. See Cesari 2005: 1019; Kepel 1991; Fetzer and Soper 2005; Koopmans et al. 2005; Buijs and Rath, 2006; Maussen 2007; Rath et al. 2001; Sunier 2009; Tatari 2009; Klausen 2005; Joppke 2009a; Joppke and Torpey 2013.
10. Quoted in Uitmark, Duyvendak, and Rath 2014: 176.
11. Joppke 2009a; *The Economist* 2012; Uitermark 2012; Siebold 2010.
12. Roy 2010; Buruma 2010: 5; Peter van der Veer, quoted in Duyvendak et al. 2009: 138; Buruma 2006: 69; Scheffer 2000. See Duyvendak, Pels, and Rijkschroeff 2009 on the development of a progressive Dutch monoculture that has created a value gap with Muslims and a demand that they accept Dutch progressive values on gender, family, divorce, and homosexuality.
13. Klausen 2009; *The Economist* 2006.
14. Buruma 2006: 221; Buijs 2009: 434–35.

15. Wikan 2002; Kelek 2005; see Foner and Dreby 2011.

16. Cohen 2007; see Bowen 2007; Scott 2007; Renaut and Touraine 2005; Joppke 2009b; Human Rights Watch 2009.

17. Joppke 2009a: 470, 2009b; Pew Global Attitudes Project 2010.

18. Kramer 2004, see also Bowen 2009: 442; Voas and Fleischmann 2012; Maliepaard et al. 2010.

19. Leiken 2012; Bleich 2009; Pew Global Attitudes Project 2005.

20. For example, Didier Lepeyronnie, cited in Laurence and Vaisse 2006: 93; Phalet et al. 2013.

21. Rath 2011.

22. Fetzer and Soper 2005; Kastoryano 2002; Klausen 2005; Joppke 2009a; Koenig, 2005; Koopmans et al. 2005; Maussen 2007; Vertovec 1998.

23. Fetzer and Soper 2005: 48; Bowen 2012: 76.

24. Rath, 2005: 31; see also Buruma, 2006.

25. Vermeulen and Penninx 2000: 28. The system of pillarization began to break down in the 1960s in response to increasing social and geographical mobility as well as secularization in Dutch society.

26. Maussen 2012; Rath 2005: 32; Duyvendak 2011: 86–88; Buijs 2009: 426–27; Koopmans et al. 2005: 55–58; see also Carol and Koopmans 2013.

27. Laurence 2012: 137–39; 182–84, 196; Laurence and Vaisse 2006: 138. See also Joppke and Torpey 2013: 79–83 and Conclusions on the German Islam Conference plenary held on May 17, 2010, www.deutsche-islam-konferenz.de/ . . . /Plenum-arbeits programm-en.pdf?

28. Koopmans et al. 2005: 57; Fetzer and Soper 2005: 129; Joppke and Torpey 2013: 48–83.

29. Bennhold 2014.

30. Joppke and Torpey 2013: 145.

31. Crul and Mollenkopf 2012: 253.

32. Wuthnow 2005: 217–20; Gallup Center for Muslim Studies 2010.

33. Pew Forum on Religion and Public Life 2013; ACLU 2013; see also Bakalian and Bozorgmehr 2009; Cainkar 2009; Detroit Arab American Study Team 2009; Goodstein 2010.

34. Cesari 2013: 2, 11; Crul and Mollenkopf 2012; Duyvendak 2011.

35. Portes and Rumbaut 2006: 300; Alba, Raboteau, and DeWind 2009; Hirschman 2004.

36. Herberg 1960 [1955]: 27–28; Casanova 2007: 68; Alba 2009; Hirschman 2004: 1207; see also Portes and Rumbaut 2006.

37. Chen 2006, 2008; Suh 2009.

38. Kurien 1998: 37; Levitt 2007.

39. Bakalian and Bozorgmehr 2009: 2, 249.

40. Eck 2007; Warner and Wittner 1998; Ebaugh and Chafetz 2000; Fischer and Hout 2006; Leonard 2003; for a critique of the "congregational" argument, see Foley and Hoge 2007.

41. Hirschman 2004: 1215–16; see also George 1998; Hepner 1998.

42. Casanova 2007: 73.

43. Foner 2014.

44. Min 2001: 186.

45. Foley and Hoge 2007.

46. Cainkar 2009: 264.

47. Zhou and Bankston 1998; Lopez 2009.

48. Pew Forum on Religion and Public Life 2008, 2011, 2012a, 2012b; Laurence 2012; see also Buijs and Rath 2006:7; Eumap 2007. The estimated number of Muslims in Western Europe refers to those in the EU-15, before enlargement in 2004.

49. Pew Research Center for People and the Press 2011; Pew Forum on Religion and Public Life 2012a, 2012c Pew Research Center 2014; Bakalian and Bozorgmehr 2009: 95; for estimates on the proportion of U.S. Muslims who are African American, see Pew Research Center for People and the Press 2011; Pew Research Center 2007; Gallup Organization 2009; and Kosmin and Keysar 2006.

50. European Monitoring Centre for Racism and Xenophobia 2006; Pew Research Center for People and the Press 2011; Pew Research Center 2007; see also Bakalian and Bozorgmehr 2009.

51. Fischer and Hout 2006.

52. Pew Global Attitudes Project 2012; Smith 2012; Ford 2005; Gallup/The Coexist Foundation 2009.

53. Fischer and Hout 2014; Pew Forum on Religion and Public Life 2012b.

54. Casanova 2007: 67.

55. Jones et al. 2011; Bowen 2012: 57–58; Edgell, Gerteis, and Hartmann 2006.

56. Casanova 2007: 65; Cesari 2004: 176; Koopmans et al. 2005: 155, 175.

57. Casanova and Zolberg 2002; Pew Forum on Religion and Public Life 2008; see also Putnam and Campbell (2010: 501), who report that 30 percent of the respondents in their Faith Matters survey were evangelical Protestants, and Wolfe and Katznelson (2010) on the role of religion in American politics.

58. Eck 2001: 384.

59. On this view of Catholicism, see McGreevey 2003.

60. Wolfe 2006: 159; Gerstle forthcoming; Higham 1955.

61. Alba 2005: 30–31; Wuthnow 2005: 32–33.

62. Bloomberg, quoted in Elliott 2010. Cesari 2004: 84; see also Joppke and Torpey 2013: 126.

63. Casanova 2007: 74; Zolberg and Woon 1999; see also Joppke and Torpey 2013: 116, 136; Obama quoted in Los Angeles Times 2010.

64. Cainkar 2009: 265; Bakalian and Bozorgmehr 2009: 249.

65. We are grateful to Martin Baumann for comments on this question in an earlier version of this chapter (Foner and Alba 2008).

66. Laurence and Vaisse 2006: 83.

67. Alba 2005: 32, 34; Laurence and Vaisse 2006: 83; Laurence 2012: 142–43; Cesari 2013: 121.

68. Rath, quoted in Klausen, 2005:146; Maussen 2012: 344–45, 350.

69. U.K. Department for Education 2010; Maussen 2012: 346–47; Sciolino 2003; Klausen 2005: 144; Nixey 2009. The figures on the number of state-funded religious schools in Britain are for England.

70. Klausen 2005; Joppke and Torpey 2013: 73; Smale 2014.

71. Ujimoto 1999; Bloemraad 2006; Beyer 2005; Model and Lin 2002; Pew Forum on Religion and Public Life 2011.

72. Gallup survey reported in Ray 2003; Norris and Inglehart 2007; see also Pew Global Attitudes Project 2002.

73. Reitz et al. 2009: 721; Seljak 2000: 132; Bramadat 2005; CBC News Online 2.

74. Khan 2007; Milot 2009; Reitz et al. 2009: 722; Mooney 2013: 100.

75. Bramadat 2005: 4–5; Seljak 2005:181.

76. Seljak 2005; Ontario Ministry of Education 1994.

77. John Webster Grant, quoted in Christiano 2000: 75–76.

78. Seljak 2005: Young 2009; Reitz et al. 2009; Wilson 2007.

79. Boyd 2007; Reitz et al. 2009.

80. Gerstle forthcoming.

81. See Putnam and Campbell 2010; Kalkan, Layman, and Uslaner 2009.

82. Laurence 2012.

83. Cf. Laurence 2012: 270.

84. Uitermark, Duyvendak, and Rath 2014.

85. For example, Lucassen 2005:157–58, 207.

86. On one side are: Jacob and Kalter 2013; Lewis and Kashyap 2013; Maliepaard, Gijsberts, and Lubbers 2012; Phalet et al. 2013; Voas and Fleischmann 2012; on the other: Maliepaard, Lubbers, and Gijsberts 2010; Connor and Koenig 2013; Diehl and Schnell 2006; Tribalat 1995; Van der Bracht, van de Putte, and Verhaeghe 2013.

87. Crul and Mollenkopf 2012: 252.

88. Joppke and Torpey 2013: 81–83.

89. Laurence 2012: 265; see also Leiken 2012 and *Der Spiegel* 2014.

7: ENTERING THE PRECINCTS OF POWER

1. Hochschild and Mollenkopf 2009.

2. Soysal 1994; Chung 2005; Hooghe 2005; Koopmans and Statham 2000b; Koopmans 2004.

3. But see Bloemraad and Schönwälder 2013; Bird, Saalfeld, and Wust 2011; Givens and Maxwell 2012.

4. Bloemraad and Schönwälder 2013.

5. For example, Joppke and Morawska 2003, Soysal 1994, Weil 2001; Brubaker 2001; see also Freeman 1995.

6. Alba and Foner 2009.

7. Bloemraad 2006; Brubaker 1992; Castles and Davidson 2000: 85; Joppke 1999; Weil 2001, 2002.

8. Weil 2001: 30; Bauböck and Honohan 2010; Howard 2009; Joppke 2010.

9. Vink and de Groot 2010: 720; Castles and Davidson 2000: 92–93.

10. Weil 2001; Castles and Davidson 2000: 94; see also Triadafilopoulos 2012.

11. Howard 2009: 198; Kivisto and Faist 2010: 218–23.

12. Vink and de Groot 2010; Jones-Correa 2001: 1012; Howard 2005: 709; Schuck 2007b.

13. Brubaker 2001; Joppke 2004, 2010, 2012; Schain 2008.

14. Buruma 2006; Prins and Saharso 2010; Vermeulen, Michon, and Tillie 2014; Hurenkamp, Tonkens, and Duyvendak 2012; Joppke 2004, 2010, 2012; Goodman 2010, 2012; Nana 2007; Leise, 2007; Strik et al. 2010.

15. Quoted in Ersanilli and Koopmans 2010: 775; Bauböck et al. 2007.

16. Vertovec and Wessendorf 2010; Kymlicka 2012.

17. Alba and Nee 2003.

18. Portes and Zhou 1993; Hochschild and Mollenkopf 2009.

19. Bloemraad 2013.

20. Bird 2011; Wust 2011.

21. Glazer and Moynihan [1963] 1970.

22. Erie 1988; Waldinger 1996.

23. Bloemraad 2013.

24. Alba 2005; Lucassen 2005.

25. We follow the main electoral studies in including in the non-Western population the migrants to the French mainland from overseas departments and territories, even though these are French citizens by birth who are not migrating across an international border. But they are mostly nonwhites. They make up a small proportion of the non-Western total, in any event.

26. Beauchemin, Hamel, and Simon 2010.

27. Diehl and Blohm 2003; Statistisches Bundesamt 2010.

28. Bloemraad 2006.

29. Portes and Rumbaut 2006.

30. Alba and Foner 2009; Amadieu n.d; Schönwälder, Volkert, and Sinanoglu 2011.

31. Schönwälder, Sinanoglu, and Volkert 2013; Schönwälder, Volkert, and Sinanoglu 2011; Schönwälder 2013.

32. Alba and Foner 2009.

33. We depend here on the results reported by Schönwälder and her colleagues (2011, 2013), which are presented mainly in terms of all individuals with a migration background, whether European or non-European. For the largest German cities, such individuals are an estimated 27 percent of the population. Individuals with non-European origins are about a third of this large group.

34. Schönwälder, Volkert and Sinanoglu 2011; Schönwälder, Sinanoglu, and Volkert 2013.

35. Geiger and Spohn 2001.

36. Garbaye 2000, 2004, 2005; on the riots, see, for example, *The Economist* 2005 and Gordon 2005; on the survey, Amadieu n.d., see also Geisser and Oriol 2001; on regional councils, Keslassy 2010.

37. Geisser and Kelfaoui 2001: 55.

38. Amadieu n.d.

39. Andrew et al. 2008.

40. Kettlewell and Phillips 2014; Doughty, 2006; Van Heelsum 2002; Institute for Political Participation 2006; Foner et al. 2014; Vermeulen, Michon, and Tillie 2014; Michon and Vermeulen 2013.

41. The data on Hispanic elected officials come from the data series maintained by the National Association of Latino Elected Officials [NALEO], and we are grateful to Luis Fraga for pointing us in this direction.

42. Taylor et al. 2012.

43. Grenier and Perez 2003: 98; Stepick et al. 2003.
44. Mollenkopf 2014.
45. Bloemraad and Schönwälder 2013; Garbaye 2000; Geisser and Soum 2008; Tiberj and Michon 2013.
46. Schönwälder 2012; Laurence and Maxwell 2012; Migazin 2013.
47. Bloemraad 2006.
48. Bloemraad and Schönwälder 2012; Fennema et al. 2001; Vermeulen, Michon, and Tillie 2014; Michon and Vermeulen 2013; Maxwell 2013.
49. See Amadieu, n.d.; Keslassy 2010; Sobolewska 2013; Rath 1988; Vermeulen, Michon, and Tillie 2014.
50. Bird 2004; Martiniello 2000; Saggar and Geddes 2000; Saggar 2013.
51. Mollenkopf 2014; Skerry 1993.
52. Garbaye 2004; 2005: 32; 2000: 296; Geisser and Kelfaoui 2001; Geisser and Soum 2008; on the impact of the party system in Canada, see Bird 2011.
53. Koopmans and Statham 2000a: 38.
54. Vermeulen, Michon, and Tillie 2014; Entzinger 2003; Lijphart 1968; Buijs 2009: 426; Duyvendak 2011: 86–88; see also Duyvendak and Scholten 2012.
55. Joppke 1999: 224–25; Favell 1998; Koopmans and Statham 2000b: 221; Erie 1988.
56. Kramer 2005: 41; Geiger and Spohn 2001.
57. Geisser and Soum 2012: 56; see also Brouard and Tiberj 2011.
58. Bloemraad 2013: 662.
59. See Michon and Vermeulen 2013.
60. Brubaker 1992.
61. Laurence and Maxwell 2012.
62. Birnbaum 2013.
63. Sciolino 2004.
64. Geisser and Soum 2008, 2012.

8: EDUCATING THE SECOND GENERATION

1. Jiménez and Horowitz 2013.
2. Lucas 2001; Raftery and Hout 1993.
3. Van de Werfhorst and Mijs 2010; Alba and Holdaway 2013; Hochschild and Scovronick 2003; Phillips and Chin 2004.
4. Almendinger 1989; also Kristen, Reimer, and Kogan 2008; Shavit and Müller 1998; Suárez-Orozco, Suárez-Orozco, and Todorova 2008; Van de Werfhorst and Mijs 2010. In discussing systems, we must of necessity focus on their predominant patterns and ignore numerous variants within each one
5. Almendinger 1989: 233; Lessard-Phillips, Fleischmann, and van Elsas 2014.
6. Heath and Brinbaum 2014.
7. Almendinger 1989: 234; OECD 2013e: 220; Shavit and Müller 1998: 12.
8. Goldin and Katz 2008.
9. Porter 2013: B13; also Hochschild and Skovronick 2003; Kozol 1991.
10. Suárez-Orozco, Suárez-Orozco, and Todorova 2008.
11. Gibson et al. 2013.

12. Maaz et al. 2008.
13. Crul 2011; Hanushek and Woessmann 2005.
14. Crul et al. 2013.
15. Goldin and Katz 2008.
16. Alba et al. 2013.
17. Alba, Sperling, and Sloan 2011; Alba and Holdaway 2013: chap. 1.
18. Gibson et al 2013.
19. Crul 2011.
20. *The Economist* 2009; also Friedman 2012.
21. Downey, von Hippel, and Broh 2004; Entwisle and Alexander 1992; Heyns 1979.
22. Benabou, Kramarz, and Prost 2004; Goldenberg 2008.
23. Feliciano 2005.
24. Kao and Tienda 1995; Kasinitz et al. 2008.
25. Heath and Brinbaum 2014; see in particular Lessard-Phillips, Fleischmann, and van Elsas 2014 and also Ichou 2014.
26. All the data we use have limitations. The credentials data have been gathered on a country-by-country basis in ways that are not entirely consistent (for example, different countries use different schemes to collect data about immigrant and ethnic origins, and these can have consequences for the average educational performance that we observe). In analyzing the PISA data, moreover, we generally cannot identify specific national origins of immigrant-origin children. To limit our tabulations to low-status groups, we therefore resort to controlling for parental education, by defining second-generation groups as those where parents did not complete secondary education. This control, it should be noted, is broadly accurate but does eliminate the highly educated families that are present in virtually all low-status immigration flows.
27. Heath, Rothon, and Kilpi 2008; Heath and Brinbaum 2014; Waters et al. 2013.
28. OECD 2006.
29. OECD 2006: 171.
30. National Equality Panel 2010: 345
31. Zhou 2009.
32. The studies involved are: Alba et al. 2013; Crul et al. 2013; Waters et al. 2013; Yu and Heath 2007.
33. Alba, Müller, and Handl 1994; Clauss and Nauck 2010; Diehl, Friedrich, and Hall 2009; Faist 1995.
34. See also Kalter and Granato 2007.
35. Lutz 2014; Tesser and Dronkers 2007.
36. See in this context Kristen 2008.
37. Lopez and Fry 2013; Murnane 2013; the available data do not show Mexican Americans separately from other Hispanics.
38. Kasinitz et al. 2008.
39. Heath and Brinbaum 2014.
40. Ibid.
41. Massey et al. 2007.
42. Mouguérou, Brinbaum, and Primon 2010.
43. Alba et al. 2013.
44. Yu and Heath 2007; Reitz and Zhang 2011.

45. Reitz, Zhang, and Hawkins 2011.

46. Vasagar 2011; Waters et al. 2013.

47. Waters et al. 2013: 128–31.

48. Cheung 2014.

49. Crul 2011.

50. Silberman 2011.

51. Fleischmann and Kristen 2014; Kasinitz et al. 2008; Portes and Rumbaut 2001.

52. See, for example, Feliciano and Rumbaut 2005; Foner 2005; Lopez 2003; Waters 1999.

53. Fleischmann and Kristen 2014.

54. For example, Kasinitz et al. 2008. In addition, the data we have for Canada are neither recent enough nor sufficiently detailed to allow conclusions on a par with those in the text; see Boyd 2009.

55. Kasinitz et al. 2008; see also Luthra and Waldinger 2010; White and Glick 2009.

56. Cheung and Heath 2007; Cheung 2014; Heath and Martin 2013; Model and Lin 2002.

57. Luthra and Waldinger 2010.

58. Kochhar 2014.

59. Batalova and Fix 2011; Lopez and Fry 2013.

60. Alba et al. 2013; Lhommeau, Meurs, and Primon 2010; Okba 2010; Silberman, Alba, and Fournier, 2007; Silberman 2011; Simon 2003.

61. Kalter and Granato 2007; Kalter 2011.

62. Crul et al. 2013.

63. Modood 2011; Zhou 2009.

64. Van de Werfhorst, van Elsas, and Heath 2014.

65. Tribalat 1995; Condon and Régnard 2010.

66. Crul et al. 2013.

67. Covello 1972; Steinberg 1974; Glazer and Moynihan [1963] 1970.

68. Alba 1985; see also Perlmann 2005.

69. Alba 2009.

70. Corcoran et al. 2004; Phillips and Chin 2004.

71. Rice 2003.

72. OECD 2013e.

73. Sahlberg 2011.

9: WHO ARE THE "WE"? IDENTITY AND INTERMARRIAGE

1. Kasinitz et al. 2008: 81; see also Schneider et al. 2012a.

2. Schneider et al. 2012a: 232; on different emphases in immigration and ethnicity research in Western Europe and the United States, see Morawska 2009.

3. Schneider et al. 2012a, 2012b. The data are from the IMMLA (Immigration and Intergenerational Mobility in Metropolitan Los Angeles) and TIES (the Integration of the European Second Generation) surveys.

4. Schneider et al. 2012a: 219; see also Crul and Schneider 2010.

5. Alba 2005; Tajfel and Turner 1986; Deaux 2009.

6. Taylor et al. 2013.
7. Waldinger 2007: 141; Duyvendak 2011.
8. Tuan 1998.
9. Boswell 2008; Reitz 2012; see also Reitz and Banerjee 2007; and Soroka, Johnston, and Banting 2007.
10. Citrin et al. 2007; Schildkraut 2011: 152.
11. Schildkraut 2011: 153.
12. Segal and Segal 2007; Leal 2005; see also Batalova 2008.
13. Schneider et al. 2012a: 215–16; see also Faist and Ulbricht forthcoming.
14. Simon 2012: 11; see also Schnapper 1991.
15. Simon 2012: 9–14.
16. Duyvendak 2011: 98–99; Slootman and Duyvendak forthcoming.
17. Duyvendak 2013; Grunberg 2013; see also Wekker 2009.
18. Home Office report, quoted in Grillo 2007: 989; Meer, Uberoi, and Modood forthcoming; Heath and Demirava 2014; Gallup Poll 2009.
19. Bloemraad forthcoming.
20. Weil 2001: 21.
21. Howard 2009.
22. Troper 2003.
23. Foner 2012: 488; Jacobson 2006: 9.
24. Gerstle forthcoming.
25. Alba 2009: 80; Gerstle 2001, forthcoming; Foner 2005.
26. Fitzgerald 1979; Alba 2009: 46; Gabaccia 2008; Jacobson 2006.
27. Jacobson 2006: 19–20.
28. Bloemraad forthcoming.
29. Gerstle forthcoming.
30. Fitzgerald 1979: 93; Jacobson 2006: 10.
31. Government of Canada 2012; Bloemraad 2006, forthcoming; Li 2003; Reitz 2004, 2012.
32. See chap. 5; Foner and Fredrickson; Foner et al. 2014.
33. Alba and Nee 2003.
34. Blau 1977; Kalmijn and Van Tubergen 2010; Qian and Lichter 2007, 2011; Lucassen and Laarman 2009; Fishman 2004; Model and Fisher 2002; Perlmann and Waters 2007.
35. Lucassen and Laarman 2009; Muttarak and Heath 2010.
36. For example, Telles and Ortiz 2008.
37. In general, the data in the literature count mixed unions, including married couples and cohabitating pairs. The United States is an exception in that the available data count only intermarriages. In addition, the data in the table for the broad Latino category are incidence rates, counting only marriages contracted in the year before the 2008 American Community Survey. All of the other data are prevalence data, which are based on all unions existing at a given moment in time.
38. Qian and Lichter 2011.
39. Kalmijn and Van Tubergen 2006.
40. Loozen, de Valk, and Wobma 2012.
41. See Hamel et al. 2010, 2012.

42. Tribalat 1995; also Phalet and Heath 2011.

43. Dale 2008.

44. Beck-Gernsheim 2007; Carol, Ersanilli, and Wagner 2014; Van Kerckem et al. 2013; Kogan 2010b; Charsley et al. 2012; Foner and Dreby 2011.

45. Min and Kim 2010.

46. Loozen et al. 2012.

47. Hamel et al. 2012; cf. Kalter and Schroedter 2010.

48. Foner and Dreby 2011.

49. See Song 2010; Song and Parker 2009; Chito Childs 2005.

50. Bennett 2011.

51. Lee and Bean 2010; Telles and Ortiz 2008; Chito Childs 2005; see also Alba and Islam 2009; Duncan and Trejo 2011.

52. Wang 2012; Qian and Lichter 2011.

53. Wang 2012.

54. Passel, Wang, and Taylor 2010.

55. On the slowing of intermarriage by Asians and Hispanics, see Qian and Lichter 2011; Lichter 2013. To understand the paradox of overall increasing intermarriage with declining rates of intermarriage by minorities, imagine the following highly stylized, hypothetical example. In a society that is divided 90/10 between two groups, whose members marry without regard to group membership, 90 percent of the smaller group will marry out but the overall proportion of intermarriages among all marriages will be just 18 percent. (That is, if a society consists of one hundred individuals altogether and everyone marries, there will be fifty marriages, of which nine are intermarriages.) If, at a later date, the division between the two groups has shifted to 50/50, then 50 percent of either group will marry out, obviously a decline in the intermarriage rate of the previous numerical minority; but now 50 percent of all marriages will cross group lines.

56. Alba and Nee 2003.

57. Crul and Mollenkopf 2012: 256.

58. Lucassen 2005: 208.

59. On the United States, see Gans 1999.

60. Alba and Nee 2003.

61. Murat Isik, quoted in Crul, Schneider and Lelie 2013: 91–92.

10: THE CHANGING FACE OF THE WEST

1. See, for example, Sassen 1988. New immigrants are likely to be needed to continue to fill these critical roles in the labor force; see Bean et al. 2013.

2. Alba 2005.

3. Corak 2013.

4. OECD 2006.

5. Cheung 2014; Cheung and Heath 2007; Heath and Martin 2013.

6. Silberman 2011; Alba et al. 2013.

7. Castle 2013.

8. Lessard-Phillips, Fleischmann, and van Elsas 2014.

9. Bean et al. 2013; Passel and Cohn 2011; Yoshikawa 2011.

10. Agius Vallejo 2012; Alba 2009; Alba and Yrizar Barbosa 2013; Vasquez 2011.

11. Duyvendak and Scholten 2012; Heath and Demireva 2014; Cesari 2013; Uberoi and Modood 2013.

12. Banting and Kymlicka 2006; Kymlicka 2012.

13. Banting and Kymlicka 2006.

14. Laurence 2012; see also Bertossi 2014; Bertossi and Duyvendak 2012.

15. Bloemraad 2006; Schnapper 1991.

16. Bloemraad 2006.

17. Alba and Holdaway 2013; Goldin and Katz 2008; Ringer 1967.

18. Snel, Burgers, and Leerkes 2007; Van Amersfort and Van Niekerk 2006.

19. Bloemraad forthcoming.

20. Zweigenhaft and Domhoff 2006.

21. Bloemraad 2006.

22. Chopin and Do 2012; Ellis and Watson 2013.

23. Freeman 2004: 960.

24. Borjas 1999; see also Papademetriou 2007.

25. Bean et al. 2013.

26. Waldinger 1996; Waldinger and Lichter 2003; Zhou 2009.

27. Portes and Zhou 1993: 86.

28. Portes and Stepick 1994.

29. Zhou 2009; Kasinitz et al. 2008: 169–70; Louie 2012: chap. 4.

30. Logan, Alba, and McNulty 1994; Waldinger and Lichter 2003; Zhou 2009.

31. Kalter 2011; Phalet and Heath 2011.

32. Jordan 2014.

33. Ravitch 2012, 2013.

34. Migrant Policy Index 2014.

35. Sotomayor 2013: 191.

36. Massey et al. 2013.

37. Dreier, Mollenkopf, and Swanstrom 2001; Sampson 2012.

38. Lyons et al. 2013.

39. See also Hochschild, Weaver, and Burch 2012.

REFERENCES

Aalbers, Manuel, and Rinus Deurloo. 2003. "Concentrated and Condemned? Residential Patterns of Immigrants from Industrial and Non-industrial Countries in Amsterdam." *Housing, Theory and Society* 20: 197–208.

Abdouni, Sarah, and Edouard Fabre. 2012. "365,000 Domiens Vivent en Metropole." *INSEE Première*, no. 1389.

ACLU [American Civil Liberties Union]. 2013. "Rights Groups File Lawsuit Challenging NYPD's Muslim Surveillance Program as Unconstitutional." June 13. http://www.aclu.org/national-security/rights-groups-file-lawsuit-challenging-nypds-muslim-surveillance-program.

Agius Vallejo, Jody. 2012. *Barrios to Burbs: The Making of the Mexican American Middle Class*. Stanford: Stanford University Press.

Alba, Richard. 1985. "The Twilight of Ethnicity among Americans of European Ancestry: The Case of Italians." *Ethnic and Racial Studies* 8: 134–58.

———. 1990. *Ethnic Identity: The Transformation of White America*. New Haven: Yale University Press.

———. 2005. "Bright vs. Blurred Boundaries: Second-generation Assimilation and Exclusion in France, Germany, and the United States." *Ethnic and Racial Studies* 28: 20–49.

———. 2009. *Blurring the Color Line: The New Chance for a More Integrated America*. Cambridge: Harvard University Press.

Alba, Richard, Glenn Deane, Nancy Denton, Ilir Disha, Brian McKenzie, and Jeffrey Napierala. 2014. "The Role of Immigrant Enclaves for Latino Residential Inequalities." *Journal of Ethnic and Migration Studies* 40: 1–20.

Alba, Richard, and Nancy Foner. 2009. "Entering the Precincts of Power: Do National Differences Matter for Immigrant-Minority Political Participation?" In Jennifer Hochschild and John Mollenkopf (eds.), *Bringing Outsiders In: Transatlantic Perspectives on Immigrant Political Incorporation*. Ithaca: Cornell University Press.

Alba, Richard, and Jennifer Holdaway (eds.). 2013. *The Children of Immigrants at School: A Comparative Look at Integration in the United States and Western Europe*. New York: New York University Press.

Alba, Richard, and Tariqul Islam. 2009. "The Case of the Disappearing Mexican Americans: An Ethnic-Identity Mystery." *Population Research and Policy Review* 28: 109–21.

Alba, Richard, Tomás Jiménez, and Helen Marrow. 2014. "Mexican Americans as a Paradigm for Contemporary Intergroup Heterogeneity." *Ethnic and Racial Studies* 37: 446–66.

Alba, Richard, John Logan, and Brian Stults. 2000. "The Changing Neighborhood Contexts of the Immigrant Metropolis." *Social Forces* 79: 587–621.

Alba, Richard, Walter Müller, and Johann Handl. 1994. "Ethnische Ungleicheit im Deutschen Bildungssystem." *Kölner Zeitschrft für Soziologie und Sozialpsychologie* 46: 209–37.

Alba, Richard, and Victor Nee. 2003. *Remaking the American Mainstream: Assimilation and Contemporary Immigration.* Cambridge: Harvard University Press.

Alba, Richard, Albert Raboteau, and Josh DeWind. 2009. "Introduction: Comparisons of Migrants and Their Religions, Past and Present." In Richard Alba, Albert Raboteau, and Josh DeWind (eds.), *Immigration and Religion in America: Comparative and Historical Perspectives.* New York: New York University Press.

Alba, Richard, Jeffrey Reitz, and Patrick Simon. 2012. "National Conceptions of Assimilation, Integration and Cohesion." In Maurice Crul and John Mollenkopf (eds.), *The Changing Face of World Cities: Young Children of Immigrants in Europe and the United States.* New York: Russell Sage Foundation.

Alba, Richard, and Steven Romalewski. 2012. *The End of Segregation? Hardly.* New York: Center for Urban Research. http://www.gc.cuny.edu/Page-Elements/Academics -Research-Centers-Initiatives/Centers-and-Institutes/Center-for-Urban-Research /CUR-research-initiatives/The-End-of-Segregation-Hardly.

Alba, Richard, and Roxane Silberman. 2002. "Decolonization Immigrations and the Social Origins of the Second Generation: The Case of North Africans in France." *International Migration Review* 36: 1169–93.

Alba, Richard, Roxane Silberman, Dalia Abdelhady, Yaël Brinbaum, and Amy Lutz. 2013. "How Similar Educational Inequalities Are Constructed in Two Different Systems, France and the U.S., and Why They Lead to Disparate Labor-market Outcomes." In Richard Alba and Jennifer Holdaway (eds.), *The Children of Immigrants at School: A Comparative Look at Integration in the United States and Western Europe.* New York: New York University Press.

Alba, Richard, Jennifer Sloan, and Jessica Sperling. 2011. "The Integration Imperative: The Children of Low-Status Immigrants in the Schools of Wealthy Societies." *Annual Review of Sociology* 37: 395–415.

Alba, Richard, and Guillermo Yrizar Barbosa. 2013. "Blurring the Color Line *Redux.*" Presentation at the International Migration Section's preconference at the American Sociological Association meeting, New York, August.

Almendinger, Jutta. 1989. "Educational Systems and Labor Market Outcomes." *European Sociological Review* 5: 231–50.

Amadieu, Jean-François. N.d. "Les Elus Issus de l'Immigration dans les Conseils Municipaux (2001–2008)." Haut Conseil à l'Intégration, Paris.

Anderson, Elijah. 1999. *Code of the Street: Decency, Violence and the Moral Life of the Inner City.* New York: W.W. Norton.

Andrew, Caroline, John Biles, Myer Siemiatycki, and Erin Tolley. 2008. "Conclusion." In Andrew, Biles, Siemiatycki, and Tolley (eds.), *Electing a Diverse Canada: The Representation of Immigrants, Minorities and Women.* Vancouver: University of British Columbia Press.

Appelbaum, Eileen, Annette Bernhardt, and Richard Murnane. 2003. *Low-Wage America: How Employers Are Reshaping Opportunity in the Workplace.* New York: Russell Sage Foundation.

Attewell, Paul, Philip Kasinitz, and Kathleen Dunn. 2010. "Black Canadians and Black

Americans: Racial Income Inequality in Comparative Perspective." *Ethnic and Racial Studies* 33: 473–95.

Back, Les. 1996. *New Ethnicities and Urban Culture: Racisms and Multiculture in Young Lives.* New York: St. Martin's Press.

Bade, Klaus. 1994. *Ausländer, Aussiedler, Asyl: eine Bestandsaufnahme.* Munich, Germany: C.H. Beck.

Bakalian, Anny, and Mehdi Bozorgmehr. 2009. *Backlash 9/11: Middle Eastern and Muslim Americans Respond.* Berkeley: University of California Press.

Bakan, Abigail, and Audrey Kobayashi. 2007. "Affirmative Action and Employment Equity: Policy, Ideology, and Backlash in Canadian Context." *Studies in Political Economy* 79: 145–66.

Banting, Keith, and Will Kymlicka. 2006. *Multiculturalism and the Welfare State: Recognition and Redistribution in Contemporary Democracies.* Oxford: Oxford University Press.

Bashi, Vilna, and Averil Clarke. 2001. "Experiencing Success: Structuring the Perception of Opportunities for West Indians." In Nancy Foner (ed.), *Islands in the City: West Indian Migration to New York.* Berkeley: University of California Press.

Batalova, Jeanne. 2008. "Immigrants in the U.S. Armed Forces." *Migration Information Source* (May). http://www.migrationpolicy.org/article/immigrants-us-armed-forces.

———. 2010. "H-1B Temporary Skilled Worker Program." *Migration Information Source* (October). http://www.migrationinformation.org/USFocus/display.cfm?ID=801.

Batalova, Jeanne, and Michael Fix. 2011. "Up for Grabs: The Gains and Prospects of First- and Second-Generation Young Adults." Migration Policy Institute report, Washington, D.C.

Batalova, Jeanne, and Aaron Terrazas. 2010. "Frequently Requested Statistics on Immigrants and Immigration in the United States." *Migration Information Source* (December). http://www.migrationinformation.org/USFocus/display.cfm?ID=818#2.

Bauböck, Rainer, Eva Ersboll, Kees Groenendijk, and Harald Waldrauch (eds.). 2007. *Acquisition and Loss of Nationality: Policies and Trends in 15 European Countries.* Amsterdam: Amsterdam University Press.

Bauböck, Rainer, and Iseult Honohan. 2010. "Access to Citizenship in Europe: Birthright and Naturalisation." Paper presented at EUDO Dissemination Conference, Brussels, November 18–19. http://www.eui.eu/Projects/EUDO/Documents/12–06 -BauboeckandHonohanpresentations.pdf.

Bauder, Harald. 2014. "Re-Imagining the Nation: Lessons from the Debates of Immigration in a Settler Society and an Ethnic Nation." *Comparative Migration Studies* 2: 9–27.

Bean, Frank, James Bachmeier, Susan Brown, Jennifer van Hook, and Mark Leach. 2013. *Unauthorized Mexican Immigration and the Socioeconomic Integration of Mexican Americans.* US 2010 Report. http://www.s4.brown.edu/us2010/Data/Report /report05132013.pdf.

Bean, Frank, Mark Leach, Susan Brown, James Bachmeier, and John Hipp. 2011. "The Educational Legacy of Unauthorized Immigration: Comparisons across U.S.-Immigrant Groups in How Parents' Status Affects Their Offspring." *International Migration Review* 45: 348–85.

Bean, Frank, and Lindsay Lowell. 2007. "Unauthorized Migration." In Mary C. Waters and Reed Ueda (eds.), *The New Americans*. Cambridge: Harvard University Press.

Bean, Frank, and Gillian Stevens. 2003. *America's Newcomers and the Dynamics of Diversity*. New York: Russell Sage Foundation.

Beauchemin, Cris, Christelle Hamel, Maud Lesne, Patrick Simon, and the TEO Survey Team. 2010. "Discrimination: A Question of Visible Minorities." *Population & Societies*, no. 466: 1–4.

Beauchemin, Cris, Christelle Hamel, and Patrick Simon. 2010. *Trajectories and Origins: Survey on Population Diversity in France*. Paris: INED and INSEE.

Beck-Gernsheim, Elisabeth. 2007. "Transnational Lives, Transnational Marriages: A Review of Evidence from Migrant Communities in Europe." *Global Networks* 8: 272–88.

Benabou, R., F. Kramarz, and C. Prost. 2004. "Zones d'éducation prioritaires: quels moyens pour quels résultats." *Économie et statistique*, no. 380.

Bendix, Reinhard. 1964. *Nation-Building and Citizenship*. New York: John Wiley.

Bennett, Pamela. 2011. "The Social Position of Multiracial Groups in the United States: Evidence from Residential Segregation." *Ethnic and Racial Studies* 34: 707–29.

Bennhold, Katrin. 2014. "Reading, Writing, and Allegations: Muslim School at Center of Debate." *New York Times*, June 22.

Beriss, David. 2004. *Black Skins, Black Voices: Caribbean Ethnicity and Activism in Urban France*. Boulder, Colo.: Westview Press.

Berman, Gavin, and Aliyah Dar. 2013. "Prison Population Statistics." *House of Commons Library*. http://www.parliament.uk/briefing-papers/sn04334.

Bernhardt, Annette, Martina Morris, Mark Handcock, and Marc Scott. 2001. *Divergent Paths: Economic Mobility in the New American Labor Market*. New York: Russell Sage Foundation.

Berry, John W. 1997. "Immigration, Acculturation, and Adaptation." *Applied Psychology: An International Review* 46: 5–68.

Bertossi, Christophe. 2014. "French 'Muslim' Soldiers? Social Change and Pragmatism in a Military Institution." In John Bowen, Christophe Bertossi, Jan Willem Duyvendak, and Mona Lena Krook (eds.), *European States and Their Muslim Citizens*. New York: Cambridge University Press.

Bertossi, Christophe, and Jan Willem Duyvendak. 2012. "National Models of Immigrant Integration: The Costs for Comparative Research." *Comparative European Politics* 10: 237–47.

Beyer, Peter. 2005. "Religious Identity and Educational Attainment among Recent Immigrants to Canada: Gender, Age, and 2nd Generation." *Journal of International Migration and Integration* 6: 177–99.

Bird, Karen. 2004. "The Political Representation of Women and Ethnic Minorities in Established Democracies: A Framework for Comparative Research." Academy of Migration Studies in Denmark, Working Paper.

———. 2011. "Patterns of Substantive Representation among Visible Minorities in Canada: Evidence from Canada's House of Commons." In Karen Bird, Thomas Saalfeld, and Andreas Wust (eds.), *The Political Representation of Immigrants and Minorities*. London and New York: Routledge.

Bird, Karen, Thomas Saalfeld, and Andreas Wust (eds.). 2011. *The Political Representation of Immigrants and Minorities*. London and New York: Routledge.

Birnbaum, Michael. 2013. "Election Brings More Lawmakers of Minority Immigrant Backgrounds to German Parliament." *Washington Post*, October 5.

Blau, Peter. 1977. *Inequality and Heterogeneity: A Primitive Theory of Social Structure.* New York: Free Press.

Blauner, Robert. 1972. *Racial Oppression in America.* New York: HarperCollins.

Bleich, Erik. 2003. *Race Politics in Britain and France.* Cambridge: Cambridge University Press.

———. 2009. "State Responses to 'Muslim' Violence: A Comparison of Six West European Countries." *Journal of Ethnic and Migration Studies* 35: 361–79.

———. 2011. "What Is Islamophobia, and How Much Is There? Theorizing and Measuring an Emerging Comparative Concept." *American Behavioral Scientist* 55: 1581–600.

Bloemraad, Irene. 2006. *Becoming a Citizen: Incorporating Immigrants and Refugees in the United States and Canada.* Berkeley: University of California Press.

———. 2012. "Understanding 'Canadian Exceptionalism' in Immigration and Pluralism Policy." Washington, D.C.: Migration Policy Institute.

———. 2013. "Accessing the Corridors of Power: Puzzles and Pathways to Understanding Minority Representation." *West European Politics* 36: 652–70.

———. Forthcoming. "Re-imagining the Nation in a World of Migration: Legitimacy, Political Claims-Making and Membership in Comparative Perspective." In Nancy Foner and Patrick Simon (eds.), *Fear, Anxiety, and National Identity: Immigration and Belonging in North America and Western Europe.* New York: Russell Sage Foundation.

Bloemraad, Irene, and Karen Schönwälder. 2013. "Immigrant and Ethnic Minority Representation in Europe: Conceptual Challenges and Theoretical Approaches." *Western European Politics* 36: 564–79.

Blokland, Talja, and Gwen van Eijk. 2010. "Do People Who Like Diversity Practice Diversity in Neighbourhood Life? Neighbourhood Use and the Social Networks of 'Diversity-Seekers' in a Mixed Neighbourhood in the Netherlands." *Journal of Ethnic and Migration Studies* 36: 313–32.

Boelhouwer, Peter. 2002. "Trends in Dutch Housing Policy and the Shifting Position of the Social Rented Sector." *Urban Studies* 39: 219–35.

Bolt, Gideon, and Ronald van Kempen. 2010. "Ethnic Segregation and Residential Mobility: Relocations of Minority Ethnic Groups in the Netherlands." *Journal of Ethnic and Migration Studies* 36: 333–54.

Bolt, Gideon, A. Sule Özüekren, and Deborah Phillips. 2010. "Linking Integration and Residential Segregation." *Journal of Ethnic and Migration Studies* 36: 169–86.

Bonilla-Silva, Eduardo. 1997. "Rethinking Racism: Toward a Structural Interpretation." *American Sociological Review* 62: 465–80.

Borjas, George. 1999. *Heaven's Door: Immigration Policy and the American Economy.* Princeton: Princeton University Press.

Borjas, George, and Rachel Friedberg. 2009. "Recent Trends in the Earnings of New Immigrants to the United States." NBER Working Paper No. 15406. Cambridge, Mass.: National Bureau of Economic Research.

Borrel, Catherine. N.d. "Enquêtes annuelles de recensement 2004 et 2005: Près de 5 millions d'immigrés à la mi-2004." INSEE. http://www.insee.fr/fr/themes/document.asp ?ref_id=ip1098&reg_id=0.

Bosch, Gerhard, Ken Mayhew, and Jérôme Gautié. 2010. "Industrial Relations, Legal Regulations, and Wage Setting." In Jérôme Gautié and John Schmitt (eds.), *Low-Wage Work in the Wealthy World*. New York: Russell Sage Foundation.

Bosch, Gerhard, and Claudia Weinkopf. 2008. *Low-Wage Work in Germany*. New York: Russell Sage Foundation.

Boswell, Randy. 2008. "Immigrants Show Sense of Belonging in Canada." Canwest News Service, June 30.

Bowen, John. 2007. *Why the French Don't Like Headscarves*. Princeton: Princeton University Press.

———. 2009. "Recognizing Islam in France after 9/11." *Journal of Ethnic and Migration Studies* 35: 439–52.

———. 2012. *Blaming Islam*. Cambridge, Mass.: MIT Press.

Bowen, John, Christophe Bertossi, Jan Willem Duyvendak, and Mona Lena Krook. 2014. "An Institutional Approach to Framing Muslims in Europe." In Bowen, Bertossi, Duyvendak, and Krook (eds.), *European States and Their Muslim Citizens*. New York: Cambridge University Press.

Boyd, Marion. 2007. "Religion-Based Alternative Dispute Resolution: A Challenge to Multiculturalism." In Keith Banting, Thomas Courchene, and F. Leslie Seidle (eds.), *Belonging? Diversity, Recognition, and Shared Citizenship in Canada*. Montreal: Institute for Research on Public Policy.

Boyd, Monica. 2009. "Social Origins and the Educational and Occupational Achievements of the 1.5 and Second Generations." *Canadian Review of Sociology* 46: 339–69.

Boyd, Monica, and Diana Worts. 2016. "Comparing Immigrant Children in Canada and the United States: Similarities and Differences." In Vicki Esses and Don Abelson (eds.), *Taking Stock of a Turbulent Period and Looking Ahead: Immigration to North America in the Early Years of the 21st Century*. Montreal-Kingston: McGill-Queens University Press.

Bramadat, Paul. 2005. "Beyond Christian Canada: Religion and Ethnicity in a Multicultural Society." In Paul Bramadat and David Seljak (eds.), *Religion and Ethnicity in Canada*. Toronto: Pearson Longman.

Breton, Raymond. 1964. "Institutional Completeness of Ethnic Communities and the Personal Relations of Immigrants." *American Journal of Sociology* 70: 193–205.

Brettell, Caroline. 2003. "Bringing the City Back In: Cities as Contexts for Incorporation." In Nancy Foner (ed.), *American Arrivals: Anthropology Engages the New Immigration*. Santa Fe, N.M.: School of American Research Press.

Breuil-Genier, Pascale, Catherine Borrel, and Bertrand Lhommeau. 2011. "Les immigrés, les descendants d'immigrés et leurs enfants," *Vue d'ensemble: France, portrait social*. Paris: INSEE. http://www.insee.fr/fr/publications-et-services/sommaire.asp?codesage=IMMFRA12.

Brinbaum, Yaël, Christelle Hamel, Jean-Luc Primon, Mirna Safi, and Patrick Simon. 2010. "Discrimination." In Cris Beauchemin, Christelle Hamel, and Patrick Simon (eds.), *Trajectories and Origins: Survey on Population Diversity in France: Initial Findings*. Paris: INED and INSEE.

Britton, Marcus. 2014. "Latino Spatial and Structural Assimilation: Close Intergroup Friendships among Houston-area Latinos." *Journal of Ethnic and Migration Studies* 40: 1192–216.

Brouard, Sylvain, and Vincent Tiberj. 2011. "Yes They Can: An Experimental Approach to the Eligibility of Ethnic Minority Candidates in France." In Karen Bird, Thomas Saalfeld, and Andreas Wust (eds.), *The Political Representation of Immigrants and Minorities*. London and New York: Routledge.

Brown, Susan. 2007. "Delayed Spatial Assimilation: Multi-Generational Incorporation of the Mexican-Origin Population in Los Angeles." *City & Community* 6: 193–209.

Brub, Joachim. 2008. "Experiences of Discrimination Reported by Turkish, Moroccan and Bangladeshi Muslims in Three European Cities." *Journal of Ethnic and Migration Studies* 34: 875–94.

Brubaker, Rogers. 1992. *Citizenship and Nationhood in France and Germany*. Cambridge: Harvard University Press.

———. 2001. "The Return of Assimilation? Changing Perspectives on Immigration and Its Sequels in France, Germany, and the United States." *Ethnic and Racial Studies* 24: 531–48.

Bruquetas-Callejo, Maria, Blanca Garces-Mascareñas, Rinus Penninx, and Peter Scholten. 2007. "Policy-Making Related to Immigration and Integration: The Dutch Case." IMISCOE Working Paper: Country Report, no. 15. http://dare.uva.nl/cgi/arno/show.cgi?fid=50310.

Buettner, Elizabeth. 2008. "'Going for an Indian': South Asian Restaurants and the Limits of Multiculturalism in Britain." *Journal of Modern History* 80: 865–901.

Buijs, Frank J. 2009. "Muslims in the Netherlands: Social and Political Developments after 9/11." *Journal of Ethnic and Migration Studies* 35: 421–38.

Buijs, Frank J., and Jan Rath. 2006. *Muslims in Europe: The State of Research*. IMISCOE Working Paper. http://www.imiscoe.org/workingpapers/documents/muslims_in_europe.

Bundesagentur für Arbeit. 2013. "Existenzgründung durch Migranten." http://www.arbeitsagentur.de/nn_394714/Navigation/zentral/Veroeffentlichungen/Themenhefte-durchstarten/Existenzgruendung/Gruendung-Migranten/Gruendung-Migranten-Nav.html (accessed 10/10/13).

Bureau of Labor Statistics (BLS). 2014. "Union Members Summary." http://www.bls.gov/news.release/union2.nr0.htm.

Buruma, Ian. 2006. *Murder in Amsterdam*. New York: Penguin.

———. 2010. *Taming the Gods: Religion and Democracy on Three Continents*. Princeton: Princeton University Press.

Buzdugan, Raluca, and Shiva Halli. 2009. "Labor Market Experiences of Canadian Immigrants with Focus on Foreign Education and Experience." *International Migration Review* 43: 366–86.

Byron, Margaret, and Stephanie Condon. 2008. *Migration in Comparative Perspective: Caribbean Communities in Britain and France*. London: Routledge.

Cainkar, Louise. 2009. *Homeland Insecurity: The Arab American and Muslim American Experience after 9/11*. New York: Russell Sage Foundation.

Caldwell, Christopher. 2009. *Reflections on the Revolution in Europe: Immigration, Islam, and the West*. New York: Doubleday.

Camarota, Steven. 2011. "Welfare Use by Immigrant Households with Children: A Look at Cash, Medicaid, Housing, and Food Programs," Center for Immigration Studies. http://cis.org/immigrant-welfare-use-2011.

Capps, Randy, Kristen McCabe, and Michael Fix. 2011. "New Streams: Black African Migration to the United States." Washington, D.C.: Migration Policy Institute.

Carol, Sarah, Evelyn Ersanilli, and Marieke Wagner. 2014. "Spousal Choice among the Children of Turkish and Moroccan Immigrants in Six European Countries: Transnational Spouse or Co-ethnic Migrant." *International Migration Review* 48: 387–414.

Carol, Sarah, and Ruud Koopmans. 2013. "Dynamics of Contestation over Islamic Religious Rights in Western Europe." *Ethnicities* 13: 165–90.

Caroli, Ève, and Jérôme Gautié. 2008. *Low-Wage Work in France.* New York: Russell Sage Foundation.

Casanova, José. 2007. "Immigration and the New Religious Pluralism: A European Union/United States Comparison." In Thomas Banchoff (ed.), *Democracy and The New Religious Pluralism.* Oxford: Oxford University Press.

Casanova, José, and Aristide Zolberg. 2002. "Religion and Immigrant Incorporation in New York." Paper presented at Conference on Immigrant Incorporation in New York, The New School.

Castle, Stephen. 2013. "Britain Is Pulled, Reluctantly, into Debate over Wearing Full-Face Veils in Public." *New York Times*, September 16.

Castles, Stephen, and Alastair Davidson. 2000. *Citizenship and Migration: Globalization and the Politics of Belonging.* New York: Routledge.

Castles, Stephen, and Mark J. Miller. 2009. *The Age of Migration: International Population Movements in the Modern World.* 4th ed. New York: Guilford Press.

CBC News Online. "Quebec Catholics," October 2, 2003. http://www.cbc.ca/news2/background/catholicism/quebeccatholics.html.

Central Bureau for Statistics. 2012. *Jaarrapport Integratie 2012.* The Hague.

———. 2013. "Huishoudens naar herkomstgroepering," http://statline.cbs.nl/StatWeb/publication/?VW=T&DM=SLNL&PA=70067NED&D1=21,23,43,45&D2=a&D3=0&D4=0,l&HD=120419–1407&HDR=T,G2,G3&STB=G1.

Centre for Contemporary Cultural Studies. 1982. *The Empire Strikes Back: Race and Racism in 70s Britain.* London: Hutchinson.

Cesari, Jocelyne. 2004. *When Islam and Democracy Meet: Muslims in Europe and the United States.* New York: Palgrave Macmillan.

———, (ed.). 2005. "Special Issue on Mosque Conflicts in European Cities." *Journal of Ethnic and Migration Studies* 31:1015–179.

———. 2013. *Why The West Fears Islam.* New York: Palgrave Macmillan.

Chagnon, Jonathan. 2013. "Migration International, 2010 and 2011." *Statistics Canada.* http://www.statcan.gc.ca/pub/91-209-x/2013001/article/11787-eng.htm.

Challinor, A. E. 2011. "Canada's Immigration Policy: A Focus on Human Capital." *Migration Information Source* (September). http://www.migrationinformation.org/feature/display.cfm?ID=853.

Charsley, Katharine, Brooke Storer-Church, Michaela Benson, and Nicholas van Hear. 2012. "Marriage-Related Migration to the UK." *International Migration Review* 46: 861–90.

Chavez, Leo. 2008. *The Latino Threat: Constructing Immigrants, Citizens, and the Nation.* Stanford, Calif.: Stanford University Press.

Chen, Carolyn. 2006. "From Filial to Religious Piety: Evangelical Christianity Reconstructing Taiwanese Immigrant Families in the United States." *International Migration Review* 40: 573–602.

————. 2008. *Getting Saved in America: Taiwanese Immigration and Religious Experience*. Princeton: Princeton University Press.

Cheung, Sin Yi. 2014. "Ethno-religious Minorities and Labour Market Integration: Generational Advancement or Decline?" *Ethnic and Racial Studies* 37: 140–60.

Cheung, Sin Yi, and Anthony Heath. 2007. "Nice Work If You Can Get It: Ethnic Penalties in Great Britain." In Heath and Cheung (eds.), *Unequal Chances: Ethnic Minorities in Western Labor Markets*. Proceedings of the British Academy. Oxford: Oxford University Press.

Chiswick, Barry, and P. W. Miller. 2008. "Why is the Payoff to Schooling Smaller for Immigrants?" *Labour Economics* 15: 1317–40.

Chito Childs, Erica. 2005. *Navigating Interracial Borders: Black-White Couples and Their Social Worlds*. New Brunswick, N.J.: Rutgers University Press.

Chopin, Isabelle, and Thien Uyen Do. 2012. "Developing Anti-Discrimination Law in Europe." Report for European Network of Legal Experts in the Non-Discrimination Field, European Commission, Brussels. http://www.migpolgroup.com/wp_mpg/wp content/uploads/2013/07/Developing-Anti-Discrimination-Law-in-Europe-2012 -EN-.pdf.

Christiano, Kevin. 2000. "Church and State in Institutional Flux: Canada and the United States." In David Lyon and Marguerite van Die (eds.), *Rethinking Church, State, and Modernity: Canada between Europe and America*. Toronto: University of Toronto Press.

Chung, Angie. 2005. " 'Politics without the Politics': The Evolving Political Cultures of Ethnic Non-profits in Koreatown, Los Angeles," *Journal of Ethnic and Migration Studies* 31: 911–29.

Citizenship and Immigration Canada. 2008. "Annual Report to Parliament on Immigration. 2008." http://www.cic.gc.ca/english/pdf/pub/immigration2008_e.pdf.

Citrin, Jack, Amy Lerman, Michael Murakami, and Kathryn Pearson. 2007. "Testing Huntington: Is Hispanic Immigration a Threat to American Identity?" *Perspectives on Politics* 5: 31–48.

Clandestino Research Project. 2009. "Comparative Policy Brief: Size of Irregular Migration," Prepared for the European Commission. http://irregular- migration.net// typo3_upload/groups/31/4.Background_Information/4.2.Policy_Briefs_EN/ComparativePolicyBrief_SizeOfIrregularMigration_Clandestino_Nov09_2.pdf.

Clark, Ken, and Stephen Drinkwater. 2007. *Ethnic Minorities in the Labour Market: Dynamics and Diversity*. Bristol, England: Policy Press.

Clauss, Susanne, and Bernhard Nauck. 2010. "Immigrant and Native Children in Germany." *Childhood Indicators Research* 3: 471–501.

CLIP Network. 2007. *Housing and Integration of Migrants in Europe*. Dublin: European Foundation for the Improvement of Living and Working Conditions.

Cohen, Mitchell. 2007. "France Uncovered." *New York Times Book Review*, April 1.

Cole, Mike. 2009. "A Plethora of 'Suitable Enemies': British Racism at the Dawn of the Twenty-First Century." *Ethnic and Racial Studies* 32: 1671–85.

Coleman, David. 2006. "Immigration and Ethnic Change in Low-Fertility Countries: A Third Demographic Transition." *Population and Development Review* 32: 401–46.

Condon, Stéphanie, and Corinne Régnard. 2010. "Diversity of Linguistic Practices." In Cris Beauchemin, Christelle Hamel, and Patrick Simon (eds.), *Trajectories and Origins. Survey on Population Diversity in France*. Paris: INED and INSEE.

Connor, Phillip, and Matthias Koenig. 2013. "Bridges and Barriers: Religion and Occupational Attainment across Integration Contexts." *International Migration Review* 47: 3–38.

Constant, Fred. 2009. "Talking Race in Color-Blind France: Equality Denied, 'Blackness' Reclaimed." In Darlene Clark Hine, Trica D. Keaton, and Stephen Small (eds.), *Black Europe and the African Diaspora*. Urbana: University of Illinois Press.

Corak, Miles. 2013. "Income Inequality, Equality of Opportunity, and Intergenerational Mobility." *Journal of Economic Perspectives* 27: 79–102.

Corcoran, Sean, William Evans, and Robert Schwab. 2004. "Women, the Labor Market, and the Declining Quality of Teachers." *Journal of Policy Analysis and Management* 23: 449–70.

Cornelius, Wayne, Thomas Espenshade, and Idean Salehyan (eds.). 2001. *The International Migration of the Highly Skilled*. Boulder, Colo.: Lynn Reiner.

Cornelius, Wayne, and Takeyuki Tsuda. 2004. "Controlling Immigration: The Limits of Government Intervention." In Wayne Cornelius, Takeyuki Tsuda, Philip Martin, and James Hollifield (eds.). *Controlling Immigration: A Global Perspective*. 2nd ed. Stanford: Stanford University Press.

Cornell, Stephen, and Douglas Hartmann. 2007. *Ethnicity and Race: Making Identities in a Changing World*. 2nd ed. Thousand Oaks, Calif.: Pine Forge Press.

Covello, Leonard. 1972. *The Social Background of the Italo-American School Child*. Totowa: Rowman & Littlefield.

Crawford, Kyle. 2011. "Diversity in the 41st Parliament." http://www2.samaracanada.com/blog/post/Inside-the-41st-Parliament-NDP-now-most-diverse-Liberals-least-diverse.aspx.

Crul, Maurice. 2011. "How Do Educational Systems Integrate? Integration of Second-generation Turks in Germany, France, the Netherlands, and Austria." In Richard Alba and Mary C. Waters (eds.), *The Next Generation: Immigrant Youth in Comparative Perspective*. New York: New York University Press.

Crul, Maurice, Jennifer Holdaway, Helga de Valk, Norma Fuentes, and Mayida Zaal. 2013. "Educating the Children of Immigrants in Old and New Amsterdam." In Richard Alba and Jennifer Holdaway (eds.), *The Children of Immigrants at School: A Comparative Look at Integration in the United States and Western Europe*. New York: New York University Press.

Crul, Maurice, and John Mollenkopf. 2012. "Challenges and Opportunities." In Crul and Mollenkopf (eds.), *The Changing Face of World Cities: The Second Generation in Western Europe and the United States*. New York: Russell Sage Foundation.

Crul, Maurice, and Jens Schneider. 2010. "Comparative Integration Context Theory: Participation and Belonging in New Diverse European Cities." *Ethnic and Racial Studies* 33: 1249–68.

Crul, Maurice, Jens Schneider, and Frans Lelie. 2013. *Super-diversity: A New Perspective on Integration*. Amsterdam: VU University Press.

Crul, Maurice, Philipp Schnell, Barbara Herzog-Punzenberger, Maren Wilmes, Marieke Slootman, and Rosa Aparicio Gómez. 2012. "School Careers of Second-Generation Youth in Europe: Which Education Systems Provide the Best Chances for Success." In Maurice Crul, Jens Schneider, and Frans Lelie (eds.), *The European Second Generation Compared: Does the Integration Context Matter?* Amsterdam: University of Amsterdam Press.

Dale, Angela. 2008. "Migration, Marriage and Employment amongst Indian, Pakistani and Bangladeshi Residents in the UK." University of Manchester: CCSR Working Paper 2008–02.

Deaux, Kay. 2009. *To Be an Immigrant*. New York: Russell Sage Foundation.

Dekker, Lisette. 2006. "Vrouwen en Allochtonen in de Nieuw Gekozen Tweede Kamer 2006." Institute for Political Participation, Amsterdam, November 30.

Delhaye, Christine, Sawitri Saharso, and Victor van de Ven. 2014. "Immigrant Youths' Contribution to Urban Culture in Amsterdam." In Nancy Foner et al., *New York and Amsterdam: Immigration and the New Urban Landscape*. New York: New York University Press.

Demireva, Neli. 2009. "Ethnic Minority Representation in the Public Sectors of the UK, France, Germany, Sweden and the US." Equalsoc Reports. http://www.academia.edu/2555691/Equalsoc_Reports_Ethnic_Minority_Representation_in_the_Public_Sectors_of_the_UK_France_Germany_Sweden_and_the_US.

Demireva, Neli, and Christel Kesler. 2011. "The Curse of Inopportune Transitions: The Labour Market Behaviour of Immigrants and Natives in the UK." *International Journal of Comparative Sociology* 52: 306–26.

Der Spiegel. 2014. "Wie junge Männer aus dem Ruhrgebiet nach Syrien in den Dschihad zogen," July 14.

Desiderio, Maria, and John Salt. 2010. "Main Findings of the Conference on Entrepreneurship and Employment Creation of Immigrants in OECD Countries, 9–10 June 2010." In *Open for Business: Migrant Entrepreneurship in OECD Countries*. Paris: OECD.

Detroit Arab American Study Team. 2009. *Citizenship and Crisis: Arab Detroit After 9/11*. New York: Russell Sage Foundation.

DeVoretz, Don. 2004. "Commentary." In Wayne Cornelius, Takeyuki Tsuda, Philip Martin, and James Hollifield (eds.), *Controlling Immigration: A Global Perspective*. 2nd ed. Stanford: Stanford University Press.

Diehl, Claudia, and Michael Blohm. 2003. "Rights or Identity? Naturalization Processes among 'Labor Migrants' in Germany." *International Migration Review* 27: 133–62.

Diehl, Claudia, Michael Friedrich, and Anja Hall. 2009. "Jugendliche ausländische Herkunft beim Übergang in die Berufsausbildung: Vom Wollen, Können und Dürfen." *Zeitschrift für Soziologie* 38: 48–67.

Diehl, Claudia, and Rainer Schnell. 2006. "'Reactive Ethnicity' or 'Assimilation?' Statements, Arguments, and First Empirical Evidence for Labor Migrants in Germany." *International Migration Review* 40: 786–816.

Dobbin, Frank. 2009. *Inventing Equal Opportunity*. Princeton: Princeton University Press.

Doughty, Steve. 2006. "One Third of London Population is Non-white." *Daily Mail*, August 4.

Dowling, Julie. 2014. *Mexican Americans and the Question of Race*. Austin: University of Texas Press.

Downey, Douglas, Paul von Hippel, and Beckett Broh. 2004. "Are Schools the Great Equalizer? Cognitive Inequality during the Summer Months and the School Year." *American Sociological Review* 69: 613–35.

Dreier, Peter, John Mollenkopf, and Todd Swanstrom. 2001. *Place Matters: Metropolitics for the Twenty-First Century*. Lawrence: University Press of Kansas.

Drew, Catherine, and Dhananjayan Sriskandarajah. 2007. "EU Enlargement in 2007: No Warm Welcome for Labor Migrants." *Migration Information Source* (January). http// www.migrationinformation.org/Feature/.

Duncan, Brian, and Stephen Trejo. 2007. "Ethnic Identification, Intermarriage, and Unmeasured Progress by Mexican Americans." In George Borjas (ed.), *Mexican Immigration to the United States*. Cambridge, Mass.: National Bureau of Economic Research.

———. 2011. "Intermarriage and the Intergenerational Transmission of Ethnic Identity and Human Capital for Mexican Americans." *Journal of Labor Economics* 29: 195–227.

Duyvendak, Jan Willem. 2011. *The Politics of Home: Belonging and Nostalgia in Western Europe and the United States*. Houndmills, Basingstoke: Palgrave Macmillan.

———. 2012. "Holland as Home: Racism and/or Nativism." *Krisis*, no. 2: 75–77.

———. 2013. "Are All Dutch Racists? A Country's Struggle with a Black-Face Tradition." http://www.gc.cuny.edu/CUNY_GC/media/CUNY-Graduate-Center/PDF/Voices%20of%20the%20GC/Are-All-Dutch-Racists.pdf.

Duyvendak, Jan Willem, Trees Pels, and Rally Rijkschroeff. 2009. "A Multicultural Paradise? The Cultural Factor in Dutch Integration Policy." In Jennifer Hochschild and John Mollenkopf (eds.), *Bringing Outsiders In: Transatlantic Perspectives on Immigrant Political Incorporation*. Ithaca: Cornell University Press.

Duyvendak, Jan Willem, and Peter Scholten. 2012. "Deconstructing the Dutch Multicultural Model: A Frame Perspective on Dutch Integration Policymaking." *Comparative European Politics* 10: 266–82.

Ebaugh, Helen Rose, and Janet Saltzman Chafetz. 2000. *Religion and the New Immigrants: Continuities and Adaptation in Immigrant Congregations*. Walnut Creek, Calif.: Altamira.

Eck, Diana. 2001. *A New Religious America*. New York: HarperCollins.

———. 2007. "Religion." In Mary C. Waters and Reed Ueda (eds.), *The New Americans: A Guide to Immigration since 1965*. Cambridge, Mass.: Harvard University Press.

The Economist. 2004. "A Civil War on Terrorism." November 25.

———. 2005. "An Underclass Rebellion." November 12.

———. 2006. "Cartoon Wars." February 9.

———. 2009. "The Underworked American." June 11.

———. 2012. "Culture Matters More." August 11.

———. 2013. "The Polish Paradox." December 14.

Edgell, Penny, Joseph Gerteis, and Douglas Hartmann. 2006. "Atheists as 'Other': Moral Boundaries and Cultural Membership in American Society." *American Sociological Review* 71: 211–34.

Elliott, Justin. 2010. "Mayor Bloomberg Delivers Stirring Defense of Mosque." *Salon*, August 3. http://www.salon.com/2010/08/03/mayor_bloomberg_on_mosque/.

Ellis, Evelyn, and Philippa Watson. 2013. *EU Anti-Discrimination Law*. New York: Oxford University Press.

Emerson, Michael, Jenifer Bratter, Junia Howell, Wilner Jeanty. N.d. "Houston Region Grows More Ethnically Diverse, with Small Declines in Segregation: A Joint Report Analyzing Census Data from 1990, 2000, and 2010." The Kinder Institute for Urban Research and the Hobby Center for the Study of Texas, Rice University, Houston.

http://kinder.rice.edu/uploadedFiles/Kinder_Institute_for_Urban_Research/Gabriel/Houston%20Region%20Grows%20More%20Ethnically%20Diverse%201–22.pdf.

Engelen, Ewald. 2003. "Conceptualizing Economic Incorporation: From Institutional Linkages to Institutional Hybrids." Center for Migration and Development Working Paper, Princeton University.

Entwisle, Doris, and Karl Alexander. 1992. "Summer Setback: Race, Poverty, School Composition, and Mathematics Achievement in the First Two Years of School." *American Sociological Review* 57: 72–84.

Entzinger, Han. 2003. "The Rise and Fall of Multiculturalism: The Case of the Netherlands." In Christian Joppke and Ewa Morawska (eds.), *Toward Assimilation and Citizenship*. London: Palgrave Macmillan.

Erie, Stephen. 1988. *Rainbow's End: Irish-Americans and the Dilemma of Urban Machine Politics, 1840–1985*. Berkeley: University of California Press.

Ersanilli, Evelyn. 2007. "Country Profile: The Netherlands." *Focus Migration*, no. 11 (November). http://focus-migration.hwwi.de/The-Netherlands.2644.0.html?I.=1

Ersanilli, Evelyn, and Ruud Koopmans. 2010. "Rewarding Integration? Citizenship Regulations and the Socio-Cultural Integration of Immigrants in the Netherlands, France and Germany." *Journal of Ethnic and Migration Studies* 36: 773–91.

Esping Andersen, Gosta. 1990. *The Three Worlds of Welfare Capitalism*. Princeton: Princeton University Press.

Essed, Philomena, and Sandra Trienekens. 2008. "'Who Wants to Feel White?' Race, Dutch Culture and Contested Identities." *Ethnic and Racial Studies* 31: 52–72.

Eumap. 2007. "Muslims in the EU: Executive Summaries." Open Society Institute. http://www.eumap.org/topics/minority/reports/eumulsims.

European Monitoring Centre for Racism and Xenophobia (EUMC). 2006. "Muslims in the European Union: Discrimination and Islamophobia." http://fra.europa.eu/sites/default/files/fra_uploads/156-Manifestations_EN.pdf.

Eurostat. 2011. *Migrants in Europe: A Statistical Portrait of the First and Second Generation*, 2011 ed. Luxembourg: European Union.

———. 2012a. "Glossary: At-risk-of-poverty rate." Brussels: Eurostat: http://epp.eurostat.ec.europa.eu/statistics_explained/index.php/Glossary:At-risk-of-poverty_rate (accessed 7/15/12).

———. 2012b. "Asylum Decisions in the EU27: EU Member States Granted Protection to 84,100 Asylum Seekers in 2011." Eurostat Press Office.

Faist, Thomas. 1995. *Social Citizenship for Whom? Young Turks in Germany and Mexican Americans in the United States*. Aldershot, England: Avebury.

Faist, Thomas, and Christian Ulbricht. Forthcoming. "Constituting National Identity through Transnationality: Categorizations of Inequality in German Integration Debates." In Nancy Foner and Patrick Simon (eds.), *Fear, Anxiety, and National Identity: Immigration and Belonging in North America and Western Europe*. New York: Russell Sage Foundation.

Favell, Adrian. 1998. *Philosophies of Integration: Immigration and the Idea of Citizenship in France and Britain*. London: Palgrave.

———. 2008. *Eurostars and Eurocities: Free Movement and Mobility in an Integrating Europe*. Malden, Mass.: Blackwell.

Feagin, Joe. 2006. *Systemic Racism: A Theory of Oppression*. New York: Routledge.

Fekete, Liz. 2009. *A Suitable Enemy: Racism, Migration and Islamophobia in Europe.* London: Pluto.

Feliciano, Cynthia. 2005. "Does Selective Migration Matter? Explaining Ethnic Disparities in Educational Attainment among Immigrants' Children." *International Migration Review* 39: 841–71.

Feliciano, Cynthia, and Rubén Rumbaut. 2005. "Gendered Paths: Educational and Occupational Expectations and Outcomes among Adult Children of Immigrants." *Ethnic and Racial Studies* 28: 1087–118.

Fennema, Meindert, Jean Tillie, Anja van Heelsum, Maria Berger, and Rick Wolff. 2001. "L'intégration politique des minorités ethniques aux Pays-Bas." *Migrations/Société* 13: 109–29.

Fenton, Steve. 2010. *Ethnicity.* Cambridge: Polity.

Fetzer, Joel, and J. Christopher Soper. 2005. *Muslims and the State in Britain, France, and Germany.* Cambridge and New York: Cambridge University Press.

Fiscal Policy Institute. 2012. *Immigrant Small Business Owners: A Significant and Growing Part of the Economy.* New York: Fiscal Policy Institute.

Fischer, Claude, and Michael Hout. 2006. *A Century of Difference: How America Changed in the Last One Hundred Years.* New York: Russell Sage Foundation.

———. 2014. "Explaining Why More Americans Have No Religious Preference: Political Backlash and Generational Succession, 1987–2012." *Sociological Science* 1: 423–47.

Fishman, Silvia Barack. 2004. *Double or Nothing? Jewish Families and Mixed Marriage.* Hanover, N.H.: Brandeis University Press.

Fitoussi, Jean-Paul, Eloi Laurent, and Joël Maurice. 2004. *Ségrégation urbaine et integration sociale.* Paris: La Documentation Française.

Fitzgerald, David. 2009. *A Nation of Emigrants: How Mexico Manages Its Migration.* Berkeley: University of California Press.

Fitzgerald, Frances. 1979. *America Revised.* Boston: Little Brown.

Fleischmann, Fenella, and Cornelia Kristen. 2014. "Gender and Ethnic Inequalities across the Educational Career." In Anthony Heath and Yaël Brinbaum (eds.), *Unequal Attainments: Ethnic Educational Inequalities in Ten Western Countries.* Proceedings of the British Academy. Oxford: Oxford University Press.

Foley, Michael, and Dean Hoge. 2007. *Religion and the New Immigrants: How Faith Communities Form Our Newest Citizens.* New York: Oxford University Press.

Foner, Nancy. 1978. *Jamaica Farewell: Jamaican Migrants in London.* Berkeley: University of California Press.

———. 2000. *From Ellis Island to JFK: New York's Two Great Waves of Immigration.* New Haven: Yale University Press.

——— (ed.). 2001. *Islands in the City: West Indian Migration to New York.* Berkeley: University of California Press.

———. 2005. *In a New Land: A Comparative View of Immigration.* New York: New York University Press.

———. 2007. "How Exceptional Is New York? Migration and Multiculturalism in the Empire City." *Ethnic and Racial Studies* 30: 999–1023.

———. 2011. "Black Identities and the Second Generation: Afro-Caribbeans in Britain and the United States." In Richard Alba and Mary Waters (eds.), *The Next Generation: Immigrant Youth in a Comparative Perspective.* New York: New York University Press.

———. 2012. "Models of Integration in a Settler Society: Caveats and Complications in the US Case." *Patterns of Prejudice* 46: 486–99.

———. 2013a. "Introduction: Immigrants in New York City in the New Millennium." In Nancy Foner (ed.), *One Out of Three: Immigrant New York in the Twenty-First Century.* New York: Columbia University Press.

———. 2013b. *One Out of Three: Immigrant New York in the Twenty-First Century.* New York: Columbia University Press.

———. 2014. "Immigration History and the Remaking of New York." In Nancy Foner, Jan Rath, Jan Willem Duyvendak, and Rogier van Reekum (eds.), *New York and Amsterdam: Immigration and the New Urban Landscape.* New York: New York University Press.

Foner, Nancy, and Richard Alba. 2008. "Immigrant Religion in the U.S. and Western Europe: Bridge or Barrier to Inclusion?" *International Migration Review:* 42: 360–92.

———. 2010. "Immigration and the Legacies of the Past: The Impact of Slavery and the Holocaust on Contemporary Immigrants in the United States and Western Europe." *Comparative Studies in Society and History* 52: 798–819.

Foner, Nancy, and Joanna Dreby. 2011. "Relations between the Generations in Immigrant Families." *Annual Review of Sociology* 37: 545–64.

Foner, Nancy, and George Fredrickson. 2004. "Immigration, Race, and Ethnicity in the United States: Social Constructions and Social Relations." In Foner and Fredrickson (eds.), *Not Just Black and White: Historical and Contemporary Perspectives on Immigration, Race, and Ethnicity in the United States.* New York: Russell Sage Foundation.

Foner, Nancy, Jan Rath, Jan Willem Duyvendak, and Rogier van Reekum (eds.). 2014. *New York and Amsterdam: Immigration and the New Urban Landscape.* New York: New York University Press.

Foner, Nancy, and Patrick Simon (eds.). Forthcoming. *Fear, Anxiety, and National Identity: Immigration and Belonging in North America and Western Europe.* New York: Russell Sage Foundation.

Foner, Nancy, and Roger Waldinger. 2013. "New York and Los Angeles as Immigrant Destinations: Contrasts and Convergence." In David Halle and Andrew Beveridge (eds.), *New York and Los Angeles: The Uncertain Future.* New York: Oxford University Press.

Fong, Eric, and Rima Wilkes. 2003. "Racial and Ethnic Residential Patterns in Canada." *Sociological Forum* 18: 577–602.

Ford, Peter. 2005. "What Place for God in Europe?" *The Christian Science Monitor,* February 22.

Fox, Cybelle, and Thomas Guglielmo. 2012. "Defining America's Racial Boundaries: Blacks, Mexicans, and European Immigrants, 1890–1945." *American Journal of Sociology* 118: 327–79.

Fredrickson, George. 1997. *The Comparative Imagination: On the History of Racism, Nationalism, and Social Movements.* Berkeley: University of California Press.

———. 2002. *Racism: A Short History.* Princeton: Princeton University Press.

———. 2005. "Diverse Republics: French and American Responses to Racial Pluralism." *Daedalus* 134: 88–101.

Freeman, Gary. 1995. "Modes of Immigration Politics in Liberal Democratic States. Rejoinder." *International Migration Review* 29: 909–13.

———. 2004. "Immigrant Incorporation in Western Democracies." *International Migration Review* 38: 945–69.

Friedman, Howard Steven. 2012. *The Measure of a Nation: How to Regain America's Edge and Boost Our Global Standing.* Amherst, N.Y.: Prometheus Books.

Friedrichs, Jürgen. 2008. "Ethnische Segregation." *Kölner Zeitschrift für Soziologie und Sozialpsychologie* 48 (Sonderheft): 380–411.

Gabaccia, Donna. 1998. *We Are What We Eat: Ethnic Food and the Making of Americans.* Cambridge, Mass.: Harvard University Press.

———. 2008. "Nations of Immigrants: Do Words Matter?" Paper presented at New York Immigration Seminar, Sociology Program, CUNY Graduate Center, October 28.

Galarneau, Diane, and Rene Morrissette. 2008. "Immigrants' Education and Required Job Skllls." *Statistics Canada.* http://www.statcan.gc.ca/pub/75–001-x/2008112/article /10766-eng.htm.

Gallup Center for Muslim Studies. 2010. "In U.S. Religious Prejudice Stronger Against Muslims." January 21. http://www.gallup.com/poll/125312/religious-prejudice -stronger-against-muslims.aspx.

Gallup Organization. 2009. "Muslim Americans: A National Portrait." http://www .gallup.com/strategicconsulting/153572/report-muslim-americans-national -portrait.aspx.

Gallup/The Coexist Foundation. 2009. "The Gallup Coexist Index 2009: A Global Study of Interfaith Relations." http://www.olir.it/areetematiche/pagine/documents/News _2150_Gallup2009.pdf.

Gans, Herbert. 1979. "Symbolic Ethnicity: The Future of Ethnic Groups and Cultures in America." *Ethnic and Racial Studies* 2: 1–20.

———. 1992. "Second Generation Decline: Scenarios for the Economic and Ethnic Futures of Post-1965 American Immigrants." *Ethnic and Racial Studies* 15: 173–92.

———. 1999. "The Possibility of a New Racial Hierarchy in the Twenty-First Century United States." In Michele Lamont (ed.), *The Cultural Territories of Race.* Chicago: University of Chicago Press.

Garbaye, Romain. 2000. "Ethnic Minorities, Cities and Institutions: A Comparison of the Modes of Management of Ethnic Diversity of a French and British City." In Ruud Koopmans and Paul Statham (eds.), *Challenging Immigration and Ethnic Relations Politics: Comparative European Perspectives.* Oxford: Oxford University Press.

———. 2004. "Ethnic Minority Local Councillors in French and British Cities: Social Determinants and Political Opportunity Structures." In Rinus Penninx et al. (eds.), *Citizenship in European Cities.* Aldershot, England: Ashgate.

———. 2005. *Getting Into Local Power: The Politics of Ethnic Minorities in British and French Cities.* Oxford: Blackwell.

Gautié, Jérôme, and John Schmitt. 2010. *Low-Wage Work in the Wealthy World.* New York: Russell Sage Foundation.

Geiger, Klaus, and Margaret Spohn. 2001. "Les parlementaires allemands issus de l'immigration." *Migrations/Société* 13: 21–30.

Geisser, Vincent, and Schérazade Kelfaoui. 2001. "Marseille 2001, la communauté réinventée par des politiques." *Migrations/Société* 13: 55–77.

Geisser, Vincent, and Paul Oriol. 2001. "Les français d' 'origine étrangère' aux élections municipales de 2001." *Migrations/Société* 13: 41–53.

Geisser, Vincent, and El Yamine Soum. 2008. *Discriminer pour mieux régner: Enquête sur la diversité dans les partis politiques.* Paris: Éditions de l'Atelier.

———. 2012. "The Legacies of Colonialism: Migrant-Origin Minorities in French Politics." In Terri Givens and Rahsaan Maxwell (eds.), *Immigrant Politics: Race and Representation in Western Europe.* Boulder, Colo.: Lynne Rienner.

George, Sheba. 1998. "Caroling with the Keralites: The Negotiation of Gendered Spaces in an Indian Immigrant Church." In R. Stephen Warner and Judith Wittner (eds.), *Gatherings in Diaspora: Religious Communities and the New Immigration.* Philadelphia: Temple University Press.

German Marshall Fund. 2011. *Transatlantic Trends: Immigration.* Washington, D.C.: German Marshall Fund: http://trends.gmfus.org/files/2011/12/TTImmigration_final_web1.pdf.

Gerstle, Gary. 2001. *American Crucible: Race and Nation in the Twentieth Century.* Princeton: Princeton University Press.

———. Forthcoming. "The Contradictory Character of American Nationality: A Historical Perspective." In Nancy Foner and Patrick Simon (eds.), *Fear, Anxiety, and National Identity: Immigration and Belonging in North America and Western Europe.* New York: Russell Sage Foundation.

Gibson, Margaret, Silvia Carrasco, Jordic l'àmies, Maribel Ponferrada, and Anne Ríos. 2013. "Different Systems, Similar Results: Youth of Immigrant Origin at School in California and Catalonia." In Richard Alba and Jennifer Holdaway (eds.), *The Children of Immigrants at School: A Comparative Look at Integration in the United States and Western Europe.* New York: New York University Press.

Gillan, Audrey. 2005. "Ghettoes in English Cities 'Almost Equal to Chicago.'" *The Guardian*, September 23.

Giraud, Michel. 2009. "Colonial Racism, Ethnicity, and Citizenship: The Lessons of the Migration Experiences of French-Speaking Caribbean Populations." In Margarita Cervantes-Rodriguez, Ramon Grosfoguel, and Eric Mielants (eds.), *Caribbean Migration to Western Europe and the United States.* Philadelphia: Temple University Press.

Givens, Terri, and Rhonda Evans Case. 2012. "Race and Politics in the European Parliament." In Terri Givens and Rahsaan Maxwell (eds.), *Immigrant Politics: Race and Representation in Western Europe.* Boulder, Colo.: Lynne Rienner.

Givens, Terri, and Rahsaan Maxwell (eds.). 2012. *Immigrant Politics: Race and Representation in Western Europe.* Boulder, Colo.: Lynne Rienner.

Glazer, Nathan. 1997. *We Are All Multiculturalists Now.* Cambridge, Mass.: Harvard University Press.

Glazer, Nathan, and Daniel P. Moynihan. [1963] 1970. *Beyond the Melting Pot: The Negroes, Puerto Ricans, Jews, Italians, and Irish of New York City.* Cambridge, Mass.: MIT Press.

Göktürk, Deniz, David Gramling, and Anton Kaes (eds.). 2007. *Germany in Transit: Nation and Migration, 1955–2005.* Berkeley: University of California Press.

Gold, Steven. 2010. *The Store in the Hood: A Century of Ethnic Business and Conflict.* Lanham, Md.: Rowman and Littlefield.

Goldberg, David Theo. 2006 "Racial Europeanization." *Ethnic and Racial Studies* 29: 331–64.

Goldenberg, Claude. 2008. "Teaching English Language Learners: What the Research Does—and Does Not—Say." *American Educator* 32: 8–23, 42–44.

Goldin, Claudia, and Lawrence Katz. 2008. *The Race between Education and Technology.* Cambridge, Mass.: Harvard University Press.

Gonzales, Roberto. 2011. "Learning to be Illegal: Undocumented Youth and Shifting Legal Contexts in the Transition to Adulthood." *American Sociological Review* 76: 602–19.

Gonzalez-Barrera, Ana, and Mark Hugo Lopez. 2013. *A Demographic Portrait of Mexican-Origin Hispanics in the United States.* Washington, D.C.: Pew Hispanic Center.

Goodman, Sara Wallace. 2010. "Integration Requirements for Integration's Sake? Identifying, Categorizing and Comparing Civic Integration Policies." *Journal of Ethnic and Migration Studies* 36: 753–72.

———. 2012. "Fortifying Citizenship: Policy Strategies for Civic Integration in Western Europe." *World Politics* 64: 659–98.

Goodstein, Laurie. 2010. "Across America, Mosque Projects Meet Opposition." *New York Times,* August 1.

Gordon, Milton. 1964. *Assimilation in American Life.* New York: Oxford University Press.

Gordon, Philip. 2005. "On Assimilation and Economics, France Will Need New Models." *The New Republic,* November 9.

Gornick, Janet, and Marcia Meyers. 2003. *Families That Work: Policies for Reconciling Parenthood and Employment.* New York: Russell Sage Foundation.

Government of Canada. 2012. "Canadian Multiculturalism: An Inclusive Citizenship." http://www.cic.gc.ca/english/multiculturalism/citizenship.asp.

Grenier, Guillermo, and Lisandro Perez. 2003. *The Legacy of Exile: Cubans in the United States.* Boston: Allyn and Bacon.

Grieco, Elizabeth, et al. 2012. "The Foreign-Born Population in the United States, 2010: American Community Survey Reports." Washington, D.C.: U.S. Census Bureau.

Grillo, Ralph. 2007. "An Excess of Alterity? Debating Difference in a Multicultural Society." *Ethnic and Racial Studies* 30: 979–98.

Grunberg, Arnon. 2013. "Why the Dutch Love Black Pete." *New York Times,* December 4.

Guzy, Miriam. 2006. "Nurturing Immigrant Entrepreneurship." European Microfinance Network, December, Brussels. http://www.microfinancegateway.org/sites/default/files/mfg-en-toolkit-nurturing-immigrant-entrepreneurship-a-handbook-for-microcredit-and-business-support-2006.pdf.

Haines, David. 2007. "Refugees." In Mary C. Waters and Reed Ueda (eds.), *The New Americans.* Cambridge, Mass.: Harvard University Press.

Hall, Peter, and David Soskice. 2001. *Varieties of Capitalism.* Oxford: Oxford University Press.

Hamel, Christelle, Doreen Huschek, Nadja Milewski, and Helga de Valk. 2012. "Union Formation and Partner Choice." In Maurice Crul, Jens Schneider, and Frans Lelie (eds), *The European Second Generation Compared.* Amsterdam: Amsterdam University Press.

Hamel, Christelle, Bertrand Lhommeau, Ariane Pailhé, and Emmanuelle Santelli. 2010. "Union Formation between Here and There." In Cris Beauchemin, Christelle Hamel, and Patrick Simon (eds.), *Trajectories and Origins: Survey on Population Diversity in France: Initial Findings.* Paris: INED and INSEE.

Handl, Johann. 1994. *Soziale und berufliche Umschichtung der Bevölkerung in Bayern nach 1945: eine Sekundäranalyse der Mikrozensus-Zusatzerhebung von 1971.* Munich: Iudicium-Verlag.

Hansen, Randall. 2007. "The Free Economy and the Jacobin State, or How Europe Can Cope with the Coming Immigration Wave." In Carol Swain (ed.), *Debating Immigration.* New York: Cambridge University Press.

Hanushek, Eric, and Ludger Woessmann. 2005. "Does Educational Tracking Affect Performance and Inequality? Difference-in-Differences Evidence across Countries," Bonn: Institute for the Study of Labor.

Hargreaves, Alec. 1995. *Immigration, 'Race,' and Ethnicity in Contemporary France.* London: Routledge.

Heath, Anthony. 2013. Personal communication to authors about British electorate, July 15.

Heath, Anthony, and Yaël Brinbaum (eds.). 2014. *Unequal Attainments: Ethnic Educational Inequalities in Ten Western Countries.* Proceedings of the British Academy. Oxford: Oxford University Press.

Heath, Anthony, and Neli Demireva. 2014. "Has Multiculturalism Failed in Britain?" *Ethnic and Racial Studies* 37: 161–80.

Heath, Anthony, and Jean Martin. 2013. "Can Religious Affiliation Explain 'Ethnic' Inequalities in the Labour Market?" *Ethnic and Racial Studies* 36: 1005–27.

Heath, Anthony, Catherine Rothon, and Elina Kilpi. 2008. "The Second Generation in Western Europe: Education, Unemployment, and Occupational Attainment." *Annual Review of Sociology* 34: 211–35.

Hepner, Randal. 1998. "The House That Rasta Built: Church-Building and Fundamentalism among New York Rastafarians." In R. Stephen Warner and Judith Wittner (eds.), *Gatherings in Diaspora: Religious Communities and the New Immigration.* Philadelphia: Temple University Press.

Herberg, Will. 1960 [1955]. *Protestant, Catholic, Jew.* New York: Anchor Books.

Heyns, Barbara. 1979. *Summer Learning and the Effects of Schooling.* New York: Academic Press.

Higham, John. 1955. *Strangers in the Land: Patterns of American Nativism, 1860–1925.* New Brunswick, N.J.: Rutgers University Press.

Hirschman, Charles. 2004. "The Role of Religion in the Origins and Adaptation of Immigrant Groups in the United States." *International Migration Review* 38: 1206–33.

Hochschild, Jennifer, and Nathan Scovronick. 2003. *The American Dream and the Public Schools.* New York: Oxford University Press.

Hochschild, Jennifer, and John Mollenkopf (eds.). 2009. *Bringing Outsiders In: Transatlantic Perspectives on Immigrant Political Incorporation.* Ithaca: Cornell University Press.

Hochschild, Jennifer, Vesla Weaver, and Traci Burch. 2012. *Creating a New Racial Order: How Immigration, Multiracialism, Genomics, and the Young Can Remake Race in America.* Princeton: Princeton University Press.

Hollifield, James. 2004. "France: Republicanism and the Limits of Immigration Control." In Wayne Cornelius et al. (eds.), *Controlling Immigration: A Global Perspective.* 2nd ed. Stanford: Stanford University Press.

Hollifield, James, Philip Martin, and Pia Orrenius. 2014. "Introduction: The Dilemmas of Immigration Control." In James Hollifield, Philip Martin, and Pia Orrenius (eds.),

A Global Perspective on Controlling Immigration. 3rd ed. Stanford: Stanford University Press.

Hollinger, David. 1996. *Science, Jews, and Secular Culture: Studies in Mid-Twentieth-Century Intellectual History.* Princeton: Princeton University Press.

———. 2003. "Amalgamation and Hypodescent: The Question of Ethnoracial Mixture in the History of the United States." *American Historical Review* 108: 1363–90.

Hondagneu-Sotelo, Pierrette. 2001. *Domestica: Immigrant Workers Cleaning and Caring in the Shadows of Affluence.* Berkeley: University of California Press.

Hondius, Dienke. 2009. "Blacks in Early Modern Europe: New Research from the Netherlands." In Darlene Clark Hine, Trica Keaton, and Stephen Small (eds.), *Black Europe and the African Diaspora.* Urbana: University of Illinois Press.

Hooghe, Marc. 2005. "Ethnic Organizations and Social Movement Theory: The Political Opportunity Structure for Ethnic Mobilization in Flanders." *Journal of Ethnic and Migration Studies* 31: 975–90.

Hou, Feng. 2006. "Spatial Assimilation of Racial Minorities in Canada's Immigrant Gateway Cities." *Urban Studies* 43: 1191–213.

Hou, Feng, and Zheng Wu. 2009. "Racial Diversity, Minority Concentration, and Trust in Canadian Urban Neighborhoods." *Social Science Research* 38: 693–716.

House of Commons. 2011. "House of Commons FAQs." http://www.parliament.uk/about/faqs/house-of-commons-faqs/ (accessed 7/15/11).

Howard, Marc Morjé. 2005. "Variation in Dual Citizenship Policies in the Countries of the EU." *International Migration Review* 39: 697–720.

———. 2009. *The Politics of Citizenship in Europe.* New York: Cambridge University Press.

Human Rights Watch. 2009. *Discrimination in the Name of Neutrality: Headscarf Bans for Teachers and Civil Servants in Germany.* New York: Human Rights Watch.

Huntington, Samuel. 2004. *Who Are We? The Challenges to America's National Identity.* New York: Simon and Schuster.

Hurenkamp, Menno, Evelien Tonkens, and Jan Willem Duyvendak. 2012. *Crafting Citizenship: Negotiating Tensions in Modern Society.* Basingstoke and New York: Palgrave Macmillan.

Iceland, John. 2009. *Where We Live Now: Immigration and Race in the United States.* Berkeley: University of California Press.

Iceland, John, and Kyle Anne Nelson. 2008. "Hispanic Segregation in Metropolitan America: Exploring the Multiple Forms of Spatial Assimilation." *American Sociological Review* 73: 741–65.

Ichou, Mathieu. 2014. "Les origines des inégalités scolaires. Contribution à l'étude des trajectoires scolaires des enfants d'immigrés en France et en Angleterre." Ph.D. diss., Institut des Études Politiques de Paris (Science Po).

Imoagene, Onosu. 2012. "Being British vs. Being American: Identification among Second-generation Adults of Nigerian Descent in the US and UK." *Ethnic and Racial Studies* 35: 2153–73.

Innocenti Insight. 2009. *Children in Immigrant Families in Eight Affluent Countries: Their Family, National and International Context.* Florence: Innocenti Research Centre.

Institute for Political Participation. 2006. "Meer Diversiteit in de Gemeenteraden." *Nieuwsbrief,* pp. 7–9.

Ireland, Patrick. 2004. *Becoming Europe: Immigration, Integration and the Welfare State.* Pittsburgh: University of Pittsburgh Press.

Jacob, Konstanze, and Frank Kalter. 2013. "Intergenerational Change in Religious Salience among Immigrant Families in Four European Countries." *International Migration* 51: 38–56.

Jacobson, Matthew Frye. 2006. *Roots Too: White Ethnic Revival in Post–Civil Rights America.* Cambridge, Mass.: Harvard University Press.

Ji, Qingqing, and Jeanne Batalova. 2012. "College-Educated Immigrants in the United States." *Migration Information Source* (December). http://www.migrationinformation.org/Feature/display.cfm?ID=927.

Jiménez, Tomás. 2010. *Replenished Ethnicity: Mexican Americans, Immigration, and Ethnicity.* Berkeley: University of California Press.

Jiménez, Tomás, and Adam Horowitz. 2013. "When White Is Just Alright: How Immigrants Redefine Achievement and Reconfigure the Ethnoracial Hierarchy." *American Sociological Review* 78: 849–71.

Johnston, Ron, James Forrest, and Michael Poulsen. 2002. "Are There Ethnic Enclaves/Ghettos in English Cities?" *Urban Studies* 39: 591–618.

Johnston, Ron, Michael Poulsen, and James Forrest. 2013. "Multiethnic Residential Areas in a Multiethnic Country? A Decade of Major Change in England and Wales." *Environment and Planning A* 45: 753–59.

Jones, Robert, Daniel Cox, William Galston, and E. J. Dionne, Jr. 2011. *What It Means to Be an American.* Washington, D.C.: Governance Studies at the Brookings Institution and Public Religion Research Institute.

Jones-Correa, Michael. 1998. *Between Two Nations: The Political Predicament of Latinos in New York City.* Ithaca: Cornell University Press.

———. 2001. "Under Two Flags: Dual Nationality in Latin America and Its Consequences for the United States." *International Migration Review* 35: 997–1029.

Joppke, Christian. 1999. *Immigration and the Nation-State: The United States, Germany, and Britain.* Oxford: Oxford University Press.

———. 2004. "The Retreat of Multiculturalism in the Liberal State: Theory and Policy." *British Journal of Sociology* 55: 237–57.

———. 2009a. "Limits of Integration Policy: Britain and Her Muslims." *Journal of Ethnic and Migration Studies* 35: 453–72.

———. 2009b. *Veil: Mirror of Identity.* London: Polity.

———. 2010. *Citizenship and Immigration.* Cambridge: Polity.

———. 2012. "The Role of the State in Cultural Integration: Trends, Challenges, and Ways Ahead." Washington, D.C.: Migration Policy Institute.

Joppke, Christian, and Ewa Morawska. 2003. "Integrating Immigrants in Liberal Nation-States: Policies and Practices." In Joppke and Morawska (eds.), *Toward Assimilation and Citizenship.* London: Palgrave Macmillan.

Joppke, Christian, and John Torpey. 2013. *Legal Integration of Islam: A Transatlantic Comparison.* Cambridge, Mass.: Harvard University Press.

Jordan, Miriam. 2014. "Hispanics Gain at California Colleges: University System Admits More Latinos than Whites for the First Time." *Wall Street Journal*, April 20.

Judt, Tony. 2005. *Postwar: A History of Europe since 1945.* New York: Penguin.

Kalkan, Kerem Ozan, Geoffrey Layman, and Eric Uslaner. 2009. "'Bands of Others?'

Attitudes toward Muslims in Contemporary American Society." *Journal of Politics* 71: 847–62.

Kalleberg, Arne. 2000. "Nonstandard Employment Relations: Part-Time, Temporary, and Contract Work." *Annual Review of Sociology* 26: 341–65.

———. 2009. "Precarious Work, Insecure Workers: Employment Relations in Transition." *American Sociological Review* 74: 1–22.

Kalmijn, Mathijs, and Frank van Tubergen. 2006. "Ethnic Intermarriages in the Netherlands: Confirmations and Refutations of Accepted Insights." *European Journal of Population* 22: 371–97.

———. 2010. "A Comparative Perspective on Intermarriage: Explaining Differences among National Origin Groups in the United States." *Demography* 47: 459–79.

Kalter, Frank. 2006. "Auf der Suche nach einer Erklärung für die spezifischen Arbeitsmarktnachteile von Jugendlichen türkishcher Herkunft." *Zeitschrift für Soziologie* 35: 144–60.

———. 2011. "The Second Generation in the German Labor Market: Explaining the Turkish Exception." In Richard Alba and Mary Waters (eds.), *The Next Generation: Immigrant Youth in a Comparative Perspective.* New York: New York University Press.

Kalter, Frank, and Nadia Granato. 2007. "Educational Hurdles on the Way to Structural Assimilation." In Anthony Heath and Sin Yi Cheung (eds.), *Unequal Chances: Ethnic Minorities in Western Labor Markets.* Proceedings of the British Academy. Oxford: Oxford University Press.

Kalter, Frank, and Irina Kogan. 2006. "Ethnic Inequalities at the Transition from School to Work in Belgium and Spain: Discrimination or Self-exclusion?" *Research in Social Stratification and Mobility* 24: 259–74.

Kalter, Frank, and Julia Schroedter. 2010. "Transnational Marriage among Former Labour Migrants in Germany." *Journal of Family Research* 22: 12–36.

Kang, Miliann. 2010. *The Managed Hand: Race, Gender, and the Body in Beauty Service Work.* Berkeley: University of California Press.

Kao, Grace, and Marta Tienda. 1995. "Optimism and Achievement: The Educational Performance of Immigrant Youth." *Social Science Quarterly* 76:1–19.

Kasinitz, Philip. 1992. *Caribbean New York.* Ithaca: Cornell University Press.

Kasinitz, Philip, John Mollenkopf, Mary Waters, and Jennifer Holdaway. 2008. *Inheriting the City: The Children of Immigrants Come of Age.* New York and Cambridge, Mass.: Russell Sage Foundation and Harvard University Press.

Kastoryano, Riva. 2002. *Negotiating Identities: States and Immigrants in France and Germany.* Princeton: Princeton University Press.

Katznelson, Ira. 2005. *When Affirmative Action Was White: An Untold History of Racial Inequality in Twentieth Century America.* New York: W.W. Norton.

Kelek, Necla. 2005. *Die fremde Braut: Ein Bericht aus dem Inneren des türkischen Lebens in Deutschland.* Cologne: Kiepenheuer and Witsch.

Kelley, Ninette, and Michael Trebilcock. 1998. *The Making of the Mosaic: A History of Canadian Immigration Policy.* Toronto: University of Toronto Press.

Kent, Mary Mederios. 2007. "Immigration and America's Black Population." *Population Bulletin* 62: 3–16.

Kepel, Gilles. 1991. *Les banlieues de l'Islam: Naissance d'une religion en France.* Paris: Éditions du Seuil.

Keslassy, Éric. 2010. "Quelle place pour les minorités visibles? Retour sur les élections régionales de mars 2010." Institut Montaigne, September.

Kettlewell, Kelly, and Liz Phillips. 2014. *Census of Local Authority Councillors, 2013.* Slough, England: National Foundation for Educational Research.

Khan, Sheema. 2007. "Quebec Muslims: Navigating Uncharted Territory." http://www .onislam.net/english/politics/americas/435648.html.

Kim, Dae Young. 2004. "Leaving the Ethnic Economy: The Rapid Integration of Second-Generation Korean Americans in New York." In Philip Kasinitz, John Mollenkopf, and Mary C. Waters (eds.), *Becoming New Yorkers: Ethnographies of the New Second Generation.* New York: Russell Sage Foundation.

Kim, Soohan, Alexandra Kalev, and Frank Dobbin. 2012. "Progressive Corporations at Work: The Case of Diversity Programs." *Review of Law and Social Change* 36: 171–213.

King, Karen. 2009. "The Geography of Immigration in Canada: Settlement, Education, and Labour Activity and Occupation Profiles." Working Paper Series. Toronto: Martin Prosperity Institute, Rotman School of Management, University of Toronto.

Kivisto, Peter. 2002. *Multiculturalism in a Global Society.* Oxford: Wiley-Blackwell.

Kivisto, Peter, and Thomas Faist. 2010. *Beyond a Border: The Causes and Consequences of Contemporary Immigration.* Los Angeles: Pine Forge Press.

Klausen, Jyette. 2005. *The Islamic Challenge: Politics and Religion in Western Europe.* Oxford and New York: Oxford University Press.

———. 2009. *The Cartoons That Shook the World.* New Haven: Yale University Press.

Kloosterman, Robert, and Jan Rath. 2003. "Introduction." In Robert Kloosterman and Jan Rath (eds.), *Immigrant Entrepreneurs: Venturing Abroad in the Age of Globalization.* Oxford and New York: Berg.

Klostermann, Johannes. 2008. "Eliminating Racist Discrimination in Germany." Report of the Forum Menschenrechte. www2.ohchr.org/english/bodies/cerd/ . . . /Forum Menschenrechte.pdf.

Kochhar, Rakesh. 2009. "Unemployment Rose Sharply among Latino Immigrants in 2008." Washington, D.C.: Pew Hispanic Center. http://www.pewhispanic.org/files /reports/102.pdf.

———. 2014. "Latino Jobs Growth Driven by U.S. Born." Washington, D.C.: Pew Research Center's Hispanic Trends Project. www.pewhispanic.org/2014/06/19 /latino-jobs-growth-driven-by-u-s-born/.

Koenig, Matthias. 2005. "Incorporating Muslim Immigrants in Western Nation States: A Comparison of the United Kingdom, France and Germany." *Journal of International Migration and Integration* 6: 219–34.

Kogan, Irena. 2006. "Labor Markets and Economic Incorporation among Recent Immigrants in Europe." *Social Forces* 85: 697–721.

———. 2010a. "New Immigrants—Old Disadvantage Patterns? Labour Market Integration of Recent Immigrants into Germany." *International Migration* 49: 91–117.

———. 2010b. "Introduction to the Special Issue on Minority Ethnic Groups' Marriage Patterns in Europe." *Journal of Family Research* 22: 1–9.

———. 2011. "The Price of Being an Outsider: Labour Market Flexibility and Immigrants' Employment Paths in Germany." *International Journal of Comparative Sociology* 52: 264–83.

Koikkalainen, Saara. 2011. "Free Movement in Europe: Past and Present." *Migration In-*

formation Source (April). http://www.migrationinformation.org/Feature/display.cfm ?ID=836.

Kolb, Holger. 2014. "When Extremes Converge: German and Canadian Labor Migration Policy Compared." *Comparative Migration Studies* 2: 57–75.

Koopmans, Ruud. 2004. "Migrant Mobilization and Political Opportunities: Variation among German Cities and a Comparison with the United Kingdom and the Netherlands." *Journal of Ethnic and Migration Studies* 30: 449–70.

Koopmans, Ruud, and Paul Statham. 2000a. "Migration and Ethnic Relations as a Field of Political Contention: An Opportunity Structure Approach." In Koopmans and Statham (eds.), *Challenging Immigration and Ethnic Relations: Comparative European Perspectives.* Oxford: Oxford University Press.

———. 2000b. "Challenging the Liberal Nation-State? Postnationalism, Multiculturalism, and the Collective Claims-Making of Migrants and Ethnic Minorities in Britain and Germany." In Ruud Koopmans and Paul Statham (eds.), *Challenging Immigration and Ethnic Relations: Comparative European Perspectives.* Oxford: Oxford University Press.

Koopmans Ruud, Paul Statham, Marco Giugni, and Florence Passy. 2005. *Contested Citizenship: Immigration and Cultural Diversity in Europe.* Minneapolis: University of Minnesota Press.

Kosmin, Barry, and Ariela Keysar. 2006. *Religion in a Free Market: Religious and Non-Religious Americans, Who, What, Why, Where.* Ithaca, N.Y.: Paramount Market Publishers.

Kozol, Jonathan. 1991. *Savage Inequalities: Children in America's Schools.* New York: Crown.

Kramer, Jane. 2004. "Taking the Veil: How France's Public Schools Became the Battleground in a Culture War." *The New Yorker*, November 22.

———. 2005. "Difference." *The New Yorker*, November 21.

Kristen, Cornelia. 2008. "Schulische Leistungen von Kindern aus türkischen Familien am Ende der Grundschulzeit: Befunde aus der IGLU-Studie." *Kölner Zeitschrift für Soziologie und Sozialpsychologie* 48: 230–51.

Kristen, Cornelia, David Reimer, and Irena Kogan. 2008. "Higher Education Entry of Turkish Immigrant Youth in Germany." *International Journal of Comparative Sociology* 49: 127–51.

Krivo, Lauren, Ruth Peterson, and Danielle Kuhl. 2009. "Segregation, Racial Structure, and Neighborhood Violent Crime." *American Journal of Sociology* 114: 1765–802.

Krugman, Paul. 2014. "Europe's Secret Success." *New York Times*, May 25.

Kulu-Glasgow, Isik, and Arjen Leerkes. 2013. "Restricting Turkish Marriage Migration? National Policy, Couples' Coping Strategies, and International Obligations." *Migration Letters* 10: 369–82.

Kurien, Prema. 1998. "Becoming American by Becoming Hindu: Indian Americans Take Their Place at the Multicultural Table." In R. Stephen Warner and Judith Wittner (eds.), *Gatherings in Diaspora: Religious Communities and the New Immigration.* Philadelphia: Temple University Press.

Kymlicka, Will. 2012. *Multiculturalism: Success, Failure, and the Future.* Washington, D.C.: Migration Policy Institute.

Ladd, Helen, and Edward Fiske. 2011. "Weighted Student Funding in the Netherlands: A Model for the U.S.?" *Journal of Policy Analysis and Management* 30: 470–98.

Lamont, Michèle. 2000. *The Dignity of Working Men: Morality and the Boundaries of Race, Class, and Immigration*. Cambridge, Mass.: Harvard University Press.

Lamont, Michèle, and Virág Molnár. 2002. "The Study of Boundaries in the Social Sciences." *Annual Review of Sociology* 28: 167–95.

Laurence, Jonathan. 2012. *The Emancipation of Europe's Muslims: The State's Role in Minority Integration*. Princeton: Princeton University Press.

Laurence, Jonathan, and Rahsaan Maxwell. 2012: "Political Parties and Diversity in Western Europe." In Terri Givens and Rahsaan Maxwell (eds.), *Immigrant Politics: Race and Representation in Western Europe*. Boulder, Colo.: Lynne Rienner.

Laurence, Jonathan, and Justin Vaisse. 2006. *Integrating Islam: Political and Religious Challenges in Contemporary France*. Washington, D.C.: Brookings Institution Press.

Layton-Henry, Zig. 2004. "Britain: From Immigration Control to Migration Management." In Wayne Cornelius, Takeyuki Tsuda, Philip Martin, and James Hollifield (eds.), *Controlling Immigration: A Global Perspective*. 2nd ed. Stanford: Stanford University Press.

Leal, David. 2005. "American Public Opinion toward the Military: Differences by Race, Gender, and Class." *Armed Forces & Society* 32: 123–38.

Lee, Jennifer, and Frank Bean. 2010. *The Diversity Paradox. Immigration and the Color Line in Twenty-First Century America*. New York: Russell Sage Foundation.

Leiken, Robert S. 2012. *Europe's Angry Muslims: The Revolt of the Second Generation*. New York: Oxford University Press.

Leise, Eric. 2007. "Germany Strives to Integrate Immigrants with New Policies." *Migration Information Source* (July). http://www.migrationinformation.org/Feature/display .cfm?ID=610.

Le Lohe, Michel. 1998. "Ethnic Minority Participation and Representation in the British Electoral System." In Shamit Saggar (ed.), *Race and British Electoral Politics*. London: Routledge.

Leonard, Karen Isakson. 2003. *Muslims in the United States: The State of Research*. New York: Russell Sage Foundation.

Lessard-Phillips, Laurence, Fenella Fleischmann, and Erika van Elsas. 2014. "Ethnic Minorities in Ten Western Countries: Migration Flows, Policies and Institutional Differences." In Anthony Heath and Yaël Brinbaum (eds.), *Unequal Attainments: Ethnic Educational Inequalities in Ten Western Countries*. Proceedings of the British Academy. Oxford: Oxford University Press.

Levitt, Peggy. 2007. *God Needs No Passport: Immigrants and the Changing American Religious Landscape*. New York: New Press.

Lewis, Valerie, and Ridhi Kashyap. 2013. "Piety in a Secular Society: Migration, Religiosity, and Islam in Britain." *International Migration* 51: 57–66.

Lhommeau, Bertrand, Dominique Meurs, and Jean-Luc Primon. 2010. "Labor Market Situation of Persons Aged 18–50 by Sex and Origin." In Chris Beauchemin, Christelle Hamel, and Patrick Simon (eds.), *Trajectories and Origins: Survey on Population Diversity in France*. Paris: INED and INSEE.

Li, Monica, and Jeanne Batalova. 2011. "Refugees and Asylees in the United States." *Migration Information Source* (August). http://www.migrationinformation.org /USFocus/display.cfm?ID=851.

Li, Peter. 2003. *Destination Canada: Immigration Debates and Issues*. Don Mills, Ontario: Oxford University Press.

Li, Wei. 1998. "Anatomy of a New Ethnic Settlement: The Chinese Ethnoburb in Los Angeles." *Urban Studies* 35: 479–502.

Lichter, Daniel. 2013. "Integration or Fragmentation? Racial Diversity and the American Future." *Demography* 50: 359–91.

Lieberman, Robert. 2005. "Race, State, and Policy: The Development of Employment Discrimination Policy in the USA and Britain." In Glenn Loury, Tariq Modood, and Steven Teles (eds.), *Ethnicity, Social Mobility, and Public Policy*. Cambridge: Cambridge University Press.

Light, Ivan, and Steven Gold. 2000. *Ethnic Economies*. San Diego: Academic Press.

Light, Ivan, and Michael Johnston. 2009. "The Metropolitan Dispersion of Mexican Immigrants in the United States, 1980 to 2000." *Journal of Ethnic and Migration Studies* 35: 3–18.

Lijphart, Arend. 1968. *The Politics of Accommodation: Pluralism and Democracy in the Netherlands*. Berkeley: University of California Press.

Lloyd, Caroline, Geoff Mason, and Ken Mayhew. 2008. *Low-Wage Work in the United Kingdom*. New York: Russell Sage Foundation.

Logan, John. 2006. "Variations in Immigrant Incorporation in the Neighborhoods of Amsterdam." *International Journal of Urban and Regional Research* 30: 485–509.

Logan, John, Richard Alba, and Thomas McNulty. 1994. "Ethnic Economies in Metropolitan Regions: Miami and Beyond." *Social Forces* 72: 691–724.

Logan, John, Richard Alba, and Wenquan Zhang. 2002. "Immigrant Enclaves and Ethnic Communities in New York and Los Angeles." *American Sociological Review* 67: 299–322.

Logan, John, and Glenn Deane. 2003. "Black Diversity in Metropolitan America." Report of the Lewis Mumford Center, State University of Albany. http://mumford .albany.edu/census/BlackWhite/BlackDiversityReport/black-diversity01.htm.

Logan, John, and Harvey Molotch. 1987. *Urban Fortunes: The Political Economy of Place*. Berkeley: University of California Press.

Logan, John, and Brian Stults. 2011. "The Persistence of Segregation in the Metropolis: New Findings from the 2010 Census." Report, US2010 Project. http://www.s4.brown .edu/us2010/Data/Report/report2.pdf (accessed 6/15/2011).

Logan, John, and Wenquan Zhang. 2010. "Global Neighborhoods: New Pathways to Diversity and Separation." *American Journal of Sociology* 115: 1069–109.

Loozen, Suzanne, Helga de Valk, and Elma Wobma. 2012. "Demografie." In Mérove Gijsberts, Willem Huijink, and Jaco Dagevos, *Jaarrapport Integratie 2011*. The Hague: Sociaal en Cultureel Planbureau.

Lopez, David. 2009. "Whither the Flock? The Catholic Church and the Success of Mexicans in America." In Richard Alba, Albert Raboteau, and Josh DeWind (eds.), *Immigration and Religion in America: Comparative and Historical Perspectives*. New York: New York University Press.

Lopez, David, and Ricardo Stanton-Salazar. 2001. "Mexican Americans: A Second Generation at Risk." In Rubén Rumbaut and Alejandro Portes (eds.), *Ethnicities: Children of Immigrants in America*. Berkeley: University of California Press.

López, Ian Haney. 1996. *White by Law: The Legal Construction of Race*. New York: New York University Press.

Lopez, Mark Hugo, and Richard Fry. 2013. "Among Recent High School Grads, Hispanic College Enrollment Rate Surpasses That of Whites." Washington, D.C.: Pew

Research Center (September). http://www.pewresearch.org/fact-tank/2013/09/04/hispanic-college-enrollment-rate-surpasses-whites-for-the-first-time/.

Lopez, Nancy. 2003. *Hopeful Girls, Troubled Boys: Race and Gender Disparity in Urban Education*. New York: Routledge.

Louie, Vivian. 2012. *Keeping the Immigrant Bargain: The Costs and Rewards of Success in America*. New York: Russell Sage Foundation.

Los Angeles Times. 2010. "At Ramadan Iftar Dinner Obama Supports New Mosque on Private Property near Ground Zero." August 23. latimesblogs.latimes.com/ . . . / Obama-ramadan-iftar-remarks-text-html.

Lucas, Samuel. 2001. "Effectively Maintained Inequality: Education Transitions, Track Mobility, and Social Background Effects." *American Journal of Sociology* 106: 1642–90.

Lucassen, Leo. 2005. *The Immigrant Threat: The Integration of Old and New Migrants in Western Europe since 1850*. Urbana: University of Illinois Press.

Lucassen, Leo, and Charlotte Laarman. 2009. "Immigration, Intermarriage and the Changing Face of Europe in the Post War Period." *History of the Family* 14: 52–68.

Lucassen, Jan, and Rinus Penninx. 1997. *Newcomers: Immigrants and Their Descendants in the Netherlands, 1550–1995*. Amsterdam: Het Spinhuis.

Luthra, Renee Reichl, and Roger Waldinger. 2010. "Into the Mainstream? Labor Market Outcomes of Mexican Origin Workers." *International Migration Review* 44: 830–68.

Lutz, Amy. 2014. "University Completion among the Children of Immigrants." In Anthony Heath and Yaël Brinbaum (eds.), *Unequal Attainments: Ethnic Educational Inequalities in Ten Western Countries*. Proceedings of the British Academy. Oxford: Oxford University Press.

Lyon, David, and Marguerite van Die. 2000. *Rethinking Church, State, and Modernity: Canada between Europe and America*. Toronto: University of Toronto Press.

Lyons, Christopher, María Vélez, and Wayne Santoro. 2013. "Immigration, Neighborhood Violence, and City Political Opportunities." *American Sociological Review* 78: 604–32.

Ma Mung, Emmanuel, and Thomas Lacroix. 2003. "France: The Narrow Path." In Robert Kloosterman and Jan Rath (eds.), *Immigrant Entrepreneurs: Venturing Abroad in the Age of Globalization*. Oxford and New York: Berg.

Maaz, Kai, Ulrich Trautwein, Oliver Lüdtke, and Jürgen Baumert. 2008. "Educational Transitions and Differential Learning Environments: How Explicit Between-School Tracking Contributes to Social Inequality in Educational Outcomes." *Child Development Perspectives* 2: 99–106.

Maliepaard, Mieke, Merove Gijsberts, and Marcel Lubbers. 2012. "Reaching the Limits of Secularization? Turkish- and Moroccan-Dutch Muslims in the Netherlands, 1998–2006." *Journal for the Scientific Study of Religion* 51: 359–67.

Maliepaard, Mieke, Marcel Lubbers, and Merove Gijsberts. 2010. "Generational Differences in Ethnic and Religious Attachment and their Interrelation: A Study among Muslim Minorities in the Netherlands." *Ethnic and Racial Studies* 33: 451–71.

Marrow, Helen. 2011. *New Destination Dreaming: Immigration, Race, and Legal Status in the Rural American South*. Stanford: Stanford University Press.

Marsden, George. 1994. *The Soul of the American University: From Protestant Establishment to Established Nonbelief*. New York: Oxford University Press.

Martin, Philip. 2004a. "Germany: Managing Migration in the Twenty-First Century." In

Wayne Cornelius et al. (eds.), *Controlling Immigration: A Global Perspective*. 2nd ed. Stanford: Stanford University Press.

———. 2004b. "The United States: The Continuing Immigration Debate." In Wayne Cornelius et al. (eds.), *Controlling Immigration: A Global Perspective*. 2nd ed. Stanford: Stanford University Press.

Martiniello, Marco. 2000. "The Residential Concentration and Political Participation of Immigrants in European Cities." In Sophie Body-Gendrot and Marco Martiniello (eds.), *Minorities in European Cities: The Dynamics of Social Integration and Social Exclusion at the Neighborhood Level*. London: Macmillan.

Masci, David, and Gregory Smith. 2006. "God Is Alive and Well in America." Pew Research Center. http://pewresearch.org/pubs/15.

Massey, Douglas. 1985. "Ethnic Residential Segregation: A Theoretical Synthesis and Empirical Review." *Sociology and Social Research* 69: 315–50.

———— (ed.). 2008. *New Faces in New Places: The Changing Geography of American Immigration*. New York: Russell Sage Foundation.

Massey, Douglas, Len Albright, Rebecca Casciano, Elizabeth Derickson, and David Kinsey. 2013. *Climbing Mount Laurel: The Struggle for Affordable Housing and Social Mobility in an American Suburb*. Princeton: Princeton University Press.

Massey, Douglas, and Amelia Brown. 2011. "New Migration Stream between Mexico and Canada." *Migraciones Internacionales* 6: 119–44.

Massey, Douglas, Camille Charles, Garvey Lundy, and Mary Fischer. 2002. *The Source of the River: The Social Origins of Freshmen at America's Selective Colleges and Universities*. Princeton: Princeton University Press.

Massey, Douglas, and Nancy Denton. 1988. "The Dimensions of Residential Segregation." *Social Forces* 67: 281–315.

———. 1993. *American Apartheid: Segregation and the Making of the Underclass*. Cambridge, Mass.: Harvard University Press.

Massey, Douglas, Jorge Durand, and Nolan Malone. 2002. *Beyond Smoke and Mirrors: Mexican Immigration in an Era of Economic Integration*. New York: Russell Sage Foundation.

Massey, Douglas, and Mary Fischer. 2000. "How Segregation Concentrates Poverty." *Ethnic and Racial Studies* 23: 670–91.

Massey, Douglas, Margarita Mooney, Kimberly Torres, and Camille Charles. 2007. "Black Immigrants and Black Natives Attending Selective Colleges and Universities in the United States." *American Journal of Education* 113: 243–71.

Massey, Douglas, and Magaly Sanchez R. 2012. *Brokered Boundaries: Creating Immigrant Identity in Anti-Immigrant Times*. New York: Russell Sage Foundation.

Matsumoto, Noriko. 2011. "The Invention of Multiethnic Space: East Asian Immigrants in Fort Lee, New Jersey." Ph.D. diss., CUNY Graduate Center, New York.

Maurer, Marc. 2003. "Comparative International Rates of Incarceration: An Examination of Causes and Trends." Report presented to the U.S. Commission on Civil Rights, Washington, D.C., June.

Maussen, Marcel. 2007. *The Governance of Islam in Western Europe: A State of the Art Report*. IMISCOE Working Paper No. 16, June.

———. 2012. "Pillarization and Islam: Church-State Traditions and Muslim Claims for Recognition in the Netherlands." *Comparative European Politics* 10: 337–53.

Maxwell, Rahsaan. 2012. *Ethnic Minority Migrants in Britain and France.* Cambridge: Cambridge University Press.

———. 2013. "The Integration Trade-offs of Political Representation." *European Political Science* 12: 467–78.

McGreevey, John. 2003. *Catholicism and American Freedom: A History.* New York: W.W. Norton.

Meer, Nasar, Varun Uberoi, and Tariq Modood. Forthcoming. "Nationhood and Muslims in Britain." In Nancy Foner and Patrick Simon (eds.). *Fear, Anxiety, and National Identity: Immigration and Belonging in North America and Western Europe.*

Menjivar, Cecilia. 2006. "Liminal Legality: Salvadoran and Guatemalan Immigrants' Lives in the United States." *American Journal of Sociology* 111: 999–1037.

Menjivar, Cecilia, and Daniel Kanstroom (eds.). 2014. *Constructing Immigrant 'Illegality.'* New York: Cambridge University Press.

Michon, Laure. 2012. "Successful Political Integration: Paradoxes in the Netherlands." In Terry Givens and Rahsaan Maxwell (eds.), *Immigrant Politics; Race and Representation in Western Europe.* Boulder, Colo.: Lynne Rienner.

Michon, Laure, and Floris Vermeulen. 2013. "Explaining Different Trajectories in Immigrant Political Integration: Moroccans and Turks in Amsterdam." *West European Politics* 36: 597–614.

Migazin. 2013. "Der neue Bundestag: Fünf Prozent Abgeordnete mit Migrationshintergrund." http://www.migazin.de/2013/09/24/bundestag-abgeordnete-mit-migration shintergrund.

Migrant Integration Policy Index. 2014. *Anti-Discrimination.* www.mipex.eu/anti -discrimination.

Migration Information Source. 2009. "Buyer's Remorse on Immigration Continues." December. http://www.migrationinformation.org/Feature/display.cfm?id=759.

Migration News. 2000. "Germany: Immigration Policy." Vol. 8. http://migration.ucdavis |.edu/mn/more.php?id=2164_0_4_0.

Milan, Anne. 2011. "Migration: International, 2009." *Statistics Canada.* http://www .statcan.gc.ca/pub/91–209-x/2011001/article/11526-eng.htm.

Milan, Anne, Helene Maheux, and Tina Chui. 2010. "A Portrait of Couples in Mixed Unions." *Statistics Canada.* http://www.statcan.gc.ca/pub/11–008-x/2010001/article /11143-eng.htm.

Milot, Micheline. 2009. "Modus Co-vivendi: Religious Diversity in Canada." In Paul Bramadat and Matthias Koenig (eds.), *International Migration and the Governance of Religious Diversity.* Montreal: McGill-Queen's University Press.

Min, Pyong Gap. 1996. *Caught in the Middle: Korean Communities in New York and Los Angeles.* Berkeley: University of California Press.

———. 2001. "Koreans: An Institutionally Complete Community in New York." In Nancy Foner (ed.), *New Immigrants in New York.* 2nd ed. New York: Columbia University Press.

———. 2008. *Ethnic Solidarity for Economic Survival: Korean Greengrocers in New York City.* New York: Russell Sage Foundation.

Min, Pyong Gap, and Chigon Kim. 2010. "Patterns of Intermarriages and Cross-Generational In-Marriages among Native-Born Asian Americans." *International Migration Review* 43: 443–70.

Moch, Leslie Page. 2003. *Moving Europeans: Migration in Western Europe since 1650.* 2nd ed. Bloomington: Indiana University Press.

Model, Suzanne. 2008. *West Indian Immigrants: A Black Success Story?* New York: Russell Sage Foundation.

Model, Suzanne, and Gene Fisher. 2002. "Unions between Blacks and Whites: England and the U.S. Compared." *Ethnic and Racial Studies* 25: 728–54.

———. 2007. "The New Second Generation at the Turn of the New Century: Europeans and Non-Europeans in the US Labour Market." In Anthony Heath and Sin Yi Cheung (eds.), *Unequal Chances: Ethnic Minorities in Western Labor Markets.* Proceedings of the British Academy. Oxford: Oxford University Press.

Model, Suzanne and Lang Lin. 2002. "The Cost of Not Being Christian: Hindus, Sikhs, and Muslims in Britain and Canada." *International Migration Review* 36: 1061–92.

Modood, Tariq. 2005a. "Ethnicity and Political Mobilization in Britain." In Glenn Loury, Tariq Modood, and Steven Teles (eds.), *Ethnicity, Social Mobility and Public Policy: Comparing the US and UK.* Cambridge: Cambridge University Press.

———. 2005b. *Multicultural Politics: Racism, Ethnicity, and Muslims in Britain.* Minneapolis: University of Minnesota Press.

———. 2007. *Multiculturalism.* London: Verso.

———. 2011. "Capitals, Ethnic Identity, and Educational Qualifications." In Richard Alba and Mary Waters (eds.), *The Next Generation: Immigrant Youth in Comparative Perspective.* New York: New York University Press.

Mollenkopf, John. 2014. "The Rise of Immigrant Influence in New York City Politics." In Nancy Foner, Jan Rath, Jan Willem Duyvendak, and Rogier van Reekum (eds.), *New York and Amsterdam: Immigration and the New Urban Landscape.* New York: New York University Press.

Mollenkopf, John, and Jennifer Hochschild. 2010. "Immigrant Political Incorporation: Comparing Success in the United States and Western Europe." *Ethnic and Racial Studies* 33: 19–38.

Mooney, Margarita. 2013. "Religion as a Context of Reception: The Case of Haitian Immigrants in Miami, Montreal, and Paris." *International Migration* 51: 99–112.

Morawska, Ewa. 2009. *A Sociology of Immigration: (Re)Making Multifaced America.* Houndmills, Basingstoke: Palgrave Macmillan.

Morehouse, Christal, and Michael Blomfield. 2011. "Irregular Migration in Europe." Washington, D.C.: Migration Policy Institute.

Mouguérou, Laurie, Yaël Brinbaum, and Jean-Luc Primon. 2010. "Educational Attainment of Immigrants and Their Descendants." In Cris Beauchemin, Christelle Hamel, and Patrick Simon (eds.), *Trajectories and Origins: Survey on Population Diversity in France.* Paris: INED and INSEE.

Münz, Rainer. 2006. "Europe: Population and Migration 2005." *Migration Information Source* (June). http://www.migrationpolicy.org/article/europe-population-and-migration-2005.

Murdie, Robert, and Sutama Ghosh. 2010. "Does Spatial Concentration Always Mean a Lack of Integration? Exploring Ethnic Concentration and Integration in Toronto." *Journal of Ethnic and Migration Studies* 36: 293–311.

Murnane, Richard. 2013. "U.S. High School Graduation Rates." *Journal of Economic Literature* 51: 370–422.

Murphy, Kara. 2006. "France's New Law: Control Immigration Flows, Court the Highly

Skilled." *Migration Information Source* (November). http://www.migrationinforma
tion.org/feature/display.cfm?ID=486.

Musterd, Sako, and Roger Andersson. 2005. "Housing Mix, Social Mix, and Social Opportunities." *Urban Affairs Review* 40: 761–90.

Musterd, Sako, and Sjoerd de Vos. 2005. "Residential Dynamics in Ethnic Concentrations." *Housing Studies* 22: 333–53.

Musterd, Sako, and Wim Ostendorf. 2009. "Residential Segregation and Integration in
the Netherlands." *Journal of Ethnic and Migration Studies* 35: 1515–32.

Muttarak, Raya, and Anthony Heath. 2010. "Who Intermarries in Britain? Explaining
Ethnic Diversity in Intermarriage Patterns." *British Journal of Sociology* 61: 275–305.

Muus, Philip. 2004. "The Netherlands: A Pragmatic Approach to Economic Needs and
Humanitarian Considerations." In Wayne Cornelius et al. (eds.), *Controlling Immigration: A Global Perspective*. 2nd ed. Stanford: Stanford University Press.

Myers, Dowell. 2007. *Immigrants and Boomers: Forging a New Social Contract for the
Future of America*. New York: Russell Sage Foundation.

Myles, John, and Feng Hou. 2004. "Changing Colours: Spatial Assimilation and New
Racial Minority Immigrants." *Canadian Journal of Sociology* 29: 29–58.

NALEO [National Association of Latino Elected and Appointed Officials]. Education
Fund. 2009. "General Election Profile of Latinos in Congress and State Legislatures
after Election 2008. A State-By-State Summary." http://www.naleo.org/08PostElec
-Profile.pdf.

———. 2012. "Latino Opportunities in State Legislatures." http://www.naleo.org/down
loads/2012StateLegElectionProfile.pdf.

———. 2013. "2011 Directory of Hispanic Elected Officials." http://www.naleo.org
/directory.html.

Nana, Chavi Keeney. 2007. "With Strict Policies in Place, Dutch Discourse on Integration Becomes More Inclusive." *Migration Information Source* (April). http://www
.migrationinformation.org/Feature/display.cfm?ID=596.

National Equality Panel. 2010. *An Anatomy of Economic Inequality in the UK: A Report
of the National Equality Panel*. London: Government Equalities Office. http://sticerd
.lse.ac.uk/dps/case/cr/CASEreport60.pdf.

National Household Survey. 2013. *Generation Status: Canadian-born Children of Immigrants*. Ottawa: Statistics Canada. http://www.chba.ca/uploads/Urban_Council/Spring
%202013/Tab%208%20-%20Canadian-born%20children%20of%20immigrants.pdf.

Neckerman, Kathryn, Prudence Carter, and Jennifer Lee. 1999. "Segmented Assimilation and Minority Cultures of Mobility." *Ethnic and Racial Studies* 22: 945–65.

Nieuwboer, Jacky. 2003. *National Analytical Study of Housing: RAXEN Focal Point for
the Netherlands*. European Union Agency for Fundamental Rights. http://fra.europa
.eu/fraWebsite/networks/research/raxen/country_reports/cr_raxen_housing_en.htm.

Nixey, Catherine. 2009. "A School Condemned to Death." *The Guardian*, May 25.

Noah, Tim. 2012. *The Great Divergence: America's Growing Inequality Crisis and What
We Can Do about It*. New York: Bloomsbury Press.

Norris, Pippa, and Ronald Inglehart. 2007. "Uneven Secularization in the United States
and Western Europe." In Thomas Banchoff (ed.), *Democracy and the New Religious
Pluralism*. Oxford: Oxford University Press.

OECD. 2006. *Where Immigrant Students Succeed—A Comparative Review of Perfor-

mance and Engagement from PISA 2003. Paris: Organization for Economic Co-operation and Development.

———. 2010. "Entrepreneurship and Migrants." Report of the OECD Working Party on SMESs and Entrepreneurship, Paris: OECD. http:// www.oecd.org/dataoecd/34/18 /45068866.pdf.

———. 2011. "Divided We Stand: Why Inequality Keeps Rising." Paris: OECD. http:// www.oecd.org/document/10/0,3746,en_2649_33933_49147827_1_1_1_1,00.html.

———. 2012. "Benefits and Wages: OECD Indicators." Paris: OECD. http://www.oecd .org/document/3/0,3746,en_2649_37419_39617987_1_1_1_37419,00.html.

———. 2013a. "Employment Outlook 2013 Statistical Annex." Paris: OECD. http:// www.oecd.org/els/emp/employmentoutlookstatisticalannex.htm.

———. 2013b. "OECD Indicators of Employment Protection." Paris: OECD. http:// www.oecd.org/employment/emp/oecdindicatorsofemploymentprotection.htm #latest.

———. 2013c. "Social Expenditure Data Base (SOCX)." Paris: OECD. http://www.oecd .org/els/socialpoliciesanddata/socialexpendituredatabasesocx.htm.

———. 2013d. "Public Employment: Key Figures." Paris: OECD. http://www.oecd.org /gov/pem/publicemploymentkeyfigures.htm.

———. 2013e. *Education at a Glance 2013: OECD Indicators*. Paris: OECD Publishing.

Office for National Statistics. 2011a. "Neighbourhood Statistics": http://www.neigh bourhood.statistics.gov.uk/dissemination/.

———. 2011b. "Births in England and Wales by Parents' Country of Birth, 2010." http:// www.ons.gov.uk/ons/rel/vsob1/parents—country-of-birth—england-and-wales /2010/births-in-england-and-wales-by-parents—country-of-birth—2010.html.

———. 2013. "Immigration Patterns of Non-UK Born Populations in England and Wales in 2011." http://www.ons.gov.uk/ons/dcp171776_346219.pdf.

Okba, Mahrez. 2010. "Occupations of Descendants of Immigrants and Their Fathers: Is Occupational Inheritance Determined by Geographical Origin?" In Cris Beauche-min, Christelle Hamel, and Patrick Simon (eds.), *Trajectories and Origins: Survey on Population Diversity in France*. Paris: INED and INSEE.

Okihiro, Gary. 2001. *Common Ground: Reimagining American History*. Princeton: Princeton University Press.

Oliver, J. Eric. 2010. *The Paradoxes of Integration: Race, Neighborhood and Civic Life in Multiethnic America*. Chicago: University of Chicago Press.

Omi, Michael, and Howard Winant. 1994. *Racial Formation in the United States: From the 1960s to the 1990s*. 2nd ed. New York: Routledge and Kegan Paul.

Ontario Ministry of Education. 1994. "Education about Religion in Ontario Public Ele-mentary Schools." http://www.edu.gov.on.ca/eng/document/curricul/religion/religioe .html#PartA.

Oorschot, Wim van. 2006. "The Dutch Welfare State: Recent Trends and Challenges in Historical Perspective." *European Journal of Social Security* 8: 57–76.

Orfield, Gary, and Chungmei Lee. 2006. *Racial Transformation and the Changing Nature of Segregation*. Harvard University: The Civil Rights Project: http://www.civilrights project.ucla.edu/research/deseg/Racial_Transformation.pdf.

Orum, Anthony. 2005. "Circles of Influence and Chains of Command: The Social Pro-cesses Whereby Ethnic Communities Influence Host Societies." *Social Forces* 84: 921–39.

Owen, Charlie. 2007. "Statistics: The Mixed Category in Census 2001." In Jessica M. Sims (ed.), *Mixed Heritage: Identity, Policy and Practice*. London: Runnymede.

Özüekren, Sule, and Ebru Ergoz-Karahan. 2010. "Housing Experiences of Turkish (Im) migrants in Berlin and Istanbul: Internal Differentiation and Segregation." *Journal of Ethnic and Migration Studies* 36: 355–72.

Pager, Devah. 2007. *Marked: Race, Crime, and Finding Work in an Era of Mass Incarceration*. Chicago: University of Chicago Press.

Painter, Nell Irvin. 2010. *The History of White People*. New York: W.W. Norton.

Pais, Jeremy, Scott South, and Kyle Crowder. 2011. "Metropolitan Heterogeneity and Minority Neighborhood Attainment: Spatial Assimilation or Place Stratification?" *Social Problems* 59: 259–81.

Pan Ké Shon, Jean-Louis. 2011. "La ségrégation des immigrés en France: état des lieux," *Population & Sociétés* 477 (April). http://www.ined.fr/fr/publications/population-et -societes/segregation-immigres-france/.

Pan Ké Shon, Jean-Louis, and Gregory Verdugo. 2014. "Forty Years of Immigrant Segregation in France, 1968–2007: How Different Is the New Immigration?" *Urban Studies*. http://usj.sagepub.com/content/early/2014/04/22/0042098014529343.

Papademetriou, Demetrios. 2007. "Selecting Economic Stream Immigrants through Points Systems." *Migration Information Source* (May). http://www.migrationpolicy .org/article/selecting-economic-stream-immigrants-through-points-systems.

Park, Julie, and Dowell Myers. 2010. "Intergenerational Mobility in the Post–1965 Immigration Era: Estimates by an Immigrant Generation Cohort Method." *Demography* 47: 369–92.

Parsons, Craig, and Timothy Smeeding. 2006. "What's Unique about Immigration to Europe?" In Parsons and Smeeding (eds.), *Immigration and the Transformation of Europe*. Cambridge: Cambridge University Press.

Passel, Jeffrey, and D'Vera Cohn. 2009. "Mexican Immigrants: How Many Come? How Many Leave?" Washington, D.C.: Pew Hispanic Center (July). http://www.pewhispanic .org/2009/07/22/mexican-immigrants-how-many-come-how-many-leave/.

———. 2011. "Unauthorized Immigrant Population: National and State Trends, 2010." Washington, D.C.: Pew Hispanic Center (February). http://www.pewhispanic.org /files/reports/133.pdf.

Passel, Jeffrey, D'Vera Cohn, and Ana Gonzalez-Barrera. 2013. "Population Decline of Unauthorized Immigrants Stalls, May Have Reversed." Washington, D.C.: Pew Hispanic Center (September). http://www.pewhispanic.org/2013/09/23/population -decline-of-unauthorized-immigrants-stalls-may-have-reversed/.

Passel, Jeffrey, Wendy Wang, and Paul Taylor. 2010. "One-in-Seven New Marriages Is Interracial or Interethnic: Marrying Out." Washington, D.C.: Pew Research Center (June). http://www.pewsocialtrends.org/2010/06/04/marrying-out/.

Patterson, Orlando. 2005. "Four Modes of Ethno-Somatic Stratification: The Experience of Blacks in Europe and the Americas." In Glenn Loury, Tariq Modood, and Steven Teles (eds.), *Ethnicity, Social Mobility, and Public Policy*. Cambridge: Cambridge University Press.

Peach, Ceri. 1996. "Does Britain Have Ghettos?" *Transactions of the Institute of British Geographers* 22: 216–35.

———. 1998. "Trends in Levels of Caribbean Segregation, Great Britain, 1961–97." In Mary Chamberlain (ed.), *Caribbean Migration*. London: Routledge.

———. 2006. "Islam, Ethnicity and South Asian Religions in the London 2001 Census." *Transactions of the Institute of British Geographers* 31: 353–70.

———. 2009. "Slippery Segregation: Discovering or Manufacturing Ghettos?" *Journal of Ethnic and Migration Studies* 35: 138–95.

Peake, Linda, and Brian Ray. 2001. "Racializing the Canadian Landscape: Whiteness, Uneven Geographies and Social Justice." *The Canadian Geographer* 45: 180–86.

Penninx, Rinus, and Marcus Martiniello. 2004. "Integration Processes and Policies: State of the Art and Lessons." In Rinus Penninx, Karen Kraal, Marco Martiniello, and Steven Vertovec (eds.), *Citizenship in European Cities*. Ashgate, England: Aldershot.

Perlmann, Joel. 2005. *Italians Then, Mexicans Now: Immigrant Origins and Second-Generation Progress, 1890–2000*. New York: Russell Sage Foundation.

———. 2011. "The Mexican American Second Generation in Census 2000: Education and Earnings." In Richard Alba and Mary C. Waters (eds.), *The Next Generation: Immigrant Youth in a Comparative Perspective*. New York: New York University Press.

Perlmann, Joel, and Mary C. Waters. 2007. "Intermarriage and Multiple Identities." In Mary Waters and Reed Ueda (eds.), *The New Americans: A Guide to Immigration since 1965*. Cambridge, Mass.: Harvard University Press.

Pew Forum on Religion and Public Life. 2008. "U.S. Religious Landscape Survey." February. http://religions.pewform.org/reports.

———. 2011. "The Future of the Global Muslim Population." January 27. http://www.pewforum.org/The-Future-of-the-Global-Muslim-Population.aspx.

———. 2012a. "Faith on the Move: The Religious Affiliation of International Migrants." March 8. http://www.pewforum.org/faith-on-the-move.aspx.

———. 2012b. "Nones on the Rise: One in Five Adults Have No Religious Affiliation." October 9. http://www.pewforum.org/Unaffiliated/nones-on-the-rise.aspx.

_____2012c. "Asian Americans: A Mosaic of Faiths." July 19. http://www.pewforum.org/files/2012/07/Asian-Americans-religion-full-report.pdf.

———. 2013. "State Legislation Restricting Use of Foreign or Religious Law." April 8. http://features.pewforum.org/sharia-law-map/.

Pew Global Attitudes Project. 2002. "Among Wealthy Nations U.S. Stands Alone in Its Embrace of Religion." http://www.pewglobal.org/2002/12/19/among-wealthy-nations/.

———. 2005. "Islamic Extremism: Common Concern for Muslim and Western Publics." pewglobal.org/2005/07/14/Islamic-extremism-common-concern-for-muslim-and-western-publics.

———. 2010. "Widespread Support for Banning Full Islamic Veil in Western Europe." http://pewresearch.org/pubs/1658/widespread-support-for-banning-full-islamic-veil.

———. 2012. "The American-Western European Values Gap." http://www.pewglobal.org/2011/11/17/the-american-western-european-values-gap/.

Pew Research Center. 2007. "Muslim Americans: Middle Class and Mostly Mainstream." http://www.pewresearch.org/2007/05/22/muslim-americans-middle-class-and-mostly-mainstream/.

———. 2014. "The Shifting Religious Identity of Latinos in the United States." http://www.pewforum.org/files/2014/05/Latinos-and-Religion-05–06-full-report-final.pdf.

Pew Research Center for People and the Press. 2003. "Anti-Americanism: Causes and Characteristics." http://people-press.org/Commentary/display.php.3?AnalysisID=77-16k.

———. 2011. "Muslim Americans: No Signs of Growth in Alienation or Support for Extremism." http://www.people-press.org/files/2011/08/muslim-american-report.pdf.

Phalet, Karen, and Anthony Heath. 2011. "Ethnic Community, Urban Economy, and Second-Generation Attainment: Turkish Disadvantage in Belgium." In Richard Alba and Mary C. Waters (eds.), *The Next Generation: Immigrant Youth in a Comparative Perspective*. New York: New York University Press.

Phalet, Karen, Mieke Maliepaard, Fenella Fleischmann, and Derya Gungor. 2013. "The Making and Unmaking of Religious Boundaries." *Comparative Migration Studies* 1: 123–46.

Phillips, Meredith, and Tiffani Chin. 2004. "School Inequality: What Do We Know?" In Kathryn Neckerman (ed.), *Social Inequality*. New York: Russell Sage Foundation.

Philpott, T. L. 1978. *The Ghetto and the Slum*. New York: Oxford University Press.

Pichler, Florian. 2011. "Success on European Labor Markets: A Cross-national Comparison of Attainment between Immigrant and Majority Populations." *International Migration Review* 45: 938–78.

Piore, Michael. 1979. *Birds of Passage: Migrant Labor and Industrial Societies*. Cambridge: Cambridge University Press.

Platt, Lucinda. 2009. "Ethnicity and Family: Relationships within and between Ethnic Groups. An Analysis Using the Labour Force Survey." Manchester, England. Equality and Human Rights Commission.

Pontusson, Jonas. 2005. *Inequality and Prosperity: Social Europe vs. Liberal America*. Ithaca: Cornell University Press.

Porter, Eduardo. 2013. "In Public Education, Edge Still Goes to the Rich." *New York Times*, November 6.

Portes, Alejandro, and Robert Bach. 1985. *Latin Journey: Cuban and Mexican Immigrants in the United States*. Berkeley: University of California Press.

Portes, Alejandro, and Rubén Rumbaut. 2001. *Legacies: The Story of the Immigrant Second Generation*. Berkeley: University of California Press.

———. 2006. *Immigrant America*, 3rd ed. Berkeley: University of California Press.

Portes, Alejandro, and Alex Stepick. 1994. *City on the Edge: The Transformation of Miami*. Berkeley: University of California Press.

Portes, Alejandro, and Min Zhou. 1993. "The New Second Generation: Segmented Assimilation and Its Variants." *The Annals* 530: 74–96.

Poulsen, Michael, and Ron Johnston. 2006. "Ethnic Residential Segregation in England: Getting the Right Message Across." *Environment and Planning A* 38: 2195–99.

Prashad, Vijay. 2000. *The Karma of Brown Folk*. Minneapolis: University of Minnesota Press.

Préteceille, Edmond. 2009. "La ségrégation ethno-raciale a-t-elle augmenté dans la métropole parisienne?" *Revue française de sociologie* 50: 489–515.

Priemus, Hugo, and Frans Dieleman. 2002. "Social Housing Policy in the European Union: Past, Present and Perspectives." *Urban Studies* 39: 191–200.

Prins, Baukje, and Sawitri Saharso 2010. "From Toleration to Repression: The Dutch Backlash against Multiculturalism." In Steven Vertovec and Susanne Wessendorf (eds.), *The Multiculturalism Backlash: European Discourses, Policies, and Practices*. London: Routledge.

Putnam, Robert. 2007. "E Pluribus Unum: Diversity and Community in the Twenty-first Century." *Scandinavian Political Studies* 30: 137–74.

Putnam, Robert, and David Campbell. 2010. *American Grace: How Religion Divides and Unites Us.* New York: Simon and Schuster.

Qian, Zhenchao, and Daniel Lichter. 2007. "Social Boundaries and Marital Assimilation: Interpreting Trends in Racial and Ethnic Intermarriage." *American Sociological Review* 72: 68–94.

———. 2011. "Changing Patterns of Interracial Marriage in a Multiracial Society." *Journal of Marriage and Family* 73: 1065–84.

Raftery, Adrian, and Michael Hout. 1993. "Maximally Maintained Inequality: Expansion, Reform, and Opportunity in Irish Education, 1921–75." *Sociology of Education* 66: 41–62.

Rath, Jan. 1988. "Mobilization of Ethnicity in Dutch Politics." In Malcolm Cross and Hans Entzinger (eds.), *Lost Illusions: Caribbean Minorities in Britain and the Netherlands.* London: Routledge.

———. 2005. "Against the Current: The Establishment of Islam in the Netherlands." *Canadian Diversity* 4: 31–34.

———. 2011. "Debating Multiculturalism: Europe's Reaction in Context." *Harvard International Review.* http://hir.harvard.edu/print/debating-multiculturalism?page=0%2C2.

Rath, Jan, and Robert Kloosterman. 2003. "The Netherlands: A Dutch Treat." In Robert Kloosterman and Jan Rath (eds.). *Immigrant Entrepreneurs: Venturing Abroad in the Age of Globalization.* Oxford and New York: Berg.

Rath, Jan, Rinus Penninx, Kees Groenendijk, and Astrid Meyer. 2001. *Western Europe and Its Islam.* Leiden: Brill.

Rathelot, Roland, and Mirna Safi. 2014. "Local Ethnic Composition and Natives' and Immigrants' Geographic Mobility in France, 1982–1999." *American Sociological Review* 79: 43–64.

Ravitch, Diane. 2012. "Schools We Can Envy." *New York Review of Books,* March 8.

———. 2013. *Reign of Error: The Hoax of the Privatization Movement and the Danger to America's Public Schools.* New York: Alfred A. Knopf.

Ray, Julie. 2003. "Worlds Apart: Religion in Canada, Britain, U.S." www.gallup.com/poll/9016/worlds-apart-religion-canada-britain-us.

Reardon, Sean, and Kendra Bischoff. 2011. "Income Inequality and Income Segregation." *American Journal of Sociology* 116: 1092–153.

Reimers, David. 1992. *Still the Golden Door: The Third World Comes to America.* 2nd ed. New York: Columbia University Press.

Reimers, David, and Harold Troper. 1992. "Canadian and American Immigration Policy since 1945." In Barry Chiswick (ed.), *Immigration, Language and Ethnicity: Canada and the United States.* Washington, D.C.: American Enterprise Institute Press.

Reitz, Jeffrey. 2004. "Canada: Immigration and Nation-Building in the Transition to a Knowledge Economy." In Wayne Cornelius, Takeyuki Tsuda, Philip Martin, and James Hollifield (eds.), *Controlling Immigration: A Global Perspective.* 2nd ed. Stanford: Stanford University Press.

———. 2005. "Tapping Immigrants' Skills: New Directions for Canadian Immigration Policy in the Knowledge Economy." *IRPP Choices* 11 (February).

———. 2007. "Immigrant Employment Success in Canada, Part II: Understanding the Decline." *Journal of International Migration and Integration* 8: 37–62.

———. 2011. "Taxi Driver Syndrome." *Literary Review of Canada* 19: 20–22.

———. 2012. "The Distinctiveness of the Canadian Immigrant Experience." *Patterns of Prejudice* 46: 518–38.

———. 2014. "Canada: New Initiatives and Approaches to Immigration and Nation Building." In James Hollifield, Philip Martin, and Pia Orrenius (eds.), *Controlling Immigration: A Global Perspective*. 3rd ed. Stanford: Stanford University Press.

Reitz, Jeffrey, and Rupa Banerjee. 2007. "Racial Inequality, Social Cohesion and Policy Issues in Canada." In Keith Banting, Thomas Courchene, and F. Leslie Seidle (eds.), *Belonging? Diversity, Recognition and Shared Citizenship in Canada*. Montreal: Institute for Research on Public Policy.

Reitz, Jeffrey, Rupa Banerjee, Mai Phan, and Jordan Thompson. 2009. "Race, Religion, and the Social Integration of New Immigrant Minorities in Canada." *International Migration Review* 43: 695–726.

Reitz, Jeffrey, Heather Zhang, and Naoko Hawkins. 2011. "Comparisons of the Success of Racial Minority Immigrant Offspring in the United States, Canada, and Australia." *Social Science Research* 40: 1051–66.

Reitz, Jeffrey, and Ye Zhang. 2011. "National and Urban Contexts for the Integration of the Immigrant Second Generation in the United States and Canada." In Richard Alba and Mary Waters (eds.), *The Next Generation. Immigrant Youth in a Comparative Perspective*. New York: New York University Press.

Renaut, Alain, and Alain Touraine. 2005. *Un débat sur la laïcité*. Paris: Stock.

Reyneri, Emilio, and Giovanna Fullin. 2011. "Ethnic Penalties in the Transition to and from Unemployment: A West European Perspective." *International Journal of Comparative Sociology* 52: 247–63.

Rice, Jennifer. 2003. *Teacher Quality: Understanding the Effectiveness of Teacher Attributes*. Washington, D.C.: Economic Policy Institute.

Ringer, Fritz. 1967. "Cultural Transmission in German Higher Education in the Nineteenth Century." *Journal of Contemporary History* 2: 123–38.

Rodriguez-Garcia, Dan. 2007. "Intermarriage Patterns and Socio-ethnic Stratification among Ethnic Groups in Toronto." CERIS Working Paper No. 60. Toronto: CERIS, The Ontario Metropolis Center.

Rose, E.J.B., et al. 1969. *Colour and Citizenship: A Report on British Race Relations*. London: Oxford University Press.

Rosenbaum, Emily, and Samantha Friedman. 2007. *The Housing Divide: How Generations of Immigrants Fare in New York's Housing Market*. New York: New York University Press.

Roth, Wendy. 2012. *Race Migrations: Latinos and the Cultural Transformation of Race*. Stanford: Stanford University Press.

Roy, Olivier. 2010. "On Islam in Europe." *Islamineurope.blogspot.com*, May 11.

Rumbaut, Rubén. 2005. "Turning Points in the Transition to Adulthood: Determinants of Educational Attainment, Incarceration and Early Childbearing among Children of Immigrants." *Ethnic and Racial Studies* 28: 1041–86.

Rumbaut, Rubén, and Walter Ewing. 2007. *The Myth of Immigrant Criminality and the Paradox of Assimilation: Incarceration Rates among Native and Foreign-Born Men*. Washington, D.C.: American Immigration Law Foundation.

Rusinovic, Katja. 2006. *Dynamic Entrepreneurship: First- and Second-Generation Immigrant Entrepreneurs in Dutch Cities*. Amsterdam: Amsterdam University Press.

Russell, Sharon Stanton. 2002. "Refugees: Risks and Challenges Worldwide." *Migra-*

tion Information Source (November). http://www.migrationinformation.org/Feature /display.cfm?ID=64.

Sabbagh, Daniel. 2002. "Affirmative Action at Sciences Po." *French Politics, Culture, and Society* 20: 52–64.

Safi, Mirna. 2009. "La dimension spatiale de l'intégration: évolution de la ségrégation des populations immigrées en France entre 1968 et 1999." *Revue française de sociologie* 50: 521–52.

Saggar, Shamit. 2013. "Bending without Breaking the Mould: Race and Political Representation in the United Kingdom." *Patterns of Prejudice* 47: 69–93.

Saggar, Shamit, and Andrew Geddes. 2000. "Negative and Positive Racialization: Re-Examining Ethnic Minority Political Representation in the UK." *Journal of Ethnic and Migration Studies* 26: 25–44.

Sahlberg, Pasi. 2011. *Finnish Lessons: What Can the World Learn from Educational Change in Finland?* New York: Teachers College Press.

Salverda, Wiemer, Maarten van Klaveren, and Marc van der Meer. 2008. *Low-Wage Work in the Netherlands.* New York: Russell Sage Foundation.

Sampson, Robert. 2012. *Great American City: Chicago and the Enduring Neighborhood Effect.* Chicago: University of Chicago.

Sampson, Robert, and Patrick Sharkey. 2008. "Neighborhood Selection and the Social Reproduction of Concentrated Racial Inequality." *Demography* 45: 1–29.

Sanjek, Roger. 1998. *The Future of Us All: Race and Neighborhood Politics in New York City.* Ithaca: Cornell University Press.

Sassen, Saskia. 1988. *The Mobility of Labor and Capital.* Cambridge: Cambridge University Press.

Schain, Martin. 1999. "Minorities and Immigrant Incorporation in France: The State and the Dynamics of Multiculturalism." In Christian Joppke and Steven Lukes (eds.), *Multicultural Questions.* Oxford: Oxford University Press.

———. 2006. "The Politics of Immigration in France, Britain, and the United States: A Trans-Atlantic Comparison." In Craig Parsons and Timothy Smeeding (eds.), *Immigration and the Transformation of Europe.* Cambridge: Cambridge University Press.

———. 2008. *The Politics of Immigration in France, Britain, and the United States: A Comparative Study.* New York: Palgrave Macmillan.

———. 2013. "The Challenge of Illegal Immigration in Europe." *E-International Relations*, December 14. http://www.e-ir.info/2013/12/14/the-challenge-of-illegal-imigra tion-in-europe/.

Scheffer, Paul. 2000. "Het Multiculturele Drama." *NRC Handelsbad*, January 29.

Schildkraut, Deborah. 2011. *Americanism in the Twenty-First Century: Public Opinion in the Age of Immigration.* New York: Cambridge University Press.

Schnapper, Dominique. 1991. *La France de l'intégration: Sociologie de la nation en 1990.* Paris: Éditions Gallimard.

Schneider, Jens, Leo Chavez, Louis DeSipio, and Mary Waters. 2012a. "Belonging." In Maurice Crul and John Mollenkopf (eds.), *The Changing Face of World Cities.* New York: Russell Sage Foundation.

Schneider, Jens, Tineke Fokkema, Raquel Matias, Snezana Stojcic, Dusan Ugrina, and Constanza Vera-Larrucea. 2012b. "Identities: Urban Belonging and Intercultural Relations." In Maurice Crul, Jens Schneider, and Frans Lelie (eds.), *The European Second Generation Compared*. Amsterdam: Amsterdam University Press.

Schönwälder, Karen. 2012. "Cautious Steps: Minority Representation in Germany." In Terri Givens and Rahsaan Maxwell (eds.), *Immigrant Politics: Race and Representation in Western Europe*. Boulder, Colo.: Lynne Rienner.

———. 2013. "Immigrant Representation in Germany's Regional States: The Puzzle of Uneven Dynamics." *West European Politics* 36: 634–51.

Schönwälder, Karen, Cihan Sinanoglu, and Daniel Volkert. 2013. "The New Immigrant Elite in German Local Politics." *European Political Science* 12: 479–89.

Schönwälder, Karen, and Janina Söhn. 2009. "Immigrant Settlement Structures in Germany: General Patterns and Urban Levels of Concentration of Major Groups." *Urban Studies* 46: 1439–60.

Schönwälder, Karen, Daniel Volkert, and Cihan Sinanoglu. 2011. "Einwanderinnen und Einwanderer in den Räten deutscher Großstädte," Max-Planck Institute for the Study of Religious and Ethnic Diversity, Göttingen, June.

Schuck, Peter. 2007a. "The Disconnect between Public Attitudes and Policy Outcomes in Immigration." In Carol Swain (ed.), *Debating Immigration*. New York: Cambridge University Press.

———. 2007b. "The Meaning of American Citizenship in a Post 9/11 World." *Fordham Law Review* 75: 2531–40.

———. 2009. "Immigrants' Incorporation in the United States after 9/11: Two Steps Forward, One Step Back." In Jennifer Hochschild and John Mollenkopf (eds.), *Bringing Outsiders In: Transatlantic Perspectives on Immigrant Political Incorporation*. Ithaca: Cornell University Press.

Sciolino, Elaine. 2003. "Muslim Lycée Opens in Secular France, Raising Eyebrows." *New York Times*, September 9.

———. 2004. "Car of Acclaimed Muslim Appointee is Bombed in France." *New York Times,* January 19.

Scott, Joan Wallach. 2007. *The Politics of the Veil*. Princeton: Princeton University Press.

Segal, Mady Wechsler, and David Segal. 2007. "Latinos Claim Larger Share of U.S. Military Personnel." Washington, D.C.: Population Reference Bureau.

Seibert, Holger, and Heika Solga. 2005. "Gleiche Chancen dank einer abgeschlossenen Ausbildung? Zum Signalwert von Ausbildungabschlüssen bei ausländischen und deutschen jungen Erwachsenen." *Zeitschrift für Soziologie* 34: 364–82.

Seljak, David. 2000. "The Catholic Church and Public Politics in Quebec." In David Lyon and Marguerite van Die (eds.), *Rethinking Church, State, and Modernity: Canada between Europe and America*. Toronto: University of Toronto Press.

———. 2005. "Education, Multiculturalism and Religion." In Paul Bramadat and David Seljak (eds.), *Religion and Ethnicity in Canada*. Toronto: Pearson Longman.

Sharkey, Patrick. 2014. "Spatial Segmentation and the Black Middle Class." *American Journal of Sociology* 119: 903–54.

Shavit, Yossi, and Walter Müller. 1998. *From School to Work: A Comparative Study of Educational Qualifications and Occupational Destinations*. New York: Oxford University Press.

Siebold, Sabine. 2010. "Merkel Says German Multiculturalism Has Failed." Reuters, October 16.

Silberman, Roxane. 2011. "The Employment of Second Generations in France: The Republican Model and the November 2005 Riots." In Richard Alba and Mary Waters (eds.), *The Next Generation: Immigrant Youth in a Comparative Perspective*. New York: New York University Press.

Silberman, Roxane, Richard Alba, and Irène Fournier. 2007. "Segmented Assimilation in France? Discrimination in the Labor Market against the Second Generation." *Ethnic and Racial Studies* 30: 1–27.

Silberman, Roxanne, and Irène Fournier. 2006. "Les secondes générations sur le marché du travail en France: une pénalité ethnique qui persiste. Contribution à la discussion sur l'assimilation segmentée," *Revue française de sociologie* 47: 243–92.

———. 2007. "Is French Society Truly Assimilative? Immigrant Parents and Offspring on the French Labor Market." In Anthony Heath and Sin Yi Cheung (eds.), *Unequal Chances: Ethnic Minorities in Western Labor Markets*. Proceedings of the British Academy. Oxford: Oxford University Press.

Simon, Patrick. 2003. "France and the Unknown Second Generation: Preliminary Results on Social Mobility." *International Migration Review* 37: 1091–119.

———. 2012. "French National Identity and Integration: Who Belongs to the National Community?" Washington, D.C.: Migration Policy Institute.

Singer, Audrey. 2004. "The Rise of New Immigrant Gateways." Living Cities Census Series. Washington, D.C.: Brookings Institution.

Skerry, Peter. 1993. *Mexican Americans: The Ambivalent Minority*. New York: Free Press.

Skrentny, John. 1996. *The Ironies of Affirmative Action*. Chicago: University of Chicago Press.

———. 2002. *The Minority Rights Revolution*. Cambridge, Mass.: Harvard University Press.

Slootman, Marieke, and Jan Willem Duyvendak. Forthcoming. "Feeling Dutch: The Culturalization and Emotionalization of Citizenship and Second Generation Belonging in the Netherlands." In Nancy Foner and Patrick Simon (eds.), *Fear, Anxiety, and National Identity: Immigration and Belonging in North America and Western Europe*. New York: Russell Sage Foundation.

Smale, Alison. 2014. "Germany Adds Lessons in Islam to Better Blend Its Melting Pot." *New York Times*, January 6.

Small, Mario Luis. 2008. "Four Reasons to Abandon the Idea of 'The Ghetto.'" *City & Community* 7: 389–98.

Smith, Nancy. 1995. "Challenges of Public Housing in the 1990s: The Case of Ontario, Canada." *Housing Policy Debate* 6: 905–31.

Smith, Robert C. 2006. *Mexican New York: Transnational Lives of New Immigrants*. Berkeley: University of California Press.

———. 2014. "Black Mexicans, Conjunctural Ethnicity, and Operating Identities: Long-Term Ethnographic Analysis." *American Sociological Review* 79: 517–48.

Smith, Tom. 2012. "Beliefs about God across Time and Countries." Report for ISSP and GESIS. NORC, University of Chicago. http://www.norc.org/PDFs/Beliefs_about _God_Report.pdf.

Snel, Erik, Jack Burgers, and Arjen Leerkes. 2007. "Class Position of Immigrant Workers in a Post-Industrial Economy: The Dutch Case." *Journal of Ethnic and Migration Studies* 33: 1323–42.

Sobolewska, Maria. 2013. "Party Strategies and the Descriptive Representation of Ethnic Minorities: The 2010 British General Election." *West European Politics* 36: 615–33.

Solomos, John. 2003. *Race and Racism in Britain*. 3rd ed. London: Palgrave.

Song, Miri. 2003. *Choosing Ethnic Identity*. London: Polity.

———. 2010. "What Happens after Segmented Assimilation? An Exploration of Intermarriage and 'Mixed Race' Young People in Britain." *Ethnic and Racial Studies* 33: 1194–213.

Song, Miri, and David Parker. 2009. "Is Intermarriage a Good Indicator of Integration?" *Journal of Ethnic and Migrant Studies* 35: 331–48.

Soroka, Stuart, Richard Johnston, and Keith Banting. 2007. "Ties that Bind: Social Cohesion and Diversity in Canada." In Keith Banting, Thomas Courchene, and Leslie Seidle (eds.), *Belonging? Diversity, Recognition and Shared Citizenship in Canada*. Montreal: Institute for Research in Public Policy.

Sotomayor, Sonia. 2013. *My Beloved World*. New York: Knopf.

South, Scott, Kyle Crowder, and Erick Chavez. 2005a. "Migration and Spatial Assimilation among U.S. Latinos: Classical versus Segmented Trajectories." *Demography* 42: 497–521.

———. 2005b. "Exiting and Entering High-Poverty Neighborhoods: Latinos, Blacks and Anglos Compared." *Social Forces* 84: 873–900.

Soysal, Yasemin. 1994. *Limits of Citizenship: Migrants and Postnational Membership in Europe*. Chicago: University of Chicago Press.

Stainback, Kevin, and Donald Tomaskovic-Devey. 2012. *Documenting Desegregation: Racial and Gender Segregation in Private Sector Employment since the Civil Rights Act*. New York: Russell Sage Foundation.

Statistics Canada. 2013. "Immigration and Ethnocultural Diversity in Canada: National Household Survey, 2011." Ottawa: Minister of Industry.

Statistics Netherlands. 2011. "Four out of Five Turks and Moroccans Marry within their Own Circles." http://www.cbs.nl/en-GB/menu/themas/bevolking/publicaties /artikelen/archief/2011/2011–3512-wm.htm.

———. 2013. "Population: Sex, Age, Origin and Generation, 1 January." www.cbs.nl /en-GB/ . . . /population-by-origin-kc.htm.

Statistisches Bundesamt. 2010. *Bevölkerung und Erwerbstätigkeit: Bevölkerung mit Migrationshintergrund—Ergebnisse des Mikrozensus 2009*. Wiesbaden: Statistisches Bundesamt.

Steinberg, Stephen. 1974. *The Academic Melting Pot*. New York: McGraw-Hill.

Stepick, Alex, Guillermo Grenier, Max Castro, and Marvin Dunn. 2003. *This Land Is Our Land: Immigrants and Power in Miami*. Berkeley: University of California Press.

Strabac, Zan, and Ola Listhaug. 2008. "Anti-Muslim Prejudice in Europe: A Multilevel Analysis of Survey Data from 30 Countries." *Social Science Research* 37: 268–86.

Strik, Tineke, Anita Böcker, Maaike Luiten, and Ricky van Oers. 2010. *Integration and Naturalisation Tests*. Nijmegen: Radboud University Nijmegen, Centre for Immigration Law.

Suárez-Orozco, Carola, Marcelo Suárez-Orozco, and Irina Todorova. 2008. *Learning a New Land: Immigrant Students in American Society*. Cambridge, Mass.: Harvard University Press.

Suh, Sharon A. 2009. "Buddhism, Rhetoric, and the Korean American Community: The Adjustment of Korean Buddhist Immigrants to the United States." In Richard Alba,

Albert Raboteau, and Josh DeWind (eds), *Immigration and Religion in America: Comparative and Historical Perspectives*. New York: New York University Press.

Sunier, Thijl. 2009. "Houses of Worship and the Politics of Space in Amsterdam." In Liza Nell and Jan Rath (eds.), *Ethnic Amsterdam*. Amsterdam: Amsterdam University Press.

Tajfel, Henri, and John C.Turner. 1986. "The Social Identity Theory of Intergroup Behavior." In S. Worchel and W. G. Austin (eds.), *Psychology of Intergroup Relations*. Chicago: Nelson-Hall.

Tatari, Eren. 2009. "Theories of State Accommodation of Islamic Religious Practices in Western Europe." *Journal of Ethnic and Migration Studies* 35: 271–88.

Taylor, Paul, et al. 2013. *Second-generation Americans: A Portrait of Adult Children of Immigrants*. Washington, D.C.: Pew Research Center.

Taylor, Paul, Ana Gonzalez-Barrera, Jeffrey Passel, and Mark Hugo Lopez. 2012. "An Awakened Giant: The Hispanic Electorate Is Likely to Double by 2030." Report of the Pew Hispanic Research Center. http://www.pewhispanic.org/2012/11/14/an-awakened-giant-the-hispanic-electorate-is-likely-to-double-by-2030/.

Telles, Edward. 2010. "Mexican Americans and Immigrant Incorporation." *Contexts* (February): 29–35.

Telles, Edward, and Edward Murguia. 1990. "Phenotypic Discrimination and Income Differences among Mexican-Americans." *Social Science Quarterly* 71: 682–96.

Telles, Edward, and Vilma Ortiz. 2008. *Generations of Exclusion: Mexican Americans, Assimilation, and Race*. New York: Russell Sage.

Tesser, Paul, and Jaap Dronkers. 2007. "Equal Opportunities or Social Closure in the Netherlands." In Anthony Heath and Sin Yi Cheung (eds.), *Unequal Chances: Ethnic Minorities in Western Labor Markets*. Proceedings of the British Academy. Oxford: Oxford University Press.

Tiberj, Vincent, and Laure Michon. 2013. "Two-tier Pluralism in 'Colour-blind' France." *West European Politics* 36: 580–96.

Tichenor, Daniel. 2002. *Dividing Lines: The Politics of Immigration Control in America*. Princeton: Princeton University Press.

———. 2008. "Strange Bedfellows: The Politics and Pathologies of Immigration Reform." *Labor: Studies in Working Class History* 5: 39–60.

Torpey, John. 2009. "The Problem of Exceptionalism Revisited." *Journal of Classical Sociology* 9: 143–68.

Triadafilopoulos, Phil. 2012. *Becoming Multicultural: Immigration and the Politics of Membership in Canada and Germany*. Vancouver: University of British Columbia Press.

Tribalat, Michèle. 1995. *Faire France: Une enquête sur les immigrés et leurs enfants*. Paris: Éditions La Découverte.

Troper, Harold. 2003. "To Farms or Cities: A Historical Tension between Canada and Its Immigrants." In Jeffrey Reitz (ed.), *Host Societies and the Reception of Immigrants*. San Diego: Center for Comparative Immigration Studies.

Tuan, Mia. 1998. *Forever Foreigners or Honorary Whites? The Asian Ethnic Experience Today*. New Brunswick, N.J.: Rutgers University Press.

Uberoi, Varun, and Tariq Modood. 2013. "Has Multiculturalism in Britain Retreated?" *Soundings: A Journal of Politics and Culture* 53: 129–42.

Uitermark, Justus. 2012. *Dynamics of Power in Dutch Integration Politics.* Amsterdam: Amsterdam University Press.

Uitermark, Justus, Jan Willem Duyvendak, and Jan Rath. 2014. "Governing through Religion in Amsterdam: The Stigmatization of Ethnic Cultures and the Uses of Islam." In Nancy Foner, Jan Rath, Jan Willem Duyvendak, and Rogier van Reekum (eds.), *New York and Amsterdam: Immigration and the New Urban Landscape.* New York: New York University Press.

Ujimoto, Victor K. 1999. "Studies of Ethnic Identity, Ethnic Relations, and Citizenship in Canada." In Peter Li (ed.), *Race and Ethnic Relations in Canada.* 2nd ed. Toronto: Oxford University Press.

U.K. Department for Education. 2010. "Maintained Faith Schools." July. https://www.gov.uk/government/publications/maintained-faith-schools/maintained-faith-schools.

UNHCR [United Nations High Commissioner for Refugees]. 2006. "Number of UK Asylum Applicants at Lowest Level Since 1993." http://www.unhcr.org.uk/PR17/March06.htm.

———. 2007. "Asylum Levels and Trends in Industrialized Countries, 2006." http://www.unhcr.org/statistics.html.

——— . 2013. "Asylum Trends 2013: Levels and Trends in Industrialized Countries." http://www.unhcr.org/5329b15a9.html.

Van Amersfoort, Hans, and Mies van Niekerk. 2006. "Immigration as a Colonial Inheritance: Post-Colonial Immigrants in the Netherlands, 1945–2002." *Journal of Ethnic and Migration Studies* 32: 323–46.

Van der Bracht, Koen, Bart van de Putte, and Pieter-Paul Verhaeghe. 2013. "God Bless Our Children? The Role of Generation, Discrimination, and Religious Context for Migrants in Europe." *International Migration* 51: 23–37.

Van der Laan Bouma-Doff, Wenda. 2007. "Confined Contact: Residential Segregation and Ethnic Bridges in the Netherlands." *Urban Studies* 44: 997–1017.

Van de Werfhorst, Herman, and Jonathan Mijs. 2010. "Achievement Inequality and the Institutional Structure of Educational Systems: A Comparative Perspective." *Annual Review of Sociology* 36: 407–28.

Van de Werfhorst, Herman, Erika van Elsas, and Anthony Heath. 2014. "Origin and Destination Effects on the Educational Careers of Second-generation Minorities." In Anthony Heath and Yaël Brinbaum (eds.), *Unequal Attainments: Ethnic Educational Inequalities in Ten Western Countries.* Proceedings of the British Academy. Oxford: Oxford University Press.

Van Heelsum, Anja. 2002. "The Relationship between Political Participation and Civic Community of Migrants in the Netherlands." *Journal of International Migration and Integration* 3: 179–99.

Van Kerckem, Klaartje, Koen van der Bracht, Peter A. J. Stevens, and Bart van de Putte. 2013. "Transnational Marriages on the Decline: Explaining Changing Trends in Partner Choice among Turkish Belgians." *International Migration Review* 47: 1006–38.

Van Reekum, Rogier, Jan Willem Duyvendak, and Christophe Bertossi. 2012. "National Models of Integration and the Crisis of Multiculturalism: A Critical Comparative Perspective." *Patterns of Prejudice* 46: 417–26.

Van Tubergen, Frank. 2005. "Self-Employment of Immigrants: A Cross-National Study of 17 Western Societies." *Social Forces* 84: 709–32.

Van Tubergen, Frank, Ineke Maas, and Henk Flap. 2004. "The Economic Incorporation of Immigrants in 18 Western Societies: Origin, Destination and Community Effects." *American Sociological Review* 69: 704–27.

Vasagar, Jeevan. 2011. "Oxford University and David Cameron Clash over Black Student Numbers." *The Guardian*, April 11.

Vasileva, Katya. 2012. "Population and Social Conditions." Eurostat: Statistics in Focus. Luxembourg: European Commission. http://epp.eurostat.ec.europa.eu/cache/ITY _OFFPUB/KS-SF-12–031/EN/KS-SF-12–031-EN.PDF.

Vasquez, Jessica. 2011. *Mexican Americans across Generations: Immigrant Families, Racial Realities*. New York: New York University Press.

Velasco, Gabriel, and Daniel Dockterman. 2010. "Statistical Portrait of Hispanics in the United States, 2008." Washington, D.C.: Pew Hispanic Center: http://www .pewhispanic.org/2010/01/21/statistical-portrait-of-hispanics-in-the-united-states -2008/.

Verdugo, Gregory. 2011. "Public Housing and Residential Segregation of Immigrants in France, 1968–1999." *Population-E* 66: 169–94.

Vermeulen, Floris, Laure Michon, and Jean Tillie. 2014. "Immigrant Political Engagement and Incorporation in Amsterdam." In Nancy Foner, Jan Rath, Jan Willem Duyvendak, and Rogier van Reekum (eds.), *New York and Amsterdam: Immigration and the New Urban Landscape*. New York: New York University Press.

Vermeulen, Hans, and Rinus Penninx. 2000. *Immigrant Integration: The Dutch Case*. Amsterdam: Het Spinhuis.

Vertovec, Steven. 1998. "Accommodating Religious Pluralism in Britain: South Asian Religions." In Marco Martiniello (ed.), *Multicultural Policies and the State: A Comparison of Two European Societies*. Utrecht: European Research Center on Migration and Ethnic Relations.

———. 2004. "Migrant Transnationalism and Modes of Transformation." *International Migration Review* 38: 970–1001.

———. 2007. "Super-Diversity and Its Implications." *Ethnic and Racial Studies* 30: 1024 54.

———. 2013. "Reading 'Super-Diversity:' Representations Powers and Pitfalls." *Migration: The COMPAS Anthology*. Oxford: COMPAS, Oxford University. http://compas anthology.co.uk/reading-super-diversity/.

——— (ed.). Forthcoming. *Diversities Old and New*. London and New York: Palgrave Macmillan.

Vertovec, Steven, and Susanne Wessendorf (eds.). 2010. *The Multiculturalism Backlash: European Discourses, Policies and Practices*. Abingdon, England: Routledge.

Vickerman, Milton. 1999. *Crosscurrents: West Indian Immigrants and Race*. New York: Oxford University Press.

———. 2001. "Tweaking a Monolith: The West Indian Immigrant Encounter with 'Blackness.'" In Nancy Foner (ed.), *Islands in the City: West Indian Migration to New York*. Berkeley: University of California Press.

Villarrubia, Jacqueline, Nancy Denton, and Richard Alba. N.d. "Gateway State, Not Gateway City: New Immigrants in the Hudson Valley." Paper presented at the annual meeting of the Population Association of America.

Vink, Maarten, and Gerard-René de Groot. 2010. "Citizenship Attribution in Western

Europe: International Framework and Domestic Trends." *Journal of Ethnic and Migration Studies* 36: 713–34.

Voas, David, and Fenella Fleischmann. 2012. "Islam Moves West: Religious Change in the First and Second Generations." *Annual Review of Sociology* 38: 525–45.

Wacquant, Loïc. 2008. *Urban Outcasts: A Comparative Sociology of Advanced Marginality.* Cambridge, England: Polity Press.

Waldinger, Roger. 1996. *Still the Promised City? African-Americans and New Immigrants in Postindustrial New York.* Cambridge, Mass.: Harvard University Press.

———. 2007. "Transforming Foreigners into Americans." In Mary Waters and Reed Ueda (eds.), *The New Americans: A Guide to Immigration since 1965.* Cambridge, Mass.: Harvard University Press.

Waldinger, Roger, Howard Aldrich, and Robin Ward (eds). 1990. *Ethnic Entrepreneurs.* Newbury Park, Calif.: Sage.

Waldinger, Roger, and Michael Lichter. 2003. *How the Other Half Works: Immigration and the Social Organization of Labor.* Berkeley: University of California.

Wang, Wendy. 2012. "The Rise of Intermarriage: Rates, Characteristics Vary by Race and Gender." Washington, D.C.: Pew Research Center. http://www.pewsocialtrends. org/files/2012/02/SDT-Intermarriage II.pdf.

Warner, R. Stephen, and Judith Wittner (eds.). 1998. *Gatherings in Diaspora: Religious Communities and the New Immigration.* Philadelphia: Temple University Press.

Waters, Mary C. 1990. *Ethnic Options: Choosing Identities in America.* Berkeley: University of California Press.

———. 1999. *Black Identities: West Indian Immigrant Dreams and American Realities.* Cambridge, Mass.: Harvard University Press.

———. 2014. "Nativism, Racism, and Immigration in New York City." In Nancy Foner, Jan Rath, Jan Willem Duyvendak, and Rogier van Reekum (eds.), *New York and Amsterdam: Immigration and the New Urban Landscape.* New York: New York University Press.

Waters, Mary C., Anthony Heath, Van Tran, and Vikki Boliver. 2013. "The Educational Careers of the Children of Immigrants in Britain and the U.S." In Richard Alba and Jennifer Holdaway (eds.), *The Children of Immigrants at School: A Comparative Look at Integration in the United States and Western Europe.* New York: New York University Press.

Waters, Mary C., and Tomás Jiménez. 2005. "Assessing Immigrant Assimilation: New Empirical and Theoretical Challenges." *Annual Review of Sociology* 31: 105–25.

Weil, Patrick. 2001. "Access to Citizenship: A Comparison of Twenty-Five Nationality Laws." In Alexander Aleinikoff and Douglas Klusmeyer (eds.), *Citizenship Today: Global Perspectives and Practices.* Washington, D.C.: Carnegie Endowment for International Peace.

———. 2002. *Qu'est-ce qu' un français? Histoire de la nationalité française depuis la Révolution.* Paris: Grasset.

Wekker, Gloria. 2009. "Another Dream of a Common Language: Imagining Black Europe." In Darlene Clark Hine, Trica Keaton, and Stephen Small (eds.), *Black Europe and the African Diaspora.* Urbana: University of Illinois Press.

Wessendorf, Susanne. 2010. "Commonplace Diversity: Social Interactions in a Superdiverse Context." MMG Working Paper 10–11, Max Planck Institute for the Study of Religious and Ethnic Diversity, Göttingen, Germany.

———. 2013. "Commonplace Diversity and the 'Ethos of Mixing': Perceptions of Difference in a London Neighbourhood." *Identities* 20: 407–22.

West, Cornell. 1994. *Race Matters*. New York: Vintage Books.

West, Heather. 2009. "Prison Inmates at Midyear 2009—Statistical Tables." Washington, D.C.: U.S. Department of Justice, Bureau of Justice Statistics. http://www.bjs.gov/content/pub/pdf/pim09st.pdf.

Western, Bruce, and Christopher Wildeman. 2009. "The Black Family and Mass Incarceration." *The Annals of the American Academy of Political and Social Science* 621: 221–42.

White, Michael, Eric Fong, and Qian Cai. 2003. "The Segregation of Asian-origin Groups in the United States and Canada." *Social Science Research* 32: 148–67.

White, Michael, and Jennifer Glick. 2009. *Achieving Anew: How New Immigrants Do in American Schools, Jobs, and Neighborhoods*. New York: Russell Sage Foundation.

Whitehead, Christine, and Kathleen Scanlon (eds.). 2007. *Social Housing in Europe*. London: London School of Economics and Political Science.

Wikan, Unni. 2002. *A Generous Betrayal: Politics of Culture in a New Europe*. Chicago: University of Chicago Press.

Wikipedia. 2013. "Existenzgründung." http://de.wikipedia.org/wiki/Existenzgründung (accessed 10/10/13).

Wilensky, Harold. 2002. *Rich Democracies: Political Economy, Public Policy, and Performance*. Berkeley: University of California Press.

Wilpert, Czarina. 2003. "Germany: From Workers to Entrepreneurs." In Robert Kloosterman and Jan Rath (eds.), *Immigrant Entrepreneurs: Venturing Abroad in the Age of Globalization*. Oxford and New York: Berg.

Wilson, Jennifer. 2007. "Faith-based Schools." *CBCNews.ca*, September 17. http: www.cbc.ca/ontariovotes2007/features/features-faith.html.

Wilson, William Julius. 1996. *When Work Disappears*. New York: Knopf.

Wimmer, Andreas. 2013. *Ethnic Boundary Making: Institutions, Power, Networks*. Oxford: Oxford University Press.

Winant, Howard. 2002. *The World Is a Ghetto: Race and Democracy since World War II*. New York: Basic Books.

Winks, Robin. 1971. *The Blacks in Canada*. New Haven: Yale University Press.

Winter, Elke. 2014. "Traditions of Nationhood or Political Conjuncture? Debating Citizenship in Canada and Germany." *Comparative Migration Studies* 2: 29–56.

Wolfe, Alan. 2006. "Religious Diversity: The American Experiment that Works." In Michael Kazin and Joseph McCartin (eds.), *Americanism: New Perspectives on the History of an Ideal*. Chapel Hill: University of North Carolina Press.

Wolfe, Alan, and Ira Katznelson (eds.). 2010. *Religion and Democracy in the United States: Danger or Opportunity?* Princeton: Princeton University Press.

Wust, Andreas 2011. "Migrants as Parliamentary Actors in Germany." In Karen Bird, Thomas Saalfeld, and Andreas Wust (eds.), *The Political Representation of Immigrants and Minorities*. London and New York: Routledge.

Wuthnow, Robert. 2005. *America and the Challenges of Religious Diversity*. Princeton: Princeton University Press.

Yoshikawa, Hirokazu. 2011. *Immigrants Raising Citizens: Undocumented Parents and Their Young Children*. New York: Russell Sage Foundation.

Young, John. 2009. "Introduction: Faith and Politics in Canada." In John Young and

Boris DeWeil (eds.), *Faith and Democracy? Religion and Politics in Canada*. Newcastle upon Tyne, England: Cambridge Scholars Publishing.

Yu, Soojin, and Anthony Heath. 2007. "Inclusion for All but Aboriginals in Canada." In Anthony Heath and Sin Yi Cheung (eds.), *Unequal Chances: Ethnic Minorities in Western Labor Markets*. Proceedings of the British Academy. Oxford: Oxford University Press.

Zeng, Zhen and Yu Xie. 2004. "Asian Americans' Earnings Disadvantage Reexamined: The Role of Place of Education." *American Journal of Sociology* 109: 1075–108.

Zhou, Min. 2004. "Revisiting Ethnic Entrepreneurship: Convergencies, Controversies, and Conceptual Advancements." *International Migration Review* 3: 1040–74.

———. 2009. "How Neighbourhoods Matter for Immigrant Children: The Formation of Educational Resources in Chinatown, Koreatown and Pico Union, Los Angeles." *Journal of Ethnic and Migration Studies* 35: 1153–79.

Zhou, Min, and Carl Bankston III. 1998. *Growing Up American: How Vietnamese Children Adapt to Life in the United States*. New York: Russell Sage Foundation.

Zolberg, Aristide. 1999. "Matters of State: Theorizing Immigration Policy." In Charles Hirschman, Philip Kasinitz, and Josh DeWind (eds.), *The Handbook of International Migration*. New York: Russell Sage Foundation.

———. 2006. *A Nation by Design: Immigration Policy in the Fashioning of America*. Cambridge, Mass.: Harvard University Press.

———. 2007. "Immigration Control Policy: Law and Implementation." In Mary C. Waters and Reed Ueda (eds.), *The New Americans*. Cambridge, Mass.: Harvard University Press.

———. 2008. *How Many Exceptionalisms? Explorations in Comparative Macroanalysis*. Philadelphia: Temple University Press.

Zolberg, Aristide, and Litt Woon. 1999. "Why Islam Is Like Spanish: Cultural Incorporation in Europe and the United States." *Politics & Society* 27: 5–38.

Zuñiga, Victor, and Rubén Hernández-León. 2006. *New Destinations: Mexican Immigration in the United States*. New York: Russell Sage Foundation.

Zweigenhaft, Richard, and G. William Domhoff. 2006. *Diversity in the Power Elite: How It Happened, Why It Matters*. Lanham, Md.: Rowman & Littlefield.

INDEX

Aboutaleb, Ahmed, 157
affirmative action: in Britain, 112–13; in Canada, 112, 113; in France, 112; in Germany, 112; in Netherlands, 112, 113; in United States, 109–13, 185, 234, 243–44
Affordable Care Act, 52
African Americans: affirmative action for, 109–13, 243–44; and civil rights movement, 99, 109–13, 116, 236; immigrants distancing themselves from, 114–15; in carceration rates of, 105–6; Islam among, 131; mixed unions among, 104, 208, 215; one drop rule, 215, 216; political integration of, 207; segregation of, 68, 69, 74–75, 87, 100–101, 103–4; sharing neighborhoods with Hispanics, 78–79; slavery of, 98–101, 236
Afro-Caribbeans in Britain: education of, 186–87, 192–93; employment of, 189; mixed unions among, 105; national identity of, 115, 203; political integration of, 153; postcolonial migration of, 23, 30; racial discrimination against, 106; racial identity of, 102, 115; segregation of, 83–84
Afro-Caribbeans in Canada, 81–82, 105, 210
Afro-Caribbeans in France, 31, 115
Afro-Caribbeans in Netherlands, 30, 115. See also Antilleans in Netherlands; Surinamese in Netherlands
Afro-Caribbeans in United States, 80, 97, 107, 113–15, 210
Alba, Richard, 25, 61
Algerians in France: mixed unions among, 212; national identity of, 201; postcolonial migration of, 23, 30, 31; religion of, 131; segregation of, 84; transnational marriages for, 215. See also North Africans in France
American exceptionalism, 12–13, 229, 235–36
Antilleans in Netherlands: education of, 184; mixed unions among, 105, 211; mobility of, 92; political integration of, 152; post-

colonial migration of, 30; racial identity of, 101; segregation of, 85, 89
arranged marriages, 36–37, 122, 211, 219. See also transnational marriages
Aruba, 30
Asians in Canada, 27, 81–82, 90
Asians in United States: education of, 71, 228; as high-skill workers, 61; immigration data for, 26; integration of, 108; mixed unions among, 90, 104, 210, 215, 216; national identity of, 199, 200, political integration of, 165, 168; racial discrimination against, 100, 101, 107–8; religion of, 131; residential neighborhoods of, 71–72, 90, 97; segregation of, 79–80; social capital of, 71, 240
assimilation, 6–8, 70, 90, 91, 219. See also integration
asylum seekers, 33–35. See also refugee immigration
Australia, 181
Austria, 148

baby boomers, 15
Bangladeshis in Britain: education of, 53, 180, 186–87, 241; employment of, 57, 65, 189; mixed unions among, 211; political integration of, 153; religious identity of, 102, 131; segregation of, 82–83, 84
Bangladeshis in Canada, 81
Banting, Keith, 230
Bean, Frank, 238
Beck-Gernsheim, Elizabeth, 213
Bendix, Reinhard, 3
birthrates, 44. See also demographic change
Bloemraad, Irene, 102, 149, 166, 234
Bloomberg, Michael, 135
Bracero program, 25
Breton, Raymond, 71
Britain: affirmative action in, 112–13; asylum seekers in, 34; British migration to Canada, 27; Chinese in, 83, 186; citizenship re-